Festivals, Special Events, and Tourism

Donald Getz, PhD, MCIP

VNR VAN NOSTRAND REINHOLD
New York

Copyright © 1991 by Van Nostrand Reinhold

Library of Congress Catalog Number 89-78073
ISBN 0-442-23744-8

Printed in the United States of America

Van Nostrand Reinhold
115 Fifth Avenue
New York, New York 10003

Van Nostrand Reinhold International Company Limited
11 New Fetter Lane
London EC4P 4EE, England

Van Nostrand Reinhold
480 La Trobe Street
Melbourne, Victoria 3000, Australia

Nelson Canada
1120 Birchmount Road
Scarborough, Ontario M1K 5G4, Canada

16 15 14 13 12 11 10 9 8 7 6 5 4 3 2 1

Library of Congress Cataloging-in-Publication Data

Getz, Donald, 1949–
    Festivals, special events, and tourism/Donald Getz.
       p.   cm.
    Includes bibliographical references.
    ISBN 0-442-23744-8
    1. Tourist trade. 2. Festivals. I. Title.
G155.A1G44   1990
338.4′791— dc20

89-78073
CIP

To Sharon, Audrey, Christine

Contents

Preface

Festivals and public celebrations are found in all societies. Together with a variety of other special events, they are increasingly seen as unique tourist attractions and as destination image makers. Ranging in scale from mega-events such as the Olympics and world's fairs, through community festivals, to programs of events at parks and facilities, they constitute one of the most exciting and fastest growing forms of leisure- and tourism-related phenomena. Their special appeal stems in part from the innate uniqueness of each event, which distinguishes them from fixed attractions, and their celebratory and festive ambience, which elevates them above ordinary life.

This book is written to satisfy a growing international need for concepts and practical advice on the links between festivals, special events, and tourism. As noted by Clare Gunn (1988, 259), "Probably the fastest growing form of visitor activity is festivals and events." Events of all types are proliferating, many apparently springing up for no other reason than to act as a tourist attraction. And tourist organizations are increasingly developing policies and programs to capitalize on their popularity. The New Zealand Tourist and Publicity Department (1987) recognized this fact, reporting: "Event tourism is an important and rapidly growing segment of international tourism which has not been tapped to any major extent in New Zealand." As documented in a detailed case study in this book, New Zealand has launched an ambitious program to develop the potential of event tourism.

Event tourism is a relatively new term. It can be defined as the systematic planning, development, and marketing of festivals and special events as tourist attractions, development catalysts, and image builders for attractions and destination areas. *Festivals, Special Events, and Tourism* develops the definition with concepts and methods necessary to elevate event tourism to a legitimate and equal partner in the tourism planning field. But while the book advocates event tourism planning, the author does not want it to be interpreted as naive boosterism. Not all events can play a significant role in tourism, and many traditional events are probably better left unexploited, so as to preserve their cultural integrity. Also, as with any other form of development, the tourism planner must be cautious of the many potential negative effects that events can generate.

With these cautions in mind, the following are specific objectives of the book:

1. Develop a systematic approach to the planning, development, and marketing of festivals and special events as tourist attractions, catalysts, and image builders for attractions and destination areas.
2. Provide practical planning and marketing methods and techniques for use by tourist organizations and event managers and organizers.
3. Illustrate key concepts and methods through presentation of examples and case studies from many settings.
4. Illustrate the potential benefits and costs of event tourism, along with ways to maximize benefits and prevent or ameliorate costs.
5. Explore the meaning of specialness as it applies to festivals and events, and distinguish special events from other types of tourist attractions.
6. Draw conclusions as to the research, planning, and evaluation necessary to advance the field of event tourism.

A conceptual framework is developed through definitions and models, and specific methods and techniques are highlighted through case studies. The tourism official or planner will learn how to formulate event tourism strategies and marketing plans for national, regional, and local destinations, and how to use festivals and special events to promote various settings, such as heritage areas and parks. Festival and event managers and organizers will learn how to develop an event's attractiveness to tourists, and how to use tourism to improve the event.

Other practical applications of the material include: evaluation aimed at developing and improving the event product and organizational effectiveness; impact assessment, to demonstrate the value of events; preparation of feasibility studies and bids for events; and help in winning support from the public, grant-giving agencies, and sponsors.

The book does *not* comprehensively cover the details of organizing and managing special events; rather it focuses on the tourism connections. Nevertheless, managers will find a great deal of useful general material that can be adapted to a wide range of management tasks. The actual production of events is also not explicitly covered, although pertinent principles and examples are provided. Much other useful information on tourism, leisure, and events is listed in the References. It is hoped that this book will fill a void in the mainstream of leisure and tourism, without needlessly duplicating the broad background material that readers should also consult.

The book is logically organized with the intent of being read from beginning to end. Although some readers will be interested mostly in the destination planning and marketing aspects and others will be concerned primarily with specific festival and event planning and marketing, all readers will benefit from the entire book. To effectively develop event tourism for a destination, knowledge of the issues facing event organizers is essential; managers of specific events can greatly increase their marketing effectiveness through a better understanding of destination tourism and how it is planned and marketed.

As a textbook, *Festivals, Special Events, and Tourism* can be used for courses in tourism, recreation management and programming, commercial recreation, hospitality management, and arts and culture. In most cases it will be a book for specialists, requiring some previous knowledge of the field and how it relates to tourism. It is intended not to stand on its own as a complete text on festivals and events or tourism, but to be a complement to other available material.

Writing this book has been both exciting and challenging. Hundreds of articles, books, and documents, many not widely available, were collected and scrutinized. Examples from both published and unpublished sources are frequently cited, to give the reader a sampling of this background material. Original case studies and interviews were obtained from practitioners and tourism officials in five English-speaking countries. The author's own research, and that of his students, has also been valuable in shaping the contents and particularly in providing an underlying philosophy about festivals and special events.

Future researchers and writers on this subject will find considerable room for expansion and improvement, as this field is currently just emerging as a vital topic for tourism, leisure, and economic professionals. Sociologists and anthropologists have a head start, but their work has typically concentrated on the social and cultural meanings of events, not their significance in developing economies and communities. Much room for fertile interdisciplinary debate exists, but it is also likely that some barriers separate these groups. Mutual awareness and education are required, and this book can at least provide ammunition to further the debate.

The final chapter offers general conclusions on what makes some festivals and events special, assesses research needs, and speculates about the future of festivals and event tourism. Readers should realize that many of the trends evident in the 1990s have their roots in earlier decades, although some new trends and issues will materialize. By the end of the decade, festivals and special events may have taken on a whole new meaning and complexion, rendering some of this author's forecasts and admonitions obsolete. Whatever happens, I have great confidence in predicting that festivals and special events will occupy a more important place than they do today, both in tourism and in the wider dimensions of culture and community.

The book also includes a glossary, in which key terms used in the text are defined and explained. This is not an attempt to replace common dictionaries, although it is clear that they do not fully reflect the jargon and terminology in a field such as this. Readers are encouraged to use this glossary with some caution, mainly for help in interpreting the author's issues and arguments. In a few years, no doubt, this glossary will require complete revision and considerable expansion.

Also provided for the reader's assistance is a subject index, in which the main concepts, methods, and case studies are itemized for easy cross-referencing within the text.

Acknowledgments

Many people provided valuable information and ideas for this book, particularly for the case studies and interviews. I take full responsibility, however, for any errors or misinterpretation of the facts.

I want to thank the major contributors, and beg forgiveness for not naming the many others who sent me material—your assistance, though not noted here, greatly enriched this book.

A special thank-you to those who provided interviews and case study material: Don Lunday, Executive Director of The International Festivals Association; Doug Little, President of Festivals Ontario; Lesa Ukman of International Events Group; Mary-Alice Arthur, Event Tourism Coordinator for the New Zealand Tourist and Publicity Department; Mark Sparrow, Director of Research and Planning for the Western Australian Tourism Commission; and Ann Anderson, Events Director of the Galveston Historical Society, for providing details of the Dickens on the Strand festival in Galveston, Texas.

Many others deserve thanks.

New Zealand: Monique Brocx, Research Director of NZTP, and Dr. David Simmons of Lincoln College also provided valuable reaction to my drafts. Jim Harland of Murray North Ltd. in Auckland sent me his notes on the Speight's Coast to Coast event. Dr. Neil Leiper of Massey University supplied additional comments. Dr. Doug Pearce, of the University of Canterbury, and his family provided both hospitality and advice. Dr. Grant Cushman of Lincoln College and his faculty in Parks, Recreation and Tourism assisted me in my journeys.

Australia: Steven I'anson, Manager of the Town of York Tourist Bureau, contributed details of its festivals and events. Dr. Trevor Mules, Director of the Centre for South Australian Economic Studies in Adelaide, graciously permitted extensive reference and quotation from the center's study of the Australian Grand Prix. Dr. Bill Faulkner, Director of the Australian Bureau of Tourism Research in Canberra, and Dr. Geoff Symes of the University of Western Australia provided very useful material. Dr. Colin Hall helped with his papers and ideas on festivals and special events, much of which parallels my own research and interests. Other material and advice came from the Victorian Tourism Commission and New South Wales Tourism Commission. Ellen Blunden, Director of The Canberra Festival, gave me information on that successful community event. Dr. John Pigram of the University of New England and Dr. Graham Yapp of the Commonwealth Scientific Investigation and Research Organization in Canberra provided both hospitality and help. The Australian Bicentennial Authority sent information on Expo '88 in Brisbane.

United States: Material of special value came from quite a few other sources in the United States, including the Louisiana Association of Fairs and Festivals; Baltimore Office of Promotion; South Carolina Department of Parks, Recreation and Tourism; Vermont Bicentennial Commission; Maryland Department of Economic and Employment Development; State of Oklahoma Tourism and Recreation Department; New Jersey Department of Commerce, Energy and Economic Development, Division of Travel and Tourism; Texas Department of Commerce, Tourism Division; Michigan Department of Commerce, Travel Bureau; Florida Department of Commerce, Division of Tourism; New York Department of Economic Development, Division of Tourism; Kentucky Department of Travel Development; New York State Office of Parks, Recreation and Historic Preservation; Ohio Department of Development; Nevada Commission on Tourism; Minnesota Travel Information Center; Utah Travel Council; Otsego County Tourism Bureau, Inc.; and Sunkist Fiesta Bowl.

Thanks also to James G. Walls, consultant; Dr. Geoff Godbey and Dr. Richard Gitelson at Pennsylvania State University; Dr. Don Holecek, Dr. Joe Fridgen, and Dr. Ed Mahoney at the Michigan Travel, Tourism and Recreation Resource Center; Dr. John R. Kelly, University of Illinois; the Texas A&M University Agricultural Extension Service; and J. Goldblatt of the Wonder Co.

In Great Britain, assistance and information came from the following people: Dr. John Watt, Highlands and Islands Development Board; Dr. Brian Hay, Scottish Tourist Board; Professor B. Goodall, University of Reading; Mike Williamson of Arthur Young Management Consultants, Edinburgh; and Allan Williams, University of Exeter.

Thanks for Canadian material are owed to: Prince Edward Island Ministry of Tourism and Parks; Don Blair, Folklorama; Mariposa Folk Foundation; National Capital Commission; Ottawa-Carleton Board of Trade; Jim Lee, British Columbia Ministry of Tourism; Travel Alberta; Yukon Department of Tourism; Saskatchewan Tourism and Small Business Ministry; Nova Scotia Department of Tourism;

Northwest Territories Division of Tourism and Parks; Newfoundland Department of Industrial Development; Quebec Ministry of Leisure; Tourism New Brunswick; Ontario Ministry of Tourism and Recreation; Manitoba Department of Economic Development and Tourism; and Calgary Exhibition and Stampede. Tourism Canada provided valuable background material and data.

From other countries: A. M. O'Reilly, University of the West Indies; Dr. Cornelius Van der Kamp, Ministry of Economic Affairs, the Netherlands; and the Munich Tourist Office, West Germany.

From associations: Toronto Olympic Committee; International Amateur Athletic Federation; International Federation of Festival Organizations; International Festivals Association; Canadian Association of Festivals and Events; and Festivals Ontario.

Special thanks to Dr. Stephen Smith, Chairman of Recreation and Leisure Studies, University of Waterloo, for your continuous encouragement and support; to Dr. Wendy Frisby, for your partnership in research and writing about festivals and special events; and to Sharon Getz for word processing, technical assistance, and patience.

CHAPTER ONE

Event Tourism

Festivals, Special Events, and Tourism examines what makes some festivals and events truly special, and how their unique ambience can powerfully motivate travel, animate otherwise static attractions, create positive images of destinations, act as a catalyst for development, and mobilize community tourism planning. With events coming to the fore in tourism developments, along with a proliferation of new events and global media coverage of mega-events, the time is right to examine this field in depth.

Events can be packaged and sanitized or fresh and authentic. They can be tourist traps or community celebrations. Not all events can be special, nor can they all play a significant role in tourism schemes. But their collective potential is seemingly unlimited—from the scale of world's fairs or the Olympics to the most modest of community festivals.

Specific objectives of this book have been stated in the Preface; to elaborate on them, a number of short profiles follow. Each is an introduction to one or more of the book's themes and to more detailed case studies, which are presented in later chapters.

York, Western Australia: Venturing into the streets of this small, historic town puts the visitor in touch with this young nation's built heritage. The preserved buildings—indeed, the whole look of the town—is a direct visual connection with the past. If you visit in the summer, it is too hot and uncomfortable; it seems empty. But in winter, the air cools and freshens with the enticing odor of the sandalwood workshops. Then York comes alive—with the whine and

York, Western Australia: historic street scene (Western Australian Tourism Commission).

rumble of vintage cars or ungainly, exotic camels racing through the streets, while cheering crowds lean precariously from the overlooking balconies. Add horse races, a jazz festival, more sedate chamber music, drama. Now the historical experience is real, and the town itself is alive. These events bring the tourists to York; they make the trip worthwhile and memorable. And the events animate the residents, as organizers, participants, celebrants. It is their town the visitors have come to experience.

The specialness of the place is not captured by its historic buildings and monuments alone. It requires people, color, motion, smell, taste. Visitors might enjoy the sight of the historic town when it is quiet, but they can really live it during York's season of special events.

Galveston, Texas: The problem for the Galveston Historical Foundation was to promote interest in, and generate revenue to preserve and enhance, a Victorian streetscape in a run-down waterfront area. The solution: a festival called Dickens on the Strand, which captures the flavor of Charles Dickens's Victorian London in costumes, foods, spectacle, and entertainment. Held annually the first weekend

York, Western Australia: The streets come alive with the York Flying 50s vintage car rally (Western Australian Tourism Commission).

in December, this innovative festival attracts residents and tourists to a pre-Christmas event, turns a slow season into a tourism peak, and raises substantial money for worthwhile community projects.

Dickens on the Strand is a fine example of the invented festival, which some would call spurious and inauthentic. Others might find its admission fees and merchandising not in keeping with a true public celebration. Yet it meets a real demand for entertainment and public spectacle. The quality of the product is very high, and the visitors find it satisfying. The community benefits in many ways, including the obvious value of tourism revenue and the funding of heritage preservation. Festivals come in many shapes and forms, and not all are traditional. Increasingly, the invented festival and special event will become a mainstay of both tourism schemes and public service.

New Zealand: Tourism in the South Pacific was the industry of the 1980s, and New Zealand has pursued its development and growth aggressively. Recognizing the potential value of special events to its tourism attractiveness, the country has launched an event tourism initiative on a national scale to coordinate and shape the roles of events in destination planning. Specific event tourism goals include attracting foreign tourists; enhancing the country's image as a distinct destination; and spreading tourism throughout the islands and beyond the traditional peak season. Assistance is given to help create and develop events, such as the Otago Goldfields Heritage Celebration and the Speight's Coast to Coast endurance triathlon.

In 1990 the country celebrated its 150th anniversary, marking the occasion with an outpouring of cultural and sporting festivities including the Commonwealth Games, all of which contribute to a higher international profile. Although New Zealand is blessed with superb natural attractions, the lesson for other countries is that events offer a viable alternative to natural resources, or a way to augment their appeal. And it can be accomplished in ways that are environmentally responsible and culturally developmental.

Canada's National Capital Region: It befits a nation's capital to be attractive to domestic and foreign tourists alike, and a major part of the attraction should be festivals and special events expressing the nation's heritage and culture. Ottawa and the other municipalities in the capital region host an impressive number and variety of festivals and events throughout the year, and recent studies have demonstrated not only their significant economic impact, but also their role in enhancing the region's image both as a capital city and as a tourist destination. The larger events are in themselves travel motivators and are successfully marketed beyond the region. Smaller events are not only important to residents as recreational and cultural activities, but are valuable spending outlets for visitors already in the area. Tourism, culture, and recreation are in partnership.

It should now be clear that this book has several interrelated themes. What makes some events special? What is their potential, singly and collectively, in developing tourism? How can each festival or event develop and market itself as a tourist attraction? How can they be used to animate different kinds of attractions and communities, or make tourist attractions of otherwise unappealing settings? What are their roles in fostering recreation, culture, and urban renewal?

Not all festivals and events reach their potential as attractions or image makers, and many organizers pay scant attention to these prospects. Others fail to become the valued community celebrations they set out to be, or do not achieve their goals as fund-raisers and community development catalysts because they are poorly planned or marketed and they fail to attract sufficient resident or tourist interest. Possible reasons for failure are examined in this book, not only the common management and planning mistakes known to event organizers and management experts, but several less obvious causes as well:

- Inadequate attention to the multiple roles, meanings, and impact of festivals and events
- Failure to integrate event marketing in destination planning and marketing schemes
- Failure of destinations to effectively utilize the attractiveness of events in product development marketing and image-making
- Insufficient data on what festival and event visitors want, and consequent inability to segment the potential markets for more effective target marketing

But this is not merely a planning and marketing handbook. It critically examines the use and abuse of special events, and provides a philosophical and methodological framework for the sensitive and responsible planning, marketing, and evaluating of events. As with tourism in general, there is considerable potential for trivialization, overcommercialization, and negative impact.

THE ROLES OF FESTIVALS AND EVENTS IN DESTINATION DEVELOPMENT

In the context of tourism destination planning, festivals and special events can play a number of important roles—as attractions, image makers, animators of static attractions, and catalysts for other developments (Fig. 1-1). Increasingly, they can also be viewed as part of the new wave of **alternative tourism,** which minimizes negative impact, contributes to sustainable development, and fosters better host-guest relations. Related to this last role is the utilization of events as planning and control mechanisms to help preserve sensitive natural or social environments.

These major roles are discussed in the following subsections. The remainder of this chapter takes a more detailed look at the potential benefits and costs of event tourism.

Tourist Attractions and Contributors to Destination Attractiveness

The most basic and important aspect of event tourism is to attract tourists, both domestic and foreign. Although the emphasis of national tourist organizations is usually placed on international tourism, there is no doubt that most festivals and events depend on local and regional audiences. Whether an event is a true tourist attraction (in other words, motivating overnight or nonlocal travel) or an activity outlet, it can have the effect of keeping people—and their money—at home, rather than traveling outside the region or country. Accordingly, event tourism must be equally part of domestic and international tourism planning.

Tourist attractions must exert a pull on potential visitors. That is, they must be able to motivate someone to want to attend. Gunn (1988) emphasized that attractions are physical settings for tourist experiences, and he distinguished between attractions that can lure people to a destination area or resort and those that provide something to do on the way or while touring. With regard to festivals and events, however, some differences must be noted. Events require physical settings, but their attractiveness is not necessarily dependent on that setting. Many other factors can be vital in creating the right ambience or atmosphere, including crowd dynamics, services, and entertainment. In Chapter

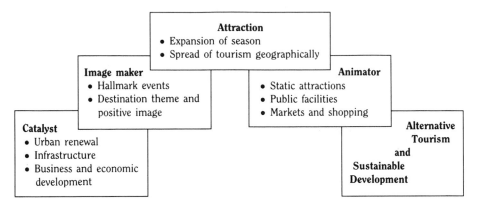

Figure 1-1. Tourism-related roles of festivals and special events.

8, as part of our discussion of product development, we will return to settings and examine the variety of places and the characteristics of settings that contribute to successful events. Motivations to attend festivals and events are considered in detail in Chapter 3.

Events do not actually have to attract tourists to the area to play an important role in tourism development. In many cases the tourist will be looking for something to do while in an area, or can be lured to an event even though he or she did not previously desire to visit it. A study of eight festivals and events in the National Capital Region of Canada (Coopers and Lybrand 1989, 21) found that visitors had specific expectations of what the capital should offer. The consultants concluded: "Festivals do contribute to a perception that Ottawa is a nice place to visit during the summer, a place where you have a good chance of coming across something interesting." In this way events can heighten visitors' experiences or induce them to stay longer and spend more.

According to Gunn (1988), destination attractions are most effective when clustered, and at a magnitude that offers variety and heightens promotional punch. Events themselves also can be clustered, both in time and space, and events can be used in conjunction with other attractions to heighten overall destination appeal.

Attractiveness is a measure of the relative strength of an attraction, in terms of the number of people drawn, the geographic spread of the market area, or its appeal compared to that of the competition. Mill and Morrison (1985) used the term *drawing power* and linked it to the distance people are willing to travel to experience the attraction. They distinguished between local, regional, and national or international market areas. We will return to this point when discussing market areas.

Event tourism must therefore seek to enhance the attractiveness of individual events and festivals and to use them to enhance destination attractiveness. These themes run throughout the book, and many factors that contribute to heightened attractiveness are identified and explained. Festivals and events play a number of specific, important roles in increasing tourist attractiveness.

Expansion of the Tourist Season

The tourism industry is in many places preoccupied with overcoming traditional problems of seasonality. Special events have become a popular method of extending the peak season or introducing a new season. Winter sports can be the basis of a new season in northern climates, involving sports competitions, winter carnivals, and alpine cultural events. In hot climates, cultural events such as Goombay in the Bahamas are an attraction for summer visits.

Events have unique advantages in this respect. They can capitalize on whatever natural appeal the off-season presents, such as winter rather than summer sports, seasonal produce and other food, and scenery or wildlife viewed in different places and under different conditions. Or events can ignore the climatic differences altogether and concentrate on indoor activities. In addition, in many destinations the residents prefer the off-season for their own celebrations, and these provide more authentic events for visitors. Of course, if this strategy is too successful, there will be no off-season!

Certain tourist segments have a natural preference for off-peak travel, because of either potential cost reductions or a desire to avoid crowds of other tourists. Retired persons and upper-income groups with more than one holiday opportunity a year are the key targets. Events can pull them for short breaks or even main holidays. Finally, dedicated music lovers, athletes, sports fans, and other special-interest travelers potentially will attend events at any time of the year to satisfy their desire for special experiences. These target markets might be smaller, but they are also more loyal and easily reached through targeted promotions.

Researchers have been able to demonstrate the success of events in lengthening tourist seasons, or in creating secondary peaks in annual travel patterns. Ritchie and Beliveau (1974) examined Quebec's famous Winter Carnival as a strategic response to seasonality. They concluded that the event, started in its modern form in 1954 by the local business community, had succeeded in turning the traditional winter low season into the peak of the tourism year. What's more, the carnival did for Quebec City what the Mardi Gras does for New Orleans— it provides a high-profile event with a strong, unique image that helps put Quebec on the tourism map.

Hanna (1981), referring to events in the United Kingdom, noted that the highly visible festivals in Edinburgh, held in September, and Bath, held in the spring, both were created deliberately to extend traditional summer tourist seasons. Also, in Scotland, Getz (1984) documented the successful efforts of the small Highland community of Carrbridge in creating an annual Ceilidh Week—

a music festival in the Highland tradition—to extend the season into September. It became the peak occupancy period of the year and generated substantial publicity and income for the village.

The strategy is not always completely successful. Lewis and Beggs (1988) reported on Bermuda's Rendezvous Time, which was created in 1960 to encourage off-season—in other words, summer—visits by offering more to do through events and other promotions. A Festival of Performing Arts was added in 1975 to make the alternative more attractive, but the researchers felt the entire campaign lacked the quality and the enthusiasm of its participants to make it truly successful. According to Blum (1989b), however, Bermudian officials believed that after twenty-three years Rendezvous Time had resulted in major off-season gains, with hotel occupancy up to 50 percent.

Spread of Tourism Geographically

Demand can be manipulated to spread visits over space as well as time. For countries such as New Zealand where international tourists traditionally concentrate in several key attraction or staging areas, special events are a natural development to help spread the demand into outlying regions. Even if the events are not powerful enough in their own right to attract international tourists, they can be important in promoting the country as a whole, and in the offering of touring packages.

Research evidence is lacking, but the work of Janiskee (1985) and Getz and Frisby (1988) reveals that in South Carolina and Ontario, respectively, community festivals are widely spread out. Their success must be attributed at least in part to their ability to draw visitors from cities. Some of the festivals documented in small-town Ontario annually attract bus tours from regional and even international markets, so it is clear that geographically spreading tourism away from the major urban concentrations is possible.

Animation of Static Attractions and Facilities

Resorts, museums, historic districts, heritage re-creations, archaeological sites, markets and shopping centers, sports stadia, convention centers, and even theme parks are all increasingly adding special events to their programs. The potential benefits are fourfold:

1. Animate the site or facility, such as through historic reenactments or cultural events that attract people who might otherwise not make a visit.
2. Encourage repeat visits by people who might otherwise think that one visit is enough for a lifetime.

3. Encourage people to bring visiting friends and relatives who might otherwise not include certain static attractions on their list of things to do.
4. Attract publicity for the site or facility.

In the following paragraphs a number of specific facilities and static attractions are covered, noting the roles of events in heightening their attractiveness. Examples are provided for each.

Resorts

A glance at the datebook or events calendar in any leisure or travel magazine quickly informs the reader of how important special events have become to resorts. The June 1989 issue of *Snow Country*, for example, listed the following festivals and events at ski resorts and four-season destinations: seventy arts workshops at Anderson Ranch Arts Center in Snowmass Village, Colorado; the Sun Valley Ice Show in Sun Valley, Idaho; the Dillon Pack Burro Race in Dillon, Colorado; an air show at Truckee/Lake Tahoe, California; the Western States 100-Mile Endurance Run in Squaw Valley, California; jazz and music festivals at Waterville Valley in New Hampshire, Whitefish in Montana, Winter Park in Colorado, and Madison/Sugarloaf in Maine; mountain bike races in Bonanza Flats, Utah; plus triathlon races, tennis, food festivals—the list goes on and on!

Winter resorts are known for ski races, but increasingly they want to be four-season destinations and permanent or second-home developments. Summer and shoulder-season special events are a natural for attracting publicity, generating accommodation demand, and raising the image of the resort above that of the competition. Aspen, Colorado, has successfully pursued this strategy with a popular arts festival, while Telluride, Colorado, has a municipally sanctioned summer festival program, which balances its successful winter skiing season (*Special Events Report* 1982, 302).

Corcoran (1988) outlined the objectives of Waterville Valley, New Hampshire, regarding their success with World Cup skiing events. The resort wanted to gain favorable media attention (television is essential!), generate shoulder-season revenues, instill employee pride, and help improve the U.S. ski team—all this at no cost to the resort, due to sponsorships. Helber (1985) linked special events to resort sales and promotions strategies with the goals of attracting guests and potential real estate buyers, and gaining media recognition.

Mayor Sonny Bono of Palm Springs, California, speaking to the 1989 annual conference of the International Festivals Association, outlined his city's plans to create an international film festival and major sporting events. The need was to overcome the image of Palm Springs as a winter resort for only the rich and famous. Increased tourism would mean increased business and city revenues acquired through the local hotel tax. Corporate sponsorship was being pursued, to avoid reliance on city coffers.

Historic and Cultural Sites

Once someone has seen the local "pioneer village" or authentic historical re-creation, what induces him or her to return? Like theme parks and museums, getting repeat visits can be the difference between profit and loss, or between quality and mediocrity. Traditional interpretive services are static, and there is only so much potential for school-group tours. But numerous site managers have progressed well beyond simple, static displays to interactive attractions, costumes and "living history," and, ultimately perhaps, festivals and major special events.

Thorburn (1986, 43) described how European cultural heritage sites were being made more attractive to foreign visitors by "using them as a stage or setting for theatre." Period costumes, parades, son et lumière, reenactments, and music festivals in cathedrals are popular. Accompanying these trends, however, is some concern that the sites themselves might be damaged by large volumes of visitors, or by the events themselves. Imagine, for example, the potential impact of increasingly popular battle reenactments!

Historic battlefields have been studied by Stevens (1989), who noted that over the past two decades there has been substantial growth in development of battle sites as visitor attractions. Special events are part of this trend, such as re-created castle sieges at historic monuments in Wales and the annual Civil War battle reenactments in the United States. Although people want truthful interpretation at such sites, Stevens felt that simulated battles tend to glorify war and ignore its unpleasant elements. After all, the real nature of war is not compatible with a fun day out for the family! Obviously, there are serious issues to be debated in this area of special event planning.

Researchers from the Michigan State University Travel, Tourism and Recreation Resource Center (Mahoney, Spotts, and Holecek 1987) studied the effects of a twelve-day special event in Genessee County, Michigan, called Christmas at Crossroads. This event was intended to attract visitors to the heritage facility at a normally slow time of year. A visitor survey found that almost half of 40,000 visitors were from outside the county, and 90 percent reported the event to be their main purpose for the trip. Christmas at Crossroads was found to be attracting many new visitors to the site, as well as repeaters. Fully 94 percent of visitors were on day-trips, but the potential for packaging tours to the site in combination with other attractions in the county, so as to encourage more overnight stays, was noted.

Dewar (1989) has documented other interesting examples concerning the role of special events in interpretation at several Canadian historic parks. At Old Fort Henry the Retreat Program held three times weekly is usually sold out, and it attracts an average of 2,000 visitors for each performance. These eventgoers constitute approximately one-third of all visitation to the site. Fort Wellington National Historic Site attracts 20 percent of its annual visitation during a two-

and-a-half-day period in August when a military pageant is presented in conjunction with Loyalist Days, a community festival. At Kitchener's Woodside National Historic Park, some 27 percent of annual attendance occurs during the six or seven special events, such as Victorian Christmas. Dewar (1989, 47) concluded that events are valuable interpretation devices, but they "must be creative, and offer the visitor a different experience."

Theme Parks

It is a well-known rule of theme park marketing that new attractions must be added periodically to attract repeat visits. Similar success can be achieved through regular entertainment programs, especially when "big names" are featured, as well as festivals and other special events. Theme parks are in fact typically designed with appropriate facilities for indoor and outdoor entertainment on a large scale, along with more intimate viewing and seating areas for minor performances.

At Epcot Center in Florida, the Disney designers used a world's fair approach to site design, maximizing potential for crowd movement, both fixed and moving entertainment, and large-scale spectacle on and surrounding the central lake. A nightly laser and fireworks show has the same effect here as it would at a once-in-a-lifetime world's fair. Elrod (1988), commenting on the Walt Disney World® strategy, said that special events were targeted to the key Florida market. A separate "special markets" department exists to develop activities for target audiences, such as graduation nights, senior citizen days, or the Salute to Floridians. The Disney "show" is changed constantly, and the staff members are viewed as show business performers.

Other theme parks can be cited. The 1989 guidebook to Canada's Wonderland, located near Toronto, lists a concert series of big-name performers (aimed at the teenage market) and assorted special events including fireworks displays, a dance day, and Italian, jazz, and gospel music festivals. Kelly (1985, 281) described the Six Flags philosophy on events at their theme parks: "Special events are employed to attract local repeat trade." The events are mostly entertainment in nature, and this element, combined with new rides and site amenities, is designed to help extend the life cycle of the product—the theme park.

Convention and Exhibition Facilities

In this book we are treating conferences, exhibitions, and meetings as special events of a sort, although where permanent facilities and convention bureaus have been established, the events are more like regular business. They are potentially special events to the visitors, of course, and this atmosphere can be made festive and more attractive through the addition of complimentary tours, parties, and nonbusiness events. Without doubt, conventiongoers examine the recreational and entertainment potential of a destination before deciding to attend, and organizers often choose their sites with this in mind. What better way to attract major conventions and meetings, therefore, than to add festivals and events directly to the package?

In Kitchener-Waterloo, Canada, home of North America's largest annual Bavarian Festival (that is, Oktoberfest), "little Oktoberfests" can be added to conventions and meetings at any time of the year, to make certain the attendees get at least a taste of the real thing. This has the added effect of promoting the festival itself. Levin (1989) also noted that conducting familiarization tours for meeting planners at festival times can be a successful strategy in attracting conventions and meetings. Indianapolis is noted as both a sporting events and convention city, illustrating the powerful synergistic effect that can be created.

A related issue is what to do with expensive convention facilities when they are not booked by those highly desired international meetings of the Shriners or Oddfellows. Using them as festival halls is a logical secondary use, assuming their design is suitable. Indeed, some cities have carefully integrated the planning of festivals, exhibitions, and conventions. A good example is Niagara Falls, New York, where the annual wintertime Festival of Lights and a summertime program of special events are fully integrated with the convention center, a public outdoor festival plaza for people to congregate, and a private shopping center.

Museums and Art Galleries

Faced with tight budgets and low visitation rates, many museums and galleries, especially those in the public sector, have turned to special touring exhibitions and other events. Successful examples include the King Tut and van Gogh exhibits that toured North America. Wall and Knapper (1981) reported that the Tutankhamen exhibition drew 780,000 visitors in Toronto, of whom 100,000 were from out of the province. The resultant spending in the city was estimated to be $26 million, mainly stemming from the use of a total of 40,000 hotel room-nights.

The difficulty with this type of facility, however, is in involving the public to an extent greater than is normally possible, given the facility's design and capacity. Creating a festive atmosphere also is more difficult for galleries and museums unless the exhibits can be housed in special settings or are presented as part of larger themed events. A noteworthy example of augmenting the potential of an exhibit was that of the Inca Empire and the Treasures of Peru, held in Montreal in the summer of 1989 and organized by the Society of Grand Events of Montreal, with significant governmental support and corporate sponsorship. Its setting was the Place des Arts cultural facility in Montreal's city center, but the event was expanded to include forty-five days of related cultural activities such as a Peruvian fiesta and a culinary festival involving a hotel.

Markets and Shopping Areas

The invention of "festival markets" has added a new dimension to shopping, dining, and entertainment. These very urban attractions are often indoors, or might include or abut plazas and courts, in which special events or regular entertainment programs encourage spending in a festive atmosphere. Probably the first of these, created by the Rouse Corporation in 1974, is Faneuil Hall/Quincy Market in Boston. It has been considered "the quintessential model of sensitive and profitable urban redevelopment" (McNulty 1986, 34). We will explore this connection with urban development and renewal in more detail later.

Another connection is with the marketing of shopping centers and downtown areas. Benson (1985) described the use of special events such as shows, performances, food festivals, exhibitions, and samplings to attract targeted consumer segments to malls. Denver's Sixteenth Street Mall is a prime example of how downtown areas can compete with suburban malls by creating attractive shopping and cultural environments. Regular programming of special music events and festivals by Downtown Denver adds life and helps foster a more favorable image (McNulty 1986).

To a degree, festival markets and the types of food festivals found in malls are often a misuse of the term *festival*. They occur in private, not public, settings and are focused on selling, not celebration. On the other hand, it is really the audience, or shoppers, who must decide if the atmosphere or event is a special or festive experience.

There is another inherent problem in this and other applications of festivals and special events—namely, when do special events become mere entertainment? Is there a dividing line between special events and programmed entertainment? What about the daily Main Street parades at Disney World—are they special in any way? Or the costumed military displays at Colonial Williamsburg—are they unique events or a routine part of the set?

One answer, of course, is that it hardly matters. The managers might realize their objectives regardless of whether or not the event is a festival or a public celebration. On the other hand, is it not obvious that it is becoming more and more difficult to create truly special events because of the proliferation of programmed entertainment and media-oriented events? Marketing experts and event programmers might very well be engaged in an ever-diminishing competition for visitors' interest and media attention. Part of what makes an event special is its infrequency, its uniqueness, even its spontaneity—all of which are antithetical to total programming and control.

Fair and Exhibition Grounds

The annual fair or exhibition was once the most common special event—the one of greatest significance to people born in rural areas and small towns, and to those born before the more recent wave of festivals and other special events eclipsed the fair's appeal. Some traditional fairs have failed, or at least declined, as the population urbanized and entertainment tastes and cultural preferences became more sophisticated. But others have kept up and adapted by introducing festival-like elements to their attractions and setting. In some areas, such as Louisiana, fairs and festivals are joined in the same professional association.

A major distinction between fairs and festivals is the traditional fairground, usually devoted to agricultural purposes as well as the annual fair or exhibition. In many small towns the fairground has also been the focal point of recreational and entertainment activities, and many have developed impressive community-oriented facilities. This infrastructure can provide a resource for festivals and special events; yet it appears that many festival organizers keep their distance from fair boards. One likely explanation is that festivals, particularly those with a cultural or arts flavor, have been initiated by recent newcomers, such as retirees, commuters, or others escaping the city. The festival or fair should be a source of community integration through celebration of common values or experiences, so this type of division should be resisted. Ways can be found to combine the old and the new, the traditional with the innovative.

Some fairs and exhibitions are big businesses. A detailed examination of the Calgary Exhibition and Stampede, a nonprofit organization devoted in part to preserving the agricultural legacy of Alberta, revealed that its grounds and numerous events attracted 3.6 million admissions in 1987, generating almost $200 million (Canadian) in expenditures and yielding $44 million in revenues (DPA Group Inc. 1988). The main draw is the annual ten-day Calgary Stampede, in reality an agricultural fair, rodeo, and entertainment event all in one, which accounts for 32 percent of the yearly revenue. Other special events are important components of the exhibition's financial health, and horse racing and professional ice hockey are permanently housed at the exhibition facilities.

It remains to be seen if traditional fairs and exhibitions can remain popular in a heavily urbanized world, particularly when the best of rural life and cultural traditions can be so well displayed and easily "consumed" in a festival format. A creative blending of the best of fairs and festivals appears to be necessary, which could result in unique attractions.

Image Makers

It is apparent that major events can have the effect of shaping an image of the host community or country, leading to its favorable perception as a potential travel destination. With global media attention focused on the host city, even for a relatively short duration, the publicity value is enormous, and some destinations will use this fact alone to justify great expenditures on attracting events. For example, Wang and Gitelson (1988, 5) observed that the annual Spoleto Festival in Charleston, South Carolina, does not in itself appear to be economically justifiable, "but the city holds it every year to maintain a desirable image."

Although mega-events can attract worldwide media attention, most festivals and other special events cannot. Nevertheless, they can hope to generate good publicity in a national or regional context, and they can strive to achieve a cumulative impact over repeated exposure. A major difference is that Olympics and other mega-events attract global attention regardless of other factors, whereas lesser events will likely have to pursue sustained and favorable publicity. As an example, many sporting events, according to Ritchie (1984, 3), "have successfully created an aura of tradition which is a major draw from a tourism perspective." The Indianapolis 500 and Kentucky Derby seem to fit this category, and it is important to note that both these sporting events have evolved into major festivals.

Viewed systematically, all special events can have an important role in developing a theme for a destination area or community. This relationship between special events and the overall, themed image of a destination is best illustrated through examples. A region short on natural attractions can develop a series of cultural events, such as ethnic and food festivals, to foster an attractive theme such as German Country. A region noted for its historic architecture can use related special events, such as re-creations of historic events, to animate and reinforce the historical theme. A wide variety of events appealing to different target markets could be used to create a general Festival Country theme, or a theme based on outdoor sports or competitions. For example, Kamloops, Canada, has deliberately created the theme of Tournament Capital of British Columbia (Kujat 1989).

Cameron (1989) noted the role of festivals and events, and cultural tourism in general, in altering the image of the Lehigh Valley in Pennsylvania. There, old industrial towns had to struggle to develop new economic activity, and overcoming a negative image was part of the challenge. By fostering cultural attractions and events, the towns successfully began to attract both investment and tourists, leading to increased community pride, higher tax revenues, heritage preservation, more business for the downtowns, and decreased crime as a result of more activity.

Another angle on image-making is illustrated by Munich, West Germany. It is a major urban tourist attraction, welcoming 30 million day visitors and 2.7 million overnighters annually (Munich Tourist Office n.d.), and famous for special events such as the original Oktoberfest. Just as other cities use events to create an image to lure conventions, Munich has also developed an incentive travel marketing program aimed at encouraging businesses internationally to send employees to Munich as a reward for good work. Featured in its Incentive Travel

Manual 1988/89 (Munich Tourist Office n.d.) are color photos and descriptions of the city's great events: Oktoberfest, Fasching (Mardi Gras carnival), Starkbierzeit (Strong Beer Season), Auer Dult (flea markets with amusements), Opera Festival, and Christkindlmarkt (Christmas Market). Theme parties are also featured: incentive travel groups can be provided with staged parties reflecting Munich's festivals and foods, and even participate in an Olympic Incentive Games at the Olympic Stadium. Munich is a classic example of maximizing a city's image through events, and it has innovatively marketed this image to international tourists and specialist markets including conventions and incentive tours.

This is just a sampling of the role of festivals and special events in image-making for destinations and attractions. Other examples are found throughout the book, especially in the case studies. Chapter 6 examines ways in which destination areas can link themes and image enhancement, and demonstrate how strong, positive images can influence the consumer buying process.

Catalysts for Urban Development and Renewal

Mega-events, such as world's fairs and the Olympics, have been supported by host governments in part because of their role as catalysts in major redevelopment schemes. The Knoxville World's Fair was conceived as a catalyst for urban renewal through image enhancement and physical redevelopment; it left a legacy of improved infrastructure, a convention center, private investments, a better tax base, and new jobs for the Tennessee city (Mendell, MacBeth, and Solomon 1983).

Lesser events can be used to bring attention—and shoppers—to redeveloped markets, waterfront areas, or civic squares. Providing the right image is an essential part of the redevelopment process, and bringing people to events is an excellent means to overcome negative associations. Hillman (1986, 4) observed this to be a marked trend in North America: "As center city revitalization continues to be viewed as a major ingredient of economic development, the questions of enlivening public spaces and extending usage of downtowns after 5 o'clock have become critical issues. . . . Events are a proven animator capable of turning barren spaces into bustling places."

McNulty (1986) cited Baltimore's downtown and inner harbor area as a successful example of urban redevelopment based on tourism and culture. Now a major tourist attraction, the harbor features festivals and fairs, restaurants, an aquarium, convention and trade fair facilities, a gallery, a science center, and hotels. Harborplace, developed by the Rouse Corporation in 1980, added a festival marketplace, and two specific facilities have been created for events: the Festival Hall and Amphitheater.

Following a series of riots in 1968, the first Baltimore City Fair was held to promote urban redevelopment and get people to go downtown again. This venture

Baltimore, Maryland: events at Harborplace, an urban festival marketplace (courtesy Rouse Company).

was followed by ethnic festivals, farmers' markets, concerts, and children's programs around the downtown in newly created public places. Then attention turned to the inner harbor, where the Rouse Corporation was undertaking major projects. The Baltimore Office of Promotion and Tourism worked with the developers to stage special events to attract residents and tourists. A survey in 1980 found that about half the visitors came to Harborplace for the festivals or because they believed Baltimore to be a festival city.

Surveys of visitors to the Inner Harbor area from outside Baltimore have continued since 1980, providing data on trends in spending, activities, and visitor characteristics (Jeanne V. Beekhuis and Co. 1988). Festivals and special events have been found to be a major trip motivator, accounting for between 16.4 and 21.5 percent of all visitors in the 1985–88 summer surveys. Conventions attracted another 4 to 7 percent. A high proportion of all visitors were day-trippers (between 49.1 and 77.6 percent over the 1980–88 period, leveling off to about 57 percent after 1985), but only 5.7 percent of those staying overnight were in Baltimore for festivals and special events.

Other cities have emulated Baltimore or struck off on their own in using festivals and events to assist redevelopment. Norfolk, Virginia, is noteworthy for

Baltimore, Maryland: street performers at Harborplace Amphitheatre (photo by Roger Miller).

the degree of city assistance to festivals: it has created a nonprofit organization called Festevents to develop and manage a program of free events on the revitalized downtown waterfront. A 6.5-acre festival park and Waterside Festival Marketplace (again, developed by the Rouse Corporation) provide outstanding settings for public celebrations. This emphasis on festival settings is important, and will be examined in more detail in Chapter 8.

Like civic redevelopment schemes, special events can be tools in promoting not just resorts but other types of real estate development. It has been suggested, for example, that one factor leading to the Australian challenge for the America's Cup was the furtherance of a resort and residential development near Perth. As events attract media attention, they can make excellent public relations tools. The risk is that events must become more sensational and spectacular to gain the desired level of publicity.

Catalysts for Developing Tourism Infrastructure

Mega-events in particular are noted for their land and infrastructure requirements, often accelerating otherwise desired or needed developments and thereby potentially boosting the destination's overall attractiveness. The legacy of major events can also be in the form of new sites and facilities for other tourism or leisure uses, as well as funds for spin-off projects.

General Business and Economic Development

Trade fairs, exhibitions, and conventions are predominantly commercial events where buyers and sellers meet or professionals discuss business. Studies have found business events to be highly profitable for host communities owing to high levels of spending; this factor, together with the prestige element, has led to the proliferation of special-purpose convention centers in most major cities and many regional centers.

World's fairs and other mega-events have traditionally incorporated business and professional congresses or meetings. With the event as a lure, organizers hope that a combination of media attention and personal visits by influential people will have a positive spin-off on the destination economy. This can occur through the establishment of contacts to build networks, the display of local talent, products, and initiative, and the fostering of self-confidence among destination area businesses. The 1987 America's Cup case study, detailed later in this book, illustrates the strategy.

Mega-events can also be viewed as general economic stimulants, owing to the massive capital investment and infrastructure improvements that often accompany them. Anderson and Wachtel (1986) described how the government of British Columbia hoped to use Vancouver's Expo '86 to create sufficient employment and investment to overcome the province's economic slump, and evidence suggests it might very well have had a positive effect. The advantage of a special event, compared to other forms of public expenditure, stems from its high international profile and the mobilization of public opinion in support of the initiative.

Alternative Tourism and Sustainable Development

Considerable attention has been given to the readily documented negative impacts of tourism, especially mass tourism. Tourism has also been politicized by those who view it as morally destructive or neocolonial in nature. There have been compelling arguments for "new," "soft," "alternative," "social," "gentle," and "community-based" tourism, and for all development to be "sustainable." These changes will require a radical departure from the common forms of mass tourism development.

Rosenow and Pulsipher (1979) stated eight basic principles of sound tourism development, and these became the basis for the ideals of alternative or new tourism. Essentially, they argued that tourism should be more environmentally and culturally responsible, based on local heritage, and developed to increase both visitor satisfaction and improvements to the community. In addition, capacity to absorb tourism has to be considered, and limits imposed where necessary.

As defined by Krippendorf (1982), soft tourism also stresses local control, along with slow, self-determined development. Cost-benefit analysis governs decisions, and social, environmental, and economic factors are considered equally. Tourism based on experiences, rather than sights, is preferred.

More recently, global attention has focused on the notion of sustainable development. This can be defined as economic development that will not impede the ability of future generations to meet their needs and enjoy a comparable or better quality of life and environment. Applied to tourism, recreation, and culture, this concept is quite similar to the principles of alternative and soft tourism, with an emphasis on the ability of tourism to foster and support conservation and ecologically responsible development. Developments that require little infrastructure, do not consume nonrenewable resources, and are nonpolluting meet the criteria of sustainability. Tourism that fosters more equitable international development can help. The concept has even been extended to the principle that tourism should contribute to world peace, thereby reducing a source of conflict, just as a better allocation of the earth's resources can remove tensions.

Festivals and special events can be important in this evolution of new concepts and styles of tourism.

Local Leisure Needs

Krippendorf (1987) also suggested that some forms of so-called alternative tourism will merely take tourists into new areas, leading eventually to mass tourism. He suggested that more attention to satisfying local leisure needs will reduce pressure for needless travel. Special events and community festivals can help accomplish this goal. Ironically, however, the larger and better ones are likely to become popular tourist attractions. Even so, a major benefit could be the reduction of mass international tourism pressure on sensitive cultures and environments.

Authentic Traditions

In the face of pressure to commercialize traditions and to make community celebrations more accessible to mass tourism, special events must be assisted in maintaining their authentic meanings to the host community. As argued in detail later in this book, authentic events, rather than packaged and commercialized ones, will hold more appeal for the kinds of tourists least likely to destroy and most likely to generate positive impact.

The Host-Guest Gulf

It is well established that the larger the cultural and economic difference between hosts and guests, the more likely that negative impact will occur. Events, particularly festivals in which the host community plays a dominant organizational and support role, can be an excellent mechanism for bringing hosts and guests into meaningful, rather than subservient, contact. Krippendorf (1987, 113) expressed a similar sentiment, calling for creation of "preconditions for a fair exchange and for equal partnership."

Festivals and other events can help overcome some of the typical limitations of mass tourism, as identified by a UNESCO study (1977). Instead of transitory host-guest contact, events can foster sustained participation in cross-cultural activities. The hosts are proud of their community and event and wish to share it; guests can easily be made aware that they are participating in a celebration, and that the people they meet are welcoming hosts. The distortions and limitations of paid entertainment, in a nightclub style, can be avoided. Furthermore, the activities and setting of the event allow casual mingling of hosts and guests on an equal footing. If this celebratory and open ambience can be augmented by other forms of host-guest interaction, such as home accommodations, the gulf might be bridged.

Tourism without Physical Development

Almost every community has the potential to develop a festival or event that can attract visitors or provide an activity for those already in the area. Dependence on natural attractions and infrastructure can be minimized, with existing facilities used wherever possible. Streets, parks, fairgrounds, community centers, town halls, restaurants, and even farm fields have been used successfully to host events. Indeed, many tourists will be more interested in this kind of authentic local celebration than in more sophisticated events that depend on special-purpose facilities and large-scale infrastructure.

Conservation

Tourism and conservation are logical partners, given the critical role of both natural attractions and a clean, safe environment in luring and satisfying visitors. Festivals and events have a role to play in marketing the importance of parks and conservation areas, controlling activities, and generating revenue for conservation purposes.

So-called nature tourism or ecotourism is emerging as a high-growth segment in tourism, and events can be the focal point of the attraction. This is especially important where tourists who are not otherwise sympathetic to conservation are provided with packages to make trips to remote areas. The interpretive event should aim to satisfy the urge both to gain some firsthand experience with natural environments and to learn about them. Planned celebrations of wildlife and natural habitats can become alternatives to potentially destructive, uncontrolled access.

Similarly, events can be used to deflect travel away from sensitive natural environments, for example outside park boundaries or in park areas with high carrying capacity. Parks, communities, or rural areas subject to heavy visitor pressure can develop a program of special events during peak season, not to attract more tourists but to accommodate existing crowds. Permanent event settings would likely become necessary, but they could be combined with interpretive and reception facilities, or built at existing accommodation sites.

Boundary Maintenance

There is scope to utilize events as social and cultural planning tools. Attracting tourists away from sensitive cultures or environments can be called *boundary maintenance,* a term used by Buck (1977) to describe the role of pseudo-events in deflecting pressure from the Lancaster County Amish community in Pennsylvania. Many visitors can be satisfied with inauthentic productions, as opposed to seeking out the real object of their curiosity, but others are more demanding. This concept of authenticity and its importance to event tourism are critically examined later in the book.

Community-Based Tourism

In Chapter 2 we will examine the entire social, cultural, and community-development perspective on festivals and events. One of the key roles of events in this context is the potential to foster local organizational development, leadership, and networking, all of which are crucial if community-based tourism development is to occur. The festival or event could be the easiest form of development for many communities to launch, setting the precedent for other initiatives and, more important, providing a forum to discuss comprehensive tourism goals and strategies. The hoped-for consequence of this process would be tourism development more in keeping with community wishes, more authentic and therefore more satisfying to tourists, less destructive or costly, and sustainable over the long term.

POTENTIAL ECONOMIC BENEFITS OF EVENTS AND EVENT TOURISM

As attractions, animators, image makers, and catalysts, festivals and events can play a major role in destination development. The products of event tourism include the events themselves, packages and tours that make event-related travel more attractive, and the desired economic impact that the events stimulate. In this section evidence from research is provided to demonstrate the significance of these economic effects and, at the same time, to show that the benefits can vary enormously. Despite substantial research on the economic impact of mega-events, much less attention has been paid to community festivals and minor special events. Consequently, some of the conclusions stated in the following paragraphs must be considered tentative, pending more systematic and comparative research.

A look at the potential economic benefits that festivals and events can generate will be followed in the next section by a discussion of possible costs. Most research to date has focused on real and imputed benefits, with less available evidence to be cited on the negative side. It is also apparent to this author that some event organizers and promoters, in common with other boosters of tourism, tend to exaggerate benefits and avoid detailed documentation of costs.

Note that the cited research findings represent many different methods, and some caution is required when making comparisons; see Chapter 10 for clarification of methodological points. Dollar values are reported as given in the studies, with no attempt made to correct for inflation or international exchange rates.

Success in Attracting Tourists

Mega-events such as the Olympics and world's fairs do attract significant numbers of foreign visitors and have a major impact on domestic travel within the host nation. But all events, even the biggest, usually depend on local and regional audiences. The majority, which are community festivals and minor sporting events, generally have only a level of attractiveness capable of drawing mainly day-trippers and weekenders, although they should aim to attract bus tours and event participants from farther afield. Events of all kinds and sizes are also important activities for tourists who already happen to be in the destination area or passing through. And successful events can enhance the image of the destination, generating an important but often unmeasurable increase in general-purpose tourism.

Vanhove and Witt (1987) examined a number of mega-events and concluded that such activities can reduce tourism outflow from the host country by as much as half and increase inflow by a similar proportion. For example, evaluation of the effects of Vancouver's Expo '86 (Lee 1987) found that the event attracted approximately 22 million site visits, of which 66 percent were from outside the province and 33 percent were from the United States. Canadian domestic tourism was heavily influenced by Expo '86, changing the normal flows and resulting in a boom year for British Columbia and a downturn in some other regions. Visitation to Canada from the United States peaked in 1986, and this was directly attributable to the event. Visits to Australia surged during its bicentennial year, including Brisbane's World's Fair, in 1988. New Zealand was forecasting substantial increases for 1990, its 150th anniversary, which encompassed the Commonwealth Games.

It appears that a major event does generate at least a short-term increase in international arrivals and domestic flows, followed by either continued growth or a return to more normal trends. What is not known is the cumulative impact of events, but it is reasonable to assume that their image-enhancing role will positively affect the trends. Certainly there is no available evidence to suggest that mega-events negatively influence tourism, although they can have the effect of geographically displacing some travel.

Data from other impact assessments suggests a wide variation in the ability of events to attract true tourists, but there is no doubt that many have been successful tourist attractions. The Arts Council for Oklahoma City (1987) estimated that arts events and attractions led to $88 million in income for the city economy, of which festivals and arts-and-crafts fairs accounted for 38 percent. Approximately 26 percent of arts events patrons were found to come from outside the area, with the annual Festival of the Arts attracting the largest number of tourists: 750,000 total attendance in 1987. The impact included that of 686 visiting artists and their expenditures.

Gartner and Holecek (1983) reported on the Greater Michigan Boat and Fishing Show of 1980. It had a total attendance of 80,000, of which fully 90 percent was attributable to visitors who traveled to Detroit mainly because of the show. Kosters (1987) studied the 1985 Sail Amsterdam event, which brought 1,000 tall ships to the Dutch city over a six-day period. Over 4 million spectators were estimated to have viewed the ships; 78 percent came from outside the city, and 18 percent of them stayed overnight.

A survey by Tourism Canada of twenty-one major Canadian festivals revealed that from 5 to 15 percent of the reported audiences were foreign, mostly from the United States (Lariviere and Vachon 1989). With a smaller scale of event, Gray (1987) examined arts and crafts festivals in northeast Minnesota. Only 12.4 percent of attendees came from out of state, and very few of them said the events were very important in their travel decision.

The Target Market Area

No general rules can be formulated to help predict the attractiveness of festivals and events to tourists, but clearly only the larger ones will generate significant amounts of international or interregional travel. Others must strive to develop local and regional markets, attract special-interest groups and tours, and become high-quality activity outlets for tourists already in the area.

The Indiana Department of Commerce and Indiana State Festival Association (1988) advised that a fifty-mile radius is the normal target market area for small festivals. The Province of Saskatchewan (Saskatchewan Ministry of Tourism and Small Business n.d.) suggested that 75 percent of the attendance at special events will come from the locality during initial years of operation, but a study of events in that province (Derek Murray Consulting Associates Ltd. 1985) found that 47 percent of visitors were real tourists from beyond fifty miles away. A visitor survey by Plant (1984) of the Elmira (Ontario) Maple Syrup Festival concluded that a two-hour driving radius defined the main market area of this community festival. Furthermore, it was discovered that first-time visitors to the festival were more likely to come from a greater distance, and that 70 percent of them were paying their first visit to the area as well.

The definition of *tourists* will of course influence all measurements. From the perspective of the host community a visitor is a visitor, but higher-level tourist organizations are interested mainly in travelers from outside the region or country. The question of travel motivation is also important, as the benefits of events cannot be entirely attributed to the event if tourists did not travel because of it. This is called the attribution problem.

More Expenditures and Longer Stays

Conventioneers are commonly believed to be the big spenders of all tourism markets, but eventgoing visitors can be just as important in the spending department. A 1985 study of major events in Montreal found that direct spending by visitors was about $80 million, almost as much as the $87 million left behind by 125,000 conventioneers in the city (Colbert, 1988).

Visitors to the Antigonish (Nova Scotia) Highland Games and other cultural festivals were found to stay longer—9.65 nights on average, compared to 6 nights—and spend more—$948 compared to $450—than the average tourist to the region (Nova Scotia Department of Tourism 1987). Some 26 percent of games visitors said the event was the reason for their visit to the province, and fully 68 percent came to the town of Antigonish for the games. The Highland Games generated the best local campsite occupancy rates for the whole year.

An evaluation of events in Saskatchewan (Derek Murray Consulting Associates Ltd. 1985) revealed that event-related travel spending was double the average trip expenditure in the province. It was also found that for every dollar spent at an event, six dollars were spent in the host community. Community spending by nonlocal eventgoers was divided among dining (29 percent), shopping (26 percent), accommodation (15 percent), transport (14 percent), entertainment (10 percent), and business (4.5 percent). Themed and sporting events had the greatest tourism impact.

Vaughan (1979) undertook an extensive analysis of the impact of the Edinburgh Festival and concluded that the average daily spending of foreign tourists was considerably greater than that of British visitors. Furthermore, because of their spending patterns, the local income created (using multipliers) per visitor day was also much higher for foreign festivalgoers.

This type of conclusion should not, however, be assumed to apply everywhere. It obviously depends on the nature of the attractions, seasonal factors, and many other potential influences. Nevertheless, the lesson to be learned is that events that specifically attract visitors to one locality are bound to have a greater economic impact for the area, and likely for the surrounding region, than that of general tourists who are merely passing through or visiting friends and relatives.

The Length of the Event

One-day events are much less likely to attract overnight stays than are weekend and longer events. Many have found a ten-day format, encompassing two weekends, to be ideal for maximizing tourist attendance. Special Events Report (1983) suggested that eight to fourteen days was the best duration for festivals, allowing enough time to create momentum but remaining short enough to build a sense of urgency for the media and potential customers. Mega-events spanning weeks or months have the advantage of being able to employ early activities and related publicity to stimulate additional demand. Short-duration events do not have this potential and must rely on year-round public relations and intensive bursts of pre-event publicity and advertising to attract attention. On the other hand, longer events are often one-shot happenings, which have the potential to fail completely, whereas annual one-day festivals can build substantial repeat trade.

The Impact of Visitor Spending

To event organizers, the total expenditure of all customers is the crucial financial statistic, but in a tourism context the expenditure of visitors to the area is much more important than total revenue. There are also significant differences in impact between money spent at the event and money spent on the trip and in the community as a whole. Tourist spending is considered to be new or incremental and is therefore equivalent to the earnings of an export industry. Money spent by tourists in area hotels, shops, restaurants, and so on has a much wider economic impact than money spent at the event site, although both can be important to the community's economy. A third complication when measuring event revenue is the difference between money spent by visitors who traveled specifically or mainly for the event and by those who happened to attend the event while in the area for other reasons. Again, both types of revenue are important, but for maximum tourism impact the event must actually attract visitors—or stimulate spending that would not have occurred in the absence of the event. These issues must be kept in mind when reading the following examples; they are thoroughly discussed in Chapter 10.

To the degree that festivals and events are successful in attracting tourists, as opposed to local audiences, off-site expenditures will increase. More travelers means larger spending on travel, accommodation, and off-site attractions or retail and service businesses, although the spending will be split between the host community and outlets en route. A good example is our case study of Dickens on the Strand in Galveston, Texas, where visitor surveys were used to estimate total spending of $7.5 million, including 54 percent at the site, another 28 percent on Galveston Island, and the remainder outside the immediate area (see Chapter 9).

An assessment of the impact of eight festivals and special events in the National Capital Region (Coopers and Lybrand 1989) estimated that the festivals made a total contribution of 1,881 person-days of employment and $61 million (Canadian) to the regional economy. Nonlocal attendees ate out at restaurants more, shopped more, and visited entertainment spots more than did the local audience, but the different events resulted in different patterns. For example, visitors to the Festival of Arts were more likely to see live theater in the capital. A more detailed case study of these events is presented in Chapter 9.

Goeldner and Long (1987) reported on a 1986 survey of visitors to the 12-day annual National Western Stock Show in Denver, Colorado, an event that features livestock shows and rodeos. The research estimated that of a total attendance of over 350,000, two-thirds of all visiting households were from the Denver metropolitan area, but 86,000 tourists also were attracted, and 22 percent of them stayed overnight. This group of overnight tourists spent $27 million, out of the total estimated expenditure of $39 million by all visitors. The largest category of spending away from the events was for food and entertainment, followed by the retail and lodging sectors. Sixty percent of all expenditures were made within the city of Denver, and combined local and county tax gains were estimated to be $816,000.

An analysis of visitors to the two-day 1987 Bluegrass Music Festival in Louisville, Kentucky (Kentucky Department of Travel Development 1987), concluded that 70 percent of the patrons were from the state, and that about $500,000 in direct spending resulted in $900,000 total income to the state, using a multiplier of 1.7 (see Chapter 10 for a discussion of multipliers). About $63,000 in tax revenue was created, of which the state realized $50,000. Direct spending by attendees went to the following outlets: food, $134,000; lodging, $116,000; alcohol, $75,000; souvenirs and crafts, $44,000; gas and oil, $36,000; groceries, $18,000; other retail, $82,000.

Visitor Spending versus Capital Costs

Mega-events naturally generate much higher levels of visitor expenditure, and they are most likely to create community- and regionwide benefits, owing to longer stays and the wide spread of accommodation that high levels of demand usually necessitate. Care must be taken, however, to distinguish between the estimates of total economic value to the host community, which are likely to include the multiplier effect of construction costs, and the estimates of impact attributable to tourist expenditure alone.

For example, Toronto's bid proposal for the 1996 Summer Olympics (Toronto Ontario Olympic Council 1989) noted that 80 percent of the direct economic impact of the Montreal Summer Olympics of 1976 was attributable to capital expenditures for new facilities, whereas for the 1984 Los Angeles Games fully 60 percent of the primary economic impact stemmed from visitor spending. Approximately 600,000 visitors to Los Angeles stayed an average of six days, and there were also some 30,000 officials, participants, and media representatives, who stayed much longer. The Los Angeles Games were notable for low capital costs, as well as reliance on private sponsorships, as opposed to the heavy government funding of Montreal's Olympics.

Toronto's bid concept followed the Los Angeles example of minimizing capital costs and maximizing corporate participation. The bid consultants (Cresap Management Consultants) forecast that visitor and participant expenditures would approximate $360 million (Canadian) from 600,000 visitors, although they believed 20 percent of the visitor spending might be "displaced" from normal spending outlets in the area (Toronto Ontario Olympic Council 1989).

We will return to this issue in Chapter 10, by examining the benefit-cost ratio of the Adelaide Grand Prix. In that Australian case, only capital costs involving grants or other money made available to the state because of the event were included in the calculation of economic benefits.

Sporting Events

Although there is no systematic research evidence on this point, it appears that certain types of events attract higher spenders and generate greater on- or off-site revenues. Sports might have a higher economic impact because many competitions last more than one day, or because competitors often travel with their whole families. Several examples of research on the economic impact of sporting events follow.

Rooney (1988) reported that the annual Masters Golf Classic at Augusta, Georgia, yields between $20 million and $30 million to the local economy and the ten-day annual Kentucky Derby Festival draws three-quarters of a million in attendance and has an impact of $18 million.

A study of a ball tournament in Savannah, Georgia (Savannah Leisure Services Bureau 1987), which attracted 127 teams and 1,740 participants from thirty-five states plus Puerto Rico, documented substantial economic benefits to the city. In total, it was estimated that visitors spent $585,000 in the city, excluding spending at the city-owned ball complex, of which Savannah collected $9,000 in room taxes and another $4,000 in local sales tax. The visitors spent most on lodging, followed by restaurant meals, car rentals, food purchases, gas and oil, and car repairs. Savannah actively pursues tournaments at its own ball complex, which both generates tourism benefits for the city and helps justify first-class recreational facilities.

Even small sports events can be important sources of income to a community, agency, or league. The New Brunswick Department of Tourism (1987) studied the 1986 Canadian Midget Softball Championship, an event that had minor tourist appeal but attracted twelve teams and obviously many family members. The eight-day competition resulted in $225,000 spent in the host community, compared to only $31,000 in direct costs, half of which went into permanent facility improvements.

Other types of sporting events can yield similar benefits. Henry and McMullen (1987) examined three horse races called the Aiken (South Carolina) Triple Crown, which together generated $302,000 in direct visitor spending to Aiken and over $500,000 in total impact. The market area for each race was examined, with the finding that 60 percent of the audience came from within a range of 40 to 120 miles. Most visitors stayed for one or two nights, while 31 percent were day-trippers.

Tax Benefits

Several of the studies cited above included an estimate of the tax benefits accruing to government from expenditures at events and during related travel. Another example is given by Taylor and Gratton (1988), who reported that public authorities gained an income of $125 million from the 1984 Los Angeles Olympics. And a Coopers and Lybrand study (1989) found that of the $61 million contribution of eight festivals and events to Canada's National Capital Region, $8.8 million was direct tax income to governments.

This fact in itself is an important motivation for government assistance to events, although it applies only to events that can attract significant amounts of spending from outside the government's jurisdiction or can meet a senior government's criteria for stimulating regional development. Events that stimulate tourist spending on highly taxed goods and services obviously generate the highest taxes, so the presence of hotel room taxes or sales taxes is an important variable, as is the nature of the event attractions and spending outlets. Indirectly, taxes also accrue from improved economic performance of organizations and businesses subject to corporate tax and from increases in personal incomes subject to taxation.

Employment

Most events generate little in the way of permanent employment, although the larger annual ones require at least a small full-time staff. Mega-events requiring a lengthy planning, operating, and shutting-down period can have a more substantial impact, particularly if major construction projects are needed. Hatten (1987) reported that Expo '86 in Vancouver generated 29,000 on-site jobs during the six-month event and increased employment 7.6 percent overall in the metropolitan area.

The income generated by small events, regardless of direct job creation, does result in support jobs, both in tourism and in other sectors as well. The employment multiplier (see Chapter 10) is often used to estimate the number of jobs created for every direct job in tourism or, more appropriately for events, the number of jobs created per unit of tourist spending. These jobs are expressed as person-years of employment, as many of the jobs are temporary (for example, site construction and site staff) or part-time. For instance, the study of eight events in Canada's National Capital Region estimated that tourist income from the events generated 1,881 person-years of employment in the region, including only 20 full-time jobs (Coopers and Lybrand 1989).

The Legacy

Part of the justification for enormous capital investment in mega-events is the promise of a permanent legacy for the host community or nation. The legacy can take many forms: financial, as in the creation of a $215 million fund for youth sports created by the Los Angeles Olympic Games (Ueberroth 1985); or physical, as with the sports facilities left by the Olympics and the monuments, parks, and transportation infrastructure created by world's fairs. It can also be psychological, environmental, or cultural in nature.

Dungan (1984) gave a number of examples of the indirect and direct physical legacies of major events, including improvements to the Los Angeles airport, Montreal's subway system, Knoxville's freeways, fairground renovations in Oklahoma City, parks in Chicago, and various urban renewal schemes. He also pointed out that physical structures, particularly those created for world's fairs, such as the Eiffel Tower in Paris or Seattle's Space Needle, have become valuable permanent symbols for their cities.

Profits and Investments

Not even successful tourist-oriented events necessarily generate a surplus or profit for the organizers. Research by Getz and Frisby (1988) found that of fifty-two community-run festivals in Ontario, Canada, the average surplus revenue was a meager $2,400, with a range from zero to $30,000. But nine of the festivals had a special project or fund for surplus revenue. Examples of community projects benefiting from festivals and events are numerous, ranging from the huge legacies of the Olympics, which benefit mostly organized sports, to small improvements in community infrastructure.

For example, McIntosh (1987) documented the efforts of the Wellesley Apple Butter and Cheese Festival in raising money for local park and recreation improvements. In 1986 this festival generated a $16,000 (Canadian) surplus, of which $7,000 is committed to community center or parkland improvement. Getz (1984) reported on the efforts of residents of Carrbridge, in the Highlands of Scotland, to raise money for a community hall from an annual music festival called the Carrbridge Ceilidh Week. Janiskee (1980) reported on the many community projects supported by the Salley (South Carolina) Chitlin Strut.

Social and Cultural Legacies

Many social and cultural benefits of events have been imputed, but little research exists to support the widespread belief that a special event can create a permanent social or cultural legacy in the host community. Ritchie (1984) suggested that several positive outcomes could accrue: increased community pride and spirit; strengthening of traditions and values; greater participation in sports, arts, or other activities related to the event theme; adaptation of new social patterns or cultural forms through exposure at the event. Other long-term benefits might take the form of increased voluntarism and community group activity, intercultural interaction, and cooperation—all of which are forecast benefits in Toronto's bid for the 1996 Summer Olympics (Toronto Ontario Olympic Council 1989).

Many organizers refer to these benefits as partial justification of the event, and conceivably an economic value could be placed on some of them (for example, the value of volunteer labor), while others might have a permanent economic cost (such as increased demand for social and cultural services). Social, cultural, and recreational agencies that foster festivals and special events invariably pursue such goals.

A Legitimate Payback for Grants

Holgerson (1988) reported on a study of thirty-one festivals that the Canadian Department of Communications' Cultural Initiatives Program partially funded in 1987–88. Almost $3 million in grants from three levels of government generated at least $6.3 million in economic impact, for a nominal return-on-investment ratio of 2.3 to 1. Financial assistance to the Edinburgh Festival from the local government, according to Vaughan (1979), generated a 500 percent return on its investment, as measured in total income created by tourist spending.

Of course, governments do not normally account for their grants in this way, but increasingly they want concrete proof that their largesse is creating economic benefits, even in the arts and cultural fields.

This sampling of research findings on the economic impact of festivals and events shows the range and scale of effects that can be achieved. The nature of the event, its organization, and marketing are all important factors influencing the outcome. Chapter 10 examines ways of maximizing local and regional economic benefits, based on a knowledge of how the multiplier works.

POTENTIAL ECONOMIC COSTS AND PROBLEMS

There is a danger that only the obvious development and operating costs of events will be considered, whereas many opportunity costs and externalities must also be evaluated. In this section the types of costs are listed, with examples.

Development and Operating Costs

Huge debts can accompany mega-events, owing to the extraordinary capital and operating costs. Taylor and Gratton (1988) discussed the public debts run up by the Olympics, notably in Munich (1972) and Montreal (1976). This trend was at least checked by the surplus-generating Los Angeles Olympic Games in 1984, which have, perhaps, become the new model. World's fairs, on the other hand, have less potential for attracting huge corporate sponsorships and television contracts, so they still depend largely on government grants or the passing on of costs to other governmental operating divisions. Livable Cities (McNulty 1986) reported that of all the modern world's fairs, only Seattle's in 1962 generated a profit.

One of the great advantages of community festivals and many other special events is their independence from capital-intensive development projects. Most utilize existing facilities, and many use surplus revenue to improve community facilities and parks. Operating costs are the main worry of organizers.

Grants and sponsorships used to cover costs are potentially economic benefits to the community or region, depending on their source and whether or not the money would have been allocated to that area for some other purpose—in which case it is only a transfer. In-kind gifts, such as free publicity or food donations, can also be considered as economic benefits for the organizers, but not necessarily for the community. Our discussion of cost-benefit assessment in Chapter 10 takes a tourism perspective on this issue and sorts out the appropriate allocations of input and output in determining the cost-benefit ratio.

Opportunity Costs

Every investment could potentially be channeled elsewhere to achieve the same goals; this forfeited opportunity is called the opportunity cost. It is not always considered in economic impact assessments, but it should be included for a thorough determination of the net worth of an event.

For a business, or a group engaged in fund-raising, the event must not only show a desired surplus or profit, it must be shown to be a better investment than, say, a raffle or real estate investment. For a grant-giving government agency, money put into events must be shown to achieve the agency's goals to the same or greater extent than alternative expenditures. Otherwise, the opportunity costs exceed the benefits.

Of course, it is seldom that simple a calculation. Events can have value beyond the monetary returns, so private businesses have to give a value to the publicity and image-making roles. Fund-raising agencies might be able to generate more money in other ways, but would the alternatives be appropriate for the group, and as easy to implement? And what are the risks? Some investments pay more but carry a higher chance of failure.

There is another way to look at opportunity costs. The host community that becomes a tourist destination might find it cannot attract, or no longer wants to accommodate, certain industries or commercial businesses that are incompatible with its tourism image. A town noted for its smelly industries might not attract tourists to an arts festival! The opportunity cost is equal to the benefits that could be realized by alternatives to tourism. But in other areas, events and tourism in general might be the only alternative, as traditional industries have declined to the point where they can no longer support a viable community.

Externalities

An external cost is any expense or problem created directly or indirectly by an event, or event tourism policy, that would not be accounted for in an event budget. These can be financial, environmental, or social and cultural in nature, and it might not be practical to put a dollar value on all externalities.

It is quite possible that a successful event can actually harm certain businesses or elements in the economy. This can occur in several ways. The event might attract business from one area to another, typically from an established commercial area to a remote festival site, or from one sector to another, such as an increase in entertainment spending. Parades and street festivals can involve physical barriers that reduce accessibility to establishments; or the crowds and traffic might simply discourage customers from approaching the business area. And money normally spent with permanent businesses will likely be displaced to the temporary spending outlets associated with the event. If these negative effects are substantial, the event organizers can expect to face some hostile business leaders who have political clout.

And as noted earlier regarding Expo '86, a successful mega-event can redirect traditional tourism flows, resulting in gains for part of the destination region or country and losses for other areas. One counterstrategy to this problem is to ensure that all regions of the country get their share of major events; another is to promote tours that encompass the event attraction, its hinterland, and remote attractions for those touring to the event.

Certain costs and negative effects are often passed on to the community as a whole and not included in the event's accounts. This is particularly true for environmental consequences, especially because ecological damage often has no immediate or visible indicators, and perhaps no one even to monitor or report the problem. The kinds of damage resulting from events can include those of infrastructure and site development (for example, road improvements or waterfront dredging and fill), air and water pollution (from traffic and wastes), litter, disruption of habitat, trampling of vegetation, and property damage from vandalism or overuse. Naturally, larger events requiring physical development and attracting huge volumes of visitors will have a greater probability of causing environmental damage. Indirect negative environmental impact must also be considered, but will likely be difficult to prove. These can include the results of attitudinal change—does the event foster an exploitive approach to nature?—or permanent changes in recreational or tourism patterns that lead to ecosystem disruption.

Social problems at events are readily apparent, but external changes might also occur. Disruption to community life is perhaps the most frequent, and this can take the form of amenity loss owing to noise or crowds, changes in social and leisure habits—such as people leaving town to escape the event's impacts—and intergroup hostility arising from resentment or inequitable distribution of costs and benefits. Major events can also upset housing markets, resulting in the displacement of tenants or escalation of prices, and can cause inflation in other goods and services that most affect low-income groups.

Event Failure

Events can fail for many reasons, and the possible costs of a failure should be taken into account. The loss in monetary terms can be most easily forecast, but there might also be losses of image and prestige, credibility, and effectiveness in other areas of the organization's or sponsor's business. More significant is the possibility that an event organization might claim a surplus or a profit from an event that fails to generate the tourist benefits it claimed, so that the community pays the price. This type of external risk can be assessed only if the community is intimately involved in the decisions.

Economic impact assessment typically ignores both opportunity and external costs, which is the main reason comprehensive cost-benefit evaluations are necessary. This is easier said than done, however. As discussed in Chapter 10, a major problem is the assigning of costs to intangibles, such as amenity loss and social change.

RELATIVE ECONOMIC ADVANTAGES AND DISADVANTAGES OF EVENT TOURISM

There is no guarantee that any of the potential costs or benefits of events will be applicable in any given situation. The potential benefits should be stated as goals, complete with strategies for attaining and evaluating each of them. Goals must also be developed to avoid, minimize, and where necessary ameliorate any negative impact. Although no absolute assurance can be given that event tourism will be beneficial to a destination, its advantages and disadvantages relative to other forms of tourism development can be stated with some confidence.

Advantages

Event tourism can be a very cost-effective means of developing tourist attractions and activity outlets. Volunteer labor and the participation of numerous community groups support most events, even the largest, compared to the reliance of most service industries on paid labor. Most do not require special facilities or infrastructure improvements. They easily attract corporate sponsorships, which spreads the costs from public to private sources. Many will generate a high ratio of revenue to costs. High local-income multipliers are possible when revenue sources can be controlled and kept within the community, whereas other forms of tourism development, especially in small communities, typically have very low local-income multipliers, owing to external ownership and imported supplies. Finally, every place has the potential to develop festival and event attractions, which assist in spreading tourism geographically and seasonally.

These cost-benefit advantages are in addition to the many other possible benefits of events, including their image-making potential, their linkage to other areas of public policy (such as fostering the arts), and their contribution to sustainable and community development.

Disadvantages

Relative to other forms of tourism development, event tourism has few cost-benefit disadvantages. The main limitation is in the fact that most events and festivals depend on local and regional markets; but this is really no different from many other elements of the industry, such as restaurants, theme parks, historic sites, national parks, or cultural attractions. Mega-events are the costliest and are seldom justifiable on purely economic grounds. They offer so much opportunity as development catalysts and image makers, however, that they are sought after with a passion. Events do have the potential to cause environmental, social, and cultural problems, but this applies to tourism in general. The major risk is that externalities and opportunity costs will not be incorporated in cost-benefit evaluations.

The balance between relative economic costs and benefits seems clearly in favor of the benefits. Tourist organizations can pursue an event tourism program in addition to, and complemented by, other areas of tourism and cultural and social policy, with minimal direct costs. At a minimum, the provision of organizational expertise, marketing data, and limited funds for seed money can go a long way to encourage numerous events to fulfill their tourism potential.

SUMMARY

It was suggested early in Chapter 1 that one major reason events might fail to realize their tourism potential is inadequate attention to their multiple roles, meanings, and impacts. Other reasons were also suggested: failure to integrate event marketing in destination planning and marketing schemes; failure of destinations to utilize the inherent attractiveness of events in product development, image-making, and marketing; and insufficient marketing data to permit sophisticated segmentation for event tourism.

The bulk of Chapter 1 was devoted to a listing and discussion of the roles of festivals and events in destination development; but given the above-mentioned reasons that events can fail to realize their tourism potential, this discussion is of equal importance to event managers and organizers. These roles were graphically summarized in Figure 1-1.

As attractions, festivals and events are important for both domestic and international tourism, even though research has found that most events rely on local and regional markets. Their particular advantages in helping to spread tourism demand geographically and by season were explained, with examples. As animators of static attractions, events help to attract attention and stimulate repeat visits. Examples were given for resorts, historic and cultural sites, theme parks, convention and exhibition facilities, museums and art galleries, markets and shopping areas, fair and exhibition grounds.

Image-making or image enhancement for a destination area is another important role for festivals and events. Mega-events attract much publicity, but individual events, and events collectively, can help create or make tangible a destination theme. Hallmark events are a special case, in which the event is so closely associated with the destination or host community that the two mutually reinforce each other's attractiveness.

As catalysts, events have contributed to urban renewal and development projects, provision of infrastructure that can benefit other tourism development, and even general economic growth. Mega-events such as the Olympics and world's fairs are typically pursued for these benefits, but smaller events can collectively be catalysts because of their image-enhancing role and their ability to bring large numbers of people into targeted areas.

Events can contribute to alternative tourism, which is a reaction against all the negative effects of modern mass tourism. Festivals and events help accomplish this in several ways: by providing local leisure and enhancing the host community, thereby lessening the need to escape; by maintaining authentic traditions, which can have the effect of attracting tourists more sensitive to indigenous cultures; and by bridging the host-guest gulf, thereby facilitating understanding and more mutually beneficial exchanges. Sustainable development, which is economic and physical development that does not harm the resource base and natural environment, is closely related. Festivals and events can be held with minimal physical development, although most mega-events require substantial change. Events are also natural allies of heritage and nature conservation and can be explicitly used as interpreters, control mechanisms, or boundary maintainers—to shift or intercept travel demand—as well as in fostering positive attitudes. Finally, event tourism is a logical and simple way to encourage community-based tourism, wherein the community defines its own goals and tourism products and keeps control over the process. The underlying assumption is that communities will be more sensitive to preserving their resource base and way of life for future generations.

Evidence from a variety of research was cited to demonstrate in more concrete terms how events attract tourists, the size of market areas, tourist spending patterns, and related economic impact. The legacy was also discussed—how facilities, revenue, and social, cultural, and psychological benefits can accrue to host communities as a result of events. Important observations and conclusions from this section include the following:

Mega-events generate significant domestic and foreign tourist demand, and they can influence long-term patterns and flows of tourism to and in the host destination.

Most events, including the largest, depend on local and regional markets for success; the day-tripper market is of primary importance to small events.

The length of the event influences tourist demand; weekend and weeklong events have greater potential for stimulating overnight visits, which leads to greater economic benefits.

Of principal interest is the amount of incremental or new revenue brought into the destination because the event serves as an attraction, or because it stimulates longer stays and more spending.

Off-site and en-route tourist expenditures are often as important, or more important, to tourism than on-site spending; some types of events are better than others in generating total spending and total incremental revenue.

Governments benefit from increased tax revenue, and research has found that grants to events can have significant, positive returns to government coffers.

Care must be taken to distinguish the impact of capital costs from that of visitor expenditure, when assessing economic effects.

Only the largest events generate significant direct employment benefits, but incremental revenue from tourism or external funding sources does indirectly help create significant employment.

Capital and operating costs are not the only negatives to consider. The cost of forgoing some other opportunity when developing or investing in events also has to be considered. In addition, externalities must not be ignored; these are the costs, often in the form of pollution, ecological damage, or social or cultural disruption, that event organizers normally would exclude from their calculations. The community as a whole must bear these externalized costs. The potential costs of event failure, to organizers and the destination, also should be forecast.

Chapter 1 concluded by comparing the relative benefits and costs of event tourism to those of other forms of tourism development. It was argued that event tourism presents a low-cost, high-return option that should not be ignored. In addition to economic benefits, event tourism can stimulate community-based tourism, contribute to heritage and nature conservation, and help create or enhance a positive destination image. Event tourism can and should be advanced in partnership with social, cultural, arts, and environmental policies.

CHAPTER TWO

Perspectives and Definitions

Event tourism is concerned with the roles that festivals and special events can play in destination development and the maximization of an event's attractiveness to tourists. The primary reasons for fostering event tourism are economic, based on the facts demonstrated in Chapter 1—that events can be used like export industries to generate income and jobs and to act as catalysts for other forms of development.

It is dangerous and counterproductive, however, to concentrate on the economic dimension to the exclusion of other perspectives on festivals and events. Indeed, many event organizers are concerned only incidentally with tourism, as their events have social and cultural goals. They should nevertheless be very interested in the potential of tourism to further their causes, if only through its revenue-generating advantages. Tourist destination planners also can maximize the acceptance and development of event tourism by recognizing and building upon the nontouristic aspects of festivals and events.

This chapter addresses the other major perspectives on festivals and events, showing how they are linked to event tourism and how a sound marketing strategy for specific festivals and events must encompass all the perspectives. Examination of a model of the various perspectives is followed by various definitions and typologies, or classifications, of special events and festivals within each perspective. The intended results are a more comprehensive understanding of all the dimensions of festivals and events and a greater capability for developing the tourist potential of events.

A MODEL OF PERSPECTIVES

In the context of tourism planning, development, and marketing, special events can play a number of key roles. Each role can be important in isolation, but the combined, synergistic effect of these roles can be vital in determining the success of destination areas and individual attractions. Events have other meanings and roles as well, and although these functions might seem to be unrelated to tourism, they are nevertheless important considerations in any event tourism strategy and for every event manager. Failure to see the interconnections could weaken or impede tourism planning. Furthermore, insensitivity to the non-touristic meanings and roles of festivals and events is likely to result in cultural insensitivity and public opposition.

Main Components of the Model

Figure 2-1 illustrates the most important perspectives when discussing festivals and special events. Of principal interest in this book is the perspective of event tourism, with events filling the roles of attractions, development catalysts, and image makers. In this context, the products of festivals and events can be defined as the events themselves, packages or tours, and the desired effects on economic development, including income generation, employment, economic stimulation, regional development, and an improved balance of payments.

The **tangible product** is the program of the festival or event itself, or alternatively packages and tours of events, and the tangible merchandise sold or consumed at events. The meanings of events are superficially reflected in the names or themes, such as *arts festival* or "*Olympics.*" They can be classified by reference to their theme or by the activities and tangible products offered for consumption to the public. But this facade disguises the fact that most events are created for specific reasons—as tourist attractions, fund-raisers, advertising and promotion devices, or stimulators of community pride. They are intended to be catalysts or facilitators.

The visitor expects a special experience at festivals and events, something out of the ordinary and markedly different from other types of entertainment or attraction. The word *festival* has clear, if variable, connotations to most people in the English-speaking world, and events are perceived to be "special" when they are clearly different (or effectively promoted as being different) from the ordinary range of things to see and do. Yet there is definitely an emerging consistency in what is offered and what is expected at festivals and events—a kind of standardized package. To develop the visitor's perspective, we will examine leisure and travel motivations and develop a three-part model, which breaks the festival or event product into three categories: essential services, generic benefits

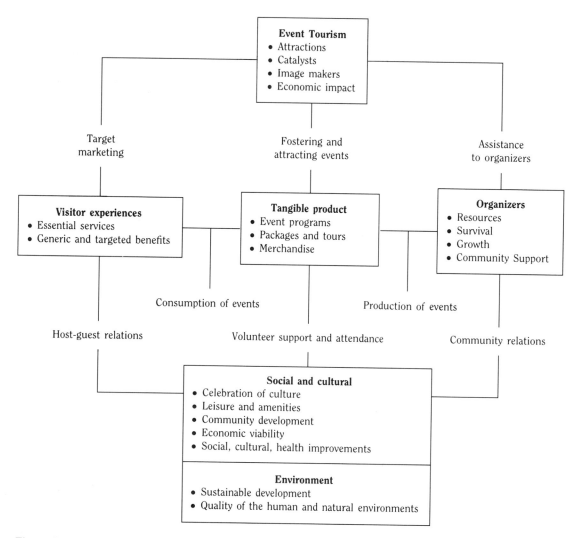

Figure 2-1. Perspectives on festivals and special events.

common to most or all festivals and events, and targeted benefits to appeal to specific segments, including tourists.

Organizers of events have many points of view on the roles and meanings of their productions, but what is unique is that most festivals and events depend on volunteer labor and are one-shot or annual occurrences of relatively short duration. This makes their organization and management quite different from those of permanent attractions and facilities, leading to an emphasis on strategies for resource acquisition, as well as development and retention of community support. Sometimes the survival of the organization itself, or advancement of the personal ambitions of organizers, can supersede the stated goals of the event. When events are developed or run by permanent attractions or the professional staff of corporations and public agencies, a different perspective is evident. The event might be indistinguishable from those launched by volunteers, but the management and impact on the organization will be categorically different.

For convenience, a range of issues has been grouped together as the social and cultural perspective, which encompasses the meaning of festivals and events as cultural celebrations, along with their roles in fostering leisure pursuits and amenities and as agents of community development, economic viability, and social, cultural, and health improvements. Included here is the issue of community control over development—in other words, a community-based approach to tourism development.

Closely linked to the host community's social and cultural concerns are issues of the environment. Both the human and natural environments have to be protected against the potential negative effects of events and tourism. Conversely, event tourism can and should be used as a positive tool in achieving sustainable development and in enhancing heritage and nature conservation.

Linkages in the Model

Now that the basic perspectives have been introduced, look again at Figure 2-1 and examine the linkages between components of the model. These linkages are management and planning operations, or interactions subject to some degree of control. Placing event tourism at the top of the model is clearly a bias derived from the title and purpose of this book, but it also serves to show that tourism organizations can take a lead role in shaping the entire field of festivals and special events. Arts and cultural agencies and sports organizations also want to be key players, and they represent logical partners for the tourism industry, community groups, and private enterprise in developing the full potential of events.

Three key operations, all of which are discussed in detail throughout the book, depend largely on coordinated action by tourism, sometimes in partnership with arts, culture, and leisure or sports interests: assistance to event organizers, the fostering or attracting of events, and market research and target marketing to identify and attract audiences and tourists. Host-guest relations, so important to the success of community-based events, and of increasing importance in alternative tourism, are subject to some degree of control or influence. Local and regional tourism bodies will likely have more success than national bodies in promoting host-guest contacts, ameliorating problems, and making certain that benefits accrue to both hosts and guests. Only in a few situations, such as at theme parks or remote settings, will this relationship not be of utmost significance. Similarly, the event organizers must develop and permanently maintain good relations with their host community. Where community groups run the event, their networking and political support should be strong. If operated by private enterprise or agencies and groups without a firm base in the community (such as imported sports competitions), much groundwork might be required. Tourist organizations, especially local ones, can mediate and enhance this process of community relations.

The consumption of events involves travel, use of information, and perhaps some reliance on intermediaries, such as travel agents, tour wholesalers, and guides. Tourism officials can influence this process to ensure a higher-quality consumer experience. Indeed, it is evident that the whole area of festival and special event packaging is very underdeveloped.

The actual production of events is the responsibility of the organizers, but it can be made more effective and efficient through advisory services, assistance packages, and objective research and evaluation supported by tourist organizations. Organizers tend to learn mostly from each other through informal contacts and their associations, and these too should be aided by tourism agencies.

Finally, volunteer support and community attendance, easily the most important elements in determining the success of most festivals and events, must be considered. If all the other operational matters are handled properly, maintaining community support should not be a problem. All too often, however, this foundation for successful events is ignored or taken for granted.

DEFINITION OF EVENTS AND SPECIAL EVENTS

In this era of mass advertising, staged media events, and bland standardization, the terms *event, special event,* and *festival* have been somewhat cheapened. The consumer is confronted with a "festival of seafood" at the local restaurant, or a "funfest" at the amusement park. So-called special events might include a sale at the shopping mall, a party, or a visit by a well-known personality. Events are created, manipulated, marketed, and sold for a variety of purposes. Yet despite the clutter, the festival or event that is a truly public celebration flourishes.

The task of defining and explaining all the terms used in the festivals and events field is so great that a glossary has been compiled for easy reference. Many terms are used loosely, or are jargonistic and not universally understood. There also seems to be an emerging competition to stylize or create new terms in order to stand out from the crowd. Hence, we see a "river*fest*" instead of festival. It is bound to get more confusing as promotional experts strive for competitive advantage.

Defining *event* is a straightforward matter; determining what makes one special is problematic. A dictionary provides basic meanings of an event: "that which happens," "affair," "result," "effect," "item at a sports meeting." More to the point is this definition: "a notable occurrence." Given that "notable" and "special" might very well be used as synonyms, we are left with this implication: to say an occurrence is an event is to say it is special! This does not help at all.

Common usage of the term *special event* is easier to clarify. Normally it refers to any event outside the normal range of programs and activities of the sponsoring or managing organization. The clear implication is that it is a onetime event, not to be repeated, or an event held infrequently. A festival can be a special event, but not all special events are festivals.

The most common special events are sports, such as tournaments, games, and Olympics. Many are entertaining or recreational in nature. It really does not matter, as it is the context that makes them special to the organizer. Similarly, it is the context that makes an event special to the customer, and it is quite possible that organizer, sponsor, and customer will not agree on the specialness of the event. As a working definition, this will suffice for this book:

> *A* special event *is a onetime or infrequently occurring event outside the normal program or activities of the sponsoring or organizing body.*
>
> *To the customer, a special event is an opportunity for a leisure, social, or cultural experience outside the normal range of choices or beyond everyday experience.*

These are good working definitions, but they do not do full justice to the meaning of *specialness*. In the concluding chapter of this book we will return to this issue, when a synthesis of all the pertinent themes can be constructed.

Other related terms, particularly *mega-event* and *hallmark event,* also can be defined only contextually. To get at the meanings of these terms, we have to develop an event tourism typology. The purpose of typologies, or classifications, is essentially scientific, but the exercise is valuable for tourism practitioners and event organizers as well. Without some way to sort out the different types of events, it is difficult to describe them in terms everyone will understand. Confusion and ineffective communications result when, for example, an organizer talks about an arts festival to foster musical appreciation in the community, but a government official interprets arts festival to mean a regular program of performances at a theater, or thinks only of the tourist potential. Attention to classification is also becoming more important as terms get modified, commercialized, and misused.

EVENT TOURISM TYPOLOGY

An event tourism typology is illustrated in Figure 2-2. It assumes that the most basic goal of event tourism is the creation of tourist attractions, capable of generating travel demand or satisfying visitor needs. The other tourism-related roles of events, as image makers, development catalysts, and control mechanisms,

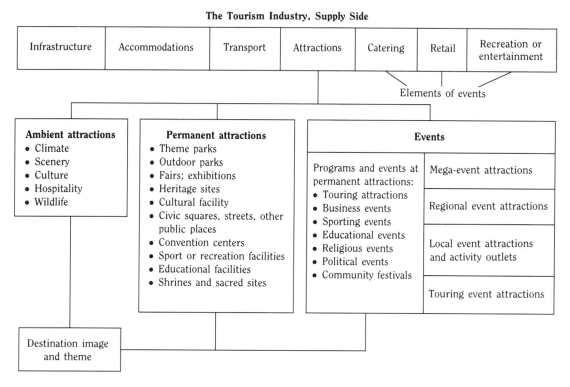

Figure 2-2. An event tourism typology.

are no less important, but they do not require inclusion in a typology of terms. Rather, the focus is on distinguishing events from other types of attractions—both ambient and permanent ones—and from other elements on the supply side of tourism.

Detailed discussion of event definitions and typologies was undertaken by the National Task Force on Tourism Data in Canada (Statistics Canada 1989). Experts from the industry and academia (including this author) were asked to assess the significance of festivals and events and recommend strategies to integrate events more fully in the national tourism planning system. Although no firm definitions and classifications emerged, some progress was made to develop a supply-side approach, and Figure 2-2 builds on this work. A related exercise in the task force reports was the listing of criteria for defining festivals and special events. The characteristics thought to be most important were the following:

- It is open to the public.
- Its main purpose is the celebration or display of a specific theme.
- It takes place once a year or less frequently.

- It has predetermined opening or closing dates.
- It does not own permanent structures.
- Its program may consist of several separate activities.
- All its activities take place in the same local area or region.

These criteria are important, but they lean more toward delimiting festivals, and they tend to exclude several important categories: fairs and exhibitions, because of their reliance on permanent facilities; circuses and other shows that travel; events more regular than once a year; and business-related meetings or conferences—all of which are important to tourism development and all of which have eventlike characteristics. We must therefore develop a classification that encompasses the full range of festivals and events.

Our event tourism typology relates to the key roles of events in destination development, primarily that of attractions. These event attractions include local ones such as community festivals, which can act as activity outlets for tourists. Events with local and regional drawing power are midway in the hierarchy, and at the top are the mega-events, which can motivate large-scale domestic and foreign travel. Mobile events exist as well, and these touring events can potentially achieve any level of tourism attractiveness. Types of programs and events are independent of the hierarchy of attractions, because any type can function at any level of tourism attractiveness. The other tourism-related roles are also relatively independent of the type of event, although larger events with greater attractiveness to tourists are likely to be more powerful image makers and development catalysts.

What Are Mega-Events?

The term *mega-event* requires some elaboration at this point, although it is almost self-defining, since *mega* means large or huge. But what exactly does this mean in the context of event tourism? Certainly world's fairs and the Olympics are big enough to earn this prefix, but what about, say, an annual festival or a political happening?

Marris (1987), summarizing a conference of the International Association of Tourism Experts on the theme of mega-events and mega-attractions, noted that mega-events can be defined by reference to their volume of visitors, cost, or psychology. Their volume should exceed one million visits, their capital cost should be at least $500 million (Canadian), and their reputation should be that of a must-see event. Marris thought the key to getting mega-events through the political approval process was the prestige factor.

Others might prefer a definition that stresses the economic effects of the event, rather than its costs, size, or image. In the same conference, Vanhove and Witt (1987) stressed that a mega-event must be able to attract worldwide publicity. A major conclusion of this conference was that mega-events and mega-attractions should be more alike, and that events could help make attractions more newsworthy.

Rooney (1988, 93) has taken an interesting perspective on mega-events. Looking only at sports, he concluded that all sporting mega-events had common features: they are "loaded with tradition" (although this might have to be fabricated for relatively new ones, such as the Super Bowl); they have profound historical significance; they have developed a mystique or taken on almost mythical proportions; they benefit from "media overload, frequently at the international level"; they are often complemented by other events, such as parades and festivals; and they are sometimes tied to specific places, and even to "hallowed ground." By way of an example, he pointed to the Kentucky Derby: "The Derby, like other mega-events, combines it all. The best athletes, a very special place, hallowed ground, tradition, prestige, mystique, and a surrounding atmosphere of revelry and frivolity" (Rooney, 1988, 96).

From a tourism perspective, the so-called mega-event (and mega-attraction, for that matter) can have only one meaning, and it must be linked to its attractiveness. A world's fair of enormous cost and prestige that attracted only a handful of tourists to the site would be a partial failure—again, only in the context of tourism. Since we know that most festivals and events rely on local and regional audiences, our definition of mega-event must focus on the proportion and number of visits made by overnight travelers to the event. An elaboration of this criterion could be the number and proportion of interstate or international visitors. The actual figures used would have to relate to averages for the destination, to have any meaning for destination tourism planning. For example, in a city or region that has a record of attracting at least 20 percent of its event audiences for overnight stays, a mega-event would have to pull 40 or 50 percent, or be an order of magnitude greater in volume.

The definition of mega-events will always remain subjective, and rather inconsequential. It is really more a question of the relative significance of an event, rather than any particular measure of events. It is placed at the top of the event attraction hierarchy in Figure 2-2 because there must be some recognition for the occasional event that is attractive enough both to generate abnormally large numbers or proportions of tourists who travel long distances and stay overnight and to shape the destination's image in a major way.

Other Elements of the Typology

Event types are often, though not always, linked to permanent facilities or attractions. An event, such as a conference at a university, might be the only reason a facility can be considered as a tourist attraction; or the event might be one element in the attractiveness to tourists of a permanent attraction, such as parades and shows at theme parks. Figure 2-2 lists certain types of attractions or facilities that are linked to types of events. For example, there are numerous programs of events and occasional special events at theme parks, heritage sites, and other such settings. Fairgrounds and exhibition facilities might have many uses, but the annual fair is an event. Although theaters and concert halls are permanent attractions, annual festivals are usually associated with them. Many arts, cultural, and entertainment productions are also taken on the road, thereby becoming touring events.

Civic squares, plazas, streets, and other public places also function occasionally as settings for special events and festivals of all kinds; even protests and demonstrations might fall into this category. Business, sporting, educational, and religious events are often held at permanent facilities, and some of these events also serve as tourist attractions. Pilgrimages and other mass movements of people for special purposes also might be considered in part as events having tourism value.

Also to be noted in this diagram are the links between events and the other supply-side elements, noted across the top. As catalysts of development and as control mechanisms, events can help shape the form of infrastructure and of other attractions. Three elements in particular—catering, retail, and recreation or entertainment—are actually provided by most special events and festivals.

Finally, there is the important category of attractions called ambient ones; that is, they are either pervasive, such as the climate and scenery, or intangible elements of the destination, including culture and hospitality, that nevertheless contribute a great deal to attractiveness. Festivals and events can act as the tangible manifestations of community culture and hospitality, and in fact could be the most important means by which tourists enjoy direct experience of the host culture.

THE TANGIBLE PRODUCT

A special event is a tangible thing encompassing visitor activities, entertainment, sensory stimulation, and products and services being sold and consumed. It usually has a theme that conveys messages about the experiences visitors might gain by attending the event. The tangible event can be considered a product to be consumed by tourists, although it is just as important to think of packages or impact as the intended products of event tourism. Because the term *product* is so important, it is worthwhile to look at the meaning of a tourism product.

Similarities and Differences

Special events share many of the attributes of other tourism products, yet they possess some characteristics that set them apart. Several authors have listed unique features of tourism products (Mill and Morrison 1985; Foster 1985;

Middleton 1988), to which we add the elements that make festivals and special events different.

Tourism products are largely intangible, consisting of personal experiences. Transport, accommodation, and attractions are used, not consumed. The products purchased or consumed at special events are also usually not as important as the atmosphere and the opportunity for a unique experience. Visitors help create the experience, as do the host-guest interactions and those between the visitors and the setting.

Festivals and events are, in common with other tourism elements, an amalgam of services and tangible products. They must be synergistic—the experience must be greater than the sum of the tangible components; individual events are often only one component in a broader travel experience.

Tourism products cannot be inspected in advance. Travel, accommodation, and activity experiences are different each time they are used. Travelers might know destination areas in advance, but not the exact nature of the visit. Special events are inspectable through repeat visits, if the events are unchanged, but the experience is still unlikely to be identical, owing to variations in the setting, social interactions, activities undertaken, or personal circumstances and motivations. Hence, long-term quality control at events is difficult, and ensuring a good visitor experience cannot be guaranteed.

Tourism products cannot be stored. Unused seats, rooms, or admissions are wasted. Special events are the same, in that surplus visitor capacity cannot be carried forward. However, the number and nature of the participants or visitors can actually change the nature of the experience, so that some people receive increased or diminished benefits depending on attendance at events.

Resources must be committed prior to consumption. The physical infrastructure, travel modes, and other sources must be provided before even one tourist can visit a destination or attraction. Special events often must be presented with no guarantee of attendance. Large amounts of organization and paid or volunteer efforts are normally expended up front. Yet events can be postponed or canceled, even though resources will be wasted by doing so.

Tourism resources are of relatively fixed quantity. Supply cannot be easily created, or reduced, as demand shifts. Festivals and events often have fixed capacities based on their physical setting or restrictions imposed for the comfort and enjoyment of customers; but flexibility can be built into some events, such as through adding more entertainment performances or moving to a larger site.

Packaging of tourism products is often difficult, owing to the large number of factors involved in the complete travel experience. Yet package holidays are a mainstay of the travel trade. Special events are themselves a package of components. They have seldom been integrated in broader trip packages, but that is changing, at least for large events.

Changes in demand, due to external influences, are common in tourism. Special events are subject to the same laws of supply and demand, but by their nature can be used to help overcome seasonality in destination areas.

Tourism products are often small of scale and dependent on intermediaries to promote them and deliver visitors. Events aimed at the tourist market have similar dependence, unless they are mega-events, which generate their own demand. On the other hand, small events, such as community festivals, are usually deemed a success if good local or regional attendance is attained.

Consumption of many tourism products is nominally free. Viewing scenery does not usually have to be paid for, although other costs are normally involved, including travel. Festivals are often "open" to the public—for example, Main Street festivals—and participation can be free. Many events, however, regulate participation and do charge admission.

Most tourism products, being experiential in nature, cannot be standardized— although some hotel chains may dispute this! Events are mostly subject to this rule, but it might actually be a strength. Those events that feel the same year after year risk losing the patronage of people who dislike standardization. The success of special events, on the other hand, can probably be attributed in part to the fact that they offer different experiences in an increasingly standardized tourist world.

This examination of tourism products helps define and classify the tangible events; more important, it shows there are some particular characteristics of events that distinguish them from other tourism products. They do require special consideration in tourism planning.

Typology Problems

The most straightforward typology of the tangible product is by theme, and any of the festival and event directories and guidebooks can be consulted on their differing systems. The *Festivals Sourcebook* (Wasserman, Herman, and Root 1984), for example, used 18 main categories and 226 terms of theme or subject material. The problem is that the names of events do not always reflect the themes, and themes do not always reflect the diversity of activity and experience provided by the event. Both a food festival and a music festival might include food and music together, although by common practice the essence of these types of events is fairly clearly denoted by their names. Many celebrations and events are not so clearly differentiated and contain a hodgepodge of subthemes.

The Glossary in this book could be considered a typology, defining key terms that include the basic types of special events and a generic definition of *festival*. Some of the event definitions include related terms that are sometimes used in the names or descriptions of events, as gleaned from numerous event calendars, guides, and promotional material. It is apparent, however, that many terms describing festivals and events in the English language are used only regionally, while others have multiple meanings. Many of the related terms, such as *fair, bazaar, mart,* and *show,* can be used as synonyms, but *show* can be applied to entertainment, exhibitions, and sales alike. It can be confusing!

Hallmark Events

Meyer (1970, 25) listed events by themes, ranging from agriculture to winter carnivals, but included a peculiar category called community festivals, which were created to publicize communities or have become closely identified with specific places. This loose category includes the New Orleans Mardi Gras, although it has many imitators. This type of event has also been called a hallmark event, which Ritchie (1984, 2) defined this way:

> Major one-time or recurring events of limited duration, developed primarily to enhance the awareness, appeal and profitability of a tourism destination in the short and/or long term. Such events rely for their success on uniqueness, status, or timely significance to create interest and attract attention.

Hallmark event is now a widely used term, but, like mega-event, it also resists precise definition. Some use it as a synonym for special event, while others suggest it is a particular class of event that has a unique image or appeal. Indeed, if we look to a dictionary, hallmark refers to a symbol of quality or authenticity that distinguishes some goods from others. But this does not really help in developing a typology of festivals and events as attractions, nor by reference to their themes or tangible components.

Accordingly, hallmark event is best used when discussing a community or destination that is known largely by an event, or where an event takes on such significance that the destination takes its tourism theme from the event. For example, Mardi Gras does give New Orleans a competitive advantage by virtue of its high profile. Stratford, Ontario, has taken its tourism theme from the successful Shakespearean Festival. A onetime event, however, will not likely become the hallmark for a destination.

The Production or Program

Other ways of classifying events relate to their form and what actually goes on during the production or celebration. These typologies are of greater interest to event producers and programmers, but they are worth mentioning here. They include a number of dichotomies: professional versus amateur performances; competitive versus noncompetitive formats; indoor versus outdoor settings; the degree of involvement by participants or spectators; and even the cost—free versus paid admission. Any of these classification systems can be useful, depending on the application.

Guidebooks are a good source of information on what happens at events. In their book *Food Festival*, Geffen and Berglie (1986) described sixty North American events with themes based around food. They observed common elements, including midways, concerts, fairs, eating contests, zany events, beauty pageants, contests and awards ceremonies, flea markets, crafts and antiques exhibits, and parades—and more eating!

Several research projects have also collected data on the most common elements of festivals. Table 2-1 lists the main themes of community festivals compared with the events and attractions at the same festivals, as indicated by fifty-two respondents in Ontario, Canada (Getz and Frisby 1988). This research and others (University of Illinois n.d., Watt and McCarville 1985) reveal the common elements of festivals to be recreation activities, entertainment (both spectator- and participant-oriented), parades, shows, exhibitions, competitions, merchandising and sales, and gambling or raffles. The possibilities are endless, but through imitation and cultural traditions, special events and festivals in regions or countries tend to take on common formats and embody common elements. Janiskee (1985) concluded from a study of food festivals in rural South Carolina that genuine thematic diversity is less than what is implied by the broad range of festival names. Most of them featured common elements, with the theme often being merely a backdrop for programming.

The art of event programming is closely related to the concepts and skills learned by recreation programmers, arts and entertainment directors, and theme park designers. It must encompass a blending of setting and activity, of structure and flexibility, of creativity and predictability. There is no one right way to do it, and trial-and-error methods probably predominate. The material covered in this book will help the programmer or performance director, insofar as the production, to be successful, must relate to the social and cultural meanings of festivals and satisfy visitor expectations.

SOCIAL AND CULTURAL MEANINGS:
DEFINITION OF FESTIVAL

The research and writings of sociologists and anthropologists must be consulted to obtain a thorough appreciation of the origins and the social and cultural meanings of festivals and other public events. In his introduction to the book *Time Out of Time: Essays on the Festival*, Falassi (1987, 1) concludes that "Festival is an event, a social phenomenon, encountered in virtually all human cultures." His discussion of the meanings of festivals is fascinating, as it highlights the variety of interpretations or connotations and the ambiguity that sometimes results when discussing festivals.

Falassi (1987, 2) summarized contemporary English-language definitions of festival as the following:

Table 2-1. Themes and Events at Community Festivals in Ontario

Main Themes Reported*		Events and Attractions Reported**	
Music	21	Contests	37
Food	18	Food	34
Culture	17	Music/concerts	26
Recreation	17	Displays and exhibitions	25
Entertainment	9	Dancing	21
History	6	Theater	19
Creative arts	4	Sports	19
Education	2	Kids' activities	19
Other	7	Parade	14
		Arts and crafts	14
		Beauty contest	12
		Sale or flea market	7
		Raffle or lottery	7
		Recreation	7
		Gambling	6
		Races	5
		Tours	4

*Number of mentions, with up to four items tabulated per respondent; sample size: fifty-two.
**Number of mentions, with up to ten items tabulated per respondent.
Source: Getz, D., and W. Frisby. 1988. Evaluating management effectiveness in community-run festivals. *Journal of Travel Research* 27 (1): 22–27 (published by the Travel and Tourism Research Association and the Business Research Division, University of Colorado).

1. A sacred or profane time of celebration, marked by special observances.
2. The annual celebration of a notable person or event, or the harvest of an important product.
3. A cultural event consisting of a series of performances of works in the fine arts, often devoted to a single artist or genre.
4. A fair.
5. Generic gaiety, conviviality, cheerfulness.

Definitions 1 and 2 are the best ones from a cultural and social perspective. The root of all festivals is public feasting and celebration (Encyclopedia Britannica 1988), and the themes of festivals are determined mostly by reference to things of shared cultural value. Falassi (1987, 2) added:

Both the social function and the symbolic meaning of the festival are closely related to a series of overt values that the community recognizes as essential to its ideology and worldview, to its social identity, its historical continuity, and to its physical survival, which is ultimately what festival celebrates.

Social scientists often used the terms *sacred* and *profane* when referring to celebrations. This distinction is essentially between events of religious significance, which are typically solemn, and those of a secular nature, which are often marked by revelry or even debauchery. More recently, however, some social scientists have argued that the sacred and the profane are not necessarily opposites or even incompatible. For example, carnivals and Mardi Gras celebrations are traditionally religious in derivation but have come to be marked by revelry. Looking at it from another angle, it can be suggested that in a predominantly secular world, many nonreligious festivals actually embody the only "sacred" rituals and solemn rites experienced by contemporary society.

Pieper (1973, 32) insisted that only a religious celebration could be a true festival, and that "through it the celebrant becomes aware of, and may enter, the greater reality which gives a wider perspective on the world of everyday work." This interpretation, stressing the sacred and lamenting the profane, seems anachronistic. Traditional festivals celebrating harvests, religious events, historic happenings, and various cultural attributes are common, but the mystical ones have clearly been supplanted by numerous so-called profane events and festivals. Indeed, communities without ancient festivals are often motivated to create them for the purpose of establishing traditions and providing a sense of roots.

Definition of Festival

A single definition of the term *festival* obviously cannot capture all the meanings and connotations explored above. We need a working definition that sums up the essence of most festivals, whatever their theme and meanings, and which separates them from other special events. At the basis of all festivals is public celebration, whether of a sacred or profane nature, and encompassing rituals and commemorations. They must be public, as opposed to private parties and celebrations, because all festivals have social and cultural meaning to the host community. And they always have a theme, even if it is hidden. The celebration must be of Something, and either this can be reflected by the name and publicized theme (for example, "a celebration of our heritage"), or it can be an unspoken celebration of shared values and experiences, as in festivals of spring and the harvest. A generic definition can be kept very simple:

A festival is a public, themed celebration.

Later sections of this book examine different kinds of festivals and special events, including detailed case studies. It would be impossible to cover all varieties, but the basic elements are generally similar. At this point, it is worth emphasizing that the main differences between a festival and a special event are not always visible. Indeed, there is a growing trend to make all kinds of events more festive in nature. In the final chapter we will return to this point to draw some conclusions.

Festival Spirit

The term *festival* can also be used as an adjective, as in "capturing the festival (or festive) spirit." Falassi (1987) referred to "gaiety, conviviality, cheerfulness" to describe this emotional aspect of celebration. Pieper (1973) stressed "joyfulness," "liberation," and "affirmation." Abrahams (1987) said that "celebrations are experiences for which people prepare and anticipate in common how they will act and feel," with openness, fun, and playfulness as key elements.

Other authors have described festival spirit as the outward expression of heritage, fear, joy, and devotion (Spicer 1958); joy, celebration, and excess (Gutowski 1978); or the sharing of community character and its feeling toward the outside world (Heenan 1978).

Designers of Vancouver's Expo '86 sought to create a celebratory experience with a number of key ingredients: festivity, exuberance, exhilaration, surprise, creativity, color, incongruity, and even outrageousness (Brissenden 1987). Clearly, the emotional and creative scope of festivals and events is almost unlimited. *Festival* can even be converted into a verb form, as in the colloquial expression "going festing," which presumably means the intent to have a good time by joining the celebration.

Festivals: Not Fairs or Mere Performances

Referring back to the Falassi (1987) summary of common definitions of a festival, at least two of them reveal public misunderstanding of the word. Using the term as a synonym of *fair* is clearly wrong, because fairs have a long tradition of their own, as periodic exhibitions and markets. Although they were often associated with early religious celebrations, and now usually contain entertainment and amusements, fairs have more to do with productivity and business than with themed public celebration. Indeed, Abrahams (1987) argued that fairs and festivals are like mirror images. But he also suggested that in modern, urban society they have become almost synonymous because the old ways of production, as celebrated in fairs, have faded. Contemporary fairs tend to be nostalgic and more oriented to how things are presented.

Art or theater festivals, which Falassi correctly identified as a series of performances, are not necessarily public celebrations. It is a misnomer to call a programmed series of performances a festival, especially if it is a permanent attraction and its program runs over a whole season. Many art and theater festivals actually did begin as one-shot festivals but became institutionalized and built facilities for their permanent accommodation. Some do manage to retain a festival atmosphere by taking the performances to the people, in parks and other public places, and by constructing a new and diverse program each year. A true arts or theater festival must also be a special event, distinct from regular programming, and it must embody elements of public celebration, as opposed to catering only to elite audiences.

Reynolds (1987, 29) cautioned that "though the arts have a natural role to play in festivity, they are not the festival itself." Arts and music are adornments, or can act as a medium of festivity, but the true nature of the festival should not be overwhelmed by them. Reynolds also complained that many arts festivals have been commercialized, or have diversified into pop and high-gloss attractions merely to lure big audiences, leaving the more mundane local arts and exhibits in the shadows. Furthermore, he said, standardization has resulted in a virtual disappearance of "the possibility of encountering the unexpected."

Symbolism

Farber (1983) argued that the study of festivals and events can reveal much about a community's symbolic, economic, social, and political life, as events create links between people and groups in a community and between the community and the world. For example, drawing on the seminal writings of Turner (e.g., 1982), Tomlinson (1986) examined the small-town festival as a performance. The parades are full of imagery and symbolism reflecting local or nationally held values: purity, beauty, humor, religion, and politics. The townsfolk are provided with a stage on which to perform for themselves, for the community, and as representatives of the community. Roles can be reversed, a person's status temporarily abandoned, and all kinds of behavior tolerated that would otherwise be socially unacceptable. Viewed by outsiders, much of the undercurrent and symbolism might be hidden or misinterpreted. The locals might appear to be quaint, when they are really playing well-known roles in a performance for the benefit of the wider community or the tourists. Intelligent visitors who catch on to this aspect of festivals and events might enter into the spirit by playing the expected role of naive outsider, and both groups can enjoy the fun. When we discuss authenticity in greater detail, we will return to this notion of visitors' expectations and reality.

Benedict (1983, 7) examined the symbolism associated with world's fairs, saying they represent a "massive display of prestige vis-a-vis other communities" and are used flagrantly to impress the public as well as rivals. This leads to consideration of the political meanings of events.

Political Meanings

Just as even the smallest community festival has social and cultural meaning that goes beyond the facade of the event, many mega-events have large, hidden political agendas and great symbolic value. Hall (1988, 6) described the Los Angeles Olympics of 1984 as being "as much a celebration of American capitalism and its achievements as a sporting event."

Ley and Olds (1988) assess world's fairs in an unfamiliar way, saying they are built in the image of society's elite and thus present a dominant ideology. Social control can be expanded by having the masses focus on "bread and circus" entertainment. In this atmosphere, opposition to events is discouraged and socially or politically punishable. Benedict (1983) also called world's fairs a modern form of international ritual reflecting power and economics, not just a cultural event reflecting distinctive ways of doing things.

Popular Culture

Events also have significance in terms of popular culture. Ludwig (1976), writing in the book *The Great American Spectaculars*, commented that certain events have an almost magical power to attract. They are not-to-be-missed social events for the in crowds, and are equally populist phenomena for the ordinary audiences. Echoing this interpretation, Reed (1980) discussed a personal attachment to the Indianapolis 500 race and festival in a book titled *Indy—Race and Ritual*. To Reed, the Indy 500 is an index to the middle-class values and aspirations of America.

A Social and Cultural Typology

Figure 2-3 illustrates an approach to classifying public events based on their social and cultural meanings. Encompassing the other two realms—of political economy and tourism and of public celebration—is that of work and everyday life, in which individuals are preoccupied with survival and routine family obligations. Leisure, commonly defined as discretionary time or a mental state marked by a feeling of freedom, is within but distinct from this realm. Private pursuits, including celebrations such as anniversaries and commemorations of a religious type such as Christmas, could be defined as either obligation or leisure, depending on the circumstances and participants' attitudes. They are distinct from public celebrations in that they are private and intimate.

Of principal interest is the realm of public celebration, which includes the portion of leisure devoted to festivals and other special events for the sheer joy of participation, as well as more solemn commemorations and rituals that might be considered by participants as being an obligation. For example, going to a food or harvest festival is generally done for the fun of it, whereas attendance at a Memorial Day commemoration or Easter religious service, however public, might be construed as being a social obligation.

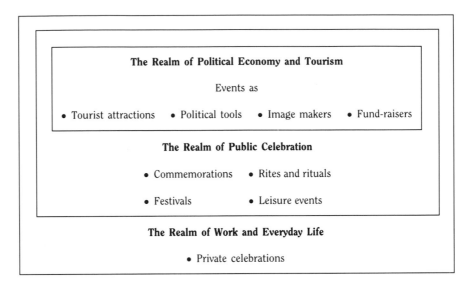

Figure 2-3. An event typology based on social and cultural meanings.

Community Development

From a community development perspective, public celebration can be valued as contributing to government policy objectives or group goals. Parks and recreation departments are commonly involved with events, as programmers or facilitators, in order to create public leisure opportunities ranging from pure games and play opportunities to organized sports and recreation, including competitions. The assumption—or conviction—is that leisure opportunities, including special events, are necessary for cultural, health, and community development. The community also gains by fostering leadership, self-esteem, identity, organizational expertise, and networking through event productions. Special-interest groups are involved to inform and educate the public about worthwhile aims, to raise money for self-perpetuation, and to facilitate the development of their pursuits. All of these goals are related in the sense that they pertain to the sharing and enhancement of a community's social and cultural values—the very root of public celebration and festivals.

Political Economy

In the third realm, that of political economy (i.e., economics) and tourism, festivals and events are created or manipulated primarily for extrinsic rather than intrinsic reasons. In other words, these types of events (or elements of them) are not necessarily rooted in public leisure or celebration, but are oriented toward economic development or private profit. Nevertheless, the events might satisfy some leisure and community development needs, so the distinction is not absolute. Indeed, all three realms can coexist.

But when events are viewed primarily as tourist attractions or image makers for destination regions, they are likely to take on a different flavor, such as being modified to emphasize spectacle and media-accessible events. This can result in spurious or inauthentic events, which eventually risk the loss of community interest and support. The same potentially holds true for political events designed to manipulate opinion or raise emotions for some chauvinistic cause, as well as for events created to generate private profit. Still, the inherent benefits of these events to the public must not be prejudged. They all have some potential to satisfy the need for public celebration and leisure opportunity.

Social and Cultural Costs

As discussed above, the social and cultural benefits of festivals and events relate to their roles in fostering community development and cultural traditions and in providing leisure opportunities. The economic benefits of event tourism also have potentially positive effects on the viability of communities and the ways in which people work and play. But there are also some significant potential costs and problems.

Social and Cultural Problems in the Community

To varying degrees, event tourism and individual events have the same potential as other forms of tourism development to introduce social and cultural changes to the host community (see, for example, de Kadt 1979; Mathieson and Wall 1982; Murphy 1985; Britton and Clarke 1987). But the infrequency and short duration of most festivals and special events, while possibly creating temporary crowding problems, are likely to minimize their potential for directly causing lasting negative effects. It is the cumulative, long-term impact of event tourism or of a large number of events that is likely to cause indirect changes in the host community.

Ritchie (1984) suggested that the sociocultural effects of hallmark events could include the benefits of an increase in activities associated with the event, such as arts or sports, and strengthening of regional values or traditions. On the negative side is the risk of commercialization and modification of the activity. This potentially negative consequence of event tourism is described in more detail in the next subsection.

Host-guest interactions, which can be improved through joint participation in festivals and events, can also be strained by events and tourism in general.

Misunderstanding can occur, or conflict over the use of local resources. Doxey (1975) invented what he called the Irridex, or irritation index, to describe the possible evolution of resident attitudes toward tourists. At first, tourists might be welcomed and the mood could be euphoric, stemming from perceived benefits. Over time, as the presence of tourists and related development become accepted, apathy can set in. Then, increasing negative impact and rising costs associated with tourism can generate resentment and even open hostility. Events that become completely tourist-oriented run the risk of generating this evolution of negative attitudes. Those that celebrate the community and permit an equal meeting of hosts and guests are more likely to preserve positive attitudes on both sides. However, there are no research conclusions available to support this contention.

Some of the direct, negative sociocultural effects of a large event on the community and its way of life are discussed further in Chapter 10 in terms of evaluation and impact assessment. Researchers examining the Australian Grand Prix in Adelaide measured amenity loss created by noise and crowding, documented accidents attributed to the psychological effects of car racing, and assigned monetary values to crime, vandalism, and loss of time.

Commercialization of Traditional Festivals and Rituals

Many authors have worried about the negative influence of tourism on traditional cultures. These effects are often most visible in the area of cultural productions such as rituals, music, dance, and festivals, and particularly those that incorporate traditional costumes. Residents of destination areas quickly learn that culture can be a commodity for which tourists will pay a great amount, resulting in either the transformation of occasional, sometimes sacred events into regular performances or the modification of rituals into forms of entertainment that are easier to perform or please the audiences more. In both cases, the rewards become monetary and divorced from their cultural meanings.

Many examples have been noted in the literature. Jordan (1980) documented a case of inauthentic maple syrup festivals held in Vermont in the summer, for the convenience of tourists and the profit of organizers. Greenwood (1972) recounted how a traditional Basque festival in Spain became an event grudgingly performed twice daily for tourists. Wilson and Udall (1982) classified folk festivals by reference to their control and orientation, observing that they range from truly indigenous (performed by and for locals) to multicultural festivals that are put on especially for tourists and other people who are not of one of the many displayed cultures.

However, there is little agreement on tourism being bad for cultural events, or on how and why negative effects occur. MacNaught (1982, 373) argued that the debasement of cultural events varies with the success people have in adopting strategies that preserve their primary values while at the same time exploiting them selectively in the marketplace. Noronha (1979) believed the Balinese of Indonesia were able to keep the meanings of sacred performances separate from the tourist shows for which they have become famous. And the Canadian Press (1989) reported how Alberta Indian bands planning a native cultural festival vowed to keep religious ceremonies out of public view. O'Reilly (1987), unhappy with the reduction of West Indian events to entertainment in tourist enclaves, argued for the bringing of tourists into the community to experience festivals on equal grounds with the residents.

An emphasis on the visually spectacular component of events can detract from their cultural meaning, as can the reduction of complex performances to simple entertainment in the nightclub style. Authenticity, however, is not always for the tourists or observer to determine. MacNaught (1982) cautioned that cultural purists are not always right in condemning new forms of music and dance, such as those found in the South Pacific, as they have found a strong base in the indigenous community.

Others have praised the positive side of tourism's impact on culture and cultural events. Boissevan (1979), referring to Malta, believed that tourism helps people rediscover their own cultural heritage. But he warned of the "romantic stylization" that can result if culture is adapted to meet tourists' expectations. Cheska (1981) wrote that the Antigonish (Nova Scotia) Highland Games were a major vehicle for preserving Scottish and Gaelic identity. Getz (1984) observed that tourism was vital in helping small Scottish communities maintain traditional Highland Games, and was an incentive for preserving other traditions because they also had commercial value.

Social Problems at Events

Wherever crowds gather there is potential for trouble, leading to the need for planned security and emergency services. Common social problems such as drinking, drugs, and rowdyism can be heightened in these situations, but other, more serious problems can actually be caused by, or become institutionalized at, events. More than one festival has had to close down or move because of bad publicity generated by drinking and related behavior; others have attracted a totally inappropriate audience.

A fascinating account of a special event gone wrong was provided by Cunneen and Lynch (1988). They described how the annual Australian Grand Prix Motorcycle Races had become the scene for institutionalized rioting, despite—or perhaps because of—the efforts of organizers and police to control crowd behavior. Hall (1988) also noted that major events, particularly those with global media coverage, tend to attract potentially violent protests and political demonstrations.

Newtonmore, Scotland: Annual Highland Games preserve heritage and boost tourism (D. Getz).

ENVIRONMENTAL PERSPECTIVE

Environmental costs and benefits of event tourism can be similar to other forms of tourism development, but there are a number of distinct differences. Many festivals and events are closely related to cultural and heritage conservation, as illustrated in examples throughout the book. They are particularly good means to raise money for conservation purposes or to interest people in their heritage, and they can be used as interpretive tools to heighten awareness in and support for nature conservation. Events also have a role to play in achieving sustainable development, as they can create economic benefits with minimal or no physical development.

From this perspective several typologies of events could be derived. A distinction should be made between events that utilize natural resources (e.g., fishing derbies) and those that are not related to direct resource consumption. Festivals and special events have great potential as educational and interpretive tools, and several categories of these can be suggested: a park festival, celebrating its creation, natural history, and values; an awareness event, stressing information dissemination through visits to sites; and an interpretive event, in which games and activities introduce visitors to concepts and issues.

THE VISITOR'S PERSPECTIVE

From a marketing point of view, the product must meet the needs and satisfy the expectations of the intended audiences. This is an especially difficult task for festivals and events, given their multiple roles and meanings, the openness of many festival settings, and the enormous difficulty of understanding all the motivations and expectations of benefits that a visitor might harbor. Chapter 3 will examine in detail the needs and motivations of potential eventgoers, trends and factors affecting them, and profiles of such people. This material is then used to develop a conceptual framework for assessing visitor benefits and relating them to product development and marketing—in other words, essential services, generic benefits, and targeted benefits.

Many special events, particularly community festivals, appear to ignore target marketing and instead try to provide a little something for every possible taste. Others label themselves as family or fun events but put the enjoyment of the host community above that of the potential visitor. It undoubtedly works for many successful festivals and events, but it is hardly an acceptable approach for those organizers and tourism industry officials who seek to maximize tourist benefits. At a bare minimum, every event organizer and programmer must have some fundamental knowledge of the range of motivations and expected benefits that might apply to the event; this applies to tourists as well as local audiences.

THE ORGANIZER'S PERSPECTIVE

This book does not detail the management and operations of events, but there is a need to appreciate the multiple perspectives of organizers. Some are not interested in tourism, although all managers should be aware of its potential to help events prosper and grow. Many are volunteers who have no capability for sophisticated management and marketing, but struggle to develop community support and resources to keep the event going. Others are producers who are devoted to creating high-quality productions.

Figure 2-4 indicates four classes of organizations commonly involved with festivals and events: public agencies, such as parks and recreation departments, that run programs of events; volunteer community festival groups, with or without professional staff; corporations set up to create profitable events; and programs of events run by corporations for reasons other than immediate profits. In addition, the role of government agencies and tourist organizations in giving grants and assistance to events must be recognized, as should the importance of private event sponsors—both of which might also be involved in producing their own events.

SUMMARY

The second chapter commenced with a model of the various perspectives on festivals and events (Fig. 2-1), showing how event tourism interrelates with the different points of view—social and cultural—of visitors, organizers, and the host community. An environmental perspective is closely linked to the social and cultural component, but that could require separate and more detailed treatment in some cases. The tangible product was shown to be the event, defined by theme, merchandise, activities, and ambience, or packages and tours of events.

Linkages in the model are also important, as they constitute processes that can be shaped or influenced by managers and organizers and by event tourism planners. These linkage processes are target marketing, fostering and attracting events, assistance to organizers, host-guest relations, volunteer support and community attendance at events, and community relations. The production and consumption of events are shown in the model as linkages between organizers and visitors.

Next, events and special events were defined. An event is a happening or occurrence, but its specialness was defined contextually. From the point of view of the organization, a special event is a onetime or infrequently occurring event outside its normal program or activities. To the visitor, a special event is an opportunity for a social, leisure, or cultural experience outside the normal range of choices or beyond everyday experience. These definitions sufficed to take us

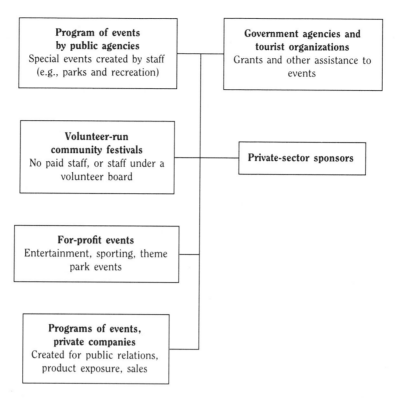

Figure 2-4. An event typology from the organizer's perspective.

through the book, but the subject of specialness is returned to in Chapter 11 to draw together all the attributes or characteristics that make some events special.

A typology of events from the event tourism perspective was then developed (Fig. 2-2), partly to help sort out the terminology being employed in the book and in the field, and partly to demonstrate how the nature or theme of individual attractions and events is not as important, in this context, as their touristic attractiveness.

Mega-events, in the event tourism context, can be defined only by reference to how successful they are as tourist attractions, although their image-making and catalytic roles are also important. A mega-event is therefore one that outperforms all others as a tourist draw, or in a particular context can be said to achieve the highest level of tourism impact. The term *hallmark event* was said to have meaning only where an event and its host community or destination area are indelibly linked in the minds of potential tourists, so as to be mutually reinforcing in their drawing power.

Festivals and events were shown to be similar to other tourism products in certain respects, but also to have unique characteristics. For example, the intangibility of the event and tourism product was stressed, but it was noted that the atmosphere or ambience of events, which is a vital component of their attractiveness, is in large part shaped by the visitors themselves.

An event typology based on social and cultural meanings was developed next (Fig. 2-3). By referring to the sociological and anthropological literature, it was revealed that festivals are an inherent part of all cultures, and have important meanings in political, symbolic, leisure, religious, and social terms.

Discussion of the social and cultural meanings of festivals enabled us to provide a simple working definition of a festival as a "public, themed celebration." This definition avoids any mystical or needlessly academic connotations. All festivals are in the public domain, as opposed to private celebrations and parties. A celebration has an object, but that is not the same as a theme. Themes are unifying concepts applied to all elements of the production and its promotion that help make an identifiable package and foster a unique experience.

Along with a model of a typology based on social and cultural meanings (Fig. 2-3), social and cultural costs or problems associated with events were also discussed. The range of potential negative impact, including social problems at events, disruption of community life, amenity loss, and commercialization, are important factors in the cost-benefit analysis that all event organizers should undertake.

Chapter 2 ended with a brief overview of the visitor's perspective and a typology from the organizer's perspective (Fig. 2-4).

CHAPTER THREE

Trends and Consumer Research

All available indicators strongly suggest that the number, diversity, and popularity of festivals and special events have grown spectacularly over the past several decades. This can also be said of many aspects of recreation, culture, and tourism, and there is no doubt that the basic reasons lie in economic prosperity, a more leisure-oriented life-style, and increasing global communications. Unfortunately, research and reliable statistics on festivals and events have not even begun to catch up to those available on other leisure and tourism phenomena.

In this chapter we will explore the evident growth, factors shaping the trends, and consumer research related to events and event tourism. (Government initiatives and policies are discussed in Chapter 4.) This material reinforces many of the points made in Chapters 1 and 2 and introduces concepts and issues of importance in the remainder of the book. In particular, our discussion of market trends and consumer research is a vital base for our later discussions of destination planning and marketing and of the marketing of specific events.

GROWTH IN THE NUMBER OF EVENTS

In the English-speaking countries profiled in Chapter 4, statistics have not been systematically collected on the number, types, distribution, or popularity of events. It is peculiar that this important component of leisure, culture, and tourism is so overlooked, but there are several obvious reasons for this. First, leisure, culture, and tourism have only recently been viewed as industries, or at least as economic activities of significance. As a consequence, government officials have shown little interest in collecting data.

Furthermore, supply-side statistics in tourism are not nearly as well developed as those on the demand side. Various regular surveys of travelers and consumers reveal important dimensions of demand for leisure, cultural, and travel activities, although specific data on festivals and events has seldom been collected. National-level inventories of events have not been taken, and it is not possible even to estimate the total demand for or use of all events.

Another reason for the data shortage is that festivals and special events are seldom considered together in their entirety. In the past there has been little interest on the part of the tourism industry to consider arts festivals and community celebrations, nor for those interested in leisure and community development to consider the tourism implications of their policies and activities. Fortunately, this is changing rapidly as new partnerships are forged in the leisure, culture, and tourism fields.

So we are left to piece together often inadequate clues as to the full scope of festivals and events, with the evidence drawn from a variety of published sources. Some of the indicators are quantified, whereas others are based on the observations of experts.

One logical place to begin is the publication *Festivals Sourcebook* (Wasserman, Herman, and Root 1977, 1984), which lists events for North America. In its 1977 edition, 3,800 festivals and events were listed; the total rose to 4,200 in 1984. Festivals, celebrations, and some fairs are included, but county fairs, horse shows, rodeos, holy days, beauty pageants, and universal holiday celebrations were excluded. Another commercial publication, *The Official 1990 Directory of Festivals, Sports and Special Events* (International Events Group 1990), provided a free listing of events. It stated there were approximately 6,000 annual events in North America. The problem with all guide and source books, obviously, is that only certain events voluntarily list themselves, and these most likely are the larger and better-organized events. Small and onetime events are more easily ignored.

Some government agencies have attempted at least to estimate the number of festivals in their jurisdiction. The Arkansas Department of Parks and Tourism (n.d.) reported a total of 750 annual festivals. From a survey for Tourism Canada, Chick (1983) reported some 1,000 festivals in Canada, most of which were found to have no orientation to tourism. A later Tourism Canada inventory in 1988 (Lariviere and Vachon 1989, 26) identified 163 major recurring festivals and events with the potential to appeal to foreign tourists, compared with 345 in the United States. These major North American events were found mostly in large cities, and half or more had a cultural theme. The same report notes that Spain claimed to offer over 3,000 festivals, and Finland offered 1,500 festivals to international markets.

A few researchers have attempted to estimate the number of events in limited areas. Getz and Frisby (1988) compiled an inventory of community-run festivals in the province of Ontario, Canada, assembling a list of approximately 300 (in a population of about eight million). Most of the 52 festivals in their survey sample were quite recent in origin, with only 22 percent predating 1970, 41 percent stemming from the 1970s, and 37 percent beginning between 1980 and 1986. That research did not attempt to estimate the number of other special events or other types of festival.

Wicks and Watt (n.d.) conducted a survey of Texas festivals and events, presumably in 1983, which found the majority to be less than twenty years old. Fully 38 percent of their sample events began in the 1973–82 period. And Janiskee (1985) reported a rapid expansion of rural festivals in South Carolina, growing from 66 in 1975 to at least 150 by 1984. They had also diffused statewide. Badders (1984) reported that many festivals in South Carolina were created during the state's tricentennial in 1970 and the U.S. bicentennial in 1976.

Evidence from other countries is sketchy. Bos, van der Kamp, and Zom (1987) reported a substantial increase in large-scale events in the Netherlands, from 1,080 to 1,345 between 1977 and 1984, while many others had grown in size. In Great Britain, Hanna (1981) noted that there had been fewer than 12 art festivals prior to World War II, but there were over 200 in 1981. The Great Britain Yearbook 1989 (1988) gave the figure of 700 arts festivals, which reveals a real explosion in their numbers. Mirloup (1983) commented on the decline of traditional community fetes and fairs in France, which he attributed to a breakdown of rural communities and more leisure choices for youth. Growth, he noted, was in fund-raising special events, especially food and wine festivals in tourism regions.

A major problem in any inventory is that of definition. Getz and Frisby (1988) found that neither the name nor its listed activities nor the use of the word *festival* or a similar term was sufficient to ensure complete confidence in the inventory. Similar difficulties are experienced when counting certain types of event. To define arts festivals requires criteria pertaining to the amount and type of artistic content, because a majority of festivals and special events contain crafts, music, dance, or other entertainment. Sporting events are not necessarily easier to define, as some criteria are required to distinguish between regular competitions and those that have something special about them. We are back to the problem of multiple perspectives, and now we can see how it impedes inventory and statistical analysis.

GROWTH IN SIZE AND ATTENDANCE

No systematic evidence can be provided to support this point, but it appears quite clear that numerous events have grown significantly in terms of both size of the production and attendance. Unfortunately, many festivals and special events do not make accurate attendance counts or estimates, either because of their open, free nature or a lack of resources to make counts. In addition, the tendency to exaggerate estimates of attendance is quite strong, so that many figures provided by organizers have to be treated with caution. A third problem is the relative newness of many events, making trend analysis difficult or impossible. Consequently, only sketchy indicators of growth in size and attendance can be found.

One example was documented by Howell (1982) concerning the development of the Salley Chitlin Strut, in South Carolina. At its modest origin in 1965 it attracted only 1,000 people; it drew a crowd of approximately 5,000 in the 1970s, and when it expanded to an all-day event the attendance soared to 20,000. In the late 1980s, around 40,000 participated. No doubt many events can relate similar growth stories, although few could express high reliability in their statistics.

Growth might be due to many factors, not just increases in demand. Expansion of the length and program has the effect of increasing capacity, although a larger event might also have greater appeal to potential customers. Well-located events have also benefited from general population growth in their market area or growth in particular market segments. Others might have declined for the same reason, or because of increased competition among events and with other types of attractions and leisure opportunities.

INCREASE IN PROFESSIONALISM

As the number of events has grown, with many expanding significantly in size and complexity, the number of volunteers and staff associated with events has mushroomed. This has given rise to regulatory and professional associations, formal education and training programs, and a still small but growing body of literature aimed at festival and event interest groups.

Sports are very well organized internationally, especially at the amateur level. The International Amateur Athletic Federation brings together all the national-level associations, and together they regulate and sanction most track and field and other amateur athletic events. The independent International Olympic Committee and other international bodies such as the Commonwealth Games Federation and Pan American Sports Organization all work with amateur athletics and hold periodic games. These bodies and their counterparts at the national level are important sources of information, training, and standardization, and their strict criteria must be satisfied when seeking approval for sanctioned sporting events.

World's fairs are regulated by the International Bureau of Exhibitions, based in Paris; it was created by international convention in 1928. In 1989 there were forty-three member nations, which agree to the regulation of types and timing of international exhibitions. The system has undergone a lot of changes, with some controversy, as countries lobbied for competitive position. The purpose of these events is nominally educational, but some authors have described them as glorified trade fairs (Benedict 1983) or political devices (Hall 1988). Two main categories have been defined (International Bureau of Exhibitions 1989): universal exhibitions (among them, Montreal in 1967, Osaka in 1970, and Seville in 1992), which have become rare owing to their scale and cost, and specialized exhibitions, which were frequent in the 1980s (such as Brisbane in 1988, Vancouver in 1986, Tsukuba in 1985, New Orleans in 1984, and Knoxville in 1982).

The International Association of Fairs and Expositions was formed in 1885 and now has about 5,000 members (Goeldner and Long 1987), which are mostly agricultural and state fairs. The organization publishes a manual on fair management. Two related groups of interest to event tourism are the International Association of Amusement Parks and Attractions and the International Association of Convention and Visitors Bureaus.

For music and arts festivals, the national, regional, and local arts associations that exist in most English-speaking countries are a principal source of funding and networking. In addition, the International Federation of Festival Organizations (FIDOF) was set up in 1967 to "serve as a means of connecting the major music festivals and cultural events of the world and to promote the importance of the festival stage" (International Federation of Festival Organizations n.d.). With a network spanning over sixty countries and 1,500 music festivals, it facilitates exchanges, coordination, and the flow of information. FIDOF is also a member organization of UNESCO's International Music Council.

The International Council of Organizations for Folklore Festivals and Folk Art, founded in 1970, is an international member organization of UNESCO involving about forty-seven countries. It concentrates on traditional and amateur arts while encouraging international understanding and friendship. Its annual activities include the organization of over one hundred international folklore festivals, exchanges among folklore groups, research into folk art, and conferences, symposia, and exhibitions.

Community festivals are the most disparate and least organized of all special events, mostly because the majority are small and almost any group can organize or sponsor a festival. The International Festivals Association was formed in 1956 to address the needs of community festivals in particular, and although its membership is primarily in the United States and Canada, it is taking steps to become international in scope. IFA's services include regional workshops, an annual conference, a newsletter, and a certified festival executive program associated with Purdue University. An interview with the executive director of IFA is included in Chapter 11.

A growing number of American states also have festival and event associations. For example, the Louisiana Association of Fairs and Festivals was created in 1934, when only a few fairs existed in the state. LAFF holds annual conventions, sends out monthly newsletters, and annually publishes 150,000 brochures listing all the member fairs and festivals. Other states have separate associations for fairs and festivals.

In Canada, the Canadian Association of Festivals and Events (CAFE) was formed in 1979 as an initiative of festival organizers, but following a recommendation of a federal task force, which thought such an association could foster national unity (Stewart 1983). A former CAFE president (Gauthier 1987) observed that a major problem has been to gain government and industry recognition of the importance of festivals for tourism, arts, and culture, as well as for communities. But the association has made important inroads, particularly in getting involved in the 1986 National Task Force on Tourism Data, which formally recognized the need for a more systematic approach to festival and event research. CAFE, like IFA, holds an annual conference, publishes a newsletter, and advises its membership on event marketing. In 1988 in Ottawa, CAFE and IFA held their first joint conference, thereby helping to build their profile and international outlook.

Some of the Canadian provinces—Ontario, British Columbia, Manitoba, and Quebec—also have festival associations, and there is a Federation of Acadian Festivals in the eastern provinces. Festivals Ontario, as an example, convenes annually and is working to establish regional seminars. Its president is interviewed in Chapter 11.

As the profession matures, we are certain to witness better-organized associations and educational and training opportunities, perhaps even formal college- and university-level courses in festival management. More literature will be needed to advance the field; most of the material published to date has been in the form of academic papers, government- or association-sponsored manuals, and hard-to-get consulting studies (see the References section of this book). A number of conferences on the subject of events have been held, and the resulting papers are herein widely cited. Tourism and recreation literature covers festivals and events rather minimally, however, and there is a clear need for general textbooks and books of case studies.

Several commercial newsletters exist, although their emphasis is on event sponsorship. *The Sponsorship Report* and *Special Events Report* advise corporations on how to communicate and advertise through event sponsorship, and event organizers on how to obtain and use corporate support. The editor of *Special Events Report* is interviewed in Chapter 11.

REASONS FOR INCREASED DEMAND

The expansion of festivals and special events parallels general economic and leisure growth, at least in the industrialized, English-speaking countries. But let's look more closely at the specific reasons. After all, not all forms of cultural and leisure activity have experienced spectacular growth. In the following subsections we will examine the main trends in factors most likely responsible for the growing demand for festivals and special events. Key marketing implications are also identified for each major trend, although we leave discussion of marketing methods for later chapters.

A major review of changing demographics and attitudes on the U.S. travel industry, called *Discover America 2000*, was conducted for the Travel Industry Association of America by the U.S. Travel Data Center (1989). Some of its findings are used in this section, and other general references are cited as appropriate. The book *Recreation Trends* (Kelly 1987), another important guide to the future, is also cited here. *The Community Tourism Industry Imperative* (Blank 1989) is a good source on travel and tourism trends affecting local planning.

Increased Income

Despite the ups and downs of economic cycles, overall productivity and wealth have increased in the industrialized world. Median family income and per capita income rose steadily in the United States and Canada through the 1980s, and they are expected to continue growing through the 1990s. For most people disposable income has become sufficient to support a wide range of leisure interests, including one or more annual vacations or many lesser recreational trips. Blank (1989, 146) concluded that increases in median family income in the United States had slowed in the late 1980s, but that some growth will likely still occur. The result is a continued broadening of travel demand to a larger share of the population. Gains being made in the less-developed nations are also resulting in a large demand for consumer goods and leisure activities.

In many places, however, the disparity between rich and poor remains great, and structural unemployment condemns many to enforced, largely unsatisfying and unoccupied time. Kelly (1987) believed the gap is possibly going to widen, resulting in a class with substantial money and growing interest in leisure, along with a poor class effectively blocked from using most commercial recreation and tourism supply.

For festivals and special events, these trends have profound implications. Demand for all forms of leisure has increased and forecasters believe this growth will continue through the 1990s. Events will continue to attract a share of this expanding market, and events that cater to upmarket people (i.e., those with higher amounts of disposable income to spend on leisure) can look forward to expanded demand. On the other hand, public festivals and free, open events will likely have heightened importance for those without large amounts of disposable income. Epperson (1986) believed that festivals and cultural events will continue to be among the top choices of the public because they offer the lowest cost per hour of any activity.

It would be a shame if polarization occurred, with a range of festivals and events for the rich and another for the poor, yet that appears to be happening already. Arts events in particular are susceptible to escalating production costs, and even with government subsidies they are sometimes priced beyond the reach of lower- and even middle-income groups. This problem could force them to become more interested in tourist markets, which might have the negative impact of alienating them from the host community—a potential tragedy that policy planners must try to avoid.

Government agencies, particularly those involved in community sports and recreation, community development, and popular culture (as opposed to those associated with so-called high culture) are most involved in creating free and inexpensive special events for the public. Their role in this respect will become more important. The big challenge is to blend the best of free, public celebration with the best of professional or other high-quality performances somehow so that no group is excluded by reason of income alone. Charleston's Spoleto Festival accomplishes this by taking free elements of the event into the city's neighborhoods.

Opportunities should increase for commercial events to draw paying audiences and for special-interest and upmarket events to grow. As leisure and cultural demand increases, the potential variety and scope of festivals and events and related packages also will increase. Because Americans spend more and save less than their counterparts in other Western nations, demand in the United States might be highest.

Leisure Time

As a result of greater productivity, legislated and negotiated holidays and fewer working hours, early retirement, and changes in employment patterns, the industrialized countries have experienced overall increases in time available for leisure pursuits. But the long-awaited "age of leisure" never materialized, as economic cycles in recent decades have created unemployment, not shorter work weeks (Kelly 1987). In addition, the demands of urban living, householding, commuting, and employment cause a majority of people to claim they do not have enough time to fulfill all their leisure desires.

Many people are still very much career- or job-oriented. In fact, the dramatic increase in the proportion of women working, in two-job families, in flexible and shift work, and in part-time employment, has meant that traditional patterns of leisure and work have been significantly altered. The results are important:

- In two-job and single-parent families, there might very well be less time for family-oriented leisure, hence the emphasis on so-called quality time, in which unique and highly rewarding social and family experiences are sought.
- Demand for leisure is spreading more evenly over the day, week, and year, although weekends and summer are still the peaks.
- Time is valued more, and more is expected from free time; for the employed, there is nothing worse than wasting time.

Festivals and special events have a number of features that make them attractive in this context. In particular, they can provide highly stimulating, short-duration leisure experiences in social settings. Each is unique in some way, whereas almost all alternatives are predictable. The public nature of many events, especially festivals, makes them ideal for last-minute attendance, and their usually open and often free or inexpensive cost makes spontaneous attendance less risky. They can provide excellent value for the modest monetary and time investment; for high-quality events, they can be satisfying, cost-effective destinations for planned trips and major expenditures.

Leisure Interests

Even casual observers can hardly fail to notice the explosion in types of leisure pursuits that have become popular and even professionalized in recent years. Not only are ball games popular, but there are numerous varieties to choose from. Arts and entertainment cater to virtually every taste, from opera to Las Vegas shows. Home leisure, associated with computers and electronics, allows limitless scope for self-discovery through hobbies. Television has been altered radically with the introduction of cable and satellite reception. It is the age of narrow-casting, in which each individual preference finds a leisure outlet.

So why not a festival or special event for every interest? Every sport has its tournaments and shows, and some of them have the potential to be the next Super Bowl! The range of festival themes is virtually endless, with specialized guidebooks now appearing to cover food, wine, music, and other specific types. This is not to suggest that each event should cater only to narrow target audiences. The marketing challenge, especially within an event tourism context, is to add specialist interests to the generic, broad appeal of festivals and events.

Sociodemographic Trends

Sociodemographic trends are having a tremendous impact on leisure, travel, and event tourism. Aided by forecasts such as *Discover America 2000* (U.S. Travel Data Center 1989), we can examine the factors most likely to affect demand for festivals and special events through the decade of the 1990s. But caution is required, as in all forecasting, because trend extrapolation assumes that current cause-effect relationships will continue. The use of American data also requires adjustments for applications to other countries, although trends in the Western nations appear to be quite similar.

Populations of all the industrialized nations are aging. Forecasters have calculated that by the year 2030, the proportion of the U.S. population in the retirement years (aged 65 and up) will be 20 percent, up from 10 percent in 1980 (Kelly 1987). The median age of the U.S. population will be 36.3 in the year 2000, compared to 33.2 in 1988. The large "baby boom" generation born in the period 1946–64, aged 24 to 42 in 1988, will constitute fully 39 percent of the U.S. population at the turn of this century. The proportion of teenagers and young adults will decline substantially (U.S. Travel Data Center 1989).

Forecasts are that 57 percent of all married couples will have two incomes in the year 2000, the number of families headed by women will grow, and the average household will be smaller, at 2.48 persons (U.S. Travel Data Center 1989). The population of North America and many other countries is also becoming more pluralistic, owing to immigration and lower birthrates among the established populations. This will affect cultural preferences and probably encourage more interest in and production of ethnic and multicultural festivals.

Seven Generational Groups

Analysis made in the *Discover America 2000* report (U.S. Travel Data Center 1989) is related to seven generational (or life cycle) groups thought to be important for shaping trends. Table 3-1 depicts characteristics of these seven groups, with a forecast of conditions in the year 2000. The "dominant decade" associated with each group refers to its members' formative period, not their greatest years of income and consumption. In the 1990s, for example, it is the early and late baby boomers who are dominant in terms of numbers, income, and travel, although the burgeoning number of older adults (aged fifty-five and older) must be given serious attention. The following paragraphs will examine the implications for life-styles, attitudes, and travel preferences among the baby boomers' and seniors' groups.

Baby Boomers

Early baby boomers, born between 1946 and 1954, will be aged forty-six to fifty-four and in their peak earning years by 2000. Their families will have moved on, they will have time and energy for leisure and travel, and they will have considerable influence on society. Late boomers, born between 1954 and 1964, will be well into the family formation and career establishment years. As this combined "big generation" ages, the whole pattern of family, work, and leisure shifts with it.

A high percentage of baby boomers are well educated, career-oriented, and upwardly mobile —the so-called yuppies. In the 1980s this phenomenon was associated with smaller families, more women in the labor force (especially in the professions and nontraditional jobs), and more single-parent families. The boomers' tastes are different from those of past generations, and they demand more for their investment of time and money. Parents with only one or two children tend to pamper the kids, take them traveling, and teach them their

Table 3-1. The Seven Generational Groups

Group	Born	Formative Years	Dominant Decade	Age in 1988	Age in 2000*	% of U.S. Pop. in 2000**
Baby boomlet	1977–88	1989–2000	1990s	0–11	12–23	17
Baby bust	1965–76	1977–1988	1980s	12–23	24–35	17
Late baby boom	1955–64	1967–1976	1970s	24–33	36–45	21
Early baby boom	1946–54	1958–1966	1960s	34–42	46–54	18
World War II babies	1935–45	1947–1957	1950s	43–53	55–65	11
Depression babies	1924–34	1936–1946	1940s	54–64	66–76	8
World War I babies	Pre-1924	Pre-1936	Pre-1940s	65 +	77 +	8

*While actual ages are presented here, statistics have been compiled using traditional age groupings as follows: 15–24, 25–34, 35–44, 45–54, 65–74, 75+.

**Based on projected population 15 years of age and over in 2000.

Source: U.S. Travel Data Center. 1989. *Discover America 2000.* Washington, D.C.: Travel Industry Association of America.

tastes in higher culture. A whole new leisure industry has responded, with dance, music, and art classes, with computer and drama camps, with the best in athletic equipment and training. Wait until this new generation (the so-called baby boomlet or echo baby boomers) become consumers!

Some of the effects of this baby boom generation have been felt in the festivals and events field. The folk festivals and antiestablishment events that were the stamp of this group in the 1960s evolved into much more sophisticated arts and entertainment festivals. Anything unchanged or associated with poor taste was spurned—tackiness was very definitely out. Nostalgia became big business, to the point where popular music seemed to have regressed twenty or thirty years. Along with nostalgia, anything rural and rustic gained popularity, as this was a very urbane generation. But this preference did not extend to traditional country fairs and exhibitions unless those events got wise to the need for new attractions and sanitized farm flavors. Craft fairs and small-town, Main Street festivals, food events, and music in pastoral settings were all in. And for the kids—children's festivals! *Macleans* magazine (1986) did a feature on the growth of children's festivals in Canada, linking them to the tastes of middle-class baby boomers and contrasting the events with declining traditional types of events. There are also performers devoting careers to the tastes of youngsters, and hotels and resorts with child-centered facilities, entertainment, and special events. The term *family event* took on new meaning, stressing variety, quality entertainment, educational value, and improved services.

Trends established in the 1980s can be expected to reach their maximum in the 1990s, but others will emerge. The middle-aged boomers, with their time, money, and tastes but with few children, will be the biggest travelers. *Discover America 2000* predicted that older boomers will desire upscale resorts combining less strenuous recreation (such as golf), second homes, and cultural events. Late baby boomers will be very active in business travel, travel with children, weekend getaways, winter trips, and city destinations. Specialty travel linked to hobbies and avocations should become more popular. All these trends bode well for festivals and events, particularly in the cultural field, off-season, and at resorts.

Seniors

Seniors have become a prime target for ever-widening forms of leisure and travel products. More older people are active and have the money and interests to be worthwhile target markets. The importance of this group was revealed in Tourism Canada's research into foreign pleasure travel markets (Lariviere and Vachon 1989), which found that almost half of the "touring" segment in the U.S. market consisted of retired people. The important "city/culture" segments of the markets in the United Kingdom, West Germany, France, and Japan were revealed to be dominated by those aged fifty or more. And among older pleasure travelers, women are predominant.

Discover America 2000 noted that the number of upscale retirees is growing and will continue to do so through the 1990s. They are likely to travel more than past generations of seniors, favoring ground transport rather than air, and will seek rewarding social experiences. They are already key targets for bus tours to special events and festivals, and this might grow substantially.

Urban Life-Styles

Most people in the industrialized world live in cities or may be considered urbanized in their outlook and life-styles. Agriculture and primary industries have declined, in terms of employment, to the point where they are not perceived to be relevant to the daily lives of the urban population. The range of urban life-styles is great, but there are commonalities that affect everyone: increasing congestion, pollution, crime, social tension, and a declining sense of community on the negative side; enhanced arts, cultural, leisure, and entertainment opportunities, as well as new forms of relationships and economic possibilities, on the positive side.

The majority of neighborhood and community festivals or events are celebrations of the special character of urban life. Some are intended to strengthen community pride or a sense of place; others are linked to ethnicity and special interests. All forms of cultural tradition are celebrated, and all forms of the arts are performed for public consumption. Most block parties, community fetes, sporting events, and fund-raisers are small and not at all oriented toward tourism. They nevertheless present a unique and attractive insight into the life-styles of the host communities, and so they can be classified as potential tourist activities with particular value in attracting former residents and others visiting friends and relatives. They are fostered for their cultural, leisure, and community development roles, but they also assist in creating the image of a vibrant community and are activity outlets for tourists. Some of them, with encouragement, can become legitimate tourist attractions.

Larger, citywide events usually have multiple purposes. They are flourishing in cities active in urban renewal and redevelopment schemes. They are more obvious tourist attractions, and tourism is generally viewed as a means to help revitalize decayed or underutilized inner-city areas. Many are linked directly to major arts, cultural, sporting, and shopping facilities, which in themselves are attractions but are static without festivals and events. This connection between tourism, urban revitalization, and events has been most noticeable in Europe and the United States, and examples are given throughout this book.

Another implication for festivals and events is the obvious growth of small-town event attractions within day-trip range of large cities. We will return to this important point when discussing market areas.

Travel and Tourism Trends

A number of sources are cited below to pull together key trends and forecasts applicable to most of the Western nations, with emphasis on implications for festival and event demand.

Long-distance travel is increasing, and periodic economic recessions have not halted the long-term growth in international travel. Archer (1989) believed the rate of increase is likely to continue or even grow, well into the next century. But the duration of pleasure trips has shortened. In the United States the average vacation trip was 4.8 nights in 1988, and Frechtling (1987) reported that weekend trips accounted for 50 percent of all U.S. vacation trips. The strong trend toward weekend pleasure trips is even stronger in dual-career families, where short breaks are easier to coordinate. And more short-break trips are being taken outside the traditional summer vacation periods.

Urban centers and their numerous services, amenities, and attractions are increasingly popular destinations for vacations, business meetings, and day or weekend pleasure trips. Cultural and heritage attractions are expanding in popularity, and there is more interest in authentic experiences, as opposed to traditional resort holidays. Schwaninger (1989) believed there will be increased demand for experiential travel, with nature and cultural attractions becoming more popular. *Discover America 2000* reported that an explosion in arts has occurred since the 1960s, leading to an ever-increasing demand for cultural tourism. Health and fitness are also strong travel motivators, and there is growing concern for safety. This holds true particularly for the expanding seniors markets.

Demand is growing in four-season resorts, especially as places for second homes, retirement, or investment properties. More short-break travel is occurring in the off-seasons, and winter sun-and-surf holidays will remain popular.

Each of these trends has been affecting festivals and special events. They have found fertile ground in the inner city, linked to other major attractions, and in the suburban and small-town belts surrounding cities. They are prime day-trip and weekend attractions, drawing on the desire either to get away from the city or to get into it.

Festivals and events cater to cultural interests of all kinds, are usually environmentally friendly, and can be promoted as safe and authentic ways to meet other people and sample different ways of living. Later we will look more closely at the whole range of human needs and travel motivations that can be satisfied through different types of events.

Certainly the opportunities will expand for developing new event attractions and packaging them more effectively to cater to diverse travel and tourism interests. Another consequence is that events will increasingly be used to bolster destination images and market positioning strategies. Travis (1989) said that increasing tourism product categorization threatens destination identities and differentiation. The more that special interests are catered to, the less relevant is a particular region or country in meeting diverse needs. Therefore, destinations able to develop an attractive image through event tourism will have a competitive advantage both for special interests (catered to by a range of targeted events) and for general touring markets.

The Media

Communications have become global and almost instantaneous in nature. This has resulted in greater international awareness and a "global village" outlook to travel, but it has also brought some unfortunate consequences. News is condensed and its presentation stresses the shock or entertainment value. The "pseudo-events" that so dismayed Boorstin (1961) have become commonplace, as various actors in the world media network strive to outdo each other in getting coverage and attracting attention to causes.

The photo opportunity has become the justification for numerous special events, each one abbreviated to a fleeting, manageable image for mass consumption, with the hope that the image is favorable publicity for the cause, the locality, or the person. Much more is now required to break through the noise and reach the target market, so events must be more spectacular and more unusual to gain the interest of the media. The Olympics, with their unrivaled spectacle and drama, are highly valued by nations and host communities, which recognize the potential for conveying political, tourist promotion, or other messages to a truly global audience. Sponsorships, which in the 1980s became a driving force in the creation or expansion of events, depend on this relationship between the evocative power of events and the resultant ability to reach target audiences with product messages and reinforcing imagery. There is potential danger in the sponsorship and media dependency of some events; we will return to that issue.

Another dimension of the media link has already been noted, that of narrowcasting. Special-interest audiences are large enough, and many are rich enough, to warrant broadcast programming or magazines aimed specifically at narrow interests. This is especially true in sports, hobbies, and entertainment, and it has helped to generate demand for new special events: tournaments for every sport; shows for every hobby; conventions on every conceivable topic; festivals to package all forms of art and entertainment.

Business Reasons
Fund-Raising

How can the myriad volunteer, nonprofit associations in today's competitive societies raise money for their operations and projects? Many have latched onto special events, with everything from teas to tourist-oriented festivals providing the vehicle to generate money. A case study of Dickens on the Strand, created by the Galveston Historical Foundation to help fund heritage conservation, is documented in Chapter 9. And although many festivals are free to the public and nonprofit in nature, participating groups often volunteer for the purpose of generating revenue. It is fairly common for event organizers to report a loss, or break-even position, while participating groups have done very well financially from the event.

Commercial Events

There are also some companies in the festival and event business for private profit, although this must be a small minority. They have to compete with civic and nonprofit organizers and therefore must provide a product of much higher quality or specialness. The most logical form of for-profit events is in the sports and entertainment fields, where special concerts and competitions are a well-established entrepreneurial activity. It is more difficult to create for-profit festivals, but the potential seems to exist for much more private-public or private-nonprofit partnerships in the management and production of events. In such cases, surplus revenue or profits can be divided.

Other Business Factors

Trade fairs, exhibitions, and conventions are predominantly commercial events at which sellers meet buyers or professionals gather to discuss their problems.

Despite communications advances, personal contacts are still highly valued, so such business events flourish. In addition, business meetings of all kinds are more and more linked to resorts, urban attractions, and leisure opportunities. One facet of this package approach to business events is the addition of other special events to the attraction, so that destinations with festivals and events might have a competitive edge in attracting conventions. Conversely, with intense competition for conventions and business meetings, numerous cities have constructed elaborate convention centers, which make great venues for other types of events. In fact, cultural and convention facilities are increasingly being joined or planned together, to maximize their potential drawing and operating power. Examples are provided later in the book.

Event Sponsorship

Sponsorship of events has become big business, complete with its own trade publications such as *Special Events Report* and *Sponsorship Report*, and a growing number of consulting firms specialize in matching events with sponsors. The editor of *Special Events Report* (Ukman 1985, 4) said that 2,500 U.S. companies would spend over $1 billion in that year on event sponsorship, a figure triple that of 1980. Sports were well developed, but not festivals. In *The Event Marketing Process: The Means to Partnership with the Corporate Sector*, Wilkinson (1988) reported a similar pattern in Canada. He suggested that 50 percent of corporate event sponsorship was aimed at sports, but this segment had become cluttered and community festivals would become the fastest growth area in corporate sponsorship.

The opportunities for targeted product exposure, sales, and image enhancement are great. But another motivator for sponsors is that of public relations and being good corporate citizens. Not all companies want, or insist on, bold media coverage. Many have legitimate interest in fostering the arts or other worthwhile causes, and do not require great publicity for their efforts.

Sponsorship can have profound implications for festivals and events, particularly with regard to their tourism potential, so we will return to this topic later in the book.

Government Policy on Festivals and Special Events

As mentioned under the heading of community development, many governmental agencies are supporting the development and growth of festivals and events as reflections of policy. Leisure and sporting events are believed to encourage community integration and healthier life-styles. Arts and music festivals contribute to cultural development. Ethnic and multicultural events can be used to reduce social or racial tensions, foster intergroup understanding, and preserve traditions.

Partly because of the influence of the media, purely political factors are contributing to the emergence of special events. Mega-events offer irresistible opportunities for posturing, pronouncing, or propagandizing, stimulating countries—for example, South Korea—to engage in large-scale development for the Olympics and an equally Olympian effort to convey the right political messages to both their allies and their enemies. More crass is the manipulation of popular events for partisan political purposes, a motivation that has been hurled at the government of British Columbia, for example, where apparently its successful Expo '86 led to the reelection of a once unpopular and troubled government (Anderson and Wachtel 1986) as a result of the economic stimulation given to the depressed provincial economy and the exuberance created by being the center of world attention.

More creatively, major political celebrations, particularly anniversaries, have led to grand programs of event development and chauvinistic display. The celebrations and associated imagery make powerful symbols to foster pride in the country and its achievements. O'Reilly (1987, 26) described the origins of the Trinidad and Tobago Carnival as a "heady symbol of freedom" from slavery and colonialism, which continues as a symbol of national pride and cultural identity. These periodic national celebrations are valuable to politicians, tourism, and events. Evidence suggests that much of the legacy of these undertakings is in the form of more and better local and regional celebrations and annual events.

Armstrong (1986) cautioned that raw civic or national boosterism often takes the place of rational planning when it comes to special events possessing high prestige value. Cost-benefit analysis is not undertaken, or the benefits—especially tourism and economic effects—are sometimes wildly exaggerated. Anyone criticizing the event can then be placed in the uncomfortable position of being branded as a doomsayer or, much worse, unpatriotic. This is the worst kind of politics, and event managers use it at their own peril.

To explore more fully the roles of governments in the growth of festivals and events, and in particular the emergence of event tourism initiatives, we will examine the situation in Australia, Canada, Great Britain, the United States, and New Zealand in the next chapter. Of these, only New Zealand has adopted a formal event tourism policy and strategy, so we will give that example extra attention. In the other countries there are varying degrees of national involvement with festivals and events, but most of the initiatives are at the state, or provincial, and municipal, or local, levels.

MARKET AND CONSUMER RESEARCH

Recent concepts and research findings from the leisure and tourism fields can help us gain a better understanding of the needs and motivations that generate demand for festivals and events, and of how this knowledge can be used for more effective event tourism marketing. Subsequent chapters will examine in depth the actual methods of using market and consumer research in event tourism planning and in festival marketing.

Needs and Travel Motivations

A great deal has been written about basic human needs and how they translate into leisure and travel motivations. But the specific subject of festivals and events has not been raised in this material, so we must break some new ground.

Table 3-2 attempts to combine commonly accepted categories of need, as suggested by Maslow (1954), with frequently cited travel motivations (e.g., Mayo and Jarvis 1981; Middleton 1988) and relate these to the benefits that festivals and special events potentially can provide to meet the needs or satisfy the motivations.

Caution is required when interpreting or applying this illustration, for several reasons. There is no firm agreement among scholars as to what actually causes people to seek out certain travel or leisure opportunities. The most compelling recent theory has been put forward by Iso-Ahola (1980, 1983; Mannell and Iso-Ahola 1987), who argued that leisure and travel behavior is stimulated by a desire both to escape undesirable conditions and, simultaneously, to realize desired experiences. Marketing people sometimes refer to "push and pull" factors, but it is wrong to think of them as acting independently.

The Maslow (1954) hierarchy of needs is widely cited, but the concept suggests that lower-order physical needs must be satisfied before higher social and personal needs become important. Iso-Ahola (1980) challenged this notion, concluding instead that any combination of needs can stimulate leisure behavior. In fact, research has discovered that social obligations motivate much leisure behavior, and that most people indicate their social needs have been satisfied more than their physical needs.

There is also no reason to believe that any given event will necessarily provide certain benefits to satisfy the listed needs and travel motivations. Rather, Table 3-2 should be used to suggest ways in which a festival or event can be improved. This relates well to the model of essential services and generic and targeted benefits that is discussed later in the book, in the context of product development and marketing.

Physical Needs and Motivations

Physical needs are the most basic, pertaining to survival, safety and comfort, and procreation. They can stimulate or shape interest in healthful activities, in relaxation to relieve stress or boredom, in sexually gratifying pursuits, and in

Table 3-2. Basic Needs, Travel Motives, and Related Benefits from Festivals and Events

Basic Needs	Travel Motivations	Benefits from Festivals and Events
Physical (based on physiological needs)	Exercise Relaxation or change of pace Safe and comfortable shelter, surroundings, food and drink Earning a living Sexual gratification	Physical activity in sporting and recreational events Relaxation at entertainment events Safe public activity Food and beverages Help in making a living (through business or trade fairs) Sexuality in entertainment and socializing
Interpersonal or Social (based on the need for belonging, love, the esteem of others)	Togetherness with family and friends Social settings Links to cultural or ethnic and religious roots Expressions of community and national identity Opportunities for achievement and recognition, status and prestige	Novel, accessible, and fun outings for families and friends Opportunities to meet people, and to see and be seen Tangible access to ethnic and cultural traditions Celebration of community or national ideals; rituals Opportunities to compete and win recognition Opportunity to be part of a prestigious event (particularly as a volunteer)
Personal (based on the need for understanding, aesthetic appreciation, growth, and selffulfillment)	Knowledge and new experiences Aesthetic experiences Fantasy Fulfillment of ambitions	Education through exhibitions, interpretation events, and conferences or meetings Aesthetic appreciation of visual and performing arts, costumes, festival displays Discovery of unfamiliar traditions, foods, crafts, and so on Opportunity to participate and to learn (e.g., sports, crafts, dance, ritual)

food and drink, all of which have obvious leisure and travel connections. At another level, basic physical needs are a constraint on leisure and travel, so that a concern for health and security definitely shapes leisure and travel behavior and is an important factor in choosing destinations and activities.

The basic concern for health and safety must be dealt with at all attractions and events, so it is one of the essential services to be provided; where lacking, it generates consumer dissatisfaction or resistance. Conversely, people are motivated to engage in public celebrations and other events where health and security are expected or taken for granted. The promise of good, healthful food and beverages and personal security at public events is in this sense an attraction.

The range of special events is so great that almost everyone's interests in health, physical activity, or relaxation can be satisfied—often all at the same event. This is a challenge to the event organizers, who can take advantage of these needs through site design, service provision, program variety, and high-quality food and beverages.

Business meetings and related events, such as trade fairs and shows, satisfy the basic need to earn a living. What might not be realized, however, is that earning a living is so fundamental a need that it can influence leisure behavior. Hence the popularity of do-it-yourself and craft shows where hobbyists can learn skills, exchange ideas, and even make some money. Flea markets also involve both work and leisure, and so do many events from the point of view of volunteers and performers. This duality of festivals and events, as both work and leisure, gives rise to interesting behavioral patterns, such as the goodhearted performance of duties by volunteers who are, in fact, playing roles; or that of performers at arts festivals, whose satisfaction comes largely from after-show jamming; or the frenzied buying and selling at shows and markets—by the same people.

The last basic physical need mentioned in the table, sexual gratification, requires more delicate consideration. In one respect, it is satisfied through normal socializing, and festivals are primarily public, social occasions. In addition, sexuality is a common and often blatant aspect of contemporary entertainment and advertising, so people are accustomed to its inclusion in all types of events. But it is also often an illicit behavior, less condemned perhaps than substance abuse and rowdyism, that is engaged in frequently in all kinds of settings. Wise event organizers do not want to encourage illicit behavior at public events, but they risk doing so if their promotion or programming is suggestive and if their security or site design is faulty (poorly lit; for example). But many successful events and promotions employ sexuality as an attraction or attention-getting device, so there is a balancing act to be achieved. Whatever the opinions and values of the event organizers, this basic need really cannot be ignored.

Interpersonal or Social Needs and Motivations

The second level of needs are interpersonal or social in nature, essentially consisting of the needs for belonging, loving, and gaining the esteem of others. This motivates people to seek social experiences, which dominate leisure behavior. Indeed, it has been argued that leisure settings must facilitate socializing to be successful. Family-oriented events meet this major need.

More specialized festival themes satisfy the desire to explore one's heritage and sense of place and to celebrate community and nation. Ritual and symbolism are important aspects of events, and they stem directly from the longing for identity. At one extreme, the Olympics foster a feeling of international community; at the other, loyalty to group or nation can be encouraged. The operative word in all these cases is *belonging,* and it is a powerful need that festival and event managers can help meet through social activities—settings that permit and encourage mixing and observing, rituals, symbolism, and the sharing of something special.

Another dimension of social needs is that of self-esteem, which can be gained through the meeting of a challenge, competition, the attainment of status and prestige. Contests and prizes are perennial favorites at all kinds of events, and they are linked to a very basic set of behavioral motives. Other connections are more subtle, including the prestige and status that come both from being part of a major event (this can affect whole communities and nations) and from volunteering. Managers who design their volunteer operations with this fact in mind will find that incentives and rewards do not always have to be tangible. Public recognition and the satisfaction that comes from helping to create a prestigious event are often adequate.

Personal Needs and Motivations

The third group of needs are personal and psychological in nature. People are naturally curious and feel the need to explore and learn and to increase mastery of their lives. At the highest level is the need for aesthetics or beauty and the fulfillment of one's ambitions and desires. Sometimes added to this list is the fantasy motivation. It is certainly a factor in many forms of leisure and travel behavior, and the industry has responded with resorts, theme parks, and shopping centers with fantasy themes, along with special events that fabricate or re-create a different time or place.

In Maslow's theory, lower needs must be met before higher ones become motivators. Except in cases where health and security are not assured, however, most people carry a mixture of all these needs into their leisure and travel pursuits. In the wealthier nations, basic needs are usually not a problem, so meeting higher-level needs has come to the fore. Festivals and special events are excellent mechanisms for satisfying higher-level needs. Education is the basic theme of many shows, exhibitions, and meetings. Ethnic and multicultural festivals, and those featuring traditional crafts or foods, allow for discovery. Aesthetic appreciation is a core benefit of arts and cultural festivals and many shows. Challenge and self-fulfillment are provided by events that feature participatory activities and elements targeted to special interests. Fantasy is easily incorporated in festival and event settings, themes, and activities. Getting away from it all need not require a trip halfway around the world; it can be experienced at an attraction or event in one's own community.

All these factors are applicable to foreign travel as well as events close to home. Safety and health needs will likely be more important to long-distance travelers, and it can be most reassuring to know that event attractions are as popular (or more so) with locals as with tourists. The atmosphere of a community festival is likely to be more conducive to fostering a sense of belonging and comfort than that found in impersonal resorts and mass-tourism facilities. The interpersonal motives are increasingly important to foreign travel, as many seasoned travelers search out authentic encounters with indigenous cultures and inhabitants. And many of the higher needs are powerful travel motivators, luring people to see the world and appreciate the accomplishments of other cultures.

Typologies of Travelers

The realization that festivals and events can satisfy or help meet all the basic human needs and leisure or travel motives is an important step in product development and marketing. But not all events will be able to meet all needs, and many events focus on specific markets. So we need a basis for segmenting the market. A good starting point is a discussion of types of travelers.

Murphy (1985, 5) observed that several typologies of travelers have been formulated, which are either *interactional* (emphasizing visitor-destination interactions) or *cognitive-normative* (stressing travel motivations) in nature. By referring to these, we gain some additional insights into travel motivations. Implications can be drawn for destination development and event tourism.

The category of interactional typologies includes that of Cohen (1972): the "explorer" class, people who desire mixing with host societies, and the "drifter" group, those who search for the exotic. The typology of Smith (1977) is similar, including "explorer," "elite," "offbeat," and "unusual" groups. Pearce (1982) labeled a "high-contact" segment, people who seek out host-guest interaction. All these types of travelers contrast sharply with mass and charter tourists, who are associated with tour packages and isolated resorts.

Among the cognitive-normative typologies is the psychographic model of Plog (1972, 1987). Psychographics, as a segmentation method, focuses on personality and attitudes and how they shape leisure and travel behavior, so it is closely related to the preceding discussion of needs. Plog argued that the population can be divided into a spectrum of types ranging from "allocentric" to "psychocentric," and that the travel preferences and behavior of each type are different. Allocentrics are interested in new experiences and are adventuresome; they are motivated most by educational and cultural factors. By contrast, psychocentrics require security and are less adventuresome; they tend to travel by car to nearby, popular destinations or attractions or to take fully packaged holidays. A third category, representing the societal norm, is labeled "midcentric." Most people typically enjoy individual travel to known attractions and areas of increasing popularity that have facilities.

There are important implications of this psychographic continuum. First, most people are not adventuresome, but tend to follow travel patterns set by others, so that destinations or attractions "discovered" by an elite can become more popular, while eventually losing appeal to those who were first attracted. Further, allocentrics seek out new experiences and destinations that are not popular with other tourists, and they can be lured to new events, even in remote areas. They are more likely to seek out the new, authentic, and high-quality events, including ethnic and multicultural events, folk music, and events in remoter locations. High price is not a problem if the quality matches. Longer-distance travel is not necessarily an impediment to these groups, as they are willing to spend time and money in satisfying their special interests. Psychocentrics, by contrast, are more likely to favor events close to home and in familiar settings, with family activities stressed. Entertainment and sporting events should have strong appeal to them, as might national celebrations, parades, and ordinary food festivals. Cost is a concern here, and traditional societal values—not the outrageous or avant-garde—will appeal to them.

Using these concepts of need, motivation, and types of traveler, the event marketer can devise an appropriate marketing strategy, including segmentation, product development, pricing, and promotion to provide benefits desired by existing or targeted market groups.

Consumer Research Applicable to Festivals and Events

Not very many surveys have been undertaken to identify consumer preferences, motivations, and reactions to events, and it is difficult collecting and comparing those that have been completed. A selection of survey results has been obtained for this book, and we use them to explore a number of key dimensions: who attends events; why; what do they do; what do they like and dislike? The starting point is at the general level of destination area research, where we look for clues concerning the size and nature of the market that is interested in event products. Unfortunately, festivals and special events are seldom handled effectively in these destination surveys.

Surveys of Potential Pleasure Travel Markets for North America

The United States Travel and Tourism Administration and Tourism Canada cooperated on a five-year research program, starting in 1986, to provide market information on potential long-haul pleasure travel to Canada and the United States. Interviews were conducted in the United Kingdom, West Germany, Switzerland, France, Japan, Hong Kong, and Singapore. Respondents were queried on their travel patterns and preferences, including specific benefits sought, and how Canada and the United States were perceived. Segmentation of the sample allowed the development of a number of profiles of those likely to be interested in festivals and events. Selected data and several examples of these profiles are cited below, using published reports (Tourism Canada 1987) and unpublished Tourism Canada analyses (Rusk 1989; Lariviere and Vachon 1989).

Long-haul travel for festivals, exhibitions, or other special events was not mentioned in most of the samples (it accounted for just 2 percent of Swiss long-distance pleasure travel), so no general conclusions can be drawn regarding the current size of the overseas event tourism market. However, data were obtained on the numbers who included attendance at festivals and events in recent long-haul travel and the proportions who said local festivals were important features in an overseas destination. A summary of the data is shown in Table 3-3. It can be seen that a very significant percentage (ranging from 16 to 47 percent) of long-haul travelers from these countries do participate in festivals while abroad, although a lesser proportion (9 to 18 percent) considers such attractions to be important attributes when selecting a destination. The table also shows that many who thought local festivals were important did not actually attend any on a previous trip (23 to 55 percent did attend), which might indicate a lack of opportunity. These statistics certainly demonstrate the importance of events as activity outlets and as satisfying means to provide other major desired destination attributes, such as sightseeing, dining, shopping, entertainment, or visiting historic sites—all of which can be linked to, or manifested through, special events.

The foreign market surveys also generated segment profiles, which add to our knowledge of the roles of events and characteristics of tourists likely to consume event tourism products. For example, in the Japanese market, which is highly prized throughout North America, Europe, and the South Pacific regions, the "culture and comfort" and "culture and nature" segments were isolated. As illustrated in Table 3-4, they seek cultural activities, good cuisine, and local festivals and crafts, among other destination attributes. These important target markets tend to consist of well-educated females (older for the culture and comfort segment) who prefer package tours in the summer or autumn.

In the huge West German market, a "sports and entertainment" cluster was found. These long-haul travelers are looking for active and spectator sports, along with nightlife, cultural groups and activities, local cuisine, and some adventure. They tend to be male (66 percent), middle-aged, married professionals. Independent travel is preferred, but in the summer. A "big city" segment was revealed in the Great Britain market. Tending to be female and over 44 years of age, these tourists desire live entertainment, theater, festivals, shopping, and culture, all in a package.

The U.S. Pleasure Travel Market

This major study (9,000 interviews) of the U.S. pleasure travel market (Tourism Canada 1986) was conducted to help shape promotion to the important American

Table 3-3. The Importance of Local Festivals for Long-Haul Travel in Selected Overseas Markets

Country	Importance (%)*	Attendance at Local Festivals (%)	
		By Those Who Thought Them Important	By All Long-Haul Travelers
Japan	18.0	23.0	16.0
West Germany	9.0	55.0	47.0
Great Britain	17.5	46.0	33.0
France	11.0	44.0	27.0

*The percentage of actual long-haul travelers in each country who considered local festivals to be somewhat or very important in selecting an overseas destination.

Source: Tourism Canada. 1987. *Pleasure travel markets to North America: Japan, United Kingdom, West Germany, France, highlights report.* Ottawa: Tourism Canada.

market. It yielded useful knowledge on how and why Americans travel and gave some insights on event tourism. Eight types of trips were predetermined (through focus groups) to represent the range of pleasure trips, and the characteristics of respondents were allocated to all the types of trips they actually took. This style of segmentation ensures that the segments represent the diversity of the population's travel habits; but the predetermination of eight trip types makes secondary analysis of the data difficult, so that we cannot go into the data base and construct an event tourist profile.

Table 3-5 presents the eight trip types, their size, and the proportion of respondents allocated to each type who said that ethnic festivals and events were very important in trip planning. Note that only five of the eight trip types provide data on the importance of ethnic events, and these figures show that a very high proportion (35 to 54 percent) believed them to be important. Perhaps if the question had been expanded to cover all festivals, the proportions would have been even greater. Also note that the specific trip type that lumps together theme park visits with exhibitions and special events is a very small component of the U.S. pleasure travel market, although these data do not show how many actually attended events. It is also not possible to separate the events component from theme parks and exhibitions.

Some information was also provided on the activities of tourists. Attending an ethnic festival (other types of event were not specified) ranked eighth in the activities of those in the city trip group, fourteenth for touring, and twentieth for resort trips.

Touring trips, which are very important regionally and of great significance in the Canadian market, and the city trip segment both clearly incorporate a strong event and festival component. Table 3-6 displays data that define these

Table 3-4. Japanese Pleasure Travelers Interested in Festivals and Events

Breakdowns	Culture and Comfort Segment	Culture and Nature Segment
The Market	987,000 Japanese in segment (21% of all long-haul tourists) 77% of these rated festivals and events as an important tourism product	611,000 Japanese in segment (16% of all long-haul tourists) 82% of these rated festivals and events as an important tourist product
Tourism Activities Sought	Historic sites Museums and galleries Local festivals Different cultures Sightseeing excursions First-class hotels Dining and shopping National parks Amusement parks	Historic sites Different cultures Interesting towns and villages Local festivals Wilderness and nature Museums and galleries Local crafts Outstanding scenery National parks
Segment Profile	72% female Age 50+ and married 44% college educated 55% take package tours Prefer summer and autumn	65% female Young and single Professional or managerial College educated 58% from Tokyo Prefer summer
Implications	High interest in cultural activities and local cuisine—benefits festivals can provide. This segment is likely to be oriented to major cities and established destinations.	Cultural events with ethnic and native groups are an ideal mix.

Source: Lariviere, M., and H. Vachon. 1989. *Festivals and events, a position paper.* Ottawa: Tourism Canada. (Data taken from *Pleasure Travel Markets to North America*, by Market Facts, 1986–87, for Tourism Canada and the U.S. Travel and Tourism Administration.)

two segments and the implications for Canadian event tourism. Similar conclusions for various U.S. destinations would be expected. The research found that respondents who took touring trips were the likeliest to agree that experiencing different cultures or ways of life is very important, and the data suggest that ethnic festivals are a major way to obtain the desired culture benefit.

Also of interest is the fact that more females (59 percent) than males (53 percent) in the touring category rated ethnic events as being important. Overall, the touring trip segment was older and included more retired people than other groups. By contrast, the city trip group comprised a younger, well-educated, mostly married population, which preferred cultural attractions including ethnic

Table 3-5. The U.S. Pleasure Travel Market by Trip Types and Importance of Ethnic Festivals

Trip Types	% of All Trips	% of Trip Nights	% Thinking Ethnic Festivals Important
Visiting friends or relatives	41	44	N.A.
Touring	7	14	53
Close-to-home leisure	21	13	43
Outdoors	12	10	N.A.
Resort	6	8	35
City	8	7	47
Theme park, exhibition, or special event	4	3	N.A.
Cruise	1	1	54

Source: Longwoods Research Group Ltd. Tourism Canada. 1985. *The U.S. pleasure travel market study.* Ottawa: Tourism Canada.

festivals, sporting events, good shopping, and quality accommodations and restaurants.

One can conclude from this large survey of American pleasure travel patterns that festivals and events are important motivators and activities for different types of trip, but precise measurement of the size and importance of event tourism as a whole cannot be made.

Canadian Tourism Attitude and Motivation Study (CTAMS)

CTAMS was a large survey (15,000 interviews) of Canadians undertaken in 1985 to determine psychographic profiles of pleasure travelers. Analysis of this data set by Burak Jacobson (1986) revealed two segments that view festivals and events as important destination attributes (see Table 3-7). A "heritage group" had strong interests in arts, culture, museums, crafts, indoor sports, and amusement parks. They seek city and touring attractions with culture and festivals or events. A "city culture" group has similar interests, plus a desire for quality restaurants, performing arts, historic sites, and first-class hotels. Both segments were found to be predominantly female, aged thirty-five and older, with good education and income. Automobile travel was preferred for these types of trips.

An analysis of this data set by Smith (1988) focused on profiling all those who had attended festivals. He found that Canadian festivalgoers were more likely to be female, unmarried, well educated, and under twenty-five or over fifty-five years old. They tend to visit festivals with one or more friends or family

Table 3-6. U.S. Pleasure Travelers Interested in Festivals and Events

Breakdown	Touring Segment	City Segment
The Market	27 million travelers in this segment	23.5 million travelers in this segment
	19.2% of all long-haul travelers are in this segment	6.4% of all long-haul travelers are in this segment
	21% of this segment rated festivals and events as an important tourism product	18% of this segment rated festivals and events as an important tourism product
Tourism Activities Sought	Trip through scenic beauty, cultural, or general interest	Trip to a major city
	Different cultures and ways of life	Museums and art galleries
	Visiting small towns and villages	Dining and shopping
	National parks and historic sites	Theater and concerts
	Museums and art galleries	Local festivals and sporting events
	Local festivals	Nightlife
	Big cities	Different cultures
		Comfortable accommodations
Segment Profile	Married	Married
	College education	College educated
	Older and retired	Younger
	Live in major urban areas	Live in major urban areas
	Average length of stay: 8 days	Average length of stay: 3 days
	Car and air travel dominate	Car and air travel dominate
Implications	Festivals and events can be used to feature different cultures, ways of life, and hospitality	Package festivals and special events with art, dining, quality accommodations, and access to different cultures and a variety of attractions
	Events should be themed to complement the regional identity	

Source: Lariviere, M., and H. Vachon. 1989. *Festivals and events, a position paper.* Ottawa: Tourism Canada. (Data taken from *U.S. Pleasure Travel Market*, by Longwoods Research Group Ltd., 1985, for Tourism Canada.)

members. General travel interests of this group include experiencing new lifestyles and cultures, trying new foods, having fun, feeling safe and welcome, and learning about local history. Smaller towns and historic sites are preferred settings for these experiences, but big cities can also be attractive. Inexpensive meals and moderately priced accommodations were commonly sought. Smith (1988, 3) also commented on the package of benefits sought by those who attend festivals: "Cultural activities, live theatre, musicals, historical displays, museums and the opportunity for outdoor recreation add significantly to the appeal of a festival. Being free to act the way they feel and having the opportunity to meet other people with similar interests are also very important."

Table 3-7. Heritage and City Culture Segments from the Canadian Tourism Attitude and Motivation Survey

Heritage Segment	City Culture Segment
Predominantly female, aged 35–54	Female, well educated, good income
Prefers domestic travel in summer	Aged 45 and older
Travels by car (68%) and air (24%)	Travels abroad, especially in U.S.A. and Europe
Uses travel agents	Takes long trips
Preferred interests and activities: arts, culture, museums, crafts, indoor sports, amusement parks	Travels by car (66%) and air (27%)
Will seek activities in city and touring destinations associated with culture, attractions, and events	Travels during summer and the shoulder seasons
	Interests and activities: museums, performing arts, historic sites, crafts, quality restaurants, first-class hotels

Source: Lariviere, M., and H. Vachon. 1989. *Festivals and events, a position paper.* Ottawa: Tourism Canada (Data taken from *Canadian Travel Attitudes and Motivation Survey*, by Burak Jacobson, 1986, for Tourism Canada.)

With CTAMS and the other surveys, it is important to keep in mind that what they tell us about festival and event consumers is shaped by the questions asked and the ways in which data have been analyzed. An ideal profiling or segmentation of the event tourism market has not been possible in any of these large data sets because the questions did not address the full range of festival and eventgoing behavior. CTAMS comes closest, but allows a look only at those who consumed the vaguely defined activities of attending sports events or cultural events.

General Observations on the Eventgoer

From the above evidence, and results of event surveys cited below and elsewhere in this book, we can draw some general conclusions about the festivalgoer and eventgoer. This is risky, as the research completed to date has not been systematic and can only be considered to reveal broad patterns. In many ways, event customers reflect general leisure and travel trends and patterns, so that it should come as no surprise that those with more money (who are also better educated and older) and more time (the retired) show up disproportionately in event visitor surveys. It is the differences that are important for target marketing, and while some differences appear to be common to festivals and events in general, others vary from one event to the next.

Gender Differences

Sports and entertainment events are more likely to attract young males, whereas arts and cultural festivals have much stronger appeal to females. Community festivals and celebrations do attract more families, with a more balanced gender distribution. In Saskatchewan, for example, it was found that 60 percent of visitors at a range of events were there with families (Derek Murray Consulting Associates Ltd. 1985). In our case study of Dickens on the Strand in Galveston, Texas, the research found that 35 percent of respondents to the on-site random survey were with a group of adults without children, while 21 percent were in a single-family group with children. Females accounted for 53 percent of the sample (Ralston and Crompton 1988a,b). In general, note that many event visitor surveys do not use random sampling, so an accurate determination of demographics is difficult.

Cultural Tourism Segment

Many surveys of travelers and the arts have found that better-educated, older females are a dominant component of regular eventgoers. This is certainly the case in the national and international research cited previously, and it is corroborated by individual event research. Mitchell and Wall (1985) surveyed visitors to a music festival—the Elora Three Centuries Festival—and concluded that the 73 percent female proportion was typical (or perhaps a bit high) of the performing arts clientele in North America. The audience was older (average age: thirty-nine), highly educated, professional, and mostly married. Of the proportion of visitors who were on vacation, 52 percent said they planned to attend other performing arts in Ontario, indicating the existence of what might be called a festival circuit in the summer months. Mitchell and Wall also observed a marked difference between weekend and weekday demographics, with weekenders being more typical cultural tourists, while weekday visitors more closely reflected the resident population's characteristics.

Race and Ethnicity

The setting, sponsors or organizers, and theme probably all have a marked bearing on attracting different racial or ethnic groups. Ethnic and multicultural festivals are often aimed directly at achieving intergroup mixing and fostering better communications and understanding, whereas it appears that different types of entertainment, cultural, and sporting events have distinct racial and ethnic appeal. For example, the Louisville, Kentucky, Bluegrass Music Festival (Kentucky Department of Travel Development 1987) had an audience that was 96 percent white. Most surveys do not record this information, and it might be inappropriate to do so in direct interviewing or self-completion questionnaires. It is nevertheless a factor organizers should consider, and nonintrusive measures can be taken by direct observation to determine if certain groups are under-represented in the audience.

Repeat Visits

Numerous festival surveys have detected a loyal group of return visitors, obviously including a high proportion of area residents. This important group includes not just a segment with strong brand loyalty to particular events, returning again and again, but also a segment that takes in many different events. Music festivals in particular seem to attract a mobile audience, and sports have dedicated traveling fans.

Research by Plant (1985) found that approximately 48 percent of the visitors to the Elmira (Ontario) Maple Syrup Festival were repeaters, with an average of 4.55 previous visits. Of the first-time customers, one-half had never been to the Elmira area previously, showing that the event was a key to enhancing awareness of the whole region. Repeaters tended to be middle-aged, married, and well educated, with fewer students, young people, and seniors. This could suggest that the product had a differential appeal.

Increasingly we are likely to see more specializing regulars traveling to sample different types of theme festivals and events; food, wine, and heritage themes are good prospects for developing regular and mobile followers. Later, we will examine whether there is an optimum mix of first-time and repeat visitors to an event.

Likes and Dislikes

Surveys typically obtain some measure of visitors' likes and dislikes, suggestions, and general satisfaction. Unless these questions are specific to event attributes, however, they tend to yield useless generalizations, such as "everything" was liked by 72 percent of the audience. Nevertheless, some patterns do appear in these various surveys.

High on lists of dislikes are crowding, long lines, sanitary conditions (especially the number and cleanliness of washrooms), the weather, parking problems, lack of information, excessive costs, and poor-quality goods, service, or attractions.

Atmosphere or ambience figures prominently in the likes of many community festivalgoers, whereas arts and cultural events are more likely to attract comments on the quality of performances and the theater or other setting. Food and beverages are such vital components of many events that their quality always attracts compliments or complaints. People-watching, socializing, entertainment, and arts and crafts are clearly popular at festivals.

Different approaches to measuring pre-event awareness and preferences and postevent customer satisfaction are documented later in the case studies. Guidance is also provided in Chapter 10 concerning impact assessment and evaluation methods, including suggested basic questions for visitor surveys.

How People Learn about Events

Personal recommendations—word of mouth—often top the lists of means by which festivalgoers find out about an event, or of the main influences on their decision to attend. As to advertising effectiveness, community festivals often do best with local newspapers, with radio and television secondary in importance. Gray (1987), researching arts and crafts festivals in Minnesota, discovered that word of mouth ranged from 28 to 56 percent and newspapers from 37 to 58 percent in response to a question on how visitors learned of the events. Plant (1985), observing that word of mouth was the most frequent source of information mentioned by tourists attending the twenty-two-year-old Elmira Maple Syrup Festival, concluded that its advertising effectiveness was low and should become more targeted.

Brochures, road signs, and posters also have been effective in some circumstances in drawing visitors. This balance varies according to the nature of the advertising and event and to its age and popularity. Over the years, repeat visitors become more important promoters.

SUMMARY

The available research on event tourism markets and related consumer attitudes or behavior has not been well developed. More systematic and comparative studies are required before anything absolute can be said about the size and characteristics of the event tourism market and its segments. But Chapter 3 made an attempt to document trends and offer explanations.

Indicators strongly suggest that rapid expansion in the number, size, and diversity of festivals and special events has occurred in the Western nations since the last world war, and particularly in the last ten to twenty years. Accompanying this phenomenon has been increasing professionalism, marked by maturing associations and industry publications, although not yet matched by research or statistics. Community festivals appear to be the primary growth sector of the 1980s and 1990s, as in many countries sports and arts events have already been well established.

Reasons for these trends were suggested, particularly how general societal and leisure changes have affected the festival and special event field. Major factors affecting trends, and their key marketing implications, were identified. These also constitute an important future perspective on trends for the 1990s: increased incomes; increased leisure and the need for quality time; diversification of leisure interests; the baby-boom and an aging population; urban life-styles; travel and tourism trends, particularly short breaks; influence of the media; and business factors.

Needs and motivations were examined, resulting in speculation, or hypothesizing, as to the benefits that festivals and special events can provide to satisfy basic human needs and related travel motives (Table 3-2). All the needs, motives, and tourist types cited in the literature potentially can be met in festivals and special events, although not necessarily all at once!

Evidence was presented from international and national-level travel research to demonstrate the importance of events in motivating travel, satisfying visitor expectations, and shaping destination images. It was shown that segmenting the tourist markets generates profiles of groups that possess strong interest in attending festivals and events, or for which events would be an important activity outlet or package tour component.

Some general observations on characteristics of the eventgoer concluded the chapter. Although some certainty can be expressed—for example, that females dominate arts-related travel and males are more attracted to sports events—a great deal remains unknown. The demographics and resulting demand are changing, and research is not keeping up.

CHAPTER FOUR

Initiatives in English-Speaking Countries

Event tourism is a new policy area for government initiatives, so there are few formal and comprehensive strategies and programs in place. The state of the art in this area can be described as newly emergent and lacking clear focus. The first English-speaking country—perhaps the first anywhere—to formulate a specific event tourism policy was New Zealand, and that country's initiatives are featured in this chapter. Then highlights from Australia, the United States, Great Britain, and Canada are presented to demonstrate the range of issues and initiatives. A fully comprehensive review of all government policy and action affecting festivals and special events has not been attempted. Nor is the coverage uniform, mainly because so little has been published and disseminated on this subject.

NEW ZEALAND

New Zealand is one of the first nations to launch a specific event tourism program, but this is not really surprising given the increasing importance of tourism to the country. Throughout the 1980s, international tourism volume grew dramatically in the South Pacific, with New Zealand and Australia experiencing rapid growth in numbers of arrivals. International travel receipts doubled between 1979 and 1986, with arrivals increasing almost 70 percent. Tourism became the country's leading foreign exchange earner in 1986. Forecasts by the

Otago Goldfields Heritage Celebrations, New Zealand: A stagecoach re-creates historic links among participating communities (G. B. Scott Photography, Auckland, New Zealand).

New Zealand Tourist and Publicity Department (NZTP) call for one million visitors in 1990, the sesquicentennial of the country, which is being marked by a host of special events including the Commonwealth Games in Auckland.

The New Zealand government welcomed and encouraged tourism growth, particularly in the context of periodic bouts of inflation, a rising national budget deficit, stagnant domestic tourism, and difficult times for agriculture, the traditional leading sector in the economy. But the tourism boom has not been without difficulty or internal criticism. New Zealand is a relatively small island nation of approximately three million residents, with limited domestic means to invest in tourism infrastructure. The quality of the natural environment is outstanding, and the NZTP has successfully fostered an international image of the country as one of the world's most beautiful, clean, friendly, and safe destinations. Ever sensitive to this quality of life, some New Zealanders have been skeptical of the tourist industry, and it seems that there is a national consensus that tourism must not grow at the expense of social or environmental quality.

Otago Goldfields Heritage Celebrations, New Zealand: making the theme real to youngsters through gold panning (New Zealand Tourist and Publicity Department).

There is also a recognition that tourism is one of the brightest stars in the national economy.

The Emergence of Event Tourism

Through the decade of the 1980s a number of important studies and policy papers were prepared by government and the industry. In 1984 the Tourist and Publicity Department and the New Zealand Tourism Council (a body of industry leaders that advises the minister of tourism) published a discussion report called *New Zealand Tourism: Issues and Policies*. Summarizing trends and issues, it recommended a series of policies to develop the industry in a manner sensitive to social and environmental concerns. Contained in this document is recognition of the potential role of festivals and events in shaping the future of tourism.

Regarding the nature of New Zealand's attractions, the dominance of spectacular scenery was acknowledged. But it was also recognized that the natural asset was "complemented by the New Zealand people, their diverse lifestyle and cultures and by the character of the manmade landscape" (New Zealand Tourist and Publicity Department and New Zealand Tourism Council 1984, 5). The writers noted a heightened interest by foreign tourists in the towns, pace of life, agricultural practices and events, foods, arts and crafts, and multicultural mix of the people. All of these cultural attributes contribute to a distinctive tourism appeal.

Product development and image enhancement were judged necessary to realize the potential of the cultural attractiveness of New Zealand. One target was to be the further development of a range of community facilities and local events, including theaters, parks, sport and recreation, education, and shopping, all of which would be of interest to the tourist. Augmenting these facilities and events would be a range of dual-purpose facilities for residents and tourists. In this category are historic sites, entertainment facilities, wildlife parks and reserves, recreation and theme parks, local recreational facilities, and museums. Also mentioned were local festivals, competitions, and street entertainers. A third product category consisted of those developed mainly for tourism, such as agricultural demonstrations and large-scale heritage and theme parks.

Product development alone is not enough. The report goes on to advocate ways to make cultural activity better known and more accessible to tourists, while avoiding negative social and cultural impact. One specific area in which this could be accomplished was that of Maori and Polynesian culture. The identified need was to increase the participation of these groups in tourism development "so as to broaden the range of activities and experiences available to all visitors. This should encourage a strengthening of cultural skills and assist Maori and Polynesian people to achieve their social and economic aspirations as they think most appropriate" (New Zealand Tourist and Publicity Department and New Zealand Tourism Council 1984, 30). Music, design, food, entertainment, traditions, and fashion were thought to be key attributes of Maori and Polynesian culture that could provide a motif for New Zealand tourism.

Also within the social and cultural milieu, the 1984 report commented (29) that "A New Zealand holiday experience provides wide-ranging opportunities for the types of social contact which can lead to better understanding." And although arts and crafts are identified as having tourist appeal, the authors suggested that "It would be unfortunate for both the arts and tourism if the quality of the arts or the authenticity of cultural expressions suffered in an attempt to meet assumed visitor requirements."

An accompanying assessment of marketing issues neatly encapsulated the themes related to events. The analysis concluded that markets were changing, with an increase noted in special-interest tourism, particularly cultural and outdoor activities, and in less structured holiday patterns. They concluded (56): "Marketing activities must, therefore, convey a widening array of attractions, such as cities, historic places, outdoor activities, opportunities to meet New Zealanders, cultural events and entertainment. They must offer an enriching experience." And emphasis had to be placed on authenticity. "The more distinctive products and experiences are provided, the more effective marketing of New Zealand as a unique destination will be" (48).

Given that New Zealand is a relatively small nation, attention to regional and local development is natural. The 1984 report called for the creation of tourism regions to cover the nation, and for planning and marketing to be undertaken in each. This would help spread tourist activity throughout the islands, both by increasing information available to tourists about local and regional attractions and by encouraging more community and regional product development such as auto touring routes. Seasonality could also be addressed at the regional and local level: "Reduced tariffs for accommodation and activities would encourage participants in special interest tours, conventions, festivals and organized sporting or cultural activities to extend their visit" (108).

To elaborate on the regional dimension, the report included an appendix containing short profiles of six regions constituting the entire nation, each including suggested regional themes and tourism opportunities of national and regional status. Special events, both existing and proposed, were highlighted in many regions and linked to the themes. For example, in the Auckland area a nationally significant theme was suggested, involving creation of a Polynesian cultural center linked to a major Maori and Pacific festival of music, arts, and crafts. Other suggested themes for various regions covered a wide scope, including agricultural and food, wine, thermal attractions, built heritage, arts and crafts, sports, entertainment, forests, flowers, energy, Scottish heritage, the gold rush, alpine activities, alternative living, spas, and winter sports.

Festivals and events figured prominently in many of these themes, demonstrating their perceived importance as theme enhancers and image makers for the regions. It is also clear that some of the themes would not have any major tangible element without associated special events. In this category would be the likes of a Scottish theme, brought to life with Highland Games and traditional sheepdog trials, food, drink, and costume. Elsewhere, such as the Tongariro region, a built facility (Timberdrome) would be in partnership with an event (Forestland Festival) to establish a theme.

The issue of the social and cultural effects of tourism was increasingly evident in the early 1980s, but little had been written on these matters in New Zealand. The NZTP commissioned an independent study, resulting in a report titled *The Socio-Cultural Impacts of Tourism* (Simmons and Devlin 1986). These researchers concluded: "A style, and indeed a level of tourism that does not have the support of the population is not sustainable" (72). Recommendations were made for creation of a social impact liaison group, to foster social impact assessment and undertake case studies, and regional tourism advisory groups, to obtain integrated local, regional, and national tourism planning.

A third major report came out in 1986, titled *Growing Pains: Current Issues Facing New Zealand Tourism* (produced by the New Zealand Tourism Council). It updated statistics contained in the 1984 report and expanded the dialogue on important issues facing New Zealand tourism. With regard to social and cultural issues, it relied on the earlier report by Simmons and Devlin.

The first problem identified was that of a shortfall in tourist accommodation. A second part of the report dealt with environmental issues, in response to some intense criticism of tourism. The third topic covered was that of tourism and its impact on people in communities. Staffing and training were addressed as the fourth major issue.

The document deals with criticism leveled at tourism by emphasizing the industry's sensitivity to the relationships between tourism and the social and physical environment. A quotation underscores this awareness (New Zealand Tourism Council 1986, 26):

> *Tourism can be considered as a resource based industry which depends on the goodwill and performance of the host community. It has to be a partnership of mutual benefit. Its performance cannot be judged solely on financial and economic criteria. Wider public interest objectives have to be accommodated and social and environmental factors must be placed alongside economic considerations.*

The council's approach to reconciling these sometimes conflicting interests was to restate its desire for creation of a regional system of tourist organizations linked to existing statutory planning units. It was felt that this would ensure "a sound basis for future community based tourism development" (26). Beyond this, event tourism was not considered. Specific attention was given to the effects on the Maori community and on the rapidly growing resort of Queenstown.

The fourth report of significance was commissioned by the Tourist and Publicity Department and called *The Implications of Tourism Growth in New Zealand* (McDermott Miller Group Ltd. 1988). This project again addressed pressing issues facing the industry, and it was followed by a series of regional workshops to discuss findings. Of particular interest was the modeling of three scenarios for development of tourism in New Zealand.

A "base scenario" forecast the results of established trends, while a "concentration scenario" predicted the impact of focusing international arrivals on the main resorts and cities. In contrast, a "dispersal scenario" charted the consequences of achieving an altered mix of international markets, which would see more independent travelers going outside the established tourist concentration points. While no consensus quickly emerged on a favored planning strategy, the dispersal of tourism was a goal already being pursued, and event tourism was expected to assist.

In this historical context, establishment of an event tourism unit in the NZTP can be seen as a logical response to considerable discussion of the nature, impact, and desired development of tourism in New Zealand. The potential value of events was clearly recognized: as attractions capable of increasing foreign arrivals, extending the season, and geographically spreading demand. The creation of regional tourism themes and images was also linked explicitly to events. Intense concern for social, cultural, and environmental quality also ensured that festivals and events would be viewed as mechanisms to enhance related goals in a community context.

Formal creation of an event tourism unit in late 1987 was preceded by a ministerial-level task force charged with exploring the feasibility of hosting a Winter Olympics; it was also likely influenced by the experience of Perth, Western Australia, in attracting high-profile exposure because of the America's Cup defense. In addition, Auckland had been successful in its bid for the 1990 Commonwealth Games, so considerable attention was being given to mega-events. The new event tourism unit was seen as one of a number of initiatives to expand New Zealand's image beyond that of beautiful scenery, outdoor recreation, and friendly people.

Goals and Policies

General tourism goals were stated in *New Zealand Tourism: Issues and Policies* (New Zealand Tourist and Publicity Department and New Zealand Tourism Council 1984, 45): "The overall goal is to expand the tourism sector, and increase the benefits that tourism brings." Objectives were listed, which can be summarized as follows:

- Increasing the number of foreign arrivals
- Increasing the length of stay for each market
- Assessing the most profitable market segments and increasing arrivals from each

- Developing greater community awareness of and participation in the benefits of tourism
- Encouraging high-quality products and investments
- Encouraging New Zealanders to spend their holidays in the country

The NZTP's direction for the future can be found in its 1989–90 Corporate Plan. The department's overall goal was defined as "The maximisation of wealth and employment benefits of tourism to the nation." To accomplish this goal, the NZTP is to provide the leadership, stimulation, information, and coordination necessary for marketing the nation. Three-year objectives were determined:

- Promoting strategic tourism planning among all parties
- Strengthening and coordinating cooperative marketing overseas
- Stimulating improvement in the quality of tourism services
- Developing an accord with land management and regulatory bodies to enhance tourism development
- Creating an internationally competitive environment for investment in tourism
- Promoting programs to increase tourism facility usage

The Event Tourism Program

A single staff position was created to coordinate event tourism within the NZTP's Tourism Marketing Division. Initial tasks consisted of creating an event data base, making contact with local and international events, determining venues with potential for hosting large events, and exploring possible research efforts and development priorities. An awareness program was launched in mid-1988, during which the coordinator traveled throughout the country to explain the concept of event tourism and the role of the event tourism unit, as well as to investigate possible initiatives at the regional and community level.

As part of a "launch kit" circulated by the new event tourism unit, the NZTP prepared a brochure titled *Making You New Zealand's Star Attraction*. It noted that funds would be available to research viable opportunities and attract suitable events. Support for planning, preparing for, and bidding on special events was offered, but it was emphasized that "Its objective is to be a catalyst in making events happen in New Zealand—it does not have the resources to organise or manage hallmark events." Eligibility for assistance was restricted to events with over 1,000 participants or the ability to generate $3 million revenue, offer a high profile for New Zealand, or have strong growth potential. Suitable facilities and a strong, New Zealand–based organizing group were also required. An application form for assistance was prepared, and a newsletter has been created to build a network for event tourism interests.

During 1988–89 the unit supported a variety of events and proposals, including a successful bid for the World Trampoline Championships for Auckland in 1992 and the holding of an International Jazz and Blues Festival in Wellington (in conjunction with the Nissan Mobil 500 saloon car street races). Assistance was also provided to Speight's Coast to Coast, an annual triathlon race on the South Island, and to the Otago Goldfields Heritage Celebrations, held in thirteen communities over a ten-day period (see Chapter 9 for details on these two events). A feasibility study for hosting an International Garden Festival in Christchurch (1993–94) was commenced, and this proposal was considered as a possible focus for a national theme year.

The 1989–90 event tourism strategy consisted of continued support for bids to get international events and facilitate their transition to New Zealand, while also targeting top New Zealand events to promote overseas in order to build a profile for New Zealand as an action destination. In addition, some "off-the-wall" events serve to highlight the humorous side of New Zealand life—such as a celebration of the gum boot! Examples of specific activities in the overall strategy included support for the Grand Traverse (a survival event in the Southern Alps), a feasibility study for hosting the 1997 World Masters Games in the Wellington region, and a report on expanding the New Zealand Racing Chariots Carnival. The unit also supported brochures and media exposure for the Mountains to the Sea triathlon, held on the North Island.

New Zealand's Sesquicentennial, 1990

A substantial increase in event tourism activity came in 1990, naturally, with the celebration of the 150th anniversary of the Treaty of Waitangi, which established New Zealand. The government formed a 1990 Commission and granted it over $20 million (N.Z.) to support a wide variety of local, regional, and national events.

The most noteworthy, held in Auckland, was the fourteenth Commonwealth Games, a sporting event that attracts almost eighty national track and field teams. Surrounding the games in January and February was the complementary Commonwealth Festival, featuring the cultures of participating countries, and a major Festival of Maori and Pacific Art and Culture. Auckland also put on its own celebrations to mark 150 years as a city.

A special brochure titled New Zealand, What's on in 1990 (New Zealand Tourist and Publicity Department n.d.) stressed that 1990 was "New Zealand's Year" and highlighted all the events being held throughout the country. Not only was a calendar of events included, but also separate, short articles on sporting events, arts and history (for example, Wellington's International Festival of the Arts), and food and wine (for example, the Marlborough Wine and Food Festival). Readers were asked "Why stay longer in New Zealand?" and were then reminded of the country's diversity, natural beauty, and various events.

Two New Zealand Cities
Wellington

The capital of New Zealand, Wellington, has the political, business, and symbolic attractions shared by all capitals, but it has lacked a positive image as a destination for pleasure travel. Being labeled Windy Wellington is not a plus factor! Although the city has cultural, shopping, and sporting amenities, there was no clear must-see attraction for tourists. Historically, international tour packages avoided the capital, and by 1989 research showed that its market share was actually declining.

Wellington had long been known as the Harbor Capital, a slogan appropriate for the city's unique physical setting; but a different image was required. Special events were revealed to be a competitive strength, as the city already hosted major events such as a biennial International Festival of the Arts and the annual Nissan Mobil 500 race with an accompanying carnival. Linked to events were the historical flavor and attractions of the capital city, and these formed the basis of a new image-building campaign.

Wellington Performing for You was adopted as the slogan in 1989, with three subthemes to be stressed in international promotions: "Wellington is renowned for scenic drives"; "Wellington, where everyone gets into the act"; and "Wellington: a great jumping-off point." Associated imagery was planned to encompass the following: festivals and special events, the harbor, heritage, hills and scenery, arts and culture, and sophistication of the capital city. Action events figure prominently, reflecting the word *performing* in the slogan and suggesting a dynamic place to visit, with much to experience. The whole campaign attempts to shift a static image to one focused on activity and experience.

Image-making of this kind actually has four target audiences: Residents must be both supportive and sensitive to the implications of the images. The travel trade is a key instrument for promotions and delivery of customers, so intermediaries must be convinced to adopt the slogans and images. Media people must be convinced to use it and promote it. And potential tourists have to be exposed to the slogans and images. Wellington's Public Relations Office uses the slogans and images to position the city better as a destination, and the New Zealand Tourist and Publicity Department carries the messages internationally.

Christchurch

Christchurch, the largest city on New Zealand's South Island, possesses a strong English flavor. It has been known as a cultured city, with popular images of gardens, parks, schoolchildren in uniforms, its cathedral, and numerous historic buildings. The slogan Garden City has often been used to describe Christchurch, and it accurately reflects the town character as well as that of the surrounding agricultural region.

Despite its serving as host of the successful Commonwealth Games of 1974, in terms of international tourism the city has acted primarily as a gateway to the major scenic and recreational attractions of the Southern Alps and Fiordland. Accordingly, the city council in 1988 appointed a promotions director to help shape a better national and international awareness of Christchurch as a destination. Included in the mandate of this new job was the creation of a hallmark event for Christchurch.

A key element in the process was the formation of a working party to link the council with business interests. Its purpose is to promote the city for tourism, trade, and investment, thereby improving the residents' standard of living. Reshaping the city image was vital, and a model was sought. It investigated the highly publicized "Memphis Miracle," which was based on the Memphis (Tennessee) Jobs Conference, and found similarities that could form the basis of progress in Christchurch. So it held its own version, called Going for Goals, which attracted 800 people. Citizens were asked what images would be appropriate for their city and how they would like to see Christchurch promoted. A variety of themes were proposed, but a more important outcome of this type of consultation is likely to be the fostering of a belief that community goals can be identified and realized.

The city developed a marketing plan, even though the Going for Goals process was to continue, and it stressed a new image-development campaign, promotion of the city as the Antarctic World Gateway, and creation of new events. Speight's Coast to Coast triathlon was already linked to Christchurch (see Chapter 9 for details of this event), and the city also hosts annual events with an agricultural theme. Logically, the idea of hosting an International Garden Festival was explored, although discussion was deemed necessary on whether a more upbeat and modern hallmark event would be better. In addition, some creative thinking was required to generate viable and attractive events to reflect the Antarctic Gateway theme.

As the examples of these two New Zealand cities illustrate, event tourism is also about the process of economic and cultural development. An event can be both an attraction and a tool in reshaping a destination image. To the residents, the implications will be more than mere tourism, encompassing all aspects of their way of life and how they feel about their community.

Plans and Prospects for New Zealand's Event Tourism

Mary-Alice Arthur, event tourism coordinator for the NZTP, provided much of the background material used in this case study. She was asked to comment upon the future of event tourism in New Zealand, and the following paragraphs reflect her ideas.

An underlying task continues to be that of working with organizers to raise the profile and professionalism of events, thereby contributing, it is hoped, to a spreading of tourism benefits beyond the traditional tourist season and concentrations. Helping communities realize their own goals for events and tourism is part of this process.

The possibility of New Zealand's winning the America's Cup, leading to a challenge in 1992, inspired cooperation throughout the tourism industry. The example of Perth, Western Australia, served to emphasize the event tourism strategy. If the America's Cup defense comes to New Zealand, the event tourism unit will play a leading role in developing plans to capitalize on its publicity value, both before and after the races.

Areas for future work that were being explored in 1989 included a greater emphasis on developing and extending the national event tourism strategy by using events to build conference and convention trade, building professional management and organizational skills among local organizers, and working with local governments to use events as a development tool. Research will have to be developed to support the event tourism unit and monitor trends, especially so that effects can be measured and events evaluated comparatively on a national basis.

Over time, New Zealand will increasingly emphasize its distinct tourist attractiveness, positioning itself as an alternative to Australia, rather than a mere add-on. Festivals and special events undoubtedly will figure prominently in this long-term tourism marketing effort.

AUSTRALIA

Australia was the world's fastest growing tourist destination in the decade of the 1980s, and special events played an obvious and major role in shaping the country's image and attracting foreign visitors. The positive contribution of the movie *"Crocodile" Dundee* must be acknowledged, as well as a favorable exchange rate, the relative safety of Down Under vacations, and a maturing tourism product (Faulkner 1988). But there can be no doubt that it was the combination of the 1987 America's Cup defense in Perth/Fremantle (see Chapter 9 for a detailed case study) followed by the Australian bicentennial celebrations and 1988 World's Fair in Brisbane that generated global media coverage and augmented Australia's image as *the* place to visit.

The Commonwealth of Australia is a federation in which the states and territories (much like Canada and the United States) possess great potential to plan for tourism and develop event tourism strategies. The central government has been involved through the enormous bicentennial celebrations and through various marketing and assistance programs. Its role has been predominantly that of facilitator and coordinator.

National Tourism Planning Issues

A major report called Directions for Tourism—a Discussion Paper was released in 1988, and in it the minister, Graham Richardson, noted that tourism is "now the jewel in the crown of Australian industry with outstanding potential to continue to develop as one of our most dynamic growth industries" (Australian Department of the Arts, Sport, the Environment, Tourism and Territories 1988, iii). The discussion paper was intended to increase recognition of tourism's importance, to assess areas of national policy that involve tourism, and to prepare objectives for the industry. It was also intended to complement policies affecting other industrial and policy areas, the development strategies of states, and the marketing strategy of the Australian Tourist Commission.

Overall goals for tourism were made clear: to develop the industry for its economic benefits and enhanced quality of life for residents, but consistent with the protection of natural and cultural heritage. The bulk of the discussion concerned the significance of tourism and how the government could facilitate orderly tourism growth, but specific environmental and cultural objectives were presented as well.

The role of special events in Australian tourism was definitely acknowledged in this important report. In a section entitled "The Arts and Special Events," it observed: "Cultural and artistic facilities such as the Sydney Opera House and events such as the America's Cup, Expo '88 and the Grand Prix, attract significant numbers of national and international visitors" (Australian Department of the Arts, Sport, the Environment, Tourism and Territories 1988, 84). The importance of these facilities and of artistic events to Australian culture is also noted, placing tourism in another main policy area of government. And on sporting events, the report commented: "The Government has also provided financial support for the conduct of major international standard sporting events in Australia that have drawn thousands of national and international visitors and provided significant economic benefits" (Australian Department of the Arts, Sport, the Environment, Tourism and Territories 1988, 85).

Other key issues under discussion included the needs for increased "user pay" approaches to heritage conservation and for increased aboriginal participation in the tourism industry. Arts and cultural attractions were thought to require additional promotion to potential foreign visitors.

Policy issues, research priorities, and the question of whether a national tourism strategy for Australia was needed—and practical—were considered at a major 1988 conference in Canberra, themed Frontiers of Australian Tourism (Australian Bureau of Tourism Research 1988). Participants from academia, government, and industry discussed tourism trends, issues, and problems, including those of infrastructure shortfalls, planning, marketing, impact assessment, and government roles and policies.

A number of contributors focused on cultural matters, making several key points: the need to show Australia as being a sophisticated destination, the need to preserve a sense of place and an authentic Australian identity, and the potential for aboriginal participation through festivals and cultural centers. The comments on arts and culture are in sharp contrast with the *"Crocodile" Dundee* stereotype of Australia that appeared to exist in the minds of potential tourists. Once established, the dominant image is difficult to change. Festivals and arts or cultural events were recognized as having the potential to broaden the tourist's experience, and to attract specialist interests. Such observations should also be interpreted in the context of the research and debate that occurred in Australia throughout the decade concerning the costs and benefits of mega-events, sporting events in particular.

The Australian Bicentennial, 1988

Seldom has a nation engaged in such a grand-scale celebration as Australia did in 1988. As expressed in one unattributed brochure aimed at foreign tourists, "It's no secret that Aussies know how to throw a good party. And you're invited to the biggest one we've ever held!" And with the international promotion of Paul Hogan, alias "Crocodile" Dundee, not to mention global media coverage of the preceding America's Cup and the New Year's events in Sydney Harbor, the world accepted the invitation.

In terms of advancing tourism, which seemed to be at least an equal goal to that of fostering national pride, the bicentennial presented an unparalleled opportunity. It was somewhat fortuitous, perhaps, that the America's Cup provided an impressive appetizer, and international promotions had already captured global attention, but the effects would have been impressive in any case.

The theme of the bicentennial was variously described as Celebration of a Nation and Living Together. The State of New South Wales simultaneously celebrated its 200th anniversary, and it appeared to compete with the rest of the country—especially Brisbane, home of the World's Fair—for the most spectacular events, projects, and media attention, boasting that 30,000 events and projects were planned in that state alone. Years of advance preparation and funding went into the production of festivals and events at all levels, along with major development projects.

The major events, and a sample of the numerous others held in 1988, are listed below:

- World Expo '88 was held in Brisbane, Queensland.
- The Australian Bicentennial Exhibition traveled to thirty-four venues around the country and included local involvement at each site.
- New South Wales launched its own First State '88 Exhibition in a new facility at Darling Harbor, Sydney.
- The First Fleet Re-enactment Voyage brought a fleet of sailing vessels from

England to Sydney, via other Australian cities, and coincided with the arrival of a Tall Ships flotilla for the amazing Australia Day celebration in Sydney Harbor. Australia Day celebrations across the country were broadcast globally and live.

- Major events toured the country, including air, relay, bicycle, yacht, and balloon races; dance and music shows; sports competitions.
- A large number of international conferences were brought to Australia in 1988, no doubt with the World's Fair and other events as part of the appeal.

Expo '88

The World's Fair was intended to be the focal point of the bicentennial celebrations, and it proved to be a great success, attracting over 18.5 million visits—double the original official estimate (World Expo '88 n.d.). Surveys of visitors determined that 8.1 percent (1.5 million visits) were international tourists, whereas the fair had been predicted to attract 13 percent from abroad (Minnikin 1987).

The prime minister in 1978, when the World's Fair was first proposed, sought a host city that would guarantee the event would be self-sufficient, developed by the host state, and located near a major city center. Brisbane met all these ambitious criteria. The city was interested in redeveloping its river frontage, and an early feasibility study suggested that all costs of the World's Fair could be recovered through final sale of the improved site plus rentals during the fair, sponsorships, and ticket sales (Minnikin 1987).

Few nations in recent years have been willing to take on the enormous costs and responsibilities of a full universal exposition as it is defined by the International Bureau of Exhibitions. Brisbane opted for a special-category fair, with the theme of Leisure in the Age of Technology; the State of Queensland was required to acquire and develop the site and to build the pavilions for rentals to participating countries and corporations.

Highlights from the official summary of the event conveyed the organizers' sense of accomplishment, stressing the feeling of ownership and the involvement that Australians had in the mega-event. National pride was heightened, and relationships with international participants were developed (World Expo '88 n.d.).

What is so remarkable about the bicentennial is that an entire year in the life of a nation became, in effect, a special event. Organizers spent years in planning and promoting the individual events that were held in almost every community, and the collective celebrations as well. The long-term impact on the image of Australia is bound to be considerable, but so too is the likelihood that many of the events will become permanent—a phenomenon observed following national and state or provincial celebrations in North America. In this sense, a major governmental funding and promotional initiative can generate enormous momentum for the arts, sports, community organization, civic pride, and festivals and events that endure.

Sporting Events

Aside from the bicentennial extravaganza, Australian tourism and other agencies have been somewhat preoccupied with sporting events. This reflects both the national culture and the belief that major sporting events are best suited to fostering tourism. The multipurpose ministry responsible for tourism is also responsible for sport, so the connection at the national level is close. Pierre Rey, who had the responsibility of developing criteria for determining ministry support of events, noted: "There is a growing awareness in Australia of the potential benefits and to some extent the costs derived from the organization of major events. There is also a better understanding of the role that these events can play in achieving certain socio-economic goals" (Rey 1986, 36).

Three major sporting events have been analyzed in depth, yielding valuable insights on the links between events and tourism. The first Australian Grand Prix (formula one auto racing), held in Adelaide in 1986, was subjected to intense scrutiny, as was the 1987 America's Cup defense (yacht racing) in Perth/Fremantle; details of these events are presented in Chapters 9 and 10. The third analysis involved the 1985 World Cup of Athletics in Canberra (Australia Department of Sport, Recreation and Tourism 1985). From this accumulating experience it was expected that the national government eventually would establish criteria for determining its involvement with proposals for sporting events.

One of the states preceded the national government. Since the 1970s, the State of South Australia had promoted itself as the Festival State. This theme was based largely on cultural events, particularly the famous Adelaide Festival of Arts. Wallis-Smith (1987), whose responsibilities in the Department of Recreation and Sport included festival and event development, observed that a 1985 investigation into the feasibility of hosting the 1994 Commonwealth Games led to a recommendation for the state to broaden its theme to include sports. This was formally added to the tasks of the Special Developments Division in the ministry, with the emphasis primarily on the economic dimension.

Hallmark events, which can generate substantial demand for services, were favored, as it was recognized that not all sporting events would generate benefits worth the investment. This had been documented by the department's research into a number of Australian events. It was also influenced by the first Australian Grand Prix. Accordingly, the department carefully examined its goals and capabilities and developed appropriate evaluation criteria for those events proposed by sporting bodies that wanted government support for their bids. The policy specifically excluded events such as the Commonwealth Games, which were thought to require major government involvement to meet broad social and economic goals.

The draft criteria can be summarized as follows:

1. The event should be of an international standard, involving international competitors and an internationally recognized sporting body.
2. Written support of state and national sporting bodies is required.
3. The sponsoring sporting bodies must demonstrate that the event fits their plans and objectives, and that they have the capability to operate it professionally.
4. Costs, social impact, risks, and likely benefits will be evaluated, in part based on previous experience.
5. Events may comprise one or more activities and also may be part of an overall festival.
6. Full financial feasibility studies are required if preliminary criteria are met. State grants are available to help prepare professional assessments.
7. Organizers must meet necessary conditions at least twelve months prior to the planned event.
8. Organizers must cooperate in postevent evaluations.

To these criteria and procedures, Wallis-Smith (1987) discussed the necessity of ensuring that events are suitable for the host city. This evaluation would cover the scale of proposed events related to the services and resources of the host city, as well as the organizational capabilities of the population. Noneconomic objectives also should be important, including the potential value of sporting events in fostering social contacts, the value of sporting participation and fitness, and increased community spirit. For those events without the economic potential to justify state support, the need for other forms of assistance were acknowledged. To this purpose, thought was given to the establishment of a special events foundation to offer advice and resource material.

State Tourism Planning

In the absence of a national tourism plan, the Australian states have developed their own policies or strategies, and several of the larger ones have undertaken regional tourism plans. None had yet produced a comprehensive approach to event tourism by 1989, but a review of plans revealed an increasing awareness of the roles of events in state and regional destination planning. The plans also establish a framework within which event tourism planning can be developed.

The most populous state, New South Wales, formulated a tourism development strategy in 1986. It was undertaken by an industry-based task force at the request of the State Development Council, so its emphasis was naturally on finding ways to facilitate growth. One of the advantages this plan listed for the state was its "variety of special events and sporting functions on a year round basis that appeal to the visitor" (New South Wales 1986, 16). A major development discussed in the plan was Sydney's Darling Harbor Convention and Exhibition Centre, which was given a fast-track planning process to ensure completion for the 1988 bicentennial celebrations. In a sense, this project was a rival to Brisbane's World Expo '88, as it hosted a major international exhibition and conferences. Looking beyond 1988 to a potential postbicentennial slump, the plan recommended strong marketing to secure events for the center. Clearly Sydney does not want its position as dominant tourist destination threatened by the global publicity created for Brisbane, nor by the absence of infrastructure for hosting major events.

The State of Victoria formulated a strategy in 1984 (Victorian Tourism Strategy 1984) as part of a series of policies on economic development. This was followed by tourism plans for seven regions identified as possessing high potential as resort areas. Criteria for designating the Victoria resort zones included resources, attractions, infrastructure, services, transport, accessibility to population centers, and an image, theme, or cultural identity. Events were considered, but in the early 1980s they evidently were not developed well enough to be a major criterion on their own. The state tourism plan did make special reference to the initiatives being taken to enhance Melbourne's status as the conference capital of the country, to develop facilities for hosting international-class sporting events, and to attract and develop special events such as a touring Spoleto Festival in 1985 and festivals for the city's Chinatown. More important was the plan's recommendation, subsequently implemented, that a festivals unit be established in the tourism commission "to provide professional advice to the organization of a selected group of festivals which can provide tourist attraction" (Victorian Tourism Strategy 1984, 28).

General aims of the state's tourism planning included the usual references to employment and income generation, but also called for "increasing the sense of attachment and belonging to the State's people, nature and cultural heritage" and "protecting and conserving the unique and irreplaceable features of the Victorian environment" (Victorian Tourism Strategy 1984, 10). Domestic tourism was obviously thought to represent a major potential for the regions, all of which are easily accessible to the metropolitan populations of Melbourne, Canberra, and Sydney.

By way of example, two of the regional tourism plans can be cited. The Goldfields Development Program (Victorian Tourism Commission 1986) contains a three-year action plan intended to capitalize on this area's colorful prospecting and mining heritage. Key goals were to make the region a destination for longer vacations by creating a new image in which preservation of the historic fabric was paramount. A special element in the background research was the compilation of a "thematic inventory," in which each of six main themes—gold discovery, phases of mining, extraction technology, life-styles, unique history, and environmental effects—and over fifty subthemes pertaining to Goldfields were matched against illustrative sites and attractions. Although festivals and events were not in existence, the potential connection to more than one of the themes is obvious, such as the depiction of unique history and life-styles through a costumed historical re-creation event in a historic gold town.

The second regional tourism plan of note is the Wine and High Mountain Country Tourism Development Program (Victorian Tourism Commission 1987). Domestic market research was the basis for creation of the Wine and High Mountain Country name and themes, with the intention being to "portray the perceptual image of the area as identified by domestic holiday-makers." (Victorian Tourism Commission 1987, 13). The research showed strong interest in authentic, in-depth experiences through stay-put holidays.

Festivals and events figured more prominently in this region's strategy, perhaps because several already existed, including the Rose Festival, Wine and Wildflower Weekend, Wine and Trout Festival, and Winery Walkabout. In addition, the then-new Festivals Unit in the Victorian Tourism Commission had proposed a Rutherglen Regional Wine Show to be held sometime in the spring season. Major sporting events were also documented, with the recommendation that more of these be promoted for the off-peak seasons.

Western Australia and the Town of York

York is a historic country town of approximately 1,100 people, situated sixty miles east of metropolitan Perth (population one million). Settled first in 1831, York became a bustling service center for the agricultural activity in the Avon River valley. Today, whereas many similar country towns have faded, York has capitalized on its built heritage and residents' skills to become a thriving tourist attraction. Festivals and special events are a major part of the attractiveness, as animators of the town's architectural and historic features. The ambience ranges from interesting but hot and quiet in the summer to festive and exciting in the cool season of events.

Residents were long aware of the popularity of York for day-trips, but they wanted to foster overnight and weekend stays. Festivals and events were the logical solution, and the populace pursued this goal with the kind of determination and success that only a fully committed community can muster.

The state's Tourism Development Plan, Midlands Region (Western Australia Tourism Commission 1985), also sets objectives, based on the recognition that the Avon Valley constitutes the cornerstone of so-called nodal development (i.e., a few concentrations of tourist attractions) in the Midlands. York was described as one of the finest historic towns in Australia, and its events were highlighted, leading to recommendations for the staging of other events in specific communities and an annual event to bring the entire region together.

York's event season begins in April (the Southern Hemisphere's autumn) with Heritage Week and winds down in November with the York Flying 50. The period in between is packed with both major and minor events guaranteed to provide choice of theme, activity, and time. A description of the main York events reads like the list for an entire tourism destination region:

Heritage Week: a celebration of the pioneers and the fine community they created, featuring parades and visits to the town's many historic buildings and museums and promoted through newspapers and radio advertising, as well as joint shopping center promotions with other Avon Valley towns

Winter Theatre Festival: presented by the University of Western Australia Drama Department, using York facilities for a two- or three-day series of productions

Western Australia Jazz Festival: the second-largest jazz festival in Australia, staged by the state's Jazz Club in conjunction with the town; a three-day event that attracts up to 15,000 visitors and is promoted via television, radio, and newspapers

The York Flying 50: a race against the clock by vintage (pre-1959) cars around the historic streets of York, attracting up to 10,000 people

The York Fair: including horse races, a camel race through the streets, and street dancing

Winter Music Festival: a weekend of recitals in a variety of historic buildings

The York Hunt: reenactment of a traditional fox hunt as organized by the Hunting Club since 1883

York Art and Craft Award

Perth-to-York Vintage Car Rally

The entire community is involved, and undoubtedly required, for the management and staging of these and other minor events. Some ninety-six clubs and associations and their numerous committees take part.

Certainly the events, as much as or more than the historic attractions, have placed this town on the tourist map of Australia. One obvious result has been the community's pride in restoration and preservation of its buildings, many of which are used for the special events. Another positive impact is the restoration of local hotels at a cost of millions of dollars, signifying success in attracting the overnight visitor.

A prospectus for Heritage Inns Australia Ltd. (1988) describes the project to acquire and restore two York hotels and interconnecting retail and catering establishments as part of a plan to develop a chain of historic hotels throughout the state and Australia. The Avon Valley was described in the prospectus as possessing considerable tourism potential, with special reference to events: "The attractiveness of the valley lies not in a once only visit, but in the potential of repeated business encouraged by the numerous sporting activities and festivals conducted in the valley" (Heritage Inns Australia Ltd. 1988, 18). The directors also foresaw an active role in fostering events: "The Avon Valley . . . is ideally placed to be promoted as the location for major hallmark events. For this reason the company will strongly promote an extension of festivals and the creation of new events attracting people from all walks of life to the valley" (Heritage Inns Australia Ltd. 1988, 19). Featured prominently in the colorful prospectus are photos of York's events, several of which are taken directly from the town's own lure brochure.

York is an excellent case study of festivals and events animating historic attractions, enhancing the community's tourism image, and being a catalyst for infrastructure development. And, it appears, successful events attract interest in creating even more events. Eventually, the people of York might have to set some limits—a problem many other towns would like to have.

THE UNITED STATES

Federal involvement in tourism development and policy in the United States has been controversial and less well developed than in other countries with full national tourism organizations (see Mill and Morrison 1985; Ronkainen and Farano 1987; and Gunn 1988 for a review of tourism organization and the federal and state roles).

The United States Travel Service was established in 1961 and housed within the Department of Commerce. The travel account deficit, stemming from more Americans spending abroad than tourists were spending in the United States, was a primary reason for this initiative. The United States Travel and Tourism Administration (USTTA) was set up in 1981 to replace the Travel Service and elevate its status, but funding since then has been kept very low, and more than once the USTTA's very survival has been threatened.

The USTTA's main function is promoting foreign travel to the country, which is accomplished through advertising, working with the industry, and researching and disseminating information. Its goals are generally to facilitate and encourage the development of travel and the tourism industry, and although the USTTA has a policy coordination function, it does not attempt to set tourism policies or make strategic plans. That activity occurs mostly at the state level.

Many other federal agencies have financial programs that are potentially available to the industry or policies that affect tourism. Those pertaining to the development of recreation or park resources and heritage conservation are of potential relevance to event tourism, as are the programs affecting cultural attractions. The National Endowment for the Arts helps fund state and local government programs and nonprofit organizations in the arts, although community festivals are likely to be more successful in getting assistance from state and local arts foundations. Annually, Arts for America, the National Assembly of Local Arts Agencies, holds an arts festival management conference. The National Endowment for the Humanities provides grants to museums or historical organizations for interpretive programs. A variety of business development financial programs are available, but these are not directed at events. Other programs pertaining to community development might be of indirect assistance.

As noted in Cameron (1989), festivals, events, and heritage conservation are closely linked. The National Historic Preservation Act of 1966 has been instrumental in sparking cultural tourism initiatives at the local level. Urban renewal assistance from the federal government has also enabled many communities to take tourism initiatives, such as the development of a tourism core in Niagara Falls, New York, including a festival plaza and commercial facilities that host annual events. Another source is the National Center for Urban Ethnic Affairs, which helps in planning ethnic festivals, and a private body called the Business Committee for the Arts, which underwrites arts events and provides management advice.

Except for an occasional special celebration, such as the bicentennial in 1976 and the 1986 celebration of the Constitution, event tourism has not been promoted or developed nationally. Even the 1984 Los Angeles Olympics had minimal federal support, resulting in a private-enterprise approach that generated a large surplus (Ueberroth 1985). At all levels, event tourism is just emerging as a recognized segment of tourism that requires separate study and development.

On the industry side, the Travel Industry Association, formerly called the Discover America Travel Organization, is an umbrella organization of travel-related groups. It seeks to promote inbound travel and represent the industry's interests (Economist Intelligence Unit 1989). One pertinent initiative of this association is the Discover America National Domestic Marketing Program, which since 1987 has published a calendar called *Discover America*. Outstanding events are listed in the calendar, which is aimed at the travel industry. Other industry groups, notably the bus associations, also have lists of top attractions in North America, and many festivals and events have benefited from recognition in this way.

Universities around the United States have been very active partners with government and industry in conducting research, development assistance, and training for tourism. A major publication called *Tourism USA, Guidelines for Tourism Development* was written by the University of Missouri's Department of Recreation and Park Administration (1986) for the USTTA and other federal agencies. This document covers the basics of tourism planning for communities, including advice on getting assistance and information on various government agencies and programs. Festivals and events are mentioned, but not afforded any specific treatment.

Other event-related material has been produced at U.S. universities, including *Festivals and Events, Information and Resource Book*, from the University of Minnesota Extension Service Tourism Center (1989); *South Carolina Tourism Development Handbook: A Primer for Local Communities* (Howell and Bemisderfer 1982) and *Small Town Tourism Development* (Howell 1987), both from

Clemson University, College of Forest and Recreation Resources; and *Planning Community-wide Special Events*, from the University of Illinois at Urbana-Champaign, Cooperative Extension Service (n.d.).

Event Tourism and the States

Every state has a tourism department or similar agency for promoting tourism, but Gunn (1988) reported that most states are not involved in supply-side tourism development, owing to a strong orientation toward private-sector initiatives. While many states do provide assistance to event tourism through the publication of advisory documents, event calendars, and coverage of events in state tourism guides, relevant policy or research has been minimal in the event tourism field. A few states have event coordinators on staff, and a number of state or regional festival associations have been established with some government support. Nevertheless, there is considerable room for expansion.

Chapter 6 documents the activities of a number of states in event-related promotions. Beyond promotions, it is clear that no consistent pattern of policies or event tourism planning exists, and that most of the activity can be considered limited in scope. Each state places a different degree of emphasis on event tourism, and only a few can be considered to have a strategic approach to developing event tourism. Examples from several active states follow.

Oklahoma created an events coordinator position in its Tourism and Recreation Department. The coordinator is responsible for producing an event calendar and news releases, taking a leading role in marketing events of statewide significance, and promoting events across the state with the intent of increasing their drawing power. Another key task is giving technical advice to event organizers and providing them with a link to the Marketing Division.

The Texas Visitor Industry and the State Tourism Division Programs and Services (Texas Department of Commerce n.d.) is a publication describing that state's assistance to tourism. Its Community Development Program focuses on local initiatives, including festivals and special events. The community development manager consults with communities and organizations, and community development workshops provide training; a one-day training workshop specifically for proposed or existing festivals and events is part of the services provided.

New York has two innovative programs related to event tourism. As part of this state's highly successful I Love New York promotional theme, a series of I Love New York festivals has been created. One is held during each season, and areas must apply well in advance for designation as an official festival. The New York State Department of Commerce then makes money available for promoting each event, enabling communities or destination areas to package existing events and attractions and create new festivals. Public relations and technical assistance are also provided.

The purposes of this program link the festivals explicitly to increasing tourism, creating jobs, fostering local pride, and educating the public on destination attractions. To be eligible, a formal organization must be established, a marketing plan developed, and a final evaluation of the festival conducted. "The festival must utilize a central theme and consist of events and activities that can be developed and widely promoted" (New York State Department of Economic Development n.d.). An example is the I Love New York Summer Festival of 1989, held in Otsego County, in what the state calls the Central Leatherstocking Region (after a nickname of James Fenimore Cooper's nineteenth-century fictional hero). It began with the celebration of the fiftieth anniversary of the Baseball Hall of Fame at Cooperstown in June, and ended with the James Fenimore Cooper Bicentennial Commemorative Weekend in September. A whole program of summer events, including shows, concerts, a music festival, and tournaments, was packaged to form this special summer for Otsego.

A second New York State program of interest is the Urban Cultural Parks System, which was established to preserve, restore, and interpret urban heritage resources, leading to both cultural and economic development (New York State Office of Parks and Recreation 1981). By 1989 there were fourteen designated urban cultural parks, each with its own physical character and programming. State funding is available for visitor centers or other investments.

Special events and festivals were an integral part of the original concept, as the parks were intended to be "the stage to draw life back into their communities" (New York State Office of Parks and Recreation 1981, 7). Many of the parks are along waterfronts, with great recreational and scenic potential. For example, each year the Whitehall Urban Cultural Park hosts Sackets Harbor Day and stages a reenactment of the War of 1812 battle. There has also been cooperation between urban cultural parks and the I Love New York festivals.

A final example is the Vermont bicentennial, which typifies many state and even interstate anniversary celebrations. Vermont established a commission to organize the celebrations in 1991, and the fostering of festivals and special events was an important part of its work (Vermont Bicentennial 1989). Working with historical organizations, the commission offered workshops to assist local historical societies and town bicentennial committees to produce events, programs, or exhibits. Corporate support for events was sought, with the commission providing a menu of endorsed projects to select from. Matching grants of up to $1,500 (in 1989) were offered to assist programs or events, thus doubling what organizers could raise. With commission help, almost one hundred towns were involved by 1989. One of the most popular forms of celebration appeared to be the local homecoming, with over ninety communities having established a homecoming committee.

These are merely a few examples of many that could be cited; but because the majority of event tourism initiatives in the United States have been at the state and local levels, and often in an ad hoc manner—not part of a permanent program—documenting them is difficult.

GREAT BRITAIN

The British Tourist Authority (BTA) is the national-level agency primarily responsible for international promotion, but it shares this task with three quasi-national bodies that are more directly concerned with tourism development: the English, Welsh, and Scottish tourist boards; Northern Ireland has a separate tourist authority. Regional tourist boards have been created to organize the industry better and to involve municipalities, many of which have their own tourism officials. Other government agencies are also important for tourism planning, including the Countryside and Forestry Commissions, Nature Conservancy Council, Department of the Environment, and Heritage, Sports, and Arts Councils. Wales and the Highlands and Islands of Scotland also have special development boards that are active in tourism promotion and development.

Perhaps as a result of the difficulty in coordinating the goals of all these bodies, no overall set of tourism policies has been developed for Great Britain. The BTA produces its own strategic plans, which provide general direction, but not physical or spatial plans. Its goals, and those of the other tourism boards, have been to create employment, earn foreign revenue, and overcome regional disparity through tourism (Shaw, Greenwood, and Williams 1988). Much effort has gone into encouraging and financially assisting tourism in remote rural areas and declining industrial centers. Through the 1980s, a decade marked by tremendous economic, social, and political changes in Britain, tourism gained elevated status as a development tool because it was creating numerous jobs while other sectors declined. In 1987, 1.4 million jobs were attributed to tourism (Great Britain Year Book 1988), and the tourist boards were told to encourage tourism in areas of high unemployment and development potential. The BTA marketing plan for 1986–87 specifically targeted the encouragement of overseas tourists, and although London would continue to be the main gateway, a better spread of tourists throughout the country and the year was to be achieved, and major attractions were to be developed outside London.

Festivals and Special Events

Arts festivals and cultural events appear to be the strongest component of event tourism in Great Britain, and the growth of events is closely linked to the nation's rich heritage of cultural attractions. Thorburn (1986) examined the rise of European cultural tourism in general, noting the significance of special events. Historic towns, museums, galleries, castles, even cathedrals are settings for festivals and events that highlight a site's attractiveness and assist in the conservation process by raising money.

Hanna (1981, 57) believed this rise in arts festivals and special cultural events in historic settings was "One of the most significant cultural and tourist developments in Britain since the war." He noted that before World War II there had been fewer than a dozen arts festivals in the country, but in 1981 there were 200 or more with professional artistic content. The official Great Britain Year Book 1989 proudly mentioned there existed over 400 arts festivals. The British Arts Council and semiautonomous arts councils for Scotland and Wales give financial assistance to festivals and work with the Association of Arts Festivals.

In *A Book of British Music Festivals*, Adams (1986, 21) claimed that "Music festivals in particular are closer to the centre of our cultural life than is perhaps the case in any other country of the world." They grew considerably after the last world war as a reflection of the country's need to celebrate in a time of austerity. Music festivals multiplied again in the 1960s and 1970s, this time more in response to the perceived remoteness of the main urban cultural centers. It is no coincidence that festivals have been successful at resorts in Britain, Adams noted, observing that festivals and tourism have a long history of mutual benefit. As early as 1859 the great Handel Centenary Festival was promoted throughout Europe at train ticketing offices, to encourage tourism. There is also a distinct festival season in Britain, from May through October, which coincides with the better weather and traditional vacation patterns.

Adams characterized British music festivals as having considerable diversity in scale, in professional or amateur content, and in competitive and noncompetitive formats. Some are held to assemble the very best musicians or biggest group of performers, while others focus on local and amateur talent. Some celebrate a single composer, while others allow premieres by new talent. Most, he claimed, are unable to be financially self-sufficient, but Adams justified government subsidies because of the cultural and educational value of festivals.

Another major trend in British event tourism is its connection to urban tourism. This is related to cultural attractions, but the emphasis is more on declining industrial cities. In fact, a major study called the Urban Tourism Project (Law and Tuppen 1986) examined European and North American experiences and discussed potential markets and development issues. The two main tourism products of cities were judged to be those of conferences and exhibitions on the one hand and culture, including museums, art galleries, sports, and shopping, on the other. Festivals and events would be one component of the culture product, aimed at several leisure tourist markets: day-trippers, people visiting friends and relatives, short-break tourists, and those using the city as a gateway to a region for touring. Examples from France were documented (Tuppen 1985) for this project, including such cities as Lyons, which was attempting to create a special identity partly through the attraction of major national and international events. Tuppen (1985, 13) wrote: "Festivals and exhibitions represent a further category of events which may generate a large number of visitors, and their impact is not confined to conventional resort centres. Thus, Nancy, Besançon, Tours and Bordeaux represent some of the many towns and cities which attract a considerable number of visitors to festivals, and have sought to enhance their image and appeal as tourist centres by this means." One important aspect of event tourism in cities was composed of festival marketplaces that bring together shopping, entertainment, and food, modeled after the U.S. example of Quincy Market, built in 1976 in Boston. The similar Covent Garden development in London, created in 1980, also was cited as an example.

Garden festivals have attracted considerable attention in Britain, owing to their direct linkage to urban regeneration in older industrial cities. Kerslake (1987) traced their origins to Germany, where in the 1950s they were part of giant postwar reclamation schemes. The British events, introduced with the Liverpool Garden Festival of 1984 (and followed in two-year intervals by Stoke on Trent, Glasgow, Gateshead, and Ebbw Vale), have been developed along different lines, however, with the intent to use the garden festivals as a means to clear or develop sites for permanent commercial or industrial purposes. The festival itself, lasting six months, is really an excuse to get things moving. It consists of garden and horticultural displays, events, and entertainment, all in a specially constructed complex.

Glasgow's site was reclaimed from obsolete industrial land along the Clyde River and made good use of the water orientation. The festival areas were themed, including water and maritime, recreation and sport, landscape and scenery. The concept is highly suggestive of a mini–world's fair. Writing in the *Weekend Guardian*, Fanshawe (1989) linked the event to Glasgow's major campaign to change its image from a decaying industrial city to a growing cultural center. The Garden Festival was to be followed by an equally ambitious European City of Culture theme in 1990, intended to bring international performers and attention to the city and to foster a renaissance of indigenous cultural expression.

The tourism value of garden festivals has been questioned. Kerslake (1987) commented that their promotion was aimed at the day-trip market; in the case of Liverpool, only a small proportion of visitors came from beyond thirty-five miles away. Stoke, however, was more successful in generating tourist traffic. The Glasgow Garden Festival was promoted by the Scottish Tourist Board mainly on the premise that it would be an activity for tourists already coming to the country. A nonrandom survey of visitors to the information center at Glasgow's Garden Festival (Scottish Tourist Board 1989) did find, however, that a substantial proportion of tourists said the festival had been the main purpose of their trip to Scotland or had caused them to stay longer.

Roberts (1989) was particularly critical of the garden festivals, saying they were intended primarily to attract industry and commerce to deindustrialized areas and to be symbols of revitalization. The festivals also have an ideological message, which Roberts interpreted as an attempt to convince the old industrial areas they had to get into a new entrepreneurial way of thinking and acting. Furthermore, he said, the festivals attempt to create an illusion of a "united, green and pleasant land," whereas Roberts believes the reality is quite different. In this context, the garden festival can be seen as a political device, rather than a cultural celebration or tourist attraction.

Festivals, Commemorations, and Anniversaries

The British Tourist Authority commissioned and published a guide to maximizing the economic benefits of the numerous celebrations and festivals held in the country for primarily cultural and local reasons (Camacho 1979). Camacho noted that local, regional, and international audiences alike were important to events, and provided examples and advice on how to develop the attractiveness of events to tourists. Most of this booklet concentrates on organizational matters, but it also includes advice on obtaining financial help from local authorities, the arts councils, private and corporate sponsors, and tourist organizations. Arts council grants are not automatic, he noted, and the tourist organizations do not normally assist individual events, although they have done so for a number of important celebrations. Promotional aid from the tourist bodies can be important, however.

Camacho documented several examples of event tourism promotions, including the unique case of the British Tourist Authority's efforts to capitalize on the U.S. bicentennial in 1976. In that year, the BTA and other tourist boards promoted the notion that Americans should visit the homeland, and they encouraged and publicized celebrations in areas that had direct American connections. This was followed by the Queen's Silver Jubilee celebrations in 1977, which stimulated domestic tourism and included special promotions to North America.

Event Tourism in the Highlands and Islands of Scotland

The Highlands and Islands Development Board (HIDB), given a mandate to promote and assist social and economic development, has had a major impact on tourism development in the remoter parts of Scotland. In this region, suffering from a long history of emigration and a marginal economic base, tourism was seen very early as a potential tool in regional development. More recently, event tourism has been fostered as a complement to more long-standing efforts to encourage the growth of other attractions and tourism infrastructure.

HIDB's *Joint Events and Festivals Scheme* (HIDB 1989) provides start-up financial assistance to tourism-related festivals and events, with the specific objectives of attracting tourists and encouraging them to stay longer and spend more. Applications for aid are channeled through the established area tourist boards, which are asked to endorse the proposals. Up to three years of assistance can be obtained, but the HIDB wants events to become self-sufficient. Up to ten thousand pounds sterling could be provided to any one event, but amounts are not to exceed 50 percent of operating costs in the first year, declining to 15 percent in the third. The HIDB also assists event promotions, under the same criteria.

CANADA

Tourism Canada is the leading federal agency responsible for tourism promotion and development, but the federal nature of Canada makes each province a key partner; in addition, many municipalities, particularly the larger cities, have taken independent action to develop tourism and establish themselves as major festival and event destinations. Other federal departments have also been active in fostering event tourism. National-level tourism planning has proved to be difficult to achieve because of this division of responsibilities, but there have been major federal initiatives with importance for event tourism.

The closest thing to a national tourism strategy was released as a discussion paper in 1985. Entitled *Tourism Tomorrow* (Canada, Minister of State, Tourism 1985), this document summarized the issues, problems, and potential solutions for Canadian tourism. Considerable attention was directed at the tourism product in Canada, much of which was felt to be in the mature or declining stages of the life cycle. Regarding events, it was noted that mega-events such as Expo '67 in Montreal and the planned Expo '86 in Vancouver and Calgary Winter Olympics in 1988 had value that was much greater than their direct economic impact. Expo '67, it was concluded, attracted worldwide attention to Montreal and Canada, which promoted not only a favorable tourist destination image but also an image of a good country in which to invest or with which to trade. Smaller events were also seen as having significance to tourism. The report said that almost 500 historical, cultural, and ethnic events in smaller communities, mostly of short duration and held in the summer, "could be promoted to provide a wider appeal, particularly when combined with the celebration of significant anniversaries, for example bicentennials" (Canada Minister of State, Tourism 1985, 47). Major regional annual events were thought to have the potential to develop into at least national, if not international, attractions.

One of the major conclusions of *Tourism Tomorrow*, and of the round of consultations and reports accompanying it, was that more attention to product development and enhancement was needed, particularly in the area of cultural attractions. The report cited the permanent theatrical festivals at Niagara-on-the-Lake (Shaw Festival) and Stratford (Shakespearean Festival) for their success in drawing American audiences. It also concluded that the tourism potential for culture had not been fully realized and that a more coordinated marketing approach was needed.

Another major policy and planning initiative was the establishment of an ambitious, federal and provincial National Task Force on Tourism Data (Statistics Canada 1989), for the purpose of analyzing and improving the research and data base for tourism planning and marketing. It addressed many issues, none more daunting than defining the tourism industry from the supply side, and included a working group on festivals and events. That team examined definitions and classifications of events (see Chapter 2 of this book) and made a number of recommendations for advancing event tourism. These included the identification of events and festivals as separate categories in travel surveys and the adoption of standard measures of the impact of events. It was emphasized that "organizers and sponsors of festivals and special events have traditionally had great difficulty in establishing credible and comparable measures of the size and impact of their attractions" (Statistics Canada 1989, 23). Because of this, the role of festivals and special events in tourism planning at all levels had not been adequately recognized, and funding was difficult to obtain. One concrete product of this working group was a manual on measurement and visitor surveys (Getz 1986a), which has been largely incorporated into various sections of this book.

By 1989 no federal policy or program on event tourism had emerged in Canada. A *Discussion Paper on a National Tourism Policy* did state as a priority the development of "key cultural/heritage attractions and major events in our cities and major touring corridors" (Tourism Canada 1989, 34). Tourism Canada was also internally evaluating the significance of festivals and special events (Lariviere and Vachon 1989; Rusk 1989), suggesting that a policy or program on event tourism might be forthcoming.

Federal Financial Assistance to Festivals and Events

The main sources of funding have been the Ministry of Industry Science and Technology (which encompasses Tourism Canada), the Department of Communications, and Multiculturalism Canada. Lariviere and Vachon (1989) noted that these federal agencies had committed over $14 million (Canadian) during the preceding several years to develop and promote festivals and events. One initiative involved five pilot projects in 1986–87 to promote cultural and multicultural activities in Nova Scotia and four large Canadian cities. The Nova Scotia project used $250,000 in federal funds, matched by provincial, local, and industrial money, to promote the Northumberland Shore and Cape Breton as a multicultural destination (Nova Scotia Department of Tourism 1987). A significant portion of the funds went toward organizing and packaging international-class events. The Antigonish Highland Games was heavily promoted, as was the 1987 International Gathering of the Clans.

Provincial Initiatives

An overview of provincial and territorial activity suggests that all of these governments have become involved in event tourism, to some extent, but that no comprehensive policies on event tourism had been developed. The Tourism Canada assessment (Lariviere and Vachon 1989) reported that all the provinces and territories made financial assistance available to festivals and events, with several placing a great deal of emphasis in this area. Quebec provided $7.3

million during 1986–87 to the festivals and events sector, and Alberta launched a $20 million program to market and promote attractions and events.

Quebec has certainly been one of the most active, presumably because of its linguistic (French) and cultural uniqueness. Funding is available to events from four ministries: to popular festivals from the Ministry of Leisure; to major events from the Ministry of Cultural Affairs; to marketing and promotion of events from the Ministry of Tourism; and to major cultural and artistic events from the Ministry of International Relations. In other provinces there is a similar pattern for agencies involved in either the tourism or cultural side, and often there is little coordination between them about goals or assistance programs.

As an example of more modest involvement in event tourism, the Province of Newfoundland and Labrador employs an events and attractions coordinator in its Department of Development and Tourism, to advise and assist events or groups wanting to set up events. Specific help is given to events for promotions and packaging. The province sees cultural events as an integral part of their tourism product mix, but it desires greater federal financial assistance to help create and develop five major events across the province. Sports events are eligible for financial help from the Provincial Department of Culture, Recreation and Youth, whereas cultural festivals have to seek federal support.

Municipal Roles

Several Canadian cities have sought for themselves a preeminence in the festivals and events field or have deliberately used events to heighten their national and international image. Toronto and Montreal compete in many ways, including by means of staging international film festivals. The National Capital Region, with federal and municipal assistance, has developed an impressive number of festivals and special events to provide tourist activities and attractions and to give the capital a national flavor and suitable image. Numerous municipalities and small communities view festivals and events as a way to foster community development and attract tourists. Kujat (1989) described the experience of Kamloops, British Columbia, which declared itself Tournament Capital of B.C. and developed incentives to attract all kinds of competitions. Palmer (1989) related the efforts of Saint John, New Brunswick, in attracting major sports events, partly to better utilize the facilities left after the Canada Games.

Getz and Frisby began a research program, assisted by the Province of Ontario, to assess the roles of municipalities in developing and fostering festivals and special events, as well as related policy issues. Surveys of municipal officials involved with events and of festival organizers, supplemented by detailed case studies, revealed a high level of event-related activity in large cities and many towns and smaller communities, but low levels of involvement in the smallest municipalities.

Certainly this pattern stems from the resources, particularly staff, that are available in cities. Parks and recreation or culture departments are the most active, with common goals to foster sports, recreation, and arts for the whole community. Increasingly, however, economic development departments, chambers of commerce, and visitor and convention bureaus are assisting and creating events to promote the municipality and attract tourists. Recreation and culture departments are also incorporating tourism goals in their policies.

Much work remains to explore the significance of municipalities in developing event tourism, but there is no doubt now that they have a very major role in many countries.

SUMMARY

One of the factors shaping events and event tourism trends is government policy. In Chapter 3 this factor was introduced, along with the variety of reasons motivating government action: fostering culture and the arts; creating leisure outlets; promoting community development and intercultural understanding; generating wealth through tourism; using events as renewal and development catalysts; and getting reelected or asserting dominant values. Chapter 4 documented the recent activities of governments in selected English-speaking countries, beginning with the pioneering New Zealand experience in event tourism. Some general conclusions can be drawn from these case studies:

Event tourism as a policy field is just emerging, with most countries and destination areas involved in modest ways, by offering limited assistance in collective advertising, some degree of advice through manuals, or financial assistance.

Image-making and mega-events dominate government thinking in most jurisdictions, when it comes to the tourism implications of events. More attention to the multiplicity of perspectives on, and roles of, festivals and special events is needed.

The potential of events to spread demand seasonally and geographically is easily understood by government policymakers, and this has been used to justify assistance. However, the potential contribution of small events, arising from community initiatives, has not been well recognized.

Event initiatives have typically accompanied national or regional anniversaries and other political celebrations, stimulating many new events and new demand for quality event attractions.

Cities are at the forefront of event and event tourism development. Numerous cities are seeking to be premier festival or event attractions. Image enhancement and renewal and development schemes are common factors influencing municipal involvement, while leisure and culture departments stress social, health, and community development reasons.

Heritage and park conservation have been closely linked to events.

There is, unfortunately, plenty of scope for governments to manipulate festivals and events for crass political reasons.

Governments have yet to match their growing interest in events with the funds and research necessary to advance the field.

CHAPTER FIVE

Destination Planning and Marketing

This chapter develops an approach to destination planning and marketing with event tourism, beginning with a model of the process and discussion of some of the main steps. The discussion is continued in the next chapter with an examination of product development and promotion, which warrant more detailed treatment.

Examination of tourism destination planning requires an integrative approach, in which all the perspectives on festivals and events are incorporated. The model that is created of the destination planning and marketing process emphasizes event tourism considerations. The destination area strategic plan and marketing plan that follow stress the ways to integrate event tourism. The chapter concludes with detailed discussions of related goals, policies and priorities, market research, and strategy revisions based on impact evaluation. There are, of course, similarities in approach between destination planning and marketing and the development of individual festivals and events.

THE NATURE OF DESTINATION PLANNING

Tourism planning has evolved as a poorly integrated collection of methods and approaches, based on the different and often conflicting perspectives of business, governments at all levels, and numerous special-interest groups. Bringing these together in a manner that establishes broad goals and priorities and sorts out the conflicts for a destination area is seldom achieved, particularly where public and private interests are both involved.

A number of traditions of tourism planning can be identified (Getz 1987), and the concepts, methods, and biases associated with each are described below. Naturally, these will be open to interpretation and debate, but they do serve to focus critical attention on aspects of tourism planning and marketing that have come to be accepted practice. They also allow examination of how festivals and special events fit into different perspectives on destination planning.

Boosterism

Too much of what passes as tourism planning is little more than raw promotion of development. It can be called boosterism, because of the analogy to booster clubs, which unabashedly support ideas, groups, or products. This tradition seems to be especially prevalent among certain business groups and government officials who promote any and all forms of economic development, usually for their own financial or political gain. It also seems to be associated more with the early stages of tourism development in a destination, a period when economic benefits loom large and the full, destructive weight of ill-planned tourism has yet to become a pressing issue.

The main implication for special events is the emphasis placed on identifying and exploiting resources for their tourism development potential. Cultural or religious festivals are thus seen as resources, and their exoticism and authenticity promoted to tourists with little regard for how such attention might destroy these very attributes. New events are created and mobile events lured to the destination as tourist attractions, without much concern for their relationship to the host community or their cultural compatibility. More odious is the often accompanying attitude that leads officials and the industry to launch campaigns intended to convince host populations to be good to tourists, without dealing with the obvious problems tourism can bring or involving residents in the decision-making process.

Boosterism is not really planning. It is an attitude that can be found anywhere, particularly where sophistication in planning is lacking. It is dangerous and has to be resisted with hard information on the negatives of unplanned development and overcommercialization.

Tourism as an Industry

In most of the world's developed nations, tourism has come to be seen as an industry deserving equal attention with other sectors, such as manufacturing and forestry. This economic approach might very well incorporate an unhealthy dose of boosterism, but the sophistication required to use tourism as a tool in national and regional development planning tends to make governments and the industry more sensitive to all types of impact and to the need for more responsible planning. Nevertheless, the emphasis resulting from this approach is on achieving economic goals, and the main tools of the trade are development and marketing.

The risk is that events will be viewed from only one perspective. The numerous studies commissioned to evaluate the economic effects of festivals and other special events serve as testament to this observation. Event organizers themselves foster this tradition by stressing the economic benefits to be achieved through sponsorship or assistance to events. If it was not for the fact that marketing has become more and more sensitive to meeting customer needs and developing high-quality products, there would be little hope for many special events—they would become nothing more than standardized products in a master development plan.

Spatial and Resource Planning

A third tradition, often mixed with the others, centers on the spatial aspects of tourism and physical resource planning. The approach of Gunn (1988) is most notable, as he has advocated regional tourism planning employing careful resource analysis and incorporating spatial models that stress the roles of attractions, services, and accessibility. In this way special events are viewed as part of the resource base, giving shape to patterns of development and tourist movement. By their nature, events can help diffuse tourism throughout a region as well as serve as an anchor to develop a resort.

Many conservationists, however, have a different perspective on tourism. Parks planners in particular have often led campaigns to oppose the development pressures brought by the tourism industry, so that concern for "capacity to absorb tourism" has grown (Getz 1983). There is a constant tension between those who seek to provide people with access to interesting and even sensitive resources and those who are charged with protecting the resource base. Increasingly, however, tourism and conservation are in partnership to further the aims of both interests. Hence the development of "nature tourism" or "ecotourism" (Fennell and Eagles, 1989), in which parks and sensitive areas are more effectively managed by encouraging and controlling visits from those who appreciate conservation. In this context, special events can help to draw attention to conservation, educate the public, and control visitors.

Community-Based Planning

Newest on the scene is the community-based approach advocated by Murphy (1985) and others. It is actually part of a broader tradition that views traditional, mass tourism as more of a blight than a blessing and advocates alternative forms of tourism development and planning—or even alternatives to tourism. The essence of the community-based model is that individual communities must take control of the process, set their own goals, and plan accordingly. It is an approach that seeks to balance economic, social, cultural, and ecological considerations. The terms *community development* or *social carrying capacity* (Cooke 1982) come into use.

One model of the community-based approach to tourism planning (Murphy 1985, 37) places at its core the "community's tourism product." This Murphy defines as an amalgam of resources and facilities "which the community, as a whole, wishes to present to the tourism market." Local hospitality is an essential ingredient of the product, along with the very culture and life-style of the community.

It is easy to see how festivals and events fit this model, and, perhaps more important, how events can be a tangible product to attract tourists, reflect the local culture, and allow adequate management. As noted previously, the festival or event can also be a useful mechanism for encouraging a community to think about its tourism product and then undertake more comprehensive tourism planning. Getz (1984) hypothesized a "social multiplier" to complement the economic multiplier in determining the effects of tourism, by demonstrating that tourism initiatives, including community-run events, can serve as community development mechanisms and increase investment in the social infrastructure of the host community. Social and economic development processes should be mutually reinforcing and balanced.

Integrated and Systematic Approach

Boosterism must be relegated to the past. One cannot consider the unquestioning promotion and development of tourism to be planning at all. The economic tradition, which everywhere predominates, is too narrow. Although good marketing should act to counter the natural tendency to exploit and overcommercialize, it cannot be relied upon to do so, especially where community festivals are concerned. The community-based approach, and tourism planning that is sensitive and complementary to nature conservation, will often come into conflict with economic development goals. And there is no track record for nature tourism or community-based planning to show exactly how they can be implemented in the face of strong development pressure. All these factors argue for a more integrative model of tourism planning.

The ideal tourism planning process is systematic, democratic, goal-oriented, and integrative with other planning processes. Viewing tourism as a separate planning exercise is counterproductive and inevitably leads to conflicts within host communities or with other interest groups. How can the process of fostering arts or multiculturalism through festivals be separated from either tourism or cultural planning? How could the enormous impacts of a world's fair or Olympics be divorced from urban planning, sports development, or industrial policy? Why should the planning of heritage areas not include special events?

A systems approach to tourism planning has been developed (Getz 1986b); it can be summarized here by stating its major components and its relationship to event tourism planning. The planning process must constantly strive to base goals, policies, and strategies on a fuller understanding of how the tourism system works. This requires blending research into the nature of the system—asking, for example, how different kinds of impact are generated through festivals and what motivates people to attend events—with evaluation of actual strategies and actions, such as determining how many jobs a special event generated and whether visitors were satisfied.

Second, the better the system is understood and modeled, the more accurate predictions will become. Goals and objectives can be revised by referring to improved understanding of how to identify and cope with problems, and what the potential of festivals and events really is. Event tourism planning then becomes more effective in achieving goals.

The various traditions of tourism planning are not necessarily sequential, as elements of each tradition can be found in destination planning. By contrast, Jafari (1988) discussed four "platforms" of research and opinion on tourism planning and development, which he suggested are chronologically sequential. The first stage he called "advocacy," which is similar to the boosterism associated with unqualified promotion of tourism development. The second is "cautionary," which encompasses the writings on tourism's costs; this stage follows or accompanies the obvious problems development can bring. Next is the "adaptancy" stage, which Jafari (1988, 5) described as "favoring those forms of tourism which are responsive to the host communities and their sociocultural, manmade, and natural environments, and at the same time provide tourists with new choices and rewarding experiences." This is the stage that involves an alternative and community-based approach. The final platform is that of "knowledge-based" opinion and policy, based on scientific, systematic planning and stressing the relationship between costs and benefits. This is very much the integrated and systems approach that is advocated in this book. To achieve it requires a much greater understanding than we now possess on how various kinds of festivals and events and event tourism strategies cause either desired or negative effects.

Essential Components of Destination Planning

Quite a few models of destination planning can be found in the tourism literature (Getz 1986b, Pearce 1989). Most are oriented to development and marketing and show how to achieve growth. As such, they do not satisfy our requirement that tourism planning be systematic and based on cost-benefit evaluation. Nevertheless, we can use them to identify key components and incorporate these in our destination planning model pertinent to event tourism. From our previous discussion of planning traditions and platforms, it will be clear that spatial and physical planning, policies, comprehensive community involvement, and marketing will all figure prominently in any comprehensive destination planning strategy.

Tourism Planning (Gunn 1988) contains much valuable advice on destination planning. Gunn's model of regional strategic planning links the need for increased volumes of tourism to increased supply, resulting in expanded markets and resource development. Events are thus seen as travel generators, or resources to develop. Gunn is also known for his destination zone concept, in which travel corridors link tourist service centers and attraction clusters. This provides a basis for spatial event tourism planning.

Gunn (1982) has discussed a number of fallacies pertaining to destination planning. He stated that destination regions or zones are often defined according to different criteria, and such zones hold varying connotations. In reality, destinations do not depend on natural resources and have fuzzy boundaries that might have to be changed over time to reflect changing conditions. They should reflect feasible, public or private capabilities to develop and promote the area through product-market matching. Service centers and attraction clusters are essential.

Product-market matching has become an essential ingredient in destination tourism planning. As outlined by Gunn (1988), there are two levels to consider. At the macro level, the desired experiences of groups most likely to be attracted to an area are matched against the destination's range of current opportunities and potential. At the micro level, the emphasis is placed on evaluating development proposals as to their potential market share, investment, feasibility, and impact. This approach is a combination of two marketing orientations that Mill and Morrison (1985) identified as product orientation, or trying to sell the resources you have, and market orientation, or trying to provide what the consumer wants. Product-market matching should result in the destination's using its resources more efficiently in catering to the known desires or needs of its optimal markets.

The third marketing orientation that Mill and Morrison identified is the societal approach, which seeks to match tourism development with the needs of the destination region. This is quite similar to the community-based approach of Murphy (1985). It differs from traditional destination planning models in several ways: there is not a preoccupation with measuring and forecasting demand or seeking potential markets, but more of a focus on identifying destination community needs and goals; there is less stress on promotion and marketing, and more of an emphasis on maintaining the authenticity and quality of the product. In effect, this approach seeks sustainable development of tourism in balance with the destination community's needs.

The Tourism System, Mill and Morrison's book, also contains a policy model of particular interest. The destination must have an overall purpose and goals for tourism planning, and the process must generate policies and priorities to regulate the system. Without attention to goals and policy formulation, the traditional progrowth models will undoubtedly prevail, leaving little scope for community control and sustainable or alternative development.

Another well-known model is called PASOLP (Baud-Bovey and Lawson 1976; Baud-Bovey 1982), which stands for Product Analysis Sequence for Outdoor Leisure Planning. It shows a process focused on the generation and feasibility testing of product alternatives. Important considerations are resources, the current tourism market, organization and financing, sites of potential tourism interest, and possible markets to develop.

In summary, a number of principles for destination planning and the special role of event tourism can be stated:

Destination planning is a systematic process of planning, developing, and marketing areas as tourist destinations; it encompasses consideration of resources, attractions, infrastructure, information and communications, services, travel patterns, and impacts.

It is integrative of the many possible roles events can play in tourism, community development, organizational development, and other perspectives not related to tourism.

It is sensitive to the inherent characteristics of cultural events and community celebrations, not exploitive of them.

It is concerned with long-term goals, policy development, and methods suitable for achieving goals.

It recognizes that conflicts over goals and methods are likely to occur and seeks to reconcile the various perspectives and priorities.

It recognizes that all forms of tourism development, including events, potentially involve costs and negative effects for the host community and environment, and it seeks to identify these and devise ways to avoid, ameliorate, or correct problems.

A MODEL OF DESTINATION PLANNING AND MARKETING

Figure 5-1 illustrates a destination planning and marketing process specific to event tourism. This model is most suited to the combined efforts of government and industry for destination areas and for general tourism and event policy formulation. (A similar process is adapted in Chapter 7 to the more specific needs of marketing planning for individual events.)

This model tries to encompass the key components of destination planning, but it must be emphasized that it is not merely a development model. Rather, it stresses policy formulation based on an understanding, gained through research and evaluation, of the roles of festivals and events and the costs and benefits they can bring to the destination.

As event tourism is but one of the major elements to be considered in des-

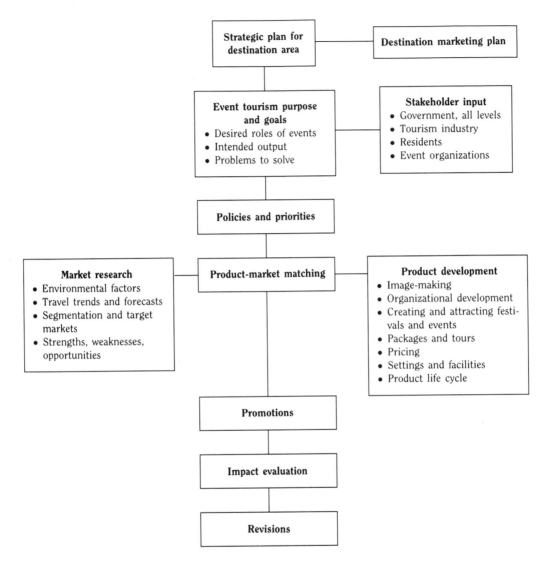

Figure 5-1. Destination planning and marketing model.

tination tourism planning, the model assumes first that an overall strategic plan will be in place to help determine the roles and goals of festivals and special events as they relate to all other sectors of destination development. That will not always be the case, however, and the event tourism planner might have to formulate a sector plan just for event tourism. In some jurisdictions strategic planning is not done at all, and the marketing plan is the only formal document to guide tourism. This is a restricted approach, although more sophisticated marketing plans encompass most of the elements shown in Figure 5-1. We should not get hung up on terminology or jargon. Marketing and planning are really part of the same process, insofar as destination tourism planning is concerned.

Destination planning begins with goals, and in a systematic process there are two standard types of goals: those pertaining to problems that must be overcome, avoided, or lessened; and those pertaining to ideal or desired conditions, such as the achievement of targets. Goals are refined through research and evaluation, and in destination planning they are achieved largely to the extent that all parties with a stake in the process—government agencies at all levels, the tourism industry, residents of the destination, and event organizations—agree to them. This is not easy to achieve, and it requires continuous input, debate, and compromise.

Once the general direction of destination planning has been set through goal statements, policies are required. A policy is a commitment to certain strategies or actions, or at least a clear guideline as to what approach will be taken toward the achievement of goals. Policies of government are sometimes legally binding, whereas typical tourism plans and strategies can only formulate goals with the hope that all concerned parties will seek to follow them and, where appropriate, adopt policies for implementation. Because so many parties are involved in tourism planning, however, policies tend to be diverse, uncoordinated, and sometimes ineffectual.

Sorting out priorities among the various goals and policies is a key issue. While all parties might agree to a set of goals and policies in principle, there can easily be disagreement over which ones are most important. For example, what happens if one goal is to create jobs through development of mega-events, which might cause some environmental disruption, while another goal is to preserve the natural environment? And how can the policies of different levels of government be reconciled?

Market research encompasses the broad and loosely defined process of identifying trends in demand, selecting target markets, and determining strategies for attracting them.

Product development goes hand in hand with market research and with marketing and promotions: research determines what products are desired, and event products are of little value to tourism without effective promotions. Indeed, some event products are actually the promotion of a package that includes events. Specific considerations are development of themes, image-making, tours and packages, creation or attraction of events, development of event sites or venues, and the spread of events geographically and seasonally. Pricing is included here, although in the context of overall destination planning it is mostly a matter of product differentiation—in other words, separating packages and attractions by major differences in their cost to consumers.

Product-market matching is identified as a separate component in the destination planning model, although in practice it is an ongoing blend of market research and product development.

Promotions, the next stage in the process, occupy much of the effort of destination tourist organizations. It is necessary to examine how event tourism fits into the broader promotional strategy for the destination and develop specific, effective ways to communicate, motivate, and encourage the consumption of event tourism products.

No planning process is complete without a permanent system of monitoring (impact research), evaluation, and feedback, all of which is intended to facilitate revising the purpose, goals, and actions as needed.

THE DESTINATION STRATEGIC PLAN

A strategic destination plan, or policy plan, is the ideal starting point in the formal process to state goals and policies, establish physical and spatial development targets, and propose an action plan for implementation. The higher the level of planning, from local to national, the less detailed the plan will be on spatial and physical development, and the more general it will be in terms of goals and policies. Small destination areas, such as individual communities, have to incorporate detailed development guidelines.

The event tourism components of a strategic destination plan should include the following:

Inventory and data base of existing and previously held events (names, types, sizes, organizers, locations, seasons, duration, sponsors, activities and components, number of visitors and participants, and impacts)

Classification of events (using all the previously discussed typologies to help sort out gaps and strengths)

Assessment of potential event organizers (groups, agencies, and destinations capable of supporting events)

Product evaluation (quantity and quality, strengths and weaknesses relative to existing and potential markets, impacts, potentials, and contribution to destination image and overall attractiveness)

Market assessment and product-market matching, target segments and their interests, and roles of events in satisfying visitors to the destination

Stakeholder input (from the industry, different levels of government and various agencies, and residents) on desired roles and outcomes of event tourism, on acceptable limits of change, and on preferred locations, timing, and scale of events and development

Purpose and goals (roles of events, intended outcomes, problems to solve, relationship to other tourism and development goals)

Policies for attracting and creating events, assisting organizers, preventing and solving problems, and maximizing desired impact

Action plan (priorities, programs for financial assistance and development, schedule of actions and who is responsible, guidelines for feasibility studies and impact assessments, performance criteria, and impact assessment and evaluation methods)

Revisions (how impact evaluation will affect goals, policies, and programs)

Thus, the destination plan should incorporate many of the elements of our planning process model, in a form that shows the basis of decisions and gives firm direction as to what must be accomplished. At what stage in the process the plan is formulated is a matter of both preference and circumstances. In some destinations the research, input, and debate will have to precede any action. In others, the plan is a convenient way to step back from what has been happening in tourism development and reassess the process. Its comprehensiveness and detail are also a matter of preference; a short, concise plan, however, will be easier to understand and might gain a better public reception. Technical appendixes can contain the details.

THE DESTINATION MARKETING PLAN

The marketing plan normally encompasses the traditional marketing mix of product, price, place, and promotion. In many destinations, promotion is all that gets done, because the tourism planning system is incomplete. In others, a marketing plan resembles a comprehensive strategic or policy plan.

Tourism marketing plans have tended to become more detailed and action-oriented. Specific, measurable performance targets are made and revised annually, such as a specific percentage increase in arrivals from a certain target market. Throughout the 1980s increasing attention was given to accountability, meaning the evaluation of what was being accomplished with money spent on marketing and promotions. Techniques have been developed for measuring both conversions, such as the number or proportion of inquiries about a destination that actually led to trips there, and calculation of the cost per arrival.

Drawing on a number of plans and texts on the subject, we can put forward the basis of a good destination marketing plan, with emphasis on the event tourism components. The following points are in addition to the marketing research and product development issues considered previously as being part of a strategic plan.

Market research and situation analysis: identification of existing markets and the current roles and attractiveness of festivals and special events; determination of the destination image; assessment of trends in demand and factors affecting trends; evaluation of competitors; consideration of growth and development of events and the factors affecting them; a SWOT analysis of current event tourism products (see Chapter 10)

Evaluation of market potential: forecasts of general and event tourism demand; segmentation to determine characteristics of prime target markets for event tourism; determination of market areas

Product-market matching: evaluation of the implications of current event tourism products for enhancing demand; assessment of how product development for event tourism could meet and create demand; determination of desirable product improvements

Marketing strategies: establishment of targets; development of strategies to manipulate price, product, promotions, and place or distribution to achieve objectives; setting of evaluative or performance criteria

Communications and promotions action plan: commitment of resources to advertising, public relations, direct selling, and sales promotions; evaluation

The important point to remember is that marketing requires the direction that comes from a strategic plan, or at least from general tourism policies. The current state of the art is rather crude, and often the only direction given to many tourism agencies is to promote growth.

GOALS AND OBJECTIVES

Event tourism goals must be broader than mere economic considerations. An integrative planning approach is based on the premise that tourism is only one perspective on special events, and that tourism goals will not be fully achievable, or sustainable, without full consideration of the other perspectives. Comprehensive event tourism goals must therefore address the following issues:

The extent to which existing events are to be developed and promoted as tourist attractions

The extent to which support will be given to develop or assist the creation of new events and the bidding for established, mobile events

The roles events are to play in extending tourist seasons and the geographic spread of tourism

The role events are to play in creating and enhancing images, particularly a destination area or attraction theme

The roles events are to play in fostering the arts, cultural goals, sports, fitness, recreation, nature and heritage conservation, and community development

The acceptable costs associated with development, and who is to pay for them

The means to identify, prevent, ameliorate, or remove negative impact

The need for organizational development at the level of interest groups, communities, destination areas, and government agencies and departments to support event tourism

Table 5-1 lists sample event tourism goals and objectives, derived from the preceding discussion and the various potential roles of festivals and events. A list of all possible goals and objectives could be enormous, so the destination planners must develop ones that are important in their circumstances and will gain support from all the stakeholder groups.

Once these broad goals have been established, in effect defining the roles of event tourism in destination planning, a second level of output goals is needed. These state the intended output or benefits the destination should obtain from various festival and event products. Table 5-2 is a starting point for writing these output goals. Different types of events should yield specific tourism benefits for the destination. A useful addition will be to include the basic development requirements associated with each type of event. For example, mega-events could have major benefits for the destination, but they also demand the highest financial commitment, longest and most complex planning process, and considerable political, corporate, and public support. Stating these requirements will greatly assist the priority assigned to each goal, as well as making clear the process by which the goals can be achieved. Accordingly, they can be termed *process goals.*

Many of the development requirements shown in Table 5-2 are aspects of product development, considered in detail in the next chapter. Others are political in nature and should be debated openly before decisions and priorities are made. Certain political and industry groups might lobby for mega-events, for example, while public support might be highest for local, recurring festivals.

Goals for Different Levels of Destination Planning

There will often be fundamental differences in goals and priorities among national, regional, and local levels of government, between government and industry sectors, and among individual attractions and events. The way in which the destination is delimited is therefore an important consideration, as is recognition that goals and priorities have to be kept quite general for most des-

Table 5-1. Sample Goals and Objectives for Event Tourism

Goals	Objectives
Create a favorable image for the destination	Attract and create high-profile events; maximize media exposure; draw attention to other attractions; reveal friendliness and modernity of the country or area; preserve authentic cultural attributes
Attract foreign visitors	Set targets for actual numbers
Generate foreign revenue	Favor events that attract above-average spenders and foreign investors or sponsors
Generate spin-off benefits for other economic sectors	Link events to technological and managerial skill development; hold trade fairs and conferences
Expand the tourism season; reinforce the peak season	Attract and create events throughout the year; stage events (length and timing) to encourage longer stays
Spread tourism benefits to all regions and localities	Attract and create events throughout the country; link to package tours and touring routes; piggyback small events on large ones
Stimulate repeat visits	Provide a sequence and variety of events; use events to introduce other attractions; foster host-guest relations; evaluate event quality and visitor satisfaction
Develop and improve the infrastructure and management skills necessary to create, attract, and sustain events	Provide assistance and advice to organizers and sponsors; foster the pooling of resources; create cooperative marketing and promotions
Foster development of the arts, sports, culture, heritage, and leisure	Assist all types of events; link events to other policy areas
Ensure maximum benefits to the host community	Conduct cost-benefit studies; follow community-based planning process
Avoid negative environmental impact; foster conservation	Stimulate nature tourism through events; require impact assessments

tination plans. One of the chief functions of strategic plans, therefore, is identifying and resolving potential conflicts and working toward a consensus. As argued previously, a bottom-up or community-based approach is recommended.

What has often happened, unfortunately, is that many destination plans have been formulated by one level of government without consideration of other levels, by a tourist organization without involvement of public officials, or by

Table 5-2. Sample Output and Process Goals for Event Tourism

Event Products	Intended Output (benefits)	Development Requirements (process goals)
Mega-event attractions Olympics World's fairs Sports Visiting VIPs Historical milestones	Image enhancement Foreign tourist influx and spending Facility and monetary legacy Enhanced pride, confidence Heightened interest in the theme	National organization Competitive bid Long-term planning Major investment Major infrastructure Large-scale promotions and market research High-level political support Large-scale sponsorship
Regional attractions Festivals Sports Fairs and exhibitions	Similar to above, but greater reliance on domestic market; national appeal Fostering of long-term growth and impacts	Permanent venue or facilities Permanent organizations Sustained marketing and promotions in conjunction with other events Possible requirement of ongoing financial assistance and sponsorships
Local attractions Community festivals and social events Local or regional competitions	Community development Leisure opportunities Activity for tourists in the area; regional and local appeal	Base of volunteers Possible need of periodic "rescue" Dependence on permanent facilities not necessary Assistance essential for marketing and promotions
Business events Conferences, conventions, meetings	Attraction of domestic and foreign visitors Suitability for off-peak seasons Spin-off business benefits Encouragement of longer stays or repeat visit for pleasure	Highly specialized conference centers and accommodations Full-time convention bureau or marketing group Ability to be piggybacked on other events
Programs Series of events at parks, resorts, attractions, and so on	Education of visitors Increased exposure Improved image Encouragement of repeat visits Encouragement of spending	Skilled programmers Specialized facilities and services not always necessary Target marketing

an industry group under the assumption that governments would endorse their plans. Individual attractions typically formulate their plans in complete isolation.

National-level destination planning is typically undertaken by national tourist organizations, or NTOs. Severe problems are encountered, particularly in federal systems, when developing national-level goals and policies. None of the examples from Australia, Canada, the United States, United Kingdom, or New Zealand that have been documented here has even attempted comprehensive policies or a physical or spatial plan for the whole country. Nevertheless, policies specific to event tourism and particular national issues are being formulated and implemented. The New Zealand case that was described illustrates the integration of event tourism planning within the broader context of national tourism strategies.

Most NTOs concentrate on marketing studies and promotion or on assistance to development of the industry. Event tourism fits into the marketing or development divisions, or it could be a separate unit. Goals are likely to be restricted to generalities affecting the entire country, such as the fostering of festival and event organizations and programs of funding, or to national-level priorities such as the hosting of mega-events. Marketing goals concentrate on developing a destination image through events and ensuring that events are integrated in all product development and promotion schemes. Where lower-level governments or the industry have formulated goals or plans, the NTO can integrate them to whatever extent is possible. What is most unlikely is any agreement on a spatial structure of tourism development covering the whole country—there will be too much competition among states, regions, and localities to accomplish that!

National-level goals for event tourism will probably be based on the potential value of events in creating a positive destination image and attracting foreign tourists, thereby helping to meet economic goals. But that would be insufficient. Event tourism relates closely to social and cultural policy, and goals must be formulated to cover these linkages. The value of festivals and events to domestic tourism also should be acknowledged. Subordinate goals concerning seasonality and the geographic spread of visitors are required, although these might have to be general and allow lower levels of government or the industry freedom in determining actual development patterns. Where the government pursues policies of regional development, event tourism goals can be connected explicitly to other strategies for spreading economic growth, such as through special financial incentives to develop events or through region-based marketing and promotion funds.

States or provinces in a federal system often have interests similar to those at the national level, but they also tend to compete against each other for tourists and developments. Regions can be defined as a state or province or as any subunit that covers more than one locality or municipality. The regional level is clearly different from the national, in that a region will seek to create a specific destination image and will make detailed tourism plans. There is usually some competition among the constituents of a region, but it is often effective for communities and industry units to cooperate in regional marketing and planning schemes.

Tourism goals at the regional level tend to be more focused than national strategies, and they are usually related to the unique characteristics of the area. Regions are thought of as destinations more than nations or localities are, except in the smallest of countries or the biggest of cities. They present the opportunity for advancing a coherent and competitive theme in which festivals and events can figure prominently. Regions are also the most logical scale at which to undertake detailed inventories, resource evaluations, impact assessments, and marketing strategies. They are not the best scale, however, at which to undertake public input or organize any but the largest of events.

Goals for destination regions tend to emphasize job creation and the spatial allocation of development, rather than national economic concerns such as the balance of payments. They also pay more attention to the domestic market, as day-trips and interregional traffic are often the biggest source of tourism income. Concern for environmental and social or cultural effects should be heightened at this level, and the goals and policies for tourism have to fit into broad, regional plans for land use, conservation, or economic development.

Specific to festivals and events, the regional tourism strategy or plan should contain goals that specify the following:

- The roles of events in image-making and theme development
- Attraction and dispersion of tourist traffic throughout the region
- Constraints on development—such as environmental, infrastructural, or social—that might restrict events
- Linkages between events and other attractions, such as historic districts or major theme parks

Because many festivals and special events are small in scale, the regional strategy at least has to consider the individual communities and their contribution to tourism.

To be realistic, the issues and goals at the most local level of tourism destination planning have to be detailed and carefully evolved from public input. The community-based approach to tourism planning requires that the public be informed, educated, and involved in the process—not to make people supportive of industry development plans, but actually to define and implement a community tourism product. Festivals and special events are among the most direct and effective ways to involve people at the grass-roots level.

Communities are naturally interested in the economic goals of higher levels of government and the industry, but they tend to be absorbed in the details of site-specific issues and visible impact on the local environment. Job creation is a vital matter of community viability and personal self-interest. Culture is not an abstract term; it is the local way of life, both at work and leisure. Environment is more than the conservation of important resources; it is the look of Main

Street, the availability of clean and open spaces, and the quality of drinking water. Every issue will be scrutinized for its potential positive and negative effects, and every tourism goal will be justifiably evaluated against the central criterion: how will it affect the way people in the community want to live? This is democratic and bottom-up planning, and it is particularly well suited to festival and event planning, in which the community must be actively involved and committed or the events will not materialize or succeed. It is also the reason most tourism plans have failed to incorporate community input in any meaningful manner—once set in motion, there is no way to predict the outcome. The community might even reject tourism developments altogether.

POLICIES AND PRIORITIES

The strategic or policy plan provides commitments, or at least guidelines, for each of the issues and goals discussed in the previous section. Policies can also be expressed as programs of assistance to an industry sector, a resource-use plan, requirements to be met by development proposals, or budgets allocated to marketing and promotions. The main difficulty encountered in tourism planning is the difference in goals and priorities among different levels of government or various stakeholders.

Two basic strategies can be employed for resolving the many conflicts likely to arise in destination tourism planning. If the driving force is a tourism or industry organization, there will be a natural tendency to focus on the tourism goals and downplay or ignore the others. In this approach, conflicts can be viewed as problems to overcome. For example: community opposition to a proposed event might be countered by promotion of the positive economic benefits to be achieved; conservationists' concerns might be countered by excluding them from the decision-making process. But how far can this approach go without arousing hostility to tourism and degrading the entire planning process?

An open, democratic planning process is essential for all forms of development, particularly in the realm of event tourism, where the host community is an integral part of the product. Planning carried out by tourist organizations in isolation from other planning systems, such as heritage, conservation, arts, culture, natural resources, land use, economic development, native rights, and so on, will inevitably be shortsighted and generate opposition.

Consequently, a top-down approach will not work. The national or regional tourist organization can certainly initiate the process and take responsibility for its implementation, but the process must be opened to public debate and must eventually become community-specific. As Murphy (1985) has demonstrated, the community must identify its goals and how they relate to tourism, then control the process by which the goals are transformed into attractions, services, and hospitality.

A major implication of this approach is that the tourist organization responsible for event tourism planning will not be responsible for much of the implementation. Its role is primarily that of facilitator—a role that Middleton (1988) suggested is more appropriate and common than that of actual developer. When it actually comes to sorting out goals, priorities, and implementation methods, the tourism planner must enter into partnerships with other agencies, industry segments, host communities, and special-interest groups.

Integrated Policies and Priorities

Logically, lower-level governments and tourism regions should share and support the national goals, and the senior levels should take into account lower-level needs and wishes in formulating their goals and policies. After all, each community will potentially benefit if more foreign visitors are attracted and if the balance of payments is favorable. And the national tourism planner will obviously want local and regional attractions like special events to flourish, thereby making the nation as a whole more attractive. But several factors intervene to make a complete integration of policies and priorities among governments and industry difficult to achieve.

First, the real or perceived mandates of different levels of government and various public or semipublic agencies are different. Many local governments do not believe it is their task to promote or support tourism. Communities are more likely to support festivals as recreational and cultural pursuits for residents, although the awareness of tourism by municipal officials is definitely increasing. Some government departments have a specific mandate to promote economic development and others to preserve the environment or foster arts and cultural growth, which can pit them against each other. Industry organizations are motivated by self-interest, and although this should encompass environmental and social responsibility, it sometimes leads to boosterism without adequate attention to negative impact.

Another problem is that senior levels of government often have considerable resources to promote tourism and assist the industry, whereas local and regional authorities might lack the resources to cope with the consequences of development and increased flow of tourism. Senior governments obtain taxation and other economic benefits, while municipalities and communities bear the direct infrastructural, environmental, and social costs. Consequently, there is potential for antagonism and even direct opposition to policies. This tends to happen only where local communities are strongly organized against development, or when negative impact is so great that the residents rebel.

Resources also affect the ability of local areas to create events or other developments to take advantage of tourism potential. There is little sense in having senior governments or the industry promote tourism if money and expertise are not provided to assist communities and small businesses to capitalize on growth.

Many government authorities are finding it essential to provide technical and financial assistance, as well as promote awareness of tourism potential, at the community and small business levels.

Politics can also enter the picture. There is a natural tendency to take credit for successful special events or promotions and to point the finger when things go wrong. Mega-events are more susceptible to this problem, as their costs and impacts are of a magnitude that ensures high levels of media attention. The potential result is a public relations contest among various interested parties, rather than cooperation and integrated planning.

Reconciling these potentially conflicting perspectives is difficult. The only reasonable way to proceed is to demonstrate that working together maximizes the degree of every stakeholder's goal attainment. Hence, there is growing interest in fostering the tourism-environment or tourism-arts partnerships and in community-based planning. Only if all parties have an equal share in the planning will effective planning result. The process must be open and consensus-building in nature. With regard to festivals and special events, which of all tourism attractions are most dependent on community goodwill and participation, the priorities are often going to evolve this way: community goals first, tourism second. To put tourism first risks a distortion of many festival or event goals and the alienation of community support.

MARKET RESEARCH

Market research is a constant process, and the research necessary for event tourism planning must become an integral part of ongoing efforts by the tourist organization. Research is necessary to identify and answer crucial planning and marketing questions, such as the following:

- Who are our potential customers? What trends are noticeable?
- What factors are affecting interest in and demand for our destination, its events, and other attractions?
- What are their needs and motives relative to festivals and events?
- How can we best reach them and influence their travel decisions?
- What is the role of events in creating or enhancing our destination theme and in increasing the attractiveness of our other tourism resources?
- What are the implications of known tourist preferences for the event tourism products?
- How can we gain a competitive advantage?
- Are customers satisfied with our products and information?

Although the planning and marketing process is continuous, in theory market research must come first. Without basic knowledge of the tourism system, no destination or event can hope to create and maintain successful tourism products.

In corporate or strategic planning, the same rule applies—only the exercise is more likely to be called "environmental scanning" or "evaluating the business environment." Others prefer to refer to this stage in the process as strategic analysis or situational analysis.

Middleton (1988, 109) outlined six main categories of marketing research: market analysis and forecasting, consumer research, product and price studies, promotion and sales studies, distribution studies, and performance evaluation. Any distinction between these categories as being strategic or evaluative is really a matter of application. The research is strategic if it is intended to establish long-term goals and strategies, and it is evaluative if it is intended primarily to determine the effectiveness and efficiency of actions and products. In a systems approach, this distinction is not meaningful, as all research and evaluation contribute to a better understanding of how the event or destination relates to its environment.

PRODUCT-MARKET MATCHING

The logic of product-market matching and its place in the destination planning model were described earlier in the chapter: at the macro level (Gunn 1988), it is the process of continuously ensuring that the destination's products and potentials are matched with real and potential consumer demand from key target segments; this ensures that a narrow product orientation (Mill and Morrison 1985) will be avoided, and that development proposals are realistic and suited to the destination. At the micro level, development proposals are evaluated as to their potential market share, investment needs, feasibility, and impact. In the event tourism context, it has several implications.

First, it requires the assessment of how events and event packages can potentially satisfy the needs of target segments. Conversely, destination planners must determine the range and attributes of existing festivals and events, and ways to package them, that would appeal to target segments.

The matching process should then evaluate suitability and feasibility, as not all existing and potential event tourism products will be practical, or desired by the host population. A community-based approach to identification of suitable community tourism products will accomplish this, but destination planners have to provide market research to enable communities to relate their event ideas to existing and realistic new target markets.

In the next chapter, which focuses on product development, additional implications for product-market matching will become apparent.

IMPACT EVALUATION AND PLAN REFINEMENT

With products in place—and even before—impact evaluation comes into play. It goes without saying that a system of evaluation forms an integral part of strategic planning at all levels and for all organizations. Its key elements are formulation of evaluative criteria and the methods to undertake evaluation, involvement of all stakeholders, and assessment of the implications of measured impact.

Feedback from the evaluation process influences goals, policies, priorities, and subsequent stages in the model. This planning process can be described as cyclical in nature, rather than linear. To make it truly systematic would require the expansion of the research and evaluation elements to a level of sophistication necessary for modeling of the system (Getz 1986b). Much more work is required by researchers, evaluators, planners, and theorists before reliable predictive models can be applied to tourism in general.

It is most important, however, that the strategic planner think systematically. To demonstrate the importance of this point, consider the following questions, which should be posed early in the planning process:

Do you know what direct and indirect effects your actions will have, both within and outside tourism? Can you predict, for example, what a mega-event will do for the cultural life of the host community?

Have you the means to detect and evaluate unintended effects of your plans and actions?

Are your goals based on what you want the nation, region, community, or organization to be in the future, or on more short-term targets? You can set goals according to what you want to happen, or what you don't want to happen.

To be systematic, the strategic planning process must at least be formulated in such a way that it learns, or adapts to new information. Planning can progress only through learning about the system in which it operates and how the planners' actions change the system for better or worse.

SUMMARY

The nature of tourism destination planning was examined first, focusing on the weaknesses inherent in boosterism, or the unquestioning promotion of tourism, and in the prevailing approach to tourism as an industry. A community-based planning approach is particularly well suited to festivals and events, because they require community commitment to be successful. Spatial and resource elements are important, but there is also potential conflict with conservation interests. In the end, an integrated and systematic approach was advocated, involving continuous research and evaluation, community-based initiatives to set goals and define the tourism product, and decisions based on cost-benefit evaluation. The ideal destination event tourism plan should not be exploitive of festivals and events, but should acknowledge all the roles and meanings of events and the potential for adverse commercialization and other negative types of impact. Long-term goals should be the basis for policy-making, with goals established in an open process involving all stakeholders—especially the host community. This approach corresponds with important elements of alternative tourism and should lead to sustainable development.

A model of event tourism destination planning and marketing (Fig. 5-1) was followed by a detailed discussion of its components. Outlines of destination strategic and marketing plans were given, with the emphasis on how event tourism considerations can be integrated. But the process itself is more important than specific plans made along the way.

Considerable attention was given in Chapter 5 to goals, objectives, policies, and priorities. Tourism planning is a political process, so these elements of policy-making are more important than master plans or event development plans. Sample goals for event tourism were suggested in Tables 5-1 and 5-2. Community-based planning works from the bottom up, based on the goals established by the community and destination residents; this results in a very different planning and marketing process from the typical top-down planning imposed by senior levels of government in concert with the tourism industry. For event tourism, both the industry and the major resource are really the population of the destination!

Ending Chapter 5 was an explanation of the roles of market research (reflecting back on the discussion in Chapter 3) and the importance of product-market matching and impact evaluation. These themes continued to be developed in later chapters.

CHAPTER SIX

Product Development and Promotion

The previous chapter introduced a model of destination planning and marketing with event tourism. This chapter examines in depth the significant elements of product development and promotion. Product development is broadly defined as encompassing the following: themes and image-making; the attraction, facilitation, and creation of events in a destination area; and the development of packages and tours. The concept of a product life cycle and a destination area cycle of evolution also has implications for event tourism planning.

Two other aspects of the traditional marketing mix are included under product development, namely, price and place; but price is less a concern at the destination level than at the level of individual events, and place relates mostly to tours and packages with a spatial component. Chapter 7 will consider the traditional marketing mix in full detail, as part of the marketing planning model for individual events, as well as integrative and internal marketing.

The promotion portion of this chapter will focus on specific ways in which the destination region can help promote events through advertising and coordination. All components of the promotion or communications mix will be considered in the next chapter.

PRODUCT DEVELOPMENT

Product development and marketing are sometimes indistinguishable in tourism, as many products do not even exist until promoted, packaged, or made accessible.

This is especially true for many community events that are not created as tourist attractions. In looking back to our model on various perspectives on festivals and events, it is also clear that the product is largely organizational in nature. Without the expertise and means to organize, the community will not be able to launch a festival. And the product in tourism is much more than an attraction or event. It is an amalgam of services, attractions, and often intangible ambience. Nowhere are the intangibles more important than in special event planning, so the product and marketing people must be skilled at identifying the attributes necessary to satisfy the target markets' needs.

The specific destination products covered in this section begin with the larger issues of creating a theme and positive image, followed by product development issues more specific to destination tourist organizations: organizational development and creation of events; attraction of events; packages and tours; distribution and accessibility; and seasonality.

Creating Destination Themes and Positive Images

Our focus here is on the role of festivals and special events in helping to create attractive destination themes and positive images. Themes and images go together for the simple reason that positive images can be conveyed more readily if they pertain to a central, coherent theme. This is why national and some large regional or state governments have such a difficult time with image-making and resort so often to easily remembered slogans, logos, and catchy tunes to associate their name with an upbeat, but vague, image. Smaller, more homogeneous destination regions or localities have it much easier, and they can create a theme that is easily identifiable with a certain area and its positive attributes.

With this key point in mind, it can be seen that large destination areas should concentrate on using festivals and events to accomplish three limited but important objectives:

1. Promote the large destination as an area that has an attractive variety of things to do, or develop broad themes such as friendliness, cultural diversity, or excitement; events can be used to create the pertinent imagery.
2. Use mega-events to attract media attention to the destination as a whole, and take long-term advantage of the so-called halo effect that sometimes results when successful events generate a lasting impression of a desirable place to visit.
3. Create or attract so many smaller events that the destination as a whole becomes known as a lively area with something attractive for all interests.

There is, of course, every good reason to pursue all three of these objectives in a comprehensive event tourism strategy. The smaller or more homogeneous destinations, right down to the level of individual resorts and communities, must be more precise in their theme and image-making efforts. Their objectives should encompass the following four points:

1. Create a theme that is important to and can be supported by the community, or is clearly consistent with the attractions of the resort area, and develop one or more festivals and events to make the theme come alive.
2. Create a hallmark event, which forever becomes identified with the destination because of its strong appeal. In this strategy, the theme and the hallmark event are indistinguishable, but the event comes first.
3. Develop many events of one type, such as sports, to create a theme such as Tournament Capital of . . . .
4. Develop many events of different types to create a destination theme such as The Most Exciting Resort in . . . .

Each of these objectives can be translated into effective destination strategies; however, pursuing more than one of them is difficult. A community cannot base its appeal on one hallmark event and then create a lot of smaller events if they distract from the main theme. Too many unlinked festivals and events might simply end up competing with each other while sending out an image of confusion to potential visitors. At a minimum, some degree of cooperative and coherent promotion of different events in one destination is important. The destination theme becomes the unifying force and acts to prevent undue competition or a cluttered, confused image.

The Destination Image

Drawing on our knowledge of the psychology of leisure and travel motivation, we can now more precisely define the nature and roles of image-making for destination and event marketing. Some clear definitions and explanations are needed first. Crompton (1979, 18) defined destination images as "the sum of beliefs, ideas and impressions that a person has of a destination." Hunt (1975) emphasized that a person's image of an area might have more to do with how the media projects the area or its attractions than with its tangible resources. Goodall (1988) stressed that a destination image is conditioned by available information. People develop preferential images of ideal vacations or experiences, according to Goodall, and this determines how they react to actual experiences.

Images are not static. They change with new information, particularly news of disasters and other bad publicity, and also in response to the firsthand reports of friends and relatives. Much of the image is based on perceptions of the destination or attraction, not reality. Accordingly, Goodall (1988, 10) says, "Personal images can therefore not only be influenced by, but can be manipulated, even created by forces external to the individual."

How is this accomplished? Both supply and demand factors have to be considered: creating an image to satisfy the needs or desired benefits of the target markets, and creating an image to highlight the best attributes of the event or destination. Uzzell (1984, 84) advised that the image be constructed in a form that appeals to the potential consumer's emotions and desires: "It is an image of something he wants to be, to have, to experience, or to achieve." In this way, both the push, or need, and pull, or attraction, factors must be addressed in image-making. The tension between wanting to get away from the ordinary or the bad and finding the extraordinary and the good can be exploited.

Actual mechanisms of image making are part science and part art. The science is in researching the needs, motives, and perceptual processes of potential customers. The art is in producing an event or products to meet the needs and in effectively communicating the strengths of the attraction. At this point it is useful to note the key, tangible elements of an image.

The Roles of Festivals and Events in Creating a Destination Image

The first key element is the visual image, conveyed through pictures, logos, and action. The destination uses imagery of festivals and events to show something tangible of culture, to convey the impression of variety, and to leave the impression of activity and sophistication. As noted by Dann (1971), some people might feel threatened by images of empty places, so festivals and events have the role of making a destination seem warm and friendly.

An event's planners highlight its most attractive components, taking care to portray a balanced image of the theme and range of experiences to be available. Festivals and events are perfect for visual communications, as they are by nature colorful and exciting. Visual media are also suitable for stimulating other sensory responses, including taste, smell, and touch. Television is an excellent medium for this, allowing both sight and sound stimulation.

The second element is the printed word. A good slogan can be a short-form message, conjuring up mental images of the event or destination attractions. Information about the destination or event can put into words the same messages depicted in visual media, or can highlight a picture. Too much information, however, will not enhance imagery.

Uzzell (1984) referred to the subject of semiotics, which is the study of the meanings of signs, symbols, and words, in explaining the image-making process. He noted that a *signifier* is a depicted object or scene that stands for something desired by the potential consumer. For example, scenes from festivals and special events can represent the good life, sophisticated cultural tastes, family fun, community spirit, or recreational excitement. Travel ads commonly feature sex appeal to signify fantasy and the good life, and entertainment events are sometimes featured in this way as well.

Authenticity is also an important consideration. Photos or scenes from community festivals and events can convey the image of a destination that provides access to residents and a look at their way of life. Scenes from events, whether tourists or locals are depicted, also generate a genuine image of the region. All too many travel ads are obviously faked, which has a negative influence on more sophisticated consumers. Festival and event images that include the audience have potentially greater credibility.

The Consumer Buying Process and Image-Making

Mill and Morrison (1985) summarized much of the thinking about how consumers make a decision to select a travel destination, and we can use this material to help in the marketing of festivals and special events. In particular, we want to identify the implications for image-making, both at the destination level and for individual events.

The buying process is a series of steps the consumer goes through in making a purchase and adopting a product: paying attention to the product or message; understanding it; adopting a positive attitude toward the product; forming an intention to purchase; making a purchase; adopting the product for regular consumption (brand loyalty).

Goals for marketing and promotion can be linked to these steps, beginning with the obvious need to inform potential markets of the event and to make certain the target markets comprehend the message. At this basic level, communicating an attractive image of the destination or event can be critical in overcoming the noise put out by competitors and all the other messages to which the consumer is exposed.

People perceive the world differently, even though they might receive the same information about it. Instead of getting their attention through detailed information, much of which will be ignored, forgotten, or misinterpreted, destination and event marketers can use a strong image that they hope will stand out, be recognized as a product offering (a potential trip or leisure experience), and stick in the mind because it is an attractive image. Something novel is likely to attract attention, and this can be the theme or the way in which it is communicated. An image of high quality, or an image appealing to a specific target market with known tastes, can also serve well at this stage.

Destination regions often use color photographs of scenery, cultural attractions—including events—and recreational activities to capture a reader's or viewer's attention and convey the image of an attractive destination choice. Little information accompanies these ads, but often there is a slogan: for example, It's Better in the Bahamas; Georgia on My Mind. This image is expected to remain in one's mind until an actual travel decision is made. For a specific event the same strategy can be employed, carefully building an attractive image over a long period of time in the hope that the event will become widely recognized. Identification of the event with a logo, slogan, mascots, or activities will help a great deal. Think of Quebec's Winter Carnival and the mascot Bonhomme Carnival, the fluffy snowman, will pop into mind. Try to think of the Olympics without an accompanying mental image of five interlocking rings.

The second goal is to persuade target markets to try the event or destination— to make a purchase. Some of the consumer research cited earlier demonstrates the importance of knowing consumer attitudes toward the destination or event, and using this to influence attitudes. Destinations that want to convey an image of an exciting place to visit, with plenty to see and do, can feature exciting events. Those developing a cultural image will prefer to illustrate arts and music festivals, among other attractions. The key at this stage of image-building (and related promotions) is to know which benefits to feature to which particular audience.

Similarly, the festival or event should aim to convince target markets that the event will provide the benefits they most desire. Promotions have to capture the essence of the event's appeal, and this can best be accomplished through development of an integrated theme. Events lacking a coherent theme will have trouble in convincing certain target groups that there is sufficient attraction to warrant a trip. Making direct comparisons with other events or attractions, or emulating their success, might work for some events.

Also important in the consumer decision process is image rectification or reorientation. Perceptions of a destination or event can be affected by bad publicity, resulting in negative attitudes. These have to be overcome through a change in image, or by building a strong image where one was absent. Given the numerous factors that influence perceptions and attitudes, most of which are beyond the control of marketing, image-making is often used defensively, when something goes wrong.

Research has found that a critical stage in the buying process is formulating the intent to purchase. This seems obvious, but consider the range of choices available to the consumer: many choices are looked upon favorably, but not all are practical. It is therefore insufficient merely to have a strong image and positive attitudes toward the product. This is why many destination tourist organizations conduct regular surveys of their target markets to measure awareness, attitude, and actual intent to travel to the destination within a fixed period of time. Some inducement might be required to convince the consumer to try a particular destination or event, and this becomes a matter of clever promotions or pricing.

Image-Making for Recurring and Onetime Events

For festival and event consumers, the purchase is a special occasion. Our earlier discussion of the tourism and event product revealed just how unique is the event experience, unlike the purchase of a tangible item at the supermarket or even the routine consumption of a hotel room or airline trip. Each festival or event "purchase" is a distinct experience in the life of the visitor, and it might be a once-in-a-lifetime experience. The image of a onetime event has to be constructed in such a way as to make it a must-see attraction. Emphasizing its uniqueness is essential, but there must be more. After all, many types of events have imitators, and television makes it possible to stay at home and witness something unique from anywhere in the world. So the image must combine uniqueness and the rewards that only being there, being part of it, can bring.

For recurring events, it is essential to make the experience so attractive and complete that repeat visits are assured and word-of-mouth promotions will be strong. Thus, the event itself is part of the image-making process. The integrated theme; high-quality goods, services, and entertainment; the setting; the staff and volunteers—all are instruments of image making. Similarly, each and every event is an integral part of the destination region's image enhancement. If the one event attended by the overseas visitor is a bad experience, the entire region will suffer the consequences.

Targeted benefits, aimed at the special interests of key market segments, are important for creating brand loyalty. Visitors who find exactly what they are after are likely to return. The image of the event or destination area should also employ the strengths of festivals and events to establish the image of a sophisticated, exciting place to come back to.

Adoption of the destination or event as a regular leisure or travel experience is vital to long-term success. This is achievable through the production of quality events or attractions and successful image-making, but it also needs reinforcement. Customers have to be reminded, comparisons have to be made to new imitators and competitors, and negative perceptions have to be corrected.

Implications for Promotion

It is now clear that the image of the destination is actually part of the product, and it can be created or enhanced by using the positive attributes of festivals and special events. Much of the work needed to create positive images is promotional, so at this point we have to get a bit ahead of ourselves and examine some practical ways in which promotions can help create the desired image.

Table 6-1 is a guide for promotion, specifically the messages and imagery associated with festivals and events, to create a favorable destination image and thereby influence the consumer buying process. Images can be used in a number of specific ways, as illustrated in the table: try to create a need or want, show how known needs of target segments can be met, create or enhance the destination theme, inform and influence perception of attractions and attractiveness, stress authenticity, correct negative images, overcome competitor noise, and encourage repeat visits.

Table 6-1. Sample Messages and Images for Destination Image-making

Objectives	Sample Messages and Images
Create a need or perceived need	Events are better than other forms of entertainment or attractions: stress uniqueness, infrequency, appeal to everyone (e.g., "this event is too special to miss!"; "everyone will be there")
Meet the needs and travel motives of target segments, both push and pull factors	Appeal to specialist interests (e.g., "for the wine connoisseur"; "only the best crafts are displayed"); appeal to common escape motives (e.g., "you're among friends here"; "don't get lost in the city crowds, come back to the country fair")
Create or enhance a destination theme	Events can make themes tangible (e.g., "sample the Games of Scottish Country"; "experience the Land of Lakes' fishing derbies, world-class regattas, and the best fish fries anywhere")
Inform consumers of the destination's attractions, and influence perceptions of attractiveness	Use the sensory stimulation of event ambience and activity to sell the area (e.g., "festival country comes alive"; "one event of many"; "your introduction to our special kind of hospitality")
Stress authenticity	(e.g., "no other place connects you to your roots the way our festival does")
Correct negative images	Create the impression that things are back to normal, or are improved (e.g., "the party continues"; "look who's got something to celebrate")
Create a hallmark event	(e.g., "Stratford and the Shakespearean Festival—inseparable, incomparable")
Overcome the noise of competition	Emphasize the spectacular, bizarre, unique (e.g., "world's only/biggest/best/first"); use events as attention-getters and lures (e.g., "come for the party, stay for the peace and quiet")
Encourage repeat visits	Stress newness and innovation (e.g., "have you tried our new food festival?"; "this is not the resort you thought you knew")

Organizational Development

Festivals and events can be looked upon as tourism products, but they cannot simply be built like a hotel, nor forced to become tourist attractions if their organizers or host communities are opposed or uninterested. The promotion of festivals or cultural celebrations and rituals as tourist attractions without regard for the wishes of the community is not only of questionable ethics, but also likely to be unproductive. To be successful tourist attractions, festivals and events must be planned and marketed as such, and the organizers must blend the elements of their production differently. In addition, more infrastructure is likely to be required for tourist-oriented events, particularly in the areas of transportation, information, communications, and safety and health services.

This is not to say that small, community festivals cannot be important tourism products. They will be discovered by some visitors even without promotion, and will be sought out specifically by others who search for authenticity and non-touristic events. And in the age of mass communications, most events could not avoid publicity of some kind.

Accordingly, the destination planners and marketers must carefully cultivate the festivals and events that are intended to be important elements in destination development and promotion strategies. This cultivation process involves organizational development, various forms of assistance to event organizers, and a respect for community wishes. In recalling our earlier discussion of community-based tourism planning, it is clear that community festivals and events provide an excellent opportunity for getting residents involved in thinking about their community tourism product and how far they want to go in balancing tourism goals with other reasons for holding the event.

Many tourist organizations and government departments have programs of assistance to festivals or communities that wish to become involved in tourism, and to groups that want to develop events for nontouristic reasons.

Manuals

The production of manuals on event planning, management, and marketing is another important way in which tourist destination organizations can assist festival and event organizers. Some basic advice and good examples are always useful, but the real value of such manuals is twofold: highlighting what is unique about the destination—its theme, history, grants programs, events already in existence, marketing research, and so on—and combining the manual with training workshops to provide personal education and counseling.

After reviewing a number of such manuals, several common weaknesses are apparent:

They tend either to be tourist-oriented or to ignore tourism. A more comprehensive approach is needed, in which all the perspectives and roles are discussed and given equal value.

Attention is not given equally to planning, marketing, organizing, management, and evaluation. Impact assessment and evaluation are sometimes ignored.

Information on what events already exist, and on good or bad examples, is sketchy. All organizers can benefit from detailed comparisons.

Model forms, planning processes, survey designs, cost-benefit methods, and other specific applications generally are not provided. The assumption seems to be that manuals are for amateurs and beginners, but this will not remain true for long, given the growth of professional organizations and formal education opportunities in the field.

Mobile Events

There are numerous mobile events that can be attracted to a destination. Sporting events predominate, but certain arts festivals, fairs, and exhibitions are also international in their venues. The Olympics and world's fairs are highly coveted, but many lesser events can also function as mega-events to the hosts. Business-related conventions and meetings fall in the category of events to be attracted, as do some visits by dignitaries or political or governmental groups.

Most mobile events have to be held regularly and so are dependent on their value as tourism attractions, image makers, or catalysts to motivate interested hosts. The most attractive ones, however, are usually in high demand and must be lured to a specific location through a bidding process. An observer can easily get the impression that many host nations or communities enter into the bidding without adequate attention to the implications, particularly to the full costs and benefits. To avoid that problem, a feasibility study is essential.

The Feasibility Study and the Bid

The term *feasibility study* has a number of connotations, often implying only an assessment of affordability or profitability. But it must also be a comprehensive evaluation of how desirable and suitable an event proposal is. All too often, so-called feasibility studies merely assess the ability of the organizers to find the facilities and generate the resources necessary to launch the event, without considering the broader and more important issues of whether or not it is in everyone's interest. The proposed event should not only play a role in the destination plan, but also be acceptable and supportable to the host community. Not only must it be financially sound, but its full costs and benefits should be evaluated.

Sparrow (1987) outlined key stages of the bidding process, based on his experience with the 1987 America's Cup defense in Western Australia. First is conceptualization of the event and how to get it, which then must be "sold" to the important authorities. Initial acceptance of the idea is likely to be based on at least a preliminary study that assigns some estimated numbers to the costs and benefits expected. Given a decision that the idea is viable and the risks acceptable, a formal commitment will be necessary. Subsequently, a bidding group, and perhaps a separate marketing group, must be established to make and sell the bid; see Ueberroth (1985), for example, on how the Los Angeles Olympics of 1984 had to be marketed to the International Olympics Committee. Competition for the event must be evaluated and countervailing strategies developed. A variety of formal and informal promotions can be used, including familiarization tours for the decision makers, lobbying, and recruitment of influential people—especially prominent politicians—as spokespersons.

Finally, if the bid is accepted, a detailed feasibility study becomes essential and a full planning and marketing process established. Sparrow said this stage requires the appointment of a key player, or group, to steer the process, imaging the event to give it profile and build support, intensive public and private sector collaboration (especially to mobilize the tourist industry), planning for impacts, and detailed market research. As described in detail in Chapter 9, Western Australia's experience with the 1987 America's Cup shows that this process takes years, and great flexibility as well.

Some organizations specify the bid format, but even so there will likely be room for embellishment or public relations. Several special cases can arise for which the destination planners should have a contingency plan. Sometimes proposals will be made independently, leaving the tourist organization to react. If the proposal is good, there might be no problem other than coordination. If it is bad, the tourist organization might have to attempt to dissuade the proponents or otherwise dispose of it.

The politics of attracting events, especially mega-events, is sometimes bizarre and frightening. Several authors have noted how irrationality, rather than sound planning, tends to accompany the pursuit of events (Armstrong 1985, Butler and Grigg 1987). In such cases there is likely to be tension or outright hostility between proponents and those who insist on detailed feasibility studies and cost-benefit assessments. Chapter 10 deals with the cost-benefit method, which can be used both before and after the event.

Although each feasibility study is likely to be almost unique, a logical sequence of steps can be recommended on the basis of the foregoing discussion.

The first step is to formulate a concept plan or description of the proposed event, its purpose and related goals, and potential impact. Specific points to cover in this event profile include

- Venue, facility, and infrastructure requirements
- Financial resources required; potential sponsors and other sources
- Human resources required
- Likely demand for the event, based on past experience
- Potential types and scale of impact: social, cultural, economic, and environmental
- Selection criteria: what does it take to get the event?

The second step examines how the proposed event relates to established destination goals and plans, and what potential roles it could play. Specific objectives should be determined, pertaining to ways to overcome seasonality; the geographic spread of tourism; theme creation and image enhancement; employment creation; income generation; methods of attracting domestic versus foreign tourists; linkages to other events; packaging and tours; and use of the event as a catalyst for economic development, infrastructure, and other tourism projects.

Could these goals and objectives be met in other ways? What are the alternatives and opportunity costs?

Proponents of the event next should demonstrate that the venue, host community, and destination area all have the capacity to absorb the event and its effects. This requires a detailed forecasting and evaluation of the potential impact, generally based on experience with other events, and consideration of how positive effects can be maximized and how negative ones or costs can be avoided or ameliorated.

More important, will the event fit the proposed venue and area? This matter of suitability is ignored too often, but it can be vital in determining the success of the event, as well as its impact. A number of points can be considered, although every situation is unique:

- Any track record of hosting successful events
- The nature of the population, such as cosmopolitanism, wealth, interests, and receptiveness to new ideas
- Availability of volunteers and leaders, sponsors and supporters
- Politics and ideology
- Sophistication in organizing events

Public input is vital at this stage, to determine levels of support or opposition and which issues must be resolved.

Detailed market research for a major event is expensive and time-consuming, so this next step might have to be undertaken in several stages. Although some indication of potential demand, which can be based on past experience, was needed at the initial stage of concept formulation, full forecasting of market potential eventually will be necessary, involving selection of target markets, consideration of price, formulation of a promotions strategy, and estimation of visitor spending. A decision to host or bid on an event could be made without marketing research, but that would not be wise. Marketing is not just promotions designed to sell the event; marketing research can help determine if the event is viable, how much it will cost, and what its impact could be.

At this stage it should be possible to estimate the likely costs and revenues, and thereby calculate financial feasibility. In other words, can we afford it? The more adventuresome might ask, if we commit ourselves, can we raise the money? A risk assessment is vital, for obvious reasons. What happens if the grants or revenues fail to materialize or costs escalate? Who pays? It would be wise to consider the potential for political disruption, the effects of bad weather, and possible organizational failure.

Economic feasibility is slightly different, pertaining more to the community or destination as a whole. Opportunity costs must be considered, as well as the possibility of adverse economic impact. Long-term gains and losses also must be assessed.

The next step is a comprehensive cost-benefit evaluation. The tangible economic costs and benefits to the destination area and host community must be compared and intangibles considered subjectively. Financial or economic considerations should not predominate, but equal consideration must be given to social, cultural, and environmental factors. Even if the benefit-to-cost ratio is favorable, that alone is not sufficient grounds to proceed; it might very well be that some costs are not acceptable under any circumstances, such as destruction of heritage or ecological damage. It is also possible to conclude that the potential benefits, however much they are in excess of costs, do not justify the effort required, or that the benefits are too concentrated in a few hands to warrant public investment. These considerations are discussed in detail in Chapter 10.

In the end, an open debate should be held on the relative merits of the proposed event, and a political decision taken on whether to proceed. If a formal bidding process is required, the major components of the bid could include the following:

- Profile of the group making the bid and accepting responsibility for the event and its financing
- Support already obtained for the bid
- Summary of the event concept
- Details of the plan—venue, facilities, investments, timing, scheduling, programming, and meeting all criteria
- Forecast of attendance, part of a marketing plan
- Assertion of financial and economic feasibility, in a financial plan and budget
- Forecast of impact, along with contingency plans
- Highlights of the legacy
- Advantages over competitors for the event

As a final key step in this process, it would be wise to have a management and marketing plan in place, or at least drafted, prior to winning a bid. Indeed, its existence might influence the bid decision. A research, monitoring, and evaluation system is an essential component, as are contingency plans for anticipatable emergencies. A detailed business plan and budget has to be formulated and constantly updated. Control mechanisms must be put in place to ensure adherence to the budget. Political lobbying, public relations, and image enhancement also cannot be overlooked.

Destination-Wide Events

Beyond organizational development and assistance to individual organizers or events, destination planners can help create events at the level of regions or nations.

So important are special events to governments for political and social reasons, and to tourism and development agencies for economic reasons, that increasingly we are witnessing the creation of events more or less out of the blue. In this category are anniversaries, such as the Australian bicentennial in 1988 and the bicentennial of the French Revolution in 1989, which are deliberately expanded into a combination of planned mega-events and an enormous number and variety of community celebrations. Grants are given, political pressures are exerted, and the media and governmental public relations corps are mobilized to maximize publicity and to foster a patriotic feeling of association with the events. These created events also tend to generate controversy over the symbolism, the theme, historical authenticity, or political interpretations. The spending of public money on such celebrations is usually criticized by some but praised by others.

As documented elsewhere in this book, anniversaries have had a significant effect on generating lasting festivals and events. However, there must be some limit to the ability of governments to stimulate more, better, or bigger events. And if the celebration is perceived to be contrived and lacks public support, the effects on event tourism might actually be negative.

Event Packages and Tours

One very noticeable gap in most destination areas is the absence of event packages and tours. The explosion of festivals and special events in communities of all sizes and in all locations seems to present unlimited opportunities for themed packages and circular tours. What has become common is the practice of attracting bus tours to specific events, but usually in an uncoordinated way, which minimizes benefit to the destination as a whole. Mega-events have also generated an array of packages and other promotions to encourage long-distance travelers to stay longer and see more of the host country or region.

Tours and packages in event tourism can be categorized as follows:

- By theme (for example, a tour of food festivals)
- By area and theme (cultural events of "Scottish Country")
- By season (fall fair tour)
- By circuits (linking gateway cities to hinterland events)
- Piggybacking (linking minor events to major event attractions)

With imagination, festivals can also be constructed of package tours, such as a touring festival of winter carnivals or village fetes. Similarly, a festival of castles, markets, country towns, or cowboy heritage can be organized to consist of a package tour to special events in each setting. But this will be a misuse of the term *festival* if there is nothing more to the package than a bus ride. The festive nature of the tour should be highlighted through various activities and creation of a celebratory atmosphere. Events can be organized at each stop in the tour, so that community celebrations match the tour group's festivities.

Geographic Distribution

To meet the goal of spreading tourist demand throughout the destination area, a number of strategies can be employed. Figure 6-1 illustrates in graphic form some of the products that can be created by linking or packaging events, although it must be stressed that none of these can be effective without strong promotion.

The first strategy consists of center-based tours radiating outward from large cities, resorts, or gateways—transportation hubs where travelers congregate— all of which have considerable potential for both daylong and weekend trips by visitors and residents alike. Events that otherwise would not have strong tourist appeal can be promoted to residents and tourists as day-trips, or as circular tours lasting one or more nights. The day-trip strategy is easier, because circular tours require a number of events to occur simultaneously or consecutively. This strategy is designed to get tourists out of the main destination, and residents out of their city. Given the existing tendency for festivals to emerge within day-trip range of major cities, there should be considerable potential to package and promote the tours.

A related strategy is the regional tour, in which the primary attraction is a sequence of stops at festivals and special events. In this case, tourists are transported to the destination region and escorted to events that, ideally, highlight the main theme or themes of the area. Alternatively, independent travelers can be provided with information to permit their own selection. In both cases, other attractions can form part of the package, but it will be most successful if the events themselves are featured. Again, the main problem will be fostering sufficient numbers of good-quality, themed events to facilitate the tours. A clustering of events in space or time could have maximum impact.

Piggybacking can be used in conjunction with tours. It is the practice of creating or promoting minor events on the back of major events occurring

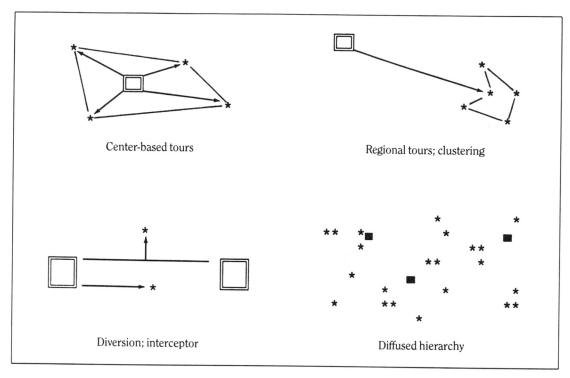

Figure 6-1. Spatial strategies for event tourism.

before or afterward, in order to extend the length of visits or expand the tourists' area of travel. If a mega-event is to be held in a large city, outlying communities can capitalize on the promotions and increased visitor numbers to pull a share of visitors their way, either singly or in tours. Joint promotions with the mega-event will work best. Although sponsors of the main attraction might not like the competition, it should actually benefit all parties by helping attract wider audiences—assuming a variety of events is offered—and spreading demand, which can avoid overcrowding.

A related idea is that of clustering small events in the same area, either in sequence or all at once, to achieve a higher level of awareness and attractiveness than could be achieved by small events independently. In this way, some destinations attempt to simulate the effects of a mega-event, without the large investment. A variation is that of spinning off subordinate events from the main anchor event. For example, the city core might host a festival of performing arts, but individual concerts and competitions could be spread out to the suburbs and regional communities. In this way, not only is the festival brought closer to the people, but target segments of tourists can be diverted to the outlying venues to performances having specialist appeal.

Another distribution strategy, the diversion, is an event created and situated to pull travelers away from established corridors. A lure is needed to call attention to an otherwise obscure event. For example, if there is considerable highway traffic between points A and B, the potential exists to lure some of the motorists to a nearby event, if only for a few hours. Signs, information at stopping places, or gimmicks such as highly visible balloons or skywriting are possible tactics that can be used.

Finally, interceptors are events designed to deflect or stop traffic from reaching another intended destination. They can be used to outperform a perceived competitor, such as where a rival event is created or scheduled specifically to draw some of the same market. For example, a town along the route between a city and another destination can hold its own events on the day of the competitor's festival. However, the regional tourist organization would be smart to encourage cooperation so this form of customer stealing is avoided.

Another example of interceptor events might be the creation of festivals or programs designed to reduce pressure on sensitive parks or natural areas. The British invented country parks to attract day-trippers from the large cities, in the hope that travel to the more sensitive national parks would be reduced. They called these "honey pots," alluding perhaps to the collection of flies around anything sweet. To be successful, however, the interceptor events must be highly attractive and timed to coincide with peak visitation to the protected area.

A variation of the interceptor might be called the interpreter. Within a park or sensitive area, interpretive events can be used to concentrate traffic that otherwise might disperse throughout the area. These events have the added advantage of permitting the education of visitors.

Figure 6-1 also illustrates what is called a diffused hierarchy of festivals and special events, consisting of major, intermediate, and minor attractions—for example, mega-events, regional attractions, and local events and activity outlets. This is a possible ultimate spatial strategy to spread benefits uniformly, and it might tend to evolve naturally in some regions.

None of the strategies for dispersing tourists will have the desired impact if the host communities cannot take advantage of their presence. Overnight stays are the most desirable, requiring suitable infrastructure and the careful scheduling of events to encourage stays. Weekend times are preferred, and planners of longer events would be wise to spread their activities over two weekends, with an anchor event at each end.

To summarize, festivals and special events have considerable potential for spreading tourism demand throughout a destination area. In this respect, they are different from permanent attractions in several ways:

Events can be sequenced to encourage repeat visits, tours, and piggyback situations.

They are often quite independent of the natural resource base or permanent facilities, and so can be held almost anywhere.

Interpretive events can usually be held without damage to sensitive environments.

Their potential for theming and image creation is also somewhat independent of the visible environment; the event theme can rub off on the community or other attractions.

Variety is potentially unlimited: events of different themes can be held in the same locations.

If necessary, events can be moved to take advantage of new opportunities, to facilitate regional tours, or to leave locations that lack community support.

Seasonality

Some of the spatial strategies discussed above actually involve scheduling decisions, especially for tours. The seasonality issue is somewhat different; in essence, it is the choice between holding events in the peak tourist season or at other times of the year.

Many destination areas and communities have opted to hold their events in the established tourist season, normally summer, whereas others prefer to create off-peak demand. Different factors must be considered in this decision, including tourism goals and feasibility.

Peak-Season Events

The main advantages of holding events in the peak tourist season can be stated simply:

Competitive advantage can be gained over destinations that are without events.

Themes are easier to establish when large numbers of visitors are exposed quickly to the images and events.

The local tourist industry is already geared up for crowds, and promotions are already in place.

The weather is generally better and more predictable; Main Street festivals and other outdoor events are best held in dry, warm weather, not the hottest or coldest or wettest times of year.

Volunteers can use vacations to help out.

In resort areas with many second homes, the seasonal visitors may feel a part of the community and want to participate.

Off-Peak Events

Advantages of the off-peak event are also significant:

Tourist demand is created when spare capacity is high.

It can encourage a four-season destination image.

It provides entertainment for residents when other opportunities are limited.

It might be easier to attract performers or displayers who are normally busy in the peak season.

Certain sports competitions are seasonal by nature.

Organizational capability might be highest, as most local groups will be meeting regularly and members will be at home.

Funding might be easier to obtain if an expanded tourist season can be created.

A destination region naturally will want to develop a range of events throughout the year, but it is restricted by the ability of communities or organizations to mount them, and by other factors such as the climate. Achieving a good seasonal balance should be one of the major goals of destination planning, but because of the relative ease of developing events in the peak season, many events or organizers might require financial or other inducements from tourist organizations to create off-season event attractions.

Resorts and built attractions might actually find it easier to create appealing off-season events, especially if they have the staff and facilities to hold indoor events, or offer indoor backup venues. To fill accommodation in slow months, many resorts have launched programs of special events combined with price discounting or other incentives. Other resorts attract events, usually sports competitions, to create the image of a major all-season attraction.

The Product Life Cycle

Just as individual events tend to go through stages of growth, maturity, and decline, so too might the destination region's themes and event tourism products. This concept, which Butler (1980) called the "tourist area cycle of evolution," suggests that a lack of planning, inability to control tourist volume and impact, or changing preferences can result in the decline of a destination's quality and popularity. Knowing this can happen, the destination planner must take measures to prevent serious problems, while the destination marketer must examine ways to broaden the area's appeal and/or adapt the product. In effect, this is a matter of long-term product-market matching.

Haywood (1986) argued that the destination cycle of evolution was unproven, particularly with respect to the question of whether or not decline is inevitable. He suggested that destination planners should examine different strategies for extension or rejuvenation and should carefully monitor the markets to detect any indication of stagnation. Haywood also put forward an interesting hypothesis: that narrow, overspecialized destinations might have a shorter life cycle than those with broader-based appeal.

To the extent that festivals and events broaden the destination's appeal and keep its attractions fresh and competitive, event tourism is one strategy for life cycle extension. However, there is a risk in constantly seeking a broader market base. If, for example, a heritage or cultural product is constantly augmented by new, unrelated attractions, it could easily result in damage to the cultural base of the area. A better strategy is to broaden appeal with events that fit the theme and do not artificially attract new segments that might be unsympathetic to heritage conservation.

Another possible strategy is to shift themes and imagery. In fact, it is common for large tourist organizations to change their slogans and themes periodically, often by imitating another's successful promotion campaign. But smaller areas, communities, and attractions cannot "change their colors" frequently. As noted already, large destinations foster general themes through vague but upbeat imagery, while smaller units must strive for specific themes and clear, distinguishable images. Events, which can be created, moved, and adapted, are potential instruments for shifting themes and adapting imagery while at the same time providing concrete, new products for tourists.

Destination tourist organizations should also specifically evaluate the need for new or improved packages and tours of events, and they must monitor the number, types, quality, and effectiveness of individual events in the area. Janiskee (1985) cautioned that the number and distribution of events in South Carolina towns and rural areas appeared to have reached a saturation level, and that increasing competition would result. Eventually, he thought, a "dynamic steady-state" would evolve, in which few new events would emerge and most existing ones would achieve stable demand; some, however, might decline or disappear. The destination tourist organization might therefore have to try continually to assess supply-demand balance in the event tourism market and develop policies and programs of assistance and promotions that strive to maintain a profitable balance for all the events.

It might help to determine the hierarchical array of events in a destination, by examining their types, sizes, and distribution. It seems logical to expect a large number of small events in communities throughout a populated area, a smaller number of events with regional attractiveness to tourists, and a few events with larger appeal (see Figure 6-1). In this diffused hierarchy, occasional mega-events could occur without disturbing the balance. This pattern approximates the "central place" distribution of retailing that researchers have documented, but there is as yet insufficient evidence to suggest any laws of event hierarchies.

PROMOTIONS

Almost all tourist organizations engage in promotion of events to some degree, but in many cases this has not gone beyond a simple and boring listing of events in annual or seasonal calendars. Providing concise, readily accessible information to the customer is important, but information and promotion are different. A sophisticated promotion mix will aim to alter the potential consumer's perceptions and images of the destination and directly affect the buying decision. Different messages and media are used to reach target segments with known preferences or motives. Promotions must also be modified according to the stage of the product in its life cycle—seeking initially to inform, then to create a demand, and finally to reinforce brand loyalty.

Creating a promotional mix consists of finding the most cost-effective balance of advertising, personal selling, sales promotion, and publicity. Research at many events has demonstrated that newspapers and word of mouth are often the primary media by which festival customers get their information, but that is partly because most festivals have a predominantly local market. Special events with more targeted appeal, such as sports or arts, might find different media are necessary to reach their primary audiences. Mega-events planned in hope of gaining national and international appeal require massive promotional campaigns of very high sophistication. All these aspects of promoting individual events are covered in detail in the next two chapters.

Destination tourist organizations have several specific promotional tasks: creating the desired image, disseminating information about events, and coordinating the promotional efforts of numerous events and assisting small events to get adequate promotion. Here we are concerned most with the information function, specifically event calendars and general travel guides for destinations, and the role of the destination tourist agency in coordinating promotions.

Dissemination of Information

A review of event calendars and travel guides for numerous destinations reveals a generally unsophisticated approach to event promotion and coordination. The prevailing mode is that of an annual or seasonal event calendar, standing alone or as part of a more comprehensive guide, which merely lists events without a description of their characteristics and without any theming or packaging. Some innovations and good examples are highlighted below to assist other destination tourist organizations.

Destination Event Calendars

North Carolina's Calendar of Events for January through August 1989 (North Carolina Department of Commerce 1989) contained photos of events and activities. It began with a message intended to stimulate an interest in reading on: "North Carolina has long been known as Variety Vacationland. And nowhere is this distinction more fitting than when it comes to our festivals, fairs and celebrations! You are cordially invited to enjoy more than 1,700 events, ranging from the traditional to the unusual."

The *Minnesota Explorer* is a seasonal (three times a year) promotion in newspaper format that embodies color photos, feature articles, and an event calendar (Minnesota Office of Tourism 1988, 1989). The format is too large for easy storage, but its promotional value is considerably greater than that of small booklets with dry listings of events. In the Spring–Summer 1989 *Minnesota Explorer* were features with these journalistic-style titles: "Minneapolis Aquatennial Turns Golden"; "Ethnic Fests"; "Past Lives on at Theme Park"; "Rendezvous Characters Preserve Lifestyle of Voyageur Era." Minnesota also publishes a separate Calendar of Events seasonally and in the same newspaper format. In the Spring–Summer 1989 issue was an article describing an innovative event: "Judy Garland's Hometown Honors 'Oz' Story With Festival."

"Nevada Events, A Guide for Travelers" (*Nevada Magazine* 1989) uses a glossy magazine format with color photos and advertisements. It is included in each issue of the more comprehensive *Nevada Magazine.* The January/February 1989 issue contained "Events Previews," which are articles on upcoming events including festivals, theater, and arts center productions. Nevada's tourist regions were themed, so that the article on "Elko's Cowboy Poetry Gathering" actually promoted the town of Elko, the festival, and the region Nevada calls Covered Wagon Territory; other territories are named Pony Express, Pioneer, Reno Tahoe, and Las Vegas, which clearly separates the two urban themes from the rural areas.

Although there is some convenience and definite cost economy in producing simple calendar listings of events, they do not do justice to individual events nor to the collective attractiveness of festivals and events in promoting the destination as a whole. Presumably many tourist organizations look upon the calendars mostly as a cheap way to assist the events, but this attitude is shortsighted. The examples cited above demonstrate that attractive formats, photos, and feature stories are far better ways to communicate and promote the excitement and diversity of special events. Even if only a small proportion of the listed events can be featured in each issue, all the others are likely to benefit from increased consumer interest in the publication. Better still would be a series of attractive event calendars for each region or theme, each including more detailed descriptions of all the listed events.

General Travel Guides

The all-purpose destination travel guide is probably the most common promotional publication, and it often contains an event section or calendar. A major problem is that the event calendar can easily get lost among the details or the advertisements. On the other hand, it provides a key opportunity to feature festivals and events, or photos of events, to enhance overall attractiveness and create a sense of excitement. After all, how many pictures just of nice scenery and outdoor recreation will the average reader pay attention to? It is probable that the imagery of group activity at special events has stronger appeal than photos with no people and no activity in them. Some examples are provided below to illustrate the potential for improving the event components in general travel guides, and for using events to enhance the guides.

The *1989 Kentucky Travel Guide* (Editorial Services Co. Inc. 1989) contained a unique section called "1989 Festivals in Kentucky." It included a short message from the Kentucky Festival Association, a map showing festival towns, and a small box for each festival in which the name, logo, and address were prominent. Full-color printing allows the different events to take advantage of attractive design and catch the reader's eye.

For 1989 the state of South Dakota and its four regional tourist associations published a *Vacation Guide Official Centennial Edition* (South Dakota Department of Tourism n.d.). The year's theme was Celebrate the Century, and the whole guide featured events of local and statewide significance, with color photos prominent. The governor, George Mickelson, introduced the guide with a stirring invitation: "If it's events you're looking for, South Dakota's centennial calendar is loaded with a potpourri of cultural celebrations and family festivities. You can celebrate your South Dakota adventure with homemade ethnic food, wagon train rides, rip-roaring rodeos, community plays, old-time threshing jamborees and much much more." Although this type of exuberance is often reserved for celebration series, typical of anniversaries, there is no reason festivals and special events cannot be as successful in promoting most destinations at other times.

Indiana also organized a created series of events, in 1988, under the theme Hoosier Celebration '88. It was actually a homecoming promotion, and in the state's travel guide, *Indiana, the Wander Book* (Indiana Department of Commerce, Tourism Development Division n.d.), the homecoming theme was featured. Over 300 communities were reported to have planned celebrations during the year, some newly created and others adapted for the theme. The effect of the travel guide was to convey the message that something special was happening, and, regardless of the theme, there is an appeal to tourists associated with being part of something special. If the celebrations are authentic community events, the appeal for some outsiders is actually greater than that of obviously tourist-oriented events.

Canada's Northwest Territories Explorer's Guide (TravelArctic, Government of the Northwest Territories n.d.) featured a special series of events in 1989. A one-page ad described the 200th anniversary of the voyage of Alexander Mackenzie down the river that now bears the explorer's name. To mark this anniversary a group from Lakehead University in Ontario re-created the canoe voyage, and the territories marked this with a summer-long celebration. Indian communities staged special events such as feasts, dances, and craft displays for visitors and residents in conjunction with the canoe expedition. A special tour package was created to take advantage of the celebrations, including the opportunity to actually canoe with the expedition.

Saskatchewan has divided the province into five distinct and named regions. In *The Great Saskatchewan Vacation Book* (Saskatchewan Department of Economic Development and Tourism n.d.), the Cowboy Country destination was introduced this way: "It's time to don your stetson and practice your western drawl. This is cowboy country. The excitement begins the moment you arrive!" How will the tourist actually experience this excitement? By sightseeing? No, by going to the featured rodeos and festivals, as well as to the historic sites and museums with interpretive events. The Saskatchewan travel guide also included detailed road maps and descriptions of individual communities in which their attractions and events were listed. Color photos were used to reinforce the themes.

Texas created an evocative promotional theme called Texas, It's a Whole Other Country. The state's travel guide (Texas Department of Commerce n.d.) described it this way: "Texas culture is a patchwork quilt stitched from the flags of six nations. . . ." The guide featured festivals, fests, regattas, fiestas, and fetes to illustrate the cultural diversity and historical richness of the destination.

The Province of Quebec is very big on special events, particularly in the main cities of Montreal and Quebec. Its Fêtes Populaires are primarily cultural and community celebrations for residents, but they also attract tourists. In its *Quebec Vacation Guide* (Quebec Ministry of Tourism 1988) the message was clear: "Summer '88 in Quebec is shaping up to be one of the most eventful ever! Big name international art, music, and entertainment of all kinds. All celebrated in a big way! So come say Bonjour and come join the celebration." The booklet began with a section on "Major Events" including festivals, concerts, art shows, and Grand Prix motorcar racing. About Montreal, the guide declared: "On any list of the world's favorite cities you're bound to find Montreal. . . . The spirit of Montreal was heralded worldwide during Expo '67, perhaps the most memorable world's fair of them all. Millions came, then returned in '76 when Montreal hosted the Olympic Games." Here is a classic example of the long-lasting image generated by mega-events, and the enduring legacy of numerous special events to capitalize on the afterglow.

Montreal's own tourist guide for 1988–89 (Greater Montreal Convention and

Tourism Bureau and Quebec Ministry of Tourism n.d.) also basked in the glory of its previous mega-events, noting that Expo '67 attracted over 50 million visits and that subsequently the city has been the host of a "plethora of international events." Cultured, cosmopolitan, and full of *joie de vivre* are themes running through the city's tourist guide. Special events of all kinds reinforce the message.

Prince Edward Island, Canada's smallest province, depends greatly on summer tourists who come for the Atlantic beaches, rural charm, cultural flavor, and history. In 1988 the province launched a special promotion of environmental attractions, called Touch Nature 1988. The *1988 Visitors Guide* (Prince Edward Island Department of Tourism and Parks n.d.) featured the theme, associated with several festivals (Irish Moss, Oysters, Fisheries, Lobster) and an Interpretive Week at provincial parks with special events such as Birds and Breakfast. The *1989 Visitors Guide* (Prince Edward Island Department of Parks and Tourism n.d.) had feature pages with color photos to promote two festivals: Festival of the Descendants was intended as a 125th anniversary of the Charlottetown Conference, which led to the Canadian Confederation; the food, music, and fun of the 1860s were re-created for the festival. The second event, called A Salute to the Irish, was a commemoration of 150 years of Irish settlement. The guidebook referred to this event as the "wildest Irish party." The province's visitor's guides also included circular motoring tours, each with a name. Among the map symbols were ones for various attractions, services, and festivals and events.

Georgia on My Mind: The Official Travel Guide for the State of Georgia (Georgia Department of Industry and Trade n.d.) in 1989 contained a page on the fairs and festivals of the state. This hardly seems significant, but the guide also included two coupons to clip and send for more information on any of the twenty listed events. This kind of inclusion may encourage readers to pursue more detailed information.

Coordination of Promotions

Most of the assistance that tourist destination organizations give to individual events appears to be related to promotions, typically through the coordination and publication of event calendars or mentions in travel guides. Some authorities have added financial assistance for promotions, either aimed at event organizations or provided generally to all tourist businesses.

Chapter 4 contained a review of selected government initiatives pertaining to assisting events, but one specific example of assistance to promotions warrants mention here: the Michigan Travel Bureau Cooperative Advertising Program (Michigan Travel Bureau n.d.). Through 1988 and 1989, $1 million was available for the purpose of promoting the state, a region, or a segment of the industry. On a matching-funds basis—the amount of assistance equals the amount of money committed by the applicant—regional or local nonprofit organizations related to the travel industry could obtain help, but individual events or businesses could not. Each promotion had to incorporate the state's logo: "Yes M!ch!gan, Celebrate! The Great Lakes." This kind of program encourages destination coordination, rather than competition, and combines state promotion with regional or local initiatives. In 1989 the Michigan Travel Bureau was also providing financial assistance to the state's Council for the Humanities to hold six festivals that reinforced the "Celebrate! The Great Lakes" theme.

SUMMARY

Product development and marketing are closely interrelated and sometimes indistinguishable; this is particularly true for festivals and events. Creation of both destination themes and positive images was explored first. Events are able to help generate positive images, attract attention, and tangibly express destination themes. An examination of how images are shaped was undertaken, concentrating on the consumer buying process. Table 6-1 provided sample messages and images for important objectives pertaining to destination image-making, using events as the image or using messages about events.

A discussion of advisory manuals revealed that an overly simplistic approach predominated. Government and tourist agencies can better assist the less well organized events by giving more comprehensive and specific advice, especially pertaining to the roles of events in destination planning and marketing. More research and evaluation case studies are needed, however.

Attracting events, especially mega-events and highly prized international events, is a role for governments and industry in partnership. Chapter 6 contained specific advice on conducting comprehensive feasibility studies and making bids for events. Much more than monetary considerations must be included, as the suitability of the event to the host community, and the potential costs and benefits, are critical factors.

Creating events, above and beyond the impact of providing assistance to event organizations, is another aspect of product development in destination event tourism. Governments are fond of anniversary celebrations, which have a potent impact on creating and enlarging events, as demonstrated in several examples mentioned throughout the book and the case study of Australia (the 1988 bicentennial). Another approach is to create packages and tours of events, or that feature events as attractions and activity outlets. Different categories of packages and tours were defined—by theme, area and theme, season, circuits, and piggybacking. Figure 6-1 illustrated several spatial strategies that can be used.

Although festivals and special events are useful in enlarging tourist seasons and overcoming seasonality problems, many are held in the peak tourist season. Relative advantages and disadvantages were discussed, with the conclusion that assistance and incentives might be required to encourage the creation of new off-season events, or the shifting of established events to different times of the year.

Concluding the discussion of destination event tourism product development was an assessment of the pertinence of the product life cycle, or tourist area cycle of evolution. The theory is that inevitably markets shift, product quality declines, or problems caused by development and crowding lead to a decline of destination popularity. Events can help avoid decline, or instigate renewal, by diversifying the attractiveness of the area or by changing or reestablishing a positive image.

The remainder of Chapter 6 dealt with promotions. Numerous examples were given to illustrate how general travel guides and event calendars could be improved to make use of the attractiveness of events, and how it is better to feature a small number of festivals and events rather than provide a boring listing of them all.

CHAPTER SEVEN

Planning and Marketing for Individual Events

This chapter and the next focus on planning and marketing for the individual festival and event, with the underlying assumption that the organizers want their event to be a tourist attraction or want tourists to be an important part of their market. Even if this is not the case, the concepts and methods will still be useful for attracting and holding local audiences.

Should festivals and events attempt to become tourist attractions? It is for the organizers and host communities to decide, but there are obvious advantages in doing at least some target marketing, if not general tourism marketing:

Tourists can be a vital component of the audience, in both the first-time and repeat visit categories.

Tourists tend to spend more, thereby enhancing an event's revenue-generating potential.

Demonstrating success as a tourist attraction is likely to increase the organization's ability to obtain grants, sponsors, and political support.

The product development and marketing concepts used to develop tourism potential can be effective in creating better community events.

Adopting a customer orientation, necessary for tourist attractions, will provide a positive philosophy to guide the organizers and volunteers.

What makes the difference between tourist-oriented and other events is the management or marketing philosophy. Some event organizers will not see any tourism potential; others will deliberately oppose it for its potential to commercialize the event or attract the "wrong" audience. Many event producers are content to sell the product they have developed; others, however, employ marketing to develop and improve the product in ways that can maximize local and tourist appeal.

Tourist organizations therefore have an educational task in fostering improved understanding of the roles of festivals and special events in tourism strategies, and in teaching marketing and product development concepts and methods. Of course, tourist organizations can simply go on promoting events as tourist attractions anyway, but that tactic can be counterproductive. Instead, a process of education and organizational development will be more positively received.

This chapter begins with a model for the marketing planning process for events, followed by a discussion of its major elements. Chapter 8 completes the examination of the marketing planning model, commencing with promotions.

One element not fully covered in this book is the actual how-to process of event production or program planning; that task is left to those with direct experience in the business of event operations. The material covered in this chapter is of value to event producers, however, and many good production ideas presented throughout the book are taken from successful events.

A MODEL OF THE MARKETING PLANNING PROCESS

In terms of marketing planning, bear in mind that several characteristics of special events set them apart from other businesses and organizations:

Tourism is often not an explicit goal, or is a minor consideration of the organizers.

Special events are often managed and produced by voluntary, not-for-profit groups or involve many volunteers.

Many events do not have professional staff or are managed by staff whose responsibility for events is a minor part of their job.

Mega-events are likely to be mobile and controlled by national or international bodies, but require massive community-level support and organization for onetime productions.

Events are services, with largely intangible products subject to direct influence by the staff and customers; management must strive to improve these relationships to create a special ambience and satisfy specific customer needs.

Event organizers and producers often participate fully in the event, so they can be seen as performers as well as managers.

The image and theme, not just the quality of service and the tangible product, are critical.

Formulating a comprehensive management or marketing plan is such an enormous task that many event organizers are likely not even to attempt it. Getz and Frisby (1988) found that most volunteer organizers of community festivals did not engage in sophisticated planning or marketing, although a majority did have formal goals and objectives in some format (Table 7-1). Many even preferred not to professionalize or become more sophisticated, for fear of losing their community foundation. Others appeared to be forced into an informal management style by the absence of resources.

For the most part, only larger event organizations will be able to fully develop a management and marketing planning process. But all organizers must be aware of the issues, concepts, and methods associated with this systematic approach. Once understood, the model will influence decision making. It is really a thought process intended to structure the ideas and analysis of the manager and decision maker.

It would be ideal if a management and marketing plan could precede all event development, but it appears that most events have rather informal or spontaneous beginnings. The main exceptions are well established, mobile events with strong organizations to back them. So planning, in practice, will often begin with rudimentary organizational development. The undertaking of a marketing study might be the introduction to more comprehensive planning, or a crisis might force the organizers to call in professional advisers to conduct a study or prepare a plan. Whatever the origins, all event organizers will evolve some style of planning, whether formal or informal. This author does not believe that all planning has to be formal and put in writing—but there are risks to the organization if it is not. Imagine, for example, what will happen to the special event manager who neglects to state goals and targets publicly. Who will judge the success or failure of the event? Will disputes arise?

The management and marketing planning process is continuous and evolving, but somewhere along the line an actual plan is probably desirable. It will fulfill the key functions of a strategic or corporate plan, but with greater emphasis on product development and target marketing.

The model illustrated in Figure 7-1 is similar to the process for event tourism destination planning, but it is much more focused on organizational development and the marketing mix. It consists of two parallel and continuously interacting processes, one dealing with the overall management of the event organization— assuming it is a separate or somewhat independent body—and the other depicting the specific marketing planning elements. This approach allows for systematic learning and adaptation of the organization and its marketing planning, with the research and evaluation findings enabling the organizers to reformulate goals and objectives, or modify the marketing mix, to grow and develop.

Each element in the model will be explained in detail, through the rest of

**Table 7-1. Organization and Management Practices
in Community-Run Festivals in Ontario**

Items	Respondents (by %) (N = 52)
Festival is legally incorporated	59
Has a main board or committee	88
Has elected board members	56
Has paid staff	31
Revenue:	
Admission charge	34
Sales of goods	59
Lottery or raffle	49
Rental of space	38
Donations	16
Other sources	35
Has formal goals and objectives	74
Marketing and promotions:	
Has a marketing plan	43
Has done a visitor survey	40
Advertises in newspapers	92
Advertises on radio	89
Advertises on posters	89
Advertises by brochures	79
Advertises on television	58
Advertises on road signs	54
Uses other means of advertising	27
Has sponsors	47
Has a policy on allocating surplus revenue	76
If yes, distribution of surplus is returned:	
to the festival (10 of 35)	
to participating organizations (10 of 35)	
to special projects (9 of 35)	

Source: Getz, D., and W. Frisby. 1988. Evaluating management effectiveness in
community-run festivals. *Journal of Travel Research* 27 (1): 22–27 (published
by the Travel and Tourism Research Association and the Business Research
Division, University of Colorado).

this chapter and the next. At the end, a very practical approach to marketing
and segmentation is presented, which will be of particular interest to small event
organizations lacking the ability to conduct sophisticated research and promotions.

PURPOSE, GOALS, AND OBJECTIVES

Marketing, and overall management of the event organization, must begin with
the statement of a purpose, mandate, or mission. This is often more difficult

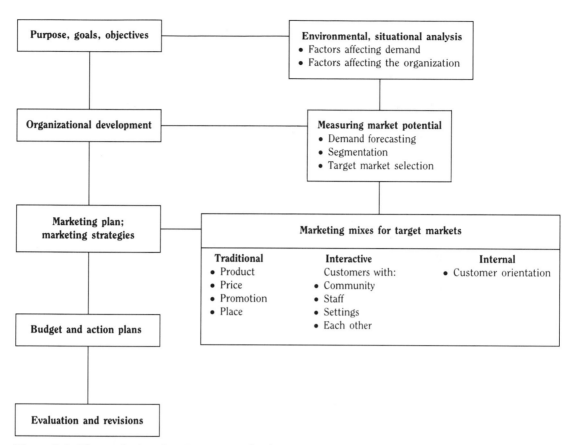

Figure 7-1. The marketing planning process for festivals and events.

than it appears, especially for new event organizations. Any of the previously described perspectives on event products can be the guiding force, and multiple purposes and goals are common. Anticipating the possibility of confusion, it is wise to develop a statement of purpose that integrates the various key perspectives. The tourism component can be either prominent, as a reason for establishing the event, or supportive, to facilitate other goals. The difference has profound implications, as events established mainly as tourist attractions, or dependent upon tourism for their success, might require quite different planning, marketing, programming, and evaluation approaches.

A good purpose statement should embody several dimensions:

The philosophical (for example, to meet community needs or to advance the cause of intercultural understanding)

Legal (to fulfill a responsibility, according to the law, assigned to the sponsoring agency or group)

Corporate orientation (to maximize profits through customer satisfaction; to promote the corporation's image)

Practical (what can realistically be accomplished by the event)

Tourism-related objectives can be fit into any of these dimensions. Seldom will tourism be the paramount purpose of an event, but if it is, the organizers or sponsors would be wise to acknowledge fully why it is deemed important to establish the event, then express these reasons in terms relating to the other perspectives.

A discussion of event tourism goals and objectives, including sample statements, was presented in Chapter 5. But individual festivals and events require a different approach, with less emphasis on the economic and touristic goals and a clearer focus on the broad range of goals that govern most events. Like the statement of purpose, the long-range goals should be sufficiently firm so as to direct the organization's activities over a period of years, but also flexible enough so as not to force the event into narrow channels. Both the mandate and long-range goals should be reviewed regularly and adapted to changing conditions and evaluation results.

Both output and process goals must be formulated. Output goals pertain to the desired results of the event, while process goals cover the ways in which the organization structures and manages itself. Improvements in process can always be made, so process and output goals must go hand in hand to advance the event.

Sample goals and objectives, along with possible indicators of success, are offered for consideration in Table 7-2. Although they merely suggest the range that is possible, they do show how tourism goals can be integrated. A direct comparison with the sample goals and objectives in Tables 5-1 and 5-2 is recommended, as well as consideration of how each of the perspectives on festivals and events can contribute to goal formulation.

ENVIRONMENTAL AND SITUATIONAL ANALYSIS

It might actually be necessary to undertake environmental and situational analysis prior to stating the purpose and goals. As more is learned about the relationships between the event and its environment, and about how the organization and event functions, the more refined the goals can become. The same applies to evaluation, which enables the organization to learn about its effectiveness and impact.

There are two major components of environmental analysis: factors affecting demand for events in general and for the specific event, and factors affecting the event organization. Situational analysis is similar, but it tends to focus on internal organizational conditions, in this case including the event itself.

Table 7-2. Sample Goals and Indicators of Success for Festivals and Events

Sample Goals	Sample Indicators of Success
Organizational	
To maximize volunteer involvement	Low turnover rate
To increase efficiency	Lower production costs
To develop and strengthen networks	Political support and numbers of participating groups
Social and cultural	
To foster the arts and sports and create leisure opportunities	Heightened awareness; numbers of participants
To strengthen local organizations and leadership	Numbers, size, and financial strength of groups; linkages
To promote heritage conservation	Money raised for projects
To improve local amenities	Investments in projects
To foster community support and pride	Attitude surveys; public input; media reports
Economic and financial	
To maximize revenues and profit	Budget surplus
To maximize local and area economic benefits	Tourist expenditures; local area income (the multiplier); cost-benefit ratio; employment multiplier
To spread benefits widely among area residents	Benefits spread widely; measure external costs
To keep costs for residents as low as possible	
Tourism and marketing	
To increase total attendance through improved marketing	Meeting specific targets of growth
To expand the market area and attract more overnight tourists	Numbers and percentages of tourists who stay
To lengthen the tourist season and increase lengths of stay by visitors	Impact on accommodation occupancy rates
To promote a strong destination image	Heightened consumer awareness and positive attitudes
Environmental	
To avoid pollution and habitat destruction	Wildlife counts; water-quality trends
To contribute to enhanced environmental quality	Conservation projects

The task of researching and providing information on general trends is that of the destination tourist organization, as most event organizers will not be able to do much in this area. Unique mega-events will have to undertake their own environmental analysis, given the onetime nature of the event, but a partnership with established tourist organizations will be most productive. General factors affecting growth and demand for festivals and special events have already been described (see Chapter 3).

This stage in the process might also include a SWOT analysis; referring to strengths, weaknesses, opportunities, and threats, the technique is good for determining the event's current and potential attractiveness. Key SWOT questions are listed in Chapter 10, as they are really a form of evaluation.

ORGANIZATIONAL DEVELOPMENT

A formal development plan—or strategic, corporate, or management plan— might be desired to provide firm direction, depending on the results of the environmental and situational analysis. It should encompass all management and marketing issues in general, but a separate marketing plan is probably necessary for larger and more sophisticated event organizations.

Marketing planning is so critical a function that it is usually assigned to a powerful and highly competent committee. Other committees will have to deal with the basic functions of staffing and volunteers, finance and fund-raising, physical arrangements and infrastructure, the program and activities of the event, and other tasks. Unless the organizational structure and processes are efficient and properly coordinated, marketing planning will be ineffectual. Advice on organization and management is available in a number of manuals mentioned in Chapter 6, and in other works cited in the References.

Care must be taken not to focus exclusively on structure and technological solutions. Organizational development is also a people-oriented process, which seeks to maximize the potential contribution of all persons involved in the organization and event. The event manager should consult the extensive literature in this area for advice on motivating, leading, and consensus-building, among other issues. Internal marketing, covered in Chapter 8, is also a form of organizational development.

MEASUREMENT OF MARKET POTENTIAL

At the most basic level, this assessment will be largely qualitative and based on readily available material, including studies of other events. More sophisticated organizations will undertake original research to quantify market potential, including segmentation studies. Whatever the level of sophistication, these key questions must be addressed:

What is the existing and potential demand for special events of this type, in this area, based on past experience?

How many customers can be expected, including local, regional, national, and international origins?

What types of people and groups are most likely to be interested in this event, or can be most easily attracted?

What are their needs and motives? What benefits will they get from the event?

What are the anticipated spending patterns of visitors or customers? What will people pay?

Note that these questions cannot even be asked if there is no preliminary definition of the nature of the event—the tangible product. If this has not been clearly defined, questions 2 through 4 can be restated to focus on a range of possible themes or an examination of what has already proved to be successful, leading to a product definition or theme.

Demand Forecasting Methods

Common tourist demand forecasting methods (see, for example, Smith 1989) can be applied to events, but they are not totally useful. Destination planners definitely want to predict volumes of domestic travel and arrivals to the region, and they should estimate the proportion of tourists potentially interested in cultural products and special events of different types. This exercise does not do much for the individual event organizer, unfortunately, as there might be little correlation between regional tourist demand and attendance at any given event.

Trend Extrapolation

For established events, a trend extrapolation is probably the only practical way to forecast next year's attendance, but many intervening factors—especially the weather—can throw predictions totally out of whack. If reliable attendance estimates are available, the growth or decline over a period of years can be projected to continue, but only if it is assumed that prevailing conditions of supply and demand that affect the event will continue. This is a method that should be used only to make short-term forecasts.

Many events are not even concerned about attendance, as they are always successful or have a limited capacity and cannot grow any more. Although they are likely to be uninterested in forecasts, they should nevertheless pay attention to trends. Complacency can be dangerous!

Comparisons

Comparison with other events is a reasonable place to start for new events whose planners want to make a demand forecast. Similar events have to be researched, particularly taking into account market area (for example, distance to cities), competitive position (are there other events at the same time or in the same area?), and attractiveness (size, quality, and diversity of the proposed event compared to the others). The comparison will be more useful if the origins and growth of comparable events can be traced, focusing on their initial attendance and their promotional efforts.

Destination planners can assist in forecasting by collecting reliable data from many events and analyzing long-term trends. Total attendance at festivals and special events has grown in many regions, so a more refined assessment of demand specific to types of events and geographic patterns of demand will help a great deal.

Market Penetration

The most difficult forecasting problem is faced by the onetime special event. Dungan (1984) showed that expected attendance at such events could be based on an estimate of market penetration, using other events and comparable attractions, such as theme parks, as guides. Market penetration is calculated as a percentage, so that if every resident in the market area attended once, the penetration would be 100 percent. Dungan reported that Expo '67 in Montreal achieved a local market penetration of 618 percent—in other words, over six visits per capita—whereas the 1964–65 World's Fair in New York achieved a low penetration of 82 percent. But all market areas and events are different, and events are different from theme parks and other attractions, so direct comparisons have obvious weaknesses.

Market surveys can be used to make better forecasts of market penetration. Chapter 9 profiles the 1987 America's Cup defense, including forecasting and associated problems. What is required are surveys in the local, regional, and national or international target markets to measure awareness of the planned event, attitudes toward it, and respondents' assessment of their likelihood or actual intention to attend. Over time, a trend and refined calculations of attendance can be derived from these market surveys. Results of Calgary's Olympulse have been published (Ritchie and Aitken 1984; Ritchie and Lyons 1987), showing how this technique was used for the 1988 Winter Olympics.

Other Forecasting Techniques

Blackorby, Ricard, and Slade (1986) undertook an interesting analysis of various world's fairs, using linear regression analysis to detect the key factors affecting attendance. They concluded that three factors—average price in U.S. dollars, size of the site in acres, and the number of foreign pavilions—accounted for 93 percent of variation in attendance at the world's fairs they examined. Using this conclusion, they predicted an attendance of 18 million paid visits to Vancouver's Expo '86, which can be compared to the official forecast of 13.5 million and the final count of 22.1 million site visits (Lee 1987).

Another novel approach to forecasting attendance at a onetime event was conducted by Louviere and Hensher (1983), using choice theory. In this research survey, respondents in one experiment were asked to select preferred mixes of event attractions, and those in another survey were required to rank choices by examining alternative locations, prices, types, and sizes of the event. From the data the researchers calculated probabilities of attendance for the population as a whole, specific to a number of event alternatives.

Whatever demand forecasting method is employed, the event planner has a difficult task. There are as yet insufficient theories and data to take event forecasting from an art to a science, and much more research will be required.

Segmentation and Selection of Target Markets

For many community events there is an underlying assumption that the whole community will be attracted. This is a naive assumption, as event visitor surveys reveal, but it is nevertheless a goal for certain types of special event. In these cases, the organizers must ask what range of products, activities, or attractions they can provide to satisfy the broadest possible market. Or it might be necessary to ask what promotions or inducements could be offered to attract the broadest possible market to a very specific theme.

Even where the event is oriented to the general community market, some segments are more likely than others to be attracted. If these segments are ignored, attendance and revenues might suffer and the event could fail without attaining its goal of reaching the whole community. It might even be that the general audiences will not attend an annual event until it proves to be popular with a sufficient number of people to generate a successful image.

More important, the tourist market should be examined in all events. Even the smallest and newest can be of interest to tourists searching for authentic local experiences. Some will respond to even minimal promotion, especially if they are already in the area and looking for activities. The event organizers might even find tourists to be more responsive than residents. Then there is the segment of residents who can be induced to bring visiting friends and relatives to community events. Finally, tourist organizations will almost always be happy to advise event organizers on the potential for attracting tourists, based on the experience of other events or their general knowledge of the volumes and flows of visitors in the region.

Definition of Segmentation and Target Marketing

Segmentation is a form of research and analysis that seeks to identify groups of people who have similar patterns of preference and/or consumption and are distinct from other groups. In the case of festivals and special events, we want to know who are the likeliest event tourists, and which types of people will most likely attend specific events. Smith (1989) said that segmentation can also answer questions about the size of potential markets, spending patterns, price sensitivity, loyalty, response to changes in the marketing mix, and the potential effectiveness of promotions. Once the segmentation analysis is completed, the most promising groups are selected as target markets, and the marketing mix should be oriented to these groups. In fact, the product and target markets must be continuously matched, as both are likely to change over time.

To be useful, a market segment must meet certain criteria (Mill and Morrison 1985). The group of people being described as a target market or segment must have homogeneity, or common characteristics, permitting ready identification of the group. It must be a measurable group in terms of numbers and of a size or with characteristics that make them worthwhile of attention—small, wealthy special-interest groups can be important! Finally, the organizers must be able to communicate effectively and affordably with the group, to make them aware of the event and interest them in it. Although the ways to identify target markets are many, and often overlapping, meeting these criteria ensures that target marketing does not get out of control. In practice, each event should focus on one or several easily defined groups. Several common and useful segmentation approaches deserve examination in detail, with emphasis on the tourist market.

Trip Purpose

Ask the audience at any event why they made the trip, and you will get two types of answer. First, several basic segments emerge that are related to the attractiveness of the event itself: some came just for the event; some tourists came to the area mainly or partially because of it; some were in the area and came to the event for something to do; others were passing through and stopped to see what was going on. All these groups are important customers, but the event marketer generally should try to attract more people to come mainly for the event, because the other groups are unpredictable and often unreachable, and because of the incremental income generated by event-motivated tourists. (See Chapter 10 for an explanation of the income multiplier and the importance of incremental income.)

Other answers will pertain to various levels of motivation, from the superficial to the specific, such as to visit friends and relatives, for the crafts, or to have a family outing. Prompting or providing suggested reasons can shape the answers to cover all kinds of possible motivations of interest to the event organizers. Segments defined in this way provide insights into the benefits sought by customers; for balance, people who are not customers should be similarly questioned. The key, however, is to determine if the groups with a trip purpose have other common characteristics, such as age, gender, or location; otherwise, not a lot can be done with the basic knowledge.

Geographic Area

As documented earlier, most events must rely on the local and regional (daytrip) market areas. Tourists coming from a distance and staying overnight are extremely valuable in generating economic benefits, but they are not likely to be the largest component. Within each of the three market zones—local, regional, and beyond—specific groups can be identified whose members are logical targets, and these overlap or combine with segments defined by trip purpose. For example, it is difficult to induce foreigners to travel abroad for a community festival, but one can arrange to bring foreign tour groups to an event as part of a package.

Most effort should be directed at the local and regional markets. From the local perspective, anyone coming from outside the host community can be considered a tourist. Tourist organizations will want to see each event become an attraction or activity outlet for tourists coming from outside the destination area.

Seasonal Approach

This is an often-ignored approach to segmentation, but it has particular relevance to events. Some groups are easier to attract in the off-season, while the largest market potential is likely to be in the summer tourist season. Another way to look at this method is to ask what would happen to an event's markets if it moved to another season. Logically, the nature of some events, such as winter carnivals or fishing derbies, actually dictates the potential market.

Demographic and Socioeconomic Characteristics

Almost all target markets are defined at least in part by reference to demographics (age, gender, marital status, family composition and size, race or ethnicity, life cycle stages) and socioeconomic variables (education, occupation, income, status). Even events aimed at families or the whole community will probably find that their audience is not that broad, or that certain segments of the population (defined by these variables) are more important.

Certain events and their activities will be gender or age specific; for example, contact sports attract mostly young males. Others have appeal mainly to the educated professional classes, or to the wealthiest segments of society. It is unwise to assume that a mixture of activities will attract a very broad audience, as the theme and image of the event, or types of activities, can have the effect of motivating or turning away certain groups.

Geodemographics is a combination of market area and demographic segmentation in which census data are mapped. This reveals more refined target areas, so promotions can be more efficiently distributed to key groups within prime market areas.

Product-Related Segments

Those with a likely interest in sporting events can be identified by the equipment they own, the magazines they read, and their recreational activities. This is an example of product-based segmentation, which is useful for event marketing. So too is the strategy of concentrating on people who are frequent users of certain facilities, on repeat visitors to an event, and on clubs with specialized product demands, such as antique car hobbyists.

Another approach is to identify target groups by *distribution channels*—that is, the ways in which the event can be linked to potential customers. Tourists might be reached most easily through specialized tour wholesalers who do their own marketing. Links with parks and recreation departments in nearby cities can pay off, as they often organize senior citizen excursions to events. In both cases, the target groups are defined by the way in which they are reached.

Psychographics

This approach was introduced in our previous discussions of needs, motivations, and benefits (see Chapter 3). Psychographics is based on assessment of personality types and the related needs, attitudes, or predispositions that generate specific leisure and travel motivations. Often these factors are combined into so-called life-style profiles, which are easier to deal with in marketing studies.

Plog (1987) identified dimensions used commonly in psychographics-based tourist segmentation: adventuresomeness (the explorer types); pleasure seeking (related to the desire for luxury); impulsivity (those who will spend a lot, without planning); self-confidence (people who will travel alone); planfulness (including package tours and bargains); masculinity (the action-oriented and outdoor groups); intellectualism (those lured by culture and history); and people orientation (related to wanting to be close to others). Whatever the psychographic factors employed in segmentation, there is a need to link these to one or more of the other segmentation methods. For example, there is an identifiable "cultural tourist" whose life-style includes frequent attendance at arts and cultural events; this group is also known to be better educated, professional, older, and urban. With more precise identification of life-style and other characteristics, event organizers will be better able to communicate with the appropriate groups.

In an amusing and subjective segmentation exercise, Gillespie (1987) observed that three basic types of people could be observed at folk festivals. There were the family types who assumed that a folk festival meant wholesome, outdoor recreation for the whole family, preferably in a rural setting. A second group was called "folkniks": they were regulars with a counterculture life-style; to them, music was a backdrop, and they preferred informal jamming. A third group was called "the outlaws": they especially liked bluegrass festivals and were disruptive, obnoxious, and often indifferent to the music. Each of the three segments reflect different life-styles, motivations, expectations, and preferred activities, yet all were found at folk festivals.

Should event organizers attempt to keep such different groups apart, or to market the event only to one segment? Research and segmentation can help identify potential problems and opportunities, but cannot automatically suggest policy decisions. It is quite possible that any event can satisfy many different interests without problems, but other events might suffer because the product does not match consumers' needs and expectations.

As a final point, Mahoney (n.d.b) argued that target marketing should result in identification of at least one segment large enough to justify special treatment, keeping in mind the criteria mentioned above. This major segment could be the key to tourist attractiveness, as special interest groups tend to travel farther. Once identified, a promotional strategy geared to the target segment must be developed, and this includes consideration of the entire marketing mix.

TRADITIONAL MARKETING MIX—THE PRODUCT

It is common to speak of the four *P*s of the marketing mix: product, price, place, and promotion. Others have expanded this list to as many as nine *P*s, adding partnership (cooperative efforts), packaging, programming, positioning, and people (Economic Planning Group of Canada n.d.). All are important, and we can consider them all in this section, although not equally. In Marketing Parks and Recreation, Mahoney (n.d.b) has argued for the inclusion of interactive and internal marketing mixes. They include some of the nine *P*s and are covered in the next chapter.

Product-market matching, which has already been discussed, is the essence of the marketing mix. Ongoing marketing planning constantly adapts the marketing mix to changes in demand, or to changes in desired target markets. This process naturally follows from, and leads to, changes in the purpose and goals of the event. Nothing stays static for long, and events that never change are likely to find that their markets have, leaving the organizers with diminishing revenues, the wrong audience, or deteriorating quality. In the tourism field a failure to adapt, to engage in product-market matching, will harm the destination's attractiveness. It is essential that established tourist markets be constantly reinforced with changing or new products, and that products be developed to meet new or shifting interests.

The general nature of tourism and event products has been thoroughly discussed. They are a blend of intangible services and experiences with tangible merchandise, settings, and performances. The festival or special event is unique, and it has a generic appeal to most cultures. Special-interest attributes can be added to the event product to give it greater attractiveness to tourists. Our three-part model of the event product from the visitor's perspective (Getz 1989a) is therefore a good starting point for this discussion. Figure 7-2 illustrates the importance of viewing the event production as a combination of essential services, elements, or attributes that provide generic benefits and elements that cater to special interests.

Essential Services

These are necessary to undertake any event or operate any permanent attraction. They cannot normally be considered as benefits, but the absence or inadequacy of any of them will cause visitor dissatisfaction. A formal evaluation system must be put in place to ensure high quality and the meeting of performance criteria for each essential service, and customers should be asked to give their opinions on adequacy. Eventgoers might even have a different perception of what is essential, for example in the important category of food and beverages. At most public events it is an expected service, at some it is essential because of the timing and setting, and at others it is part of the themed attraction.

Generic Benefits

These components of the event distinguish them from other tourist products, particularly from permanent attractions—although there is a trend toward the blending of festival elements and other attractions, as seen in the popularity of festival markets and theme parks with special event programs. The actual tangible components are potentially infinite, although we have mentioned the most common activities, attractions, and emotional components found at special events and festivals. Now let's examine these components from the perspective of visitor benefits.

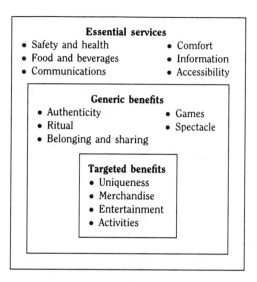

Figure 7-2. Festival and event products from the visitor's perspective.

Spectacle

MacAloon (1984) noted how the Olympics epitomize the spectacle associated with many special events. Spectacle is visually oriented, incorporating larger-than-life displays and performances, parades and ceremonies, ritual and action. It can be both a strength and a weakness, for while there is no doubt that spectacle has universal appeal, and is especially suitable for television, it can also overpower the more fundamental meanings of festival, ritual, and games.

Media-oriented events, and sports in particular, emphasize spectacle and even fabricate it when desirable. The Super Bowl is a football game, but the Super Bowl media event is a hyped-up spectacle. This might not matter in the realm of professional sports, but it can harm amateur sports and community or cultural festivals.

Spectacle is also, by definition, a spectator activity. Fireworks, parades, colorful displays, and ceremonies add vibrancy to any festival or event, and they serve to attract attention. But this type of spectator activity will not directly help to meet community or cultural development goals. Event organizers must be cautious with this element of the product, employing it for its publicity value and mass appeal, but not relying on it to the point where the remaining elements are diminished.

Belonging and Sharing

This is the core of festivals, and it is the spirit that organizers want to instill in all types of special event. Drawing from our earlier discussion of the cultural meanings of festivals, it can be stated that the essence of celebration, commemoration, and carnival is public sharing of themes having common cultural significance to the participants. Belonging and contributing to the cause is also an important motivator for the volunteers and organizers. Once the atmosphere or mood is established, merrymaking can become infectious. In more solemn ceremonies, the festivities are usually separated in setting or time.

Ritual

Most traditional, enduring festivals have a strong ritual component or are derived from religious or pagan rituals, all appealing to some higher principle, deity, or other religious meaning. It is also present in most contemporary events, regardless of their tradition, in forms such as opening and closing ceremonies, the singing of national anthems, and the inclusion of symbols such as flags and banners. Ritual can also be incorporated thematically in special events, through the employment of coordinated and mutually reinforcing symbols, ceremonies, colors, and visitor activities, so that the whole event becomes a ritualistic endorsement of community values, nationalism, or even political philosophy. One has only to remember the Nazi party rallies of the 1930s to understand the awesome power of ritual.

Games

People expect to have fun at most special events. It is part of the social meaning of public festivities, and it is expressed most directly through the myriad form of games. Games are more than sports and physical recreation. Also popular at special events are games of skill and chance, competitions, and humor.

This last element, humor, is often ignored or misunderstood. Humor can be created by entertainers, such as by clowns and costumed characters, comedians and masters of ceremony. But what of humorous sights, sounds, smells, tastes, and situations, all of which can be created or facilitated throughout the event setting and a full range of activities? Sociologists suggest that part of the attraction of carnivals and other festivals is role reversal and the elimination of behavioral norms. Celebrities and political figures can become objects of ridicule (the water-dunking event), and normally reserved settings become playgrounds (the civic square or street). Mardi Gras and other traditional carnivals probably embody this humorous flavor most.

Authenticity

Authentic means genuine, unadulterated, or real. It is much debated in the literature, both as to its meaning for tourism and events and with respect to whether or not tourists seek or can even recognize authenticity. The problem is that tourism often leads to the commercialization of events and places, and even the tourists who seek out unspoiled settings and cultures can contribute to alteration or destruction of these things.

A definition by Vallee (1987, 27) gives insight to the motivational and product-oriented nature of the term: "Authenticity is a desired and actively pursued experience by tourists which is perceived to reflect or give access to the true and unadulterated nature of everyday life in the destination." To Vallee, an authentic experience can motivate travel, and it can be considered a benefit to be derived from attendance at an event. Redfoot (1984), however, noted that lines have been drawn between those who believe that the modern tourist is generally uninterested in the authentic (e.g., Boorstin 1961) and those who have suggested that tourists are engaged in a quest for the authentic (e.g., MacCannell 1976). Both sides agree, however, that tourists usually find only pseudo-events or cultural productions, not the genuine article.

A brief review of some of the writing on authenticity as it pertains to festivals and special events will help readers to make up their own minds on this debate and, more important, to see that the pursuit of authenticity is worthwhile.

Boorstin's 1961 book, *The Image: A Guide to Pseudo-Events in America*, seems to have started the debate. In this classic, Boorstin defined *pseudo-events* as being planned for the immediate purpose of being reported or reproduced. They are not spontaneous and their meaning is ambiguous—which is part of their attraction. Clearly, many public relations events fit this definition, but so do many tourist entertainment events. Boorstin went on to say that modern tourists tend to view the whole world as a stage for these fabrications aimed at their amusement. And it is apparent that in many parts of the world the residents have acquiesced. The unfortunate consequences of tourism, in this argument, are the homogenizing of cultures everywhere and the alteration of cultural events to satisfy the preconceived notions of tourists.

In his book *The Tourist*, MacCannell (1976) suggested that modern tourists seek authenticity precisely because it has become so scarce. The tourist wants a spontaneous experience that reveals, or better yet allows, the sharing of some aspect of the daily life of a different culture or community. He used the term *backstage* to describe the physical setting in which a visitor could observe, meet, or share something authentic. Backstage is an obvious analogy to theater, where everyone knows that the visible action is a play, not real life, and that meeting the actors or seeing the activity backstage is a totally different experience.

Other researchers have explored tourist behavior and attitudes pertaining to authenticity. Cohen (1979) and Pearce (1982) suggested that visitor satisfaction will depend not only on the nature of the scene or event—whether or not it is authentic—but also on both visitors' perceptions of whether authenticity exists and their need for authentic experiences. This is obviously a complex issue. Some tourists want a festival to be an authentic cultural expression of the host community and will be disappointed to find a highly commercialized, tourist-oriented event. Other visitors, having no such expectation, presumably will not care, and still others won't know the difference. In this context authenticity partially becomes a matter of market research, trying to determine the expectations and perceptions of existing or potential target segments.

Interesting cases are documented in the literature. Buck (1977) found that staged, tourist-oriented events helped to prevent direct contact with the privacy-loving Amish residents in Lancaster County, Pennsylvania. In this way, inauthentic events can be used to maintain a social boundary between curious tourists and reluctant host communities. As long as the tourists are satisfied, even if they know they are witnessing an event put on for their entertainment or education, then it hardly seems to matter if the event is culturally genuine or not; it serves a very useful function. Indeed, in this age of mass travel and a better informed traveler, it is probably the rare, naive tourist who actually expects to discover unadulterated cultural festivals. Both hosts and guests know, in most cases, that the tourist is expected and often encouraged to attend celebrations and rituals. In other cases, the tourist is deliberately kept out.

On a related question, Moscardo and Pearce (1986) have argued that historical re-creations, as in heritage sites and events, can be considered authentic if they faithfully simulate past conditions. A similar case can be made for cultural events held far from their natural setting, such as the Polynesian Cultural Center in Hawaii. (See Stanton [1989] for a discussion of this, and other cultural centers.) At this popular tourist attraction the rituals, life-styles, and performances of many South Sea cultures are re-created for visitors, mostly by students from the depicted cultures. Certainly the entertainment value of the performances has been exaggerated, but the wise tourist probably realizes that seeing the Samoan fire-eater perform in Hawaii is little different from witnessing the same show at a hotel in Samoa. The point is, detecting and defining an authentic event is a matter not only of perception but of contemporary reality. Does the authentic ritual of the primitive, remote tribe still exist? Beloved by cultural anthropologists, these unspoiled events were first altered by Western travelers who wanted to study and record them before they could change!

Mannell and Iso-Ahola (1987, 14) concluded: "Little or no systematic research has been done to determine the factors in the setting that influence perceptions of authenticity and the resulting quality of the experience." For festivals and special events, this is a challenge for researchers.

Authenticity must be considered as a part of the event product, because it is something that can motivate certain tourists and is a benefit that at least partially can be controlled by organizers. But the definitions and arguments involving authenticity are confusing, so the event planner must have some practical advice.

Given that the essence of authenticity is its cultural meaning, the bottom line must be that host communities determine what is meaningful to them. In this perspective, authenticity is not so much the ritual, games, spectacle, or celebration itself as it is the degree to which these components have been manufactured, modified, or exploited just for tourists, the media, or financial success. In other words, has the event any cultural meaning for the host community and the participants, or is it merely a commodity to be sold? Do the hosts and performers think of the event as having importance in their lives, or are they cynically involved in a tourist rip-off?

Guidelines have been established for successful community-based tourism (e.g., Cooke 1982), and our earlier discussion of community development and the social and cultural meanings of festivals and events give us the criteria we need. The conclusion is that authenticity of a festival or event will be maximized when they:

- Reflect indigenous themes
- Are controlled by the host community
- Are valued and well attended by residents
- Offer culturally genuine goods and performances, such as local foods, costumes, dances, and crafts
- Do not exploit tourists through profit maximization at the expense of quality

From the tourism perspective, the real issue is maximizing visitor satisfaction, with the realization that events popular with the host community are likely to be more pleasing to visitors, and that authentic cultural performances, settings, food, and merchandise will be enduring attractions.

Tourist organizations should also be sensitive to the desires of cultural groups that do not want to be exploited as tourist attractions or do not want pseudo-events put on for tourists. Not all festivals and events should be viewed as tourism resources—the real event tourism resource is people, and the community must be given the right to decide for itself.

Targeted Benefits

Residents, day-trippers, and tourists in the area might attend an event out of curiosity or on impulse, as a recreational outing. They will expect certain generic benefits and basic services. To attract tourists specifically to travel to an event, however, something extra is usually required. The first step is to strive for uniqueness.

Uniqueness

The theme and name of an event are important in conveying the right message of uniqueness and special appeal. A food festival conveys a certain image, but a Great Italian Pasta Party says it with pizzazz. A Fun Day might have little appeal to tourists, but The World's Biggest Barbecue might have the desired effect. An annual tricounty ball tournament might appeal to locals, but sports-loving tourists are inundated with choice and demand the biggest, the best, or the most unusual. It is similar to establishing a brand name that ensures customer loyalty and conveys the message that here is a product one can trust. It should go without saying that the product had better be as good as the name!

Uniqueness can also be a function of rarity. Something that occurs infrequently (Olympics, World's Fair, America's Cup) or in very few places or even only one (Indy 500, Cannes Film Festival) has special appeal. Some of it is mystique, and therefore partially fabricated through promotions. Small festivals and events can try to develop this mystique by emphasizing rarity, combined with image-building based on quality, cost, or some other competitive advantage.

Specialties

Almost any component of the event production can be used to differentiate the product from those of competitors and thereby provide benefits to target segments. As indicated in Figure 7-2, entertainment, visitor activities, and merchandise can all be targeted to special-interest segments. Food and drink are essential to most events, but specialty foods, wine, beer, and bake-off events can attract gourmets, competitors, and those who are curious about ethnic products.

Most festivals have entertainment, but themed music festivals have loyal audiences and attract people who want to sample specialty art and entertainment forms. The popularity of bluegrass, jazz, classical, and folk festivals attests to this point, although tastes do change and the events must adapt. The type of counterculture folk festivals popular in the 1960s appear to be declining, forcing some to rethink and reformat their package. For example, the Mariposa Folk Festival in Ontario, Canada, has gone through tough times and reemerged as a Festival of Roots Music, expanded well beyond traditional folk music styles.

Visitor activities are the third such component that can be targeted. All aspects of spectacle, games, celebration, and ritual that are common to festivals and events can be turned into specialty benefits for the target tourist markets. Recreational pursuits such as kite flying now have their own competitions and festivals. Specialized sports such as hot-air ballooning are becoming popularized through festivals where visitors can learn, view, and even experience rides on those contraptions. And participant sports of all kinds generate their own tournaments and "classics."

The marketing principle demonstrated in our three-level model of the product from the visitor's perspective is vitally important to tourism. Very specialized events, particularly sports competitions, are adding festival benefits to expand their appeal. All-purpose, family-oriented festivals and events can create tourism demand by adding targeted benefits. All events must provide basic services to a high standard.

Themes

We have noted the importance of a good theme in product development and product-market matching. Let's take a closer look at how to develop a theme and integrate the theme in all aspects of the event and its promotions.

All festivals are themed, by definition (see Chapter 2). They celebrate or commemorate something of importance to the community, such as its heritage or way of life. But the theme is more than the mere object of celebration. As noted by Korza and Magie (1989, 10), the theme unifies an event or festival: "By permeating every aspect of a festival . . . a theme can provide programmatic direction and coherence and provide a hook which is readily understood by the media and audiences." In other words, the object of the celebration suggests a theme, but the realization of a theme is a function of coherent programming and image-making.

It is often counterproductive to impose a theme on a community; rather, it should evolve from and reflect the host community's culture and aspirations. In other words, it should be authentic. This is not to say that a consensus is required, because that is generally not possible. Instead, one or more groups or public agencies have to have faith in their theme, commitment to its principles, and a strong desire to have others participate in and enjoy the celebration. In a pluralistic society it is now expected that cultural diversity will be reflected in festivals and special events, and diversity is a strong tourism resource.

Uniqueness of theme is getting harder to create. Creativity and even a sense of humor have helped some communities find a theme that both expresses local heritage and is bound to capture attention. For example, Queenan (1989, 13) asked, "In a state where annual festivals celebrate everything from antique stoves to zucchini, why not long underwear?" She was referring to Piqua, Ohio, and its annual Great Outdoor Underwear Festival!

Event themes can be linked to destination area themes for mutual advantage. In some cases the regional theme is strong, giving rise to events that take advantage of and reinforce the destination image. Some regions have based their image making and theme on the success of one or more special events. There is no need to try to link all events into a coherent destination theme, however. Diversity is to be valued. Rather, the types of package tours described earlier can be employed to highlight and link the events that most strongly develop the destination image or theme.

Dickens on the Strand, Galveston, Texas: Visitors in costume gain free admission and help create the period atmosphere (Galveston Historical Foundation).

Other special events almost always have a specific theme based on the nature of the event, such as a sport or recreational activity. But special events do not always develop a theme fully or integrate it well in promotions. Kreag (1988) advised that all the important elements of an event have to be synthesized "into a cohesive message or statement of purpose" to ensure effective communications. Themes can be expressed in a number of ways:

- In the name of the event
- Through logos and mascots
- In the setting and design
- In the activities and attractions
- In food and beverages
- In merchandise for sale
- In consistent advertising format and style
- By stressing specified (targeted) benefits

Dickens on the Strand, Galveston, Texas: the theme represented in costumes, setting, and activities (Galveston Historical Foundation).

Our case study of Dickens on the Strand (in Chapter 9) is a great example of a fully integrated theme involving most of the abovementioned points.

PRICING

Festivals and special events are quite different from other recreational and consumer products in terms of pricing. Many events are open and free of charge, relying on merchandising, grants, sponsorships, and other forms of fund-raising to survive; profits, if any, are often gained mostly by participating groups, merchants, and suppliers. Others, especially onetime events, must employ all the common pricing strategies to ensure that maximum revenue is generated without adversely affecting demand.

Basic Price Considerations

As one key element in the marketing mix, the price of a good or service has to contribute to the meeting of overall marketing goals. Price is linked closely with promotion, as it is quite a different challenge to promote an event that has an entry fee as opposed to one that is completely open and free. Place is also linked to price, particularly because street and park festivals have a hard time controlling, and therefore charging for, admissions. Theater festivals, those involving professional performers, and events utilizing expensive-to-operate facilities probably have to adopt at least a break-even pricing policy. And price is linked closely to product, partly because consumers have different expectations of a free event, and partly because of the role of price in generating revenues for product development.

Festivals put on by community groups and public agencies are typically open to the public without charge. This is a basic part of the festival's attraction, especially to residents. As suggested in South Carolina's *Festival Planning Handbook* (South Carolina Department of Parks, Recreation and Tourism 1982, 1), "the broader your appeal, the less it should cost for visitors to participate. It is often more effective to cover your expenses or raise funds in other ways than admission charges." The free or very inexpensive event also encourages last-minute decisions to attend, along with spontaneous participation by tourists already in the area. Such events contribute to the image that a destination always has something happening, and that a particular facility or setting is a people place.

Charging admission to community festivals alters the way people think of them, and therefore potentially changes the event's markets and use patterns. The public might perceive that an admission price means less emphasis on public celebration and more on entertainment. Expectations of a higher-quality product are intensified by admission charges, and the product has to meet these expectations. Market segments with more time and money can be attracted, and planning the visit in advance will become more important. Consequently, promotion of the event will have to be modified to identify different segments, and the product reformulated to provide the benefits desired by these new segments.

From a tourism perspective, charging admission to a festival can have mixed results. On the one hand, tourists are generally in a spending mood and might very well be willing to pay for an event that residents would not. Also, high-quality events can be created with the revenue that admission fees generate, thereby making it easier to attract key target markets. On the other hand, it is highly desirable to provide free activity or spectacle for tourists in order to help create a desired destination image and to encourage host-guest interactions. A good strategy, therefore, is to have both free and paid admissions at the same event.

Organizers of festivals and events that charge admission must be prepared to accept the likely consequences for community support and participation, or to devise ways to combine both appeals. As an example of an event with an admission price, Dickens on the Strand in Galveston, Texas (see Chapter 9), has had considerable success in fostering an affluent regional tourism market without sacrificing local appeal. This is accomplished by fostering strong community volunteer support, by having interorganizational networking with numerous groups participating to raise money, and by encouraging residents to dress in costume to gain free admission. This strategy not only allows free local participation but adds to the flavor of the festival.

Setting the Price

Mahoney (n.d.a) observed that traditional economic pricing analyses, such as marginal cost and elasticity of demand, are very difficult for recreational services to use because the cost of producing a unit of service or of leisure experience is not readily quantifiable. This problem is magnified for public events, where the addition of one more person to the audience makes little or no difference to the cost. Consequently, the decisions on price are often made subjectively or for political reasons.

Even if organizers wish to maintain a free festival, they should nevertheless go through the following pricing exercise. It will encourage a more rational and coherent approach to establishing the entire marketing mix and assist in event planning.

Determination of Costs

Past experience is the best source of data on costs, but often they will have to be estimated because the event is new, changing, or subject to uncontrollable external influences. All capital and operating costs should be included, as well as any external costs (see Chapters 1 and 10 for more details) for which the organizers might become responsible. A more sophisticated organization might also consider opportunity costs, to reflect opportunities forgone by investing in the event. Allowances for various contingencies and/or a reserve fund would be prudently included. The price should also reflect long-term commitments such as debt repayment.

Specific advice on cost accounting and its importance to pricing decisions is available elsewhere (e.g., Crompton and Lamb 1986). The important point to stress here is that if price is not linked to costs, then costs can easily get out of control.

Revenue Evaluation

Without an admission price, organizers must rely on a combination of sponsorship, grants, fund-raising special events (how ironic!), licensing, and merchandising. Any of these sources can be sufficient, but how reliable are they over the long term? In our case study of festivals in Canada's National Capital Region (Chapter 9), it is noted how one event struggled chronically with revenue shortfalls because of uncertain grants and sponsorships. The more success this free event achieved, the more money it seemed to lose! Setting an admission price might have helped a great deal, and by 1990 Festival of Spring had introduced passport-type buttons at a set price.

In the absence of major, predictable revenues from other sources, most festivals and many special events have to develop an effective merchandising plan, including the licensing of products, logos, television rights, and so on. Given the popularity of arts, crafts, foods, and beverages, there is considerable potential. Indeed, it appears that many free events are simply vehicles for getting crowds to the spending outlets!

The Potential Impact of Price

Knowing that a higher price usually results in lower demand for leisure and travel products, organizers can make some forecast of the impact of rising prices on attendance and revenues. Unfortunately, little is known about the elasticity of demand for festivals and special events. Unless organizers have direct experience with price or comparisons can be made, a forecast could easily be in error. In fact, demand might actually increase!

If an admission price was charged, what would it do to the image of the event? Possibly it would become more upmarket, and any loss in total attendance could be more than compensated for by increased revenues. It is even possible that demand will increase after an admission fee is charged, particularly where the event has had a bad or weak image and the addition of a price suggests an improved product.

Other effects have to be considered. Would charging an admission fee jeopardize sponsorships or grants? What modifications, and resultant costs, would it entail for promotions? Some of this might be guesswork, but if the potential impact seems negative, then costs and benefits should be compared more thoroughly.

Some limited research into the consumer's willingness to pay for festivals and events has been undertaken, as in our case study of the festivals in Canada's National Capital Region (Chapter 9). This area requires considerably more work to help provide firm guidance on event pricing and demand forecasting.

The Potential Impact of a Revenue Shortfall

How serious will it be if the event does not meet revenue expectations, or even incurs a deficit? For the fortunate, some agency or sponsor might pick up the difference. Others could be faced with a terminal situation. The severity of the impact should influence the decision on pricing, because charging an admission fee could be the difference between self-sufficiency and insolvency.

The Existence of Competition

Other events and other competitors for leisure spending have to be considered. An expensive food festival will have a difficult time competing against a free food festival that has similar appeal and accessibility. Of course, if one has a competitive advantage in terms of timing, location, product, or promotion and image, that can be exploited. Because the majority of festivals and special events are linked to volunteers or government support of some kind, there has been a strong tendency to avoid direct competition among events. That might change in the future, and many organizers might have to adapt with a pricing strategy.

Break-Even Analysis and Cost-Recovery Pricing

Raising the price is easier to do than setting a price for the first time, as experience will reveal something about the effects of price on demand. This in itself is a good reason for having an admission fee—to help measure real economic demand. The first time a price is introduced, determining the break-even point becomes crucial.

Crompton and Lamb (1986) provided formulas for cost-recovery pricing, showing that different approaches could be taken. Full cost recovery, or average cost pricing, sets the price to regain all variable and fixed costs of the event from the users. A margin for profit can then be added. Obviously, this might not be appropriate for events considered to be a public service. A second approach is to set a price to recover from consumers only the operating costs or a portion of fixed or capital costs. This makes sense for public service events that cannot survive without some revenue from users. It is also applicable to events receiving grants or sponsorships that can be used to reduce costs.

Onetime special events have to face several complications. Organizers of most mega-events cannot hope to recover their costs from admissions, given the enormous capital investments. Instead, they will probably set admission and revenue targets that will lead to a pricing strategy. One important factor is the desire to generate strong tourism demand, thereby favoring package deals. To encourage repeat visits by residents, many events sell passes in advance. Over the duration of a longer event, pricing can be modified to reflect demand trends and public reaction to the product.

A Price for All Festivals and Events

The steps described above have avoided a technical discussion in order to focus attention on the pricing issues facing festival and event managers. Whatever the decision, it should be based on sound analysis of costs and revenues, impacts, and the contribution of pricing to the marketing mix and event goals.

This author believes that all festivals and special events can benefit from either a general admission price or a pricing policy applicable to components of the event program. The advantages are important, not only in a tourism context but for marketing and product development as well:

Without a price, economic demand cannot be determined.

Pricing can be used to influence demand, especially to help reach key target markets and avoid overuse.

Admission fees and ticket sales go hand in hand with accurate attendance counts.

Free events might develop the negative image associated with some low-quality public services.

Admission fees can make the event more self-sufficient and permit long-term financial and marketing planning.

Admission fees can permit better crowd control and foster more respect for the event, its setting, and the host community.

Pricing facilitates advance purchase of tickets and makes package deals and tours more attractive to the tourist industry.

Promotions can be linked to price discounts and free admissions; volunteers and others can be rewarded with free admissions.

The public service component of leisure events and festivals does not have to be compromised by charging admission fees. It is possible to have free general admission combined with paid admission to specialized attractions; this is likely to prove to be more popular with tourists and the tourist industry. Even elitist events with professional performers and high costs can follow the example of Charleston's Spoleto and carry free elements of the program into the city's neighborhoods. Then there is the example of Dickens on the Strand, which combines paid general admission with free admission for residents who show up in costume.

SUMMARY

In Chapters 7 and 8 our attention is directed to developing the tourism potential of individual events, from the point of view of event managers and organizers. The marketing planning process was presented in Figure 7-1, combining aspects of organizational development and management planning with more traditional marketing considerations. This integrated model ensures that marketing is viewed in its proper management context.

An initial decision for the organizer is whether to make generation of tourism a goal of the event. Some managers might fear commercialization and loss of authenticity or control; however, it was argued that not only could tourism provide revenue, but a tourist or customer orientation would help improve all events. The product development and marketing and management concepts employed to maximize attractiveness to tourists are likely to result as well in a better product for local audiences. A positive, customer-oriented philosophy must prevail in all festivals and events.

Table 7-2 described sample goals and success indicators appropriate to events, covering all the perspectives—not just tourism. The accompanying discussion of purpose, goals, and objectives led to the later examination of evaluation principles and methods.

Environmental and situational analysis was then assessed, with suggestions on what aspects of the organization and its internal and external environments should be evaluated in the marketing planning process.

Measuring market potential was the next component of the process discussed. This entails demand forecasting, which is particularly difficult for events. Trend extrapolation, comparisons, market penetration, and other methods were examined. Onetime events have the greatest problem, but forecasting demand even for recurring events is complicated by the typical absence of reliable attendance counts or estimates and inadequate event tourism market research for destinations.

The other part of assessing market potential is segmentation leading to target marketing. It was argued that very few festivals and special events actually have broad appeal, and that certain segments of the population are of particular importance. Targeting these groups will increase promotional effectiveness. The common approaches to market segmentation were presented, including trip purpose, geographic area, seasonal patterns of demand, demographic and socioeconomic characteristics, product-related segments, and psychographics.

The traditional marketing mix consists of product, price, place, and promotion. Beginning with product, we developed a three-part model of the event product from the visitor's perspective, shown in Figure 7-2. Essential services are those required by all events, the absence or inadequacy of which will disappoint customers and possibly reduce the quality of the experience and lead to lowered demand. Generic benefits are the attributes of all festivals and special events that are desired by most people. Each was discussed in turn: spectacle, belonging and sharing, ritual, games, and authenticity. This last benefit was explored in detail.

Targeted benefits are the elements of uniqueness and specialized activities, merchandise, and entertainment that provide competitive advantage to events. These benefits are most important for luring tourists, but not in the absence of essential services and generic benefits. The implications for event theming were then emphasized. The theme is important for conveying the right messages about the product. Theming is much more than a name or the object of a celebration; it is a unifying concept applied to all elements of programming, promotion, setting or design, and services.

Because so many festivals and events are free and heavily subsidized, pricing is an often overlooked aspect of festival and event marketing. Basic pricing considerations and methods were discussed, leading to the conclusion that all festivals and events should have a price. Setting a price for at least a component of the event can be very important. It will certainly help with attendance counts, and it will also provide a measure of real economic demand. Most important, from the tourism perspective, having admission fees for high-quality, specialized activities or attractions will send the right message to target markets—thus generating more revenue. In today's commercialized world, prices convey messages to consumers, and so setting the price must be an integral part of the marketing planning process.

CHAPTER EIGHT

Developing Tourism Potential

Continuing our examination of the marketing planning process for individual festivals and events, this chapter focuses on developing their tourism potential. The first section covers promotion, or the total communications mix. Though often of primary importance to event organizers, it should be considered in the context of the entire marketing mix, including product and price (see Chapter 7) and place, or setting and distribution.

Moving beyond the traditional marketing mix, this chapter next considers interactions—for example, between customers and staff—and internal marketing needs, principally staff training for a customer orientation.

Managing change, the subject of the next section, includes consideration of the product life cycle concept and the development of marketing strategies to enable an event to adapt to changes. An important element in this discussion is the question of what to do when events go bad.

Completing the marketing planning process, as shown in Figure 7-1, is the evaluation task. Organizers and others will always question the success of an event, so advice is given on how to measure success and utilize evaluation results.

Because many events are small and lack necessary resources, and because the whole marketing planning process is complex, we close our discussion of the process with a practical guide to segmentation and marketing. This simple strategy summarizes many of the key points and presents them in an easy-to-follow table.

PROMOTION

The term *promotion* is often associated with advertising, so it is more useful to think of a total communications strategy. According to Crompton and Lamb (1986), the strategy consists of the communications tasks necessary to influence the consumer buying process: informing, educating, persuading, reminding. The actual mechanisms of communications include advertising, personal selling, sales promotions, publicity, and public relations. Public relations has the added function of fostering community support and sponsorships, but that too is part of ensuring demand for the event.

Effective promotion often eludes small festival and event organizations where resources are weak and the annual planning and marketing process is condensed into too short a time period. By contrast, onetime mega-events and the largest annual events have full-time professional staff to prepare and implement sophisticated marketing strategies. We will consider the different needs of both these types of events.

A key point to remember—and it is applicable to all events—is that we are talking about the promotion of a service, an experience, not a tangible piece of merchandise. Promotion of an event has more in common with theme parks than with other components of the travel and hospitality sectors, although those too are partially engaged in creating rewarding experiences, not just selling airplane seats, hotel rooms, or meals. This is examined in detail in the sections on interactive and internal marketing, but some of those considerations have to be introduced when discussing promotions.

Organizers must determine the best ways to communicate with their main target markets, including what messages and images are to be conveyed, and by what media. A combination of paid and free advertising will be used. Table 6-1 described sample images and messages for festivals and events in destination marketing, and those ideas can be adapted for use by specific events. Consider how they can be adapted when reading the following discussion of advertising media. Also note that while the various media should be used in different ways, any of the options can be a vehicle for free or paid promotions, publicity, and public relations.

Advertising

Advertising is paid promotion of an event, usually using public media. Events commonly rely on newspapers, which are undoubtedly a very cost-effective way to reach the dominant local and regional market. The coverage might very well be undifferentiated, however, so it is not always a suitable medium for reaching specific target segments.

There is little point in paying for ads throughout the year, but much to gain by obtaining free publicity in the local papers as often as possible. Ads placed close to the event time should combine or alternate focus on attention-grabbing visual effects, in keeping with the theme, and detailed information about location, schedules, attractions, and costs. Coupons for price discounts and other incentives can be offered, and event programs circulated, through newspapers as well.

Radio is more useful to generate wide awareness of the event, along with detailed information immediately prior to the event. Audible imagery can be used effectively to convey the feeling of celebration and excitement, or to provide a sample of musical specialties. Contests with event-related prizes work well on radio and may attract sponsors or the radio station's free involvement. In large urban areas with a variety of stations, it is possible to reach target markets using radio, especially with regard to the big differences between rock, country, and middle-of-the-road programming.

Television presents the best opportunity to communicate the total visitor experience, although some things have to be left to the imagination—which is the realm of media communications experts. The event theme can be communicated well on television, encompassing visual and audio imagery from the setting, decor, activities, costumes, and participants.

Most large and ambitious events develop professionally produced videos to offer to television travel and community affairs shows and to use in attracting sponsors. Publicity stunts and unique program events can capture valuable free news coverage. Television advertising can be too expensive for smaller organizations, so free coverage has considerable publicity value—which many organizers put a dollar value on, to demonstrate their promotional efficiency. As with radio, paid advertising on television will have the most effect just prior to the event, although more distant markets need a longer lead time than the host community.

Many cities and regions have their own magazines, often with an entertainment and "what's on" emphasis. These can be used much like newspapers, although their production deadlines require extra lead time. Care is needed to check on when and how they are distributed, and what type of audience will get them.

National newsstand and subscription magazines will not be affordable to small events, but they do offer an excellent way to reach special-interest groups and targeted socioeconomic segments. The marketer must check circulation numbers and geographic distribution, determine the magazine's coverage of desired segments, and estimate costs compared to other media options. Sports and hobby magazines are often targeted precisely, but not all readers will be interested in travel. There are also travel magazines, which expanded greatly in number throughout the 1980s. Their readers are largely in the upper socioeconomic classes and travel frequently.

The event program and other brochures created for wide distribution are important components of the advertising budget. Care must be taken not to waste large numbers on people who are unlikely to read them or attend the event, so their distribution should be evaluated carefully every year. Signs, banners, and posters are often useful, to both attract local attention and provide directions. Properly sited and well-designed roadside signs can be used to lure passersby.

The secret to effective advertising is to reach the widest possible audience through the most local and inexpensive media, and to employ more costly regional or national media only to reach the most valuable target segments. Unless planners know who their existing markets are and identify their primary target markets, advertising can be a waste of money. Some events, satisfied with their annual attendance or unable to cope with a larger crowd, cease advertising completely. This saves money, but in the long run there are risks (see the discussion of the product life cycle later in this chapter).

Personal Selling

Research has proved the importance of personal selling for festivals and special events. Word-of-mouth recommendations account for a large proportion of responses whenever event patrons are asked to name their main source of information about the event or to name their reasons for attending. This is informal personal selling, but it can also be helped along by several simple techniques:

- Interorganizational networking: the more organizations are involved, the wider the potential circle of communications
- Maximization of volunteer participation, in a way that is similar to networking
- Distribution of information and promotional merchandise that participants, visitors, and performers can take home
- Recruitment incentives, such as discounts: given to residents to bring visiting friends and relatives, and to first-time visitors for a return visit with new customers

General awareness and public relations campaigns in the host community can also pay off by fostering a sense of pride and community ownership, which ensures free promotion. Paid employees must also be a part of the personal selling process; this can be encouraged through training.

Word of mouth will have its best impact on the local and regional audience, but there is definitely potential for the tourist market as well. Event marketers can focus on those people with second homes in the area, as they will have a greater personal interest in the event. Invite them to the event and encourage them to spread the message to their home communities. Expatriates are another group worth cultivating. Having occasional homecomings can get these former residents in touch with events, and they can become long-distance ambassadors.

Other techniques for direct personal selling have value for events. Door-to-door canvassing in the immediate neighborhoods around the event setting works best for community festivals, people-in-the-park events, and smaller onetime events. Personal calls or mailed-out invitations might work well for special-interest groups expected to be lured by the event theme and specialties.

Sales Promotions

This category includes a variety of activities designed to increase sales to specific groups or to the population at large. Discount coupons, contests, and specials of all kinds are sales promotions. Most destination tourist organizations conduct familiarization tours for travel writers, agents, and tour wholesalers, and events can be placed on the list of things to see. Large, annual events should conduct their own, but they must be focused very precisely. The main target will likely be coach tour operators, writers, and media personalities from key market centers and representatives of special-interest groups.

Publicity

Everyone has heard of the publicity stunt or pseudo-event fabricated to attract attention. These have their place, but the opportunities for free, image-enhancing publicity are few and have to be individually cultivated. Having an open organization, with easy access to staff and volunteers, will help the media get information. This has to be supplemented by a press kit, available anytime, and press releases timed to build interest and communicate detailed information prior to the event. Some clever festival organizers literally feed their main media contacts with samples of the event's delicacies or prized merchandise. Others are good at luring or paying celebrities to attend the event or lend their own image to its promotion.

As the number of festivals and events has grown rapidly, the opportunity for promotion at other events has increased. Many organizers do this through parade floats or permanent, mobile exhibitions. Costumed mascots or other representatives can travel more widely and promote both the event and the hospitality of the host community.

A good logo and visual graphics related to the event theme are valuable promotion devices. With imagination and entrepreneurial skill, the logo and commissioned, theme-related artwork can be licensed for profitable merchandising.

Public Relations

This is a year-round task, and it is the responsibility of every staff person and volunteer. Community-based festivals in particular must develop and maintain favorable relations with the host community and its politically influential leaders. A broad network of participants and formal, open links with stakeholder groups will yield a solid foundation. Reinvestment of surplus revenues in community projects has a dramatic impact in creating goodwill and attracting both volunteers and resident audiences.

In the tourism context, the first rule is that good community relations will enhance the image of the event and its setting as an attractive destination. Tourists arriving for an event expect the community to be supportive, and if they find conflict or inhospitable residents, tourists will not return. Word of mouth works in a negative as well as positive way.

Sponsorship and Promotions

Sponsorship provides corporations or other organizations with the opportunity to invest in the event for purposes of advertising, public relations, or sales. While this process provides the event with revenue, or in-kind services, it also can have a dramatic impact on event promotions. A case study presented in Chapter 9, the Speight's Coast to Coast triathlon in New Zealand, demonstrates the importance of major corporate sponsorship in elevating that event's advertising and building its prize money, thereby increasing its appeal to competitors and the media.

Junker (1989) noted the impact of major sponsorship on the Sunkist Fiesta Bowl in Arizona, enabling its organizers to attract better football teams and hence more tourists. Media attention increased, and this spilled over to the festival program, not just the big game. As well as the big-name sponsor (Sunkist), the Fiesta Bowl also attracts almost one thousand other sponsors, with obvious impact on the event's ability to mount its sixty-two different events in Tempe and throughout the state.

Attraction of Sponsors

To attract sponsors, and particularly to secure the ones most beneficial to the event, requires effective marketing. Readers of trade publications such as *Special Events Report* and *Sponsorship Report* can quickly gain a feeling for what sponsors seek in general, and what specific corporations' policies on sponsorship are, but each case will have to be negotiated individually.

Some basic points can be stressed about the benefits that must be offered to potential sponsors and the criteria used in searching for the right sponsors:

- The event's theme and image must fit the sponsor's.
- Sponsors want to reach their key target markets; are they the same as the event's?

Speight's Coast to Coast, New Zealand: The image of the destination, sponsors, and event can be mutually reinforcing (New Zealand Tourist and Publicity Department).

- Sponsors want one or more of the following opportunities: to sell products; to get their name associated with an attractive event; to secure free or paid advertising; to provide their staff with morale-boosting activities or rewards—how can the event facilitate these objectives?
- Are the potential benefits to the sponsor balanced against the amounts of money being sought?
- Is the quality of the event reliable enough to ensure that sponsors will be satisfied?
- Is there an established record of media exposure that will attract new sponsors?

Many issues have to be considered before rushing into the sponsorship field. Getz (1989b) outlined ways in which sponsorship could positively or negatively affect all aspects of the event organization. The product could be shaped by the sponsors' interests in maximizing exposure for their names or merchandise, for

Speight's Coast to Coast, New Zealand: Sponsorship, prizes, and high visibility go together (New Zealand Tourist and Publicity Department).

example through attracting better competitors or desiring more media-oriented spectacle. The availability of sponsors' staff and expertise could make management more effective, but financial control of the event might be lost. Organizers therefore must decide on not only a strategy for attracting sponsors, but also one for dealing with sponsors.

In general, attractiveness to tourists will be heightened by developing beneficial relationships with one or more sponsors. The correct sponsor can heighten awareness of the event, develop its product, and improve its image. In a consumer-oriented society there is often an assumption that anything good will have a big name attached to it; like it or not, this consideration of the perceived value of an event can influence leisure and travel decisions.

PLACE: THE SETTING

In the traditional marketing mix, *place* refers to the location of the business or the distribution of the goods and services, or both. For festivals and events, the setting is often an essential ingredient in creating the right atmosphere and in setting parameters of crowd control, accessibility, and essential services. Distribution—which will be considered later in this chapter—is a factor in the marketing of events through intermediaries, especially tour wholesalers, and the distribution of promotions.

Surprisingly little has been written about the festival or special event setting. Much remains to be learned about the various physical conditions that help create a festive mood or otherwise shape visitor experiences. Designers of theme parks and world's fairs probably have good insights to offer, but their experiences have to be adapted for other events and settings.

Festivals and special events often have specific requirements dictated by the nature of the program or theme. This is particularly true for sporting events, artistic performances, and exhibitions. Others make do with a hodgepodge of indoor and outdoor facilities or spaces, adapting the event to them. Street and park festivals have an appeal based in part on the inversion of normal roles— passive parks turned into busy people places, streets reclaimed from traffic for pedestrians.

Many cities have constructed festival parks, gardens, and halls, and even private enterprise has entered the picture through festival markets and themed shopping centers. They tend to be oriented to performing arts, and feature open-air amphitheaters and spaces for exhibits or related activities.

Generic Characteristics of Festival Settings

Figure 7-2, the three-level model of the event product from the visitor's perspective—essential services and generic and targeted benefits—gives us a starting point for commenting on generic characteristics of the festival setting. The focus has to be on the festival because we have defined it carefully as a themed, public celebration. A special event could be anything under the sun, which limits our ability to generalize; besides, more and more special events and permanent attractions are deliberately adding festive features to expand their appeal.

Public Nature of the Setting

The first characteristic of a festival is its public orientation. Indoor, private facilities have a role to play in staging performances, exhibitions, and catering services, but generally they cannot accommodate sufficient numbers of people to constitute the main festival place. Large, private shopping areas, so-called festival markets, are a compromise between the need for facilitating large-scale public assembly and for sustaining a business environment. Mega-malls, such as the famous West Edmonton Mall in Alberta, Canada, combine features of theme parks and festival markets, and they are undoubtedly going to become more common. But the private ownership of this type of facility and its commercial orientation limit their suitability for truly public celebrations.

Creating the theme of a festival does not completely depend on the physical setting, as many of the thematic elements are symbolic and programmatic. They can be adequately provided in indoor or outdoor settings, and increasingly we are seeing themed shopping and entertainment facilities with a festive flavor. However, certain themes are best created in public, open spaces where all facets of the everyday environment can become elements in the theme. This principle holds truest for civic and national celebrations where the theme is linked to heritage, nationalism, and community pride. In these important celebrations the use of public squares, parks, and streets adds greatly to the fostering of a spirit of community.

The Special Quality of the Setting

Falassi (1987, 4) commented on the morphology, or structure, of a festival, with important implications for producers of public celebrations. He noted that festivals open with a rite of "valorization," which "modifies the usual and daily function and meaning of time and space." The rites can be considered to purify the setting, delimit its boundaries, and forbid its use for everyday purposes.

Similarly, the end of the event is marked by rites of devalorization, much like the opening and closing ceremonies of the Olympics. During the festival, other rites are common. They may have religious or other symbolic meaning for the host culture, or they may merely structure the festival around popular activities. Falassi described them as rites of purification (religious cleansing); passage (moving from one life stage to another); reversal (inversion of normal roles, such as in masquerades); conspicuous display (of important items); conspicuous consumption (feasting); dramas (linked to mythology); exchange (economic, symbolic, or informational); and competition. These rites are obviously important in a programming context, with application to the previously discussed generic benefits, but each is linked to the setting and its suitability for the activities, rituals, and associated symbolism.

Regarding world's fairs, Benedict (1983) observed that they are held on "grounds marked off from ordinary use, and special rules apply." Other authors (Kelly 1985, Middleton 1988) have stressed the fantasy element in theme parks and festivals, where normal behavioral rules can be relaxed and everyday life forgotten. This is a quality of public settings that is very difficult, perhaps impossible, to achieve in many private facilities, which are always associated with shopping, working, or private functions, and where extraordinary behavior might not be encouraged or tolerated.

Authenticity

Authenticity is a primary consideration in heritage-themed events, particularly those held in historic districts and facilities. Here, the entire setting is an authentic-looking stage on which the public celebration is played. But it should go beyond mere window dressing, as authenticity can be greatly heightened by actual use of heritage structures, appropriate costumes, themed foods and souvenirs, and historic reenactments.

Spectacle

Some settings are more suited to spectacle, but all events can use their physical surroundings and programming to enhance spectacle. The Olympics and other sports events held in big facilities permit entertainment, processions, and ceremonies on a larger-than-life scale. Parades along main business streets offer similar grand vistas, with the added advantage that crowds are able to get very close to the spectacle. Intimacy of this kind allows for the maximum impact of visual details, artistic subtleties, and complementary features such as smells and physical contact—for example, with clowns and costumed characters—all of which are difficult to achieve in a vast facility.

The decorator and stage designer come to the fore in helping to enhance the spectacle of events. Street banners, artwork, costumes, and performances all contribute to the special ambience. Even the drabbest physical surroundings can—indeed, must—be dressed up for the successful event.

Programming should balance spectacle with the intimate. A parade is spectacular, while small groups of street performers have a different and equally attractive quality; indeed, festivals of buskers, or street performers, are gaining in popularity. Huge ceremonies can be counterbalanced with small-scale theatrical performances—big with small, mass with intimate, and so on. Otherwise, spectacle tends to dominate and eventually weaken other programming elements.

Games

Often the entertainment and amusement games are separated from other activities at events, most obviously in the carnival or midway districts attached to fairs. This makes sense for big rides and noisy, disruptive entertainments, but it is too artificial and limiting. Rather, an integrative approach to providing settings and opportunities for play, humor, entertainment, contests, risk-taking, and perhaps gambling should be the guiding principle. Contemporary consumers are becoming more demanding of quality and sophistication and are growing accustomed to the tasteful integration of these elements in theme parks and shopping areas.

The site designers can incorporate elements of surprise, exaggeration, and outrageousness to foster a humorous interpretation of the setting and event; this should be augmented with humorous performances. Playful opportunities for the visitors can be suggested by the use of sensory stimulation—the right combination of sights, sounds, smells, and tastes—or by the provision of toys and games. Almost any structure, including artwork, can be used in a playful manner if normal inhibitions are relaxed.

Risk-taking and competition are more of a challenge and potential problem. Rides, contests, and structures have to be completely safe, so the feeling of risk or chance has to be artificially created. Certain games do this, especially gambling, but there are other ways. Common to theme and amusement parks are haunted houses and fun houses, complete with scary effects, and some elements of these might be appropriate for certain events. More widely applicable is the introduction of personal or interpersonal uncertainty, challenge, and competition, all of which include an element of risk and amusement. Interactive displays with an educational value are successful when the uncertainty element is high. Challenge is present in all contests, but festival planners will generally want to rely on personal challenges, rather than team contests.

Ritual

As noted earlier, rites and rituals have both programmatic and design implications. The setting can certainly enhance the visibility, emotional impact, and symbolic importance of the rituals. Opening and closing ceremonies, the most common form of ritual at festivals and special events, require a stage and an audience where the full emotional power of the activities can be heightened. Intimacy is best, so in mega-facilities and settings with large audiences, the ritual can benefit from spectacle. For solemn and sacred rituals, the setting must convey the right imagery, incorporating both obvious and subtle messages to the audience concerning the expected behavior and mood. That is a real challenge, for it is often easier to foster a joyful celebration than a solemn mood, when crowds are involved.

Sense of Belonging and Sharing

These twin characteristics of the festival depend partly on aspects of the program and the setting. Tourists may want to mingle with residents, to feel part of the celebration and community. How can this be achieved? Feeling part of something special is an important emotion to foster, but how can this apply to visitors?

Attention to the specialness of the setting and program can similarly affect both tourists and residents. But additional attention must be paid to the different needs of people visiting a community. They are, after all, both strangers and guests, and the event organizers must treat them as honored visitors. Essential considerations are discussed below.

Basic Design Criteria for the Setting

In examining the basic design criteria for festivals and special events, we will concentrate on the tourism connection, because organizers do not often cover this important factor adequately. A useful reference on site design for arts festivals has been provided in *The Arts Festival Work Kit* (Korza and Magie 1989).

Site Suitability and Capacity

Events often disrupt normal activities and potentially have a negative impact on the physical and natural environments, so the site must be not only suitable for use by crowds but also insulated from incompatible uses and activities. One-day festivals can be tolerated easily enough, but longer events in residential neighborhoods will surely lead to complaints and conflicts. Sites that are perceived or publicized to be people places are ideal, especially if they are in commercial or waterfront settings, which normally experience high traffic volume and have little residential use.

Visitors tend to congregate and expect action in city centers and around harbors, near convention centers and hotel districts, and in specific entertainment and cultural settings. Festivals and events located elsewhere might not be discovered by visitors, or might be perceived to be for locals only.

Crowd Control and Security

Public events can get out of control and easily give rise to conditions in which accidents, illness, or crimes occur. These are major concerns for the tourist, who more than ever wants to travel to safe destinations. Crowd control and security therefore have to be seen as an element of the attractiveness of the event, and promoted—or at least prominently displayed—as such. Community-based events, attracting strong local support and attendance, are likely to be the easiest to control, while also capable of holding an appeal for tourists.

Accessibility and Traffic Control

Special attention has to be given to the needs of bus tours, the long-distance traveler who is unlikely to be familiar with the setting, and the passing tourist who might be lured to the event. If tourist and local traffic can be separated, both groups are going to be happy. Running shuttle buses from parking areas and arranging for special transportation from major regional markets will solve some problems. Signs and information, written and designed for the person who is totally unfamiliar with the area, should be posted for the traveler's convenience.

On-Site Flow

Normally this is a problem of pedestrian flow, but some events might benefit from people-mover transport. Allowing pedestrians and normal traffic to mix could be disastrous, so clear, physical separation is essential. Pedestrians coming to and leaving the site can also cause problems, particularly if the crowd arrives or leaves all at once. Police control will be necessary for these situations. Parades are especially troublesome and require considerable planning, with emergency services and police requirements specified in minute detail. The needs of tourists are different from those of residents mainly with respect to the tourists' lack of knowledge, so, once again, signs and information sources must be designed and situated to maximize their value to the stranger.

Organizers have to determine the best way to use the physical parameters of the setting to maximize safe and easy flow, allow optimal accessibility to the site, encourage visibility and use of attractions, permit convenient use of washrooms, and provide the best views or seating for performances. The social value of festivals and events has to be remembered, and it requires adequate provision for seating, mingling, people-watching, and some private, quieter places for more intimate contacts. Tourists, more than locals, will use essential services and require public rest areas, so these have to be convenient to parking and access points as well as in the main attraction and flow areas.

Concentration

Grouping events and related attractions in one main location has several advantages, including maximum control and security and minimum walking distances. Visitors to an area usually expect events and attractions to be concentrated in major parks, waterfront areas, the downtown shopping district, or civic squares and plazas, so spreading events out too widely can weaken the community's image as a people place and tourist destination. Some festivals balance the needs of tourists and residents by holding the largest events in central places and dispersing smaller, community-oriented events throughout the area. The most common downside to a concentration of activities is traffic congestion and parking shortages, so the advice given previously on maximizing accessibility becomes all the more important.

For tourism purposes, clustering festivals and special event settings in combination with other attractions will increase a destination's attractiveness. Many cities have clustered their festival sites with convention centers, arts and entertainment facilities, waterfront attractions, shopping centers, and other cultural and public buildings. In downtown locations, proximity to mass transit, commercial accommodations, and restaurants is important for tourists. Clustering will also stimulate tourist spending outside the event and increase local income and employment multipliers.

Theme

Historic settings have an advantage in providing a themed, authentic site for festivals and special events, but most towns and urban neighborhoods also have the potential for developing a themed setting. Several resort towns, for example, have modified their streetscapes to imitate a Bavarian flavor, among them Kimberley, British Columbia, and Helen, Georgia, and both hold events aimed at attracting tourists. The event itself can be the unifying factor in an otherwise uncoordinated setting. Howell (n.d.) referred to Junction City, Oregon, which has developed a coordinated and seemingly authentic Scandinavian festival in what he called a haphazard setting. The event and themed streetscaping should be mutually reinforcing, with improvements in one stimulating greater development of the other.

DISTRIBUTION

As most festivals and events do not move around, the customer must come to them; hence our emphasis on the setting. The other side of consideration of place in the marketing mix is distribution. The basic related choices available to event organizers are distributing communications and promotions; making direct contact with customers, such as providing shuttle buses or selling tickets at retail and service outlets; packaging the whole trip and event experience to make it more attractive and convenient; and fostering links with intermediaries such as travel agents, tour wholesalers, and retailers.

This section will concentrate on package tours, which constitute one of the most basic and important sources of tourists for events. The other distribution options mentioned above have been discussed in previous sections.

Tours can be subdivided into those that are formed or escorted by the wholesaler or by an interest group, or are hosted by the event. They can be all-inclusive—travel, accommodation, food, and event admission—or split between a package giving access to the event activities or program and a separate package of the other elements. The tour can be open to the public or just for a special-interest group. It can also be exclusive to the event or include one or more events as part of a broader tour.

The event organizers normally are responsible for providing a tour wholesaler with blocks of tickets or some other form of guaranteed admission for the tour customers, but much more can be done to enhance the package. Hosting the tourists should be a priority, and this entails a lot more than handing them tickets or pointing the way to the parking lot.

Hosts and Tour Groups

The tourist is an honored guest of the event and the host community, and must be made to feel as such. To enhance the tourist's experience, a number of additional benefits can be offered:

A welcome-and-departure ceremony that is distinct from that given to other customers

Easier accessibility, parking, and related directions

More detailed and better-quality information, including souvenir programs

Small gifts or extras without additional charge

Arrangements with local accommodations, restaurants, entertainment places, and the like, to offer discounts, other inducements, and better service

Emergency and amenity services aimed at the special needs of strangers, such as rest areas, food and beverages, and medical assistance

The chance for the tourists themselves to choose whether they prefer to be openly identified as guests or granted anonymity while they enjoy the event

On-site tours or guides, including a look at the backstage setting and meetings with performers, organizers, celebrities, and so on

However, event organizers should keep in mind the possibility of a public backlash if area residents are made to feel like second-class citizens compared to the tourists. If special treatment cannot be undertaken discreetly, it might cause more harm than good.

The tour wholesaler, bus driver, or travel agent involved in the packaging process should also be afforded some degree of special attention. An example is the treatment given bus tours by Winnipeg's Folklorama, one of Canada's major multicultural or ethnic festivals. Folklorama prepares special group tour booking forms and offers packages for one or more nights of attendance, food, beverages, and entertainment at different ethnic pavilions, and assistance in arranging accommodations (Folklorama n.d.). One of its main target markets comprises the nearby American states and especially the twin cities of Minneapolis/St. Paul, where links with bus tour companies have been cultivated.

Participating bus tours are given special access, reserved seating, and escorted pavilion tours. The wholesaler is provided with information kits for each tourist, itineraries, and complimentary packages for drivers and escorts.

Ways of Attracting Tour Groups

There are a number of special considerations in the attraction of tour groups. Bus tours will predominate, although larger events might be able to package other types of tour group. As observed by McConkey (1986), bus tours have many advantages but also tend to be highly price-sensitive and often consist of seniors who require extra care and might not be high spenders. In addition, the bus tour market is very competitive, and committed marketing is needed to secure and keep tours coming.

Getting involved in the bus associations and their marketplaces is a starting point, and preparing tour incentive packages is also necessary. Many destination tourist organizations will do this for events, or at least assist them. Familiarization tours can be used to get the wholesaler to the event, or at least to the setting at a different time. The wholesalers typically look for certain elements of attractiveness, from their perspective, including how well the tourists and escorts will be received. Other criteria in selecting events could include

- Distance from their markets
- Cleanliness and safety
- Uniqueness of the event
- Its established reputation
- Suitability of the event and its setting for their markets
- Value for the price, to both the tourists and the wholesaler
- Available information and its quality as well as promotions by the event itself

McConkey (1986) said that establishing personal relationships with tour wholesalers and other intermediaries is critical for success in attracting tour groups. The event's marketing people have to work to get to know the intermediaries and their needs or preferences. The atittude of event staff might be as important as the product in maintaining good relations.

A final consideration is the use of charters—bus, air, and rail—to bring groups to the event. This does not usually involve tour wholesalers or agents, but rather requires direct selling to the special-interest groups or agencies, such as parks and recreation departments, churches, schools, and homes for seniors, that put together the charter groups. Similar marketing can be directed at convention centers, which might want to add an event experience to the conference package.

INTERACTIVE MARKETING

We have already observed that a major element of festivals and events that makes them special is their public orientation and the emotional involvement of all those in attendance. In effect, much of the festival experience is created by the audience or the crowd itself. This fact makes interactive marketing essential.

There is a growing body of literature on the marketing of services (e.g., Cowell 1984), and adapting the key ideas to the field of festivals and events leads to the definition of four main components of interactive marketing: the interaction of visitors with the host community, of visitors with staff and volunteers, of visitors with their environment and the setting, and among visitors themselves.

Visitors and Hosts, Visitors and Staff

In most businesses, staff-customer interactions tend to be formalized and subject to a high level of routine duties. But at community festivals and many special events it is the host community that is actually on display, and the staff often is made up of volunteers. With an emphasis on providing an authentic experience for the visitors, the host community becomes part of the attraction, and the staff and volunteers are performers in the festival production.

Managing the host population is a rather difficult if not impossible task, so success in this area requires good public relations and strong community support for the event. Managing volunteers is more difficult than managing paid employees, given the absence of many of the rewards and disciplinary options, but there are at least several manageable elements of the visitor-host interaction that should be considered.

The first is appearance. Dress and costume of staff and volunteers can be regulated, particularly to achieve a unified theme. Functions of each staff member and volunteer should be specified, with particular attention to the degree to which each person is expected to interact with visitors or at least be visible to the guests. The latter functions include selling and ticket taking; directions and information; security and crowd control; emergency services; cleanup and maintenance; performance and entertainment. In the Disney tradition, all workers should be encouraged to think of themselves as being part of the performance and to act accordingly. To follow the Club Med approach, workers should also be prepared to act as gentle organizers, or animators, ensuring that the visitors have a good time. Direction and control should be as subtle and friendly as possible. The key point is to have all staff and volunteers realize that they are hosts, and that their visitors have literally been invited to share in the community celebration.

If the event is simply a congregation of groups and merchants, the objectives of interactive marketing will be harder to achieve. Strong interorganizational networking and the fostering of a collective commitment to the event are necessary.

Target marketing must also take into account host-visitor interactions, specifically the likely implications of attracting or hosting different market segments. Family-oriented events place specific demands on the organizers, such as entertaining children, satisfying the needs of mothers with infants, avoiding overcrowding, and having staff who can relate well to all age groups. Youth-oriented sporting or entertainment events generate a different set of requirements, for which staff, volunteers, and the host community must be prepared.

Visitors and the Environment

The importance of the setting and atmosphere in creating a festive event have been thoroughly discussed, as have basic site design criteria. From a marketing perspective, it is important to anticipate and evaluate each aspect of the visitor-setting interaction, from beginning to end, with a view to enhancing the festival atmosphere and interpersonal relations. For example, basic services can be provided either in a purely functional way or as expressions of the theme. Safety and security measures need not be intrusive. Traffic and flow controls can be made colorful and funny.

Some groups can be expected to react negatively to certain elements of the setting. There have been enough disasters at sports events, for example, to anticipate the possible outcome of excessive or inadequate crowd control. Sometimes the presence or apparent invisibility of police will make a difference to how a crowd behaves, as will the arrangement and type of crowd-control devices. Organizers have to consider both the practical and the experiential outcomes of all aspects of the setting.

Customers with Other Customers

The setting and the staff and volunteers must combine to help convey the major social and personal benefits that visitors expect from a special event. Some of these benefits will be obtained only through the intermingling, actions, and emotional response of the audience or crowd, but these too can be facilitated. A sense of belonging and sharing can be fostered by making certain that customers share the main experiences collectively, rather than in isolation. Spectacle and ritual, in balance, can be used to stimulate emotions. Being part of a unique happening is more meaningful if the experience can be shared immediately with others, so a degree of mass emotional participation is essential. Too much can be disruptive.

Some visitor segments will not mix well, and these groups have to be separated in time or space. Is it realistic to expect a rock-concert audience to mingle on equal terms with operagoers? If this trick can be achieved, a real community celebration will occur, but normally the two groups will want to be kept apart. Only certain types of event really have the potential to appeal to the total population, and to do so without crowd problems. The spectacle of parades, fireworks, and major sporting contests can accomplish this goal, but arts and cultural productions usually depend too much on tastes and peer-group preferences to have mass appeal. Targeted promotions and image-making are essential to ensure that those who are attracted to the event will be pleased with the setting, the attractions—and each other!

INTERNAL MARKETING

Organizers attuned to personnel or human resource management will already appreciate the importance of ensuring that all staff and volunteers understand their roles in creating visitor experiences. Creating the desired attitudes and work patterns will be difficult for most festival and event managers, but the implementation of a permanent system of volunteer and staff recruitment, training, and reward will eventually pay high dividends.

As noted by Mahoney (n.d.b), internal marketing consists of several components. The primary task is to create a customer-oriented environment. In our context, we have to modify this point to stress what is different about a tourist-oriented environment. Festivals and events seeking to improve their attractiveness to tourists must first adopt an attitude, or corporate philosophy, that will lead all participants, whether staff or volunteers, to value the tourist, appreciate the visitor's needs, and willingly contribute to the creation of an enjoyable travel experience. This is similar to but more difficult than catering to the resident population.

Personnel training should be oriented to ensuring that all participants understand this essential difference in attitude and how it will affect their functions and behavior. Policies should be in place to give written instructions on all the key points, such as dress codes, limits of acceptable behavior, and use of discretion when dealing with customer problems and requests.

The final aspect of internal marketing is that of communications. It is a common management problem, requiring extra efforts in a volunteer-based organization and in interorganizational situations. How the event is structured, the committee system, reporting and responsibility channels—all are vital to ensuring that all participants understand their marketing roles.

WAYS OF MANAGING CHANGE

Events can fail for many reasons, but annual and repeating events have an additional concern: no matter how good the product and its management may be, over time the established markets might lose interest. Just as important is the prospect that a never-changing product might fail to take advantage of newly developing markets. From a tourism perspective, these are serious problems.

The Product Life Cycle

The product life cycle was discussed in Chapter 6 for tourist destinations. It has also been an important model in shaping recreation programs and government and social services (e.g., Crompton and Lamb 1986). Stated simply, the concept suggests that a new product evolves through distinct stages, each with related marketing requirements. We can adapt the model to individual festivals and special events.

Introduction Stage

A new event must fight to establish its image, reputation, and market share. Growth may be slow, and promotional costs should be high, if resources permit. If there is a price, it will have to be either kept low to attract larger audiences or set high to establish an elite image immediately. A community event can lean toward nearby residents as the main market, but an event in a resort or small community has a different problem and should attempt to attract the upmarket tourists and day-trippers who are interested in new experiences and have the time and money to sample new products. For all events, special-interest groups linked to the theme and targeted benefits should be given early attention, although not at the expense of essential services and generic benefits. Visitor expectations and reactions should be tested, and the evaluation used to improve the product.

Growth Stage

There might be a takeoff point at which growth escalates rapidly, and if this happens it will likely be attributable to high-quality production and services, word-of-mouth promotions, effective target marketing, and a favorable image in the local and regional primary market area. During the rapid-growth stage, revenues or profits should be increasing, with fixed production costs paid off and promotional costs possibly reduced. Prices can be raised to match increases in demand, but price gouging will have a negative long-term impact, especially if the image of a tourist rip-off is allowed to grow.

Some festivals and events manage to tap a large well of latent demand, with a big audience materializing the very first time it is produced. It is even possible that the first year's attendance will be the maximum the event can accommodate or the organizers ever desire. This will be called an instant success, but it is worth the time to undertake full evaluations anyway, to avoid the possibility that novelty alone, or some other unanticipated factor, was the reason for quick success. Organizers with instant successes might also be tempted to change venues, expand the duration of the event, or add new activity outlets, all of which are admirably aggressive responses. But any of these actions will change the event, in effect introducing a somewhat new product, so that the life cycle model will come back into play at the introductory stage.

Maturity

There should be a period of success, or so-called gravy years, but this should be managed with care and attention to the need for adaptation. If the management fails to provide for change, and particularly if it allows the product to stagnate or decline in quality, the event's survival will be threatened.

At some point the production peak will be reached. How long this can be maintained is difficult to predict, but as long as the event is profitable, it is successful with its major markets, and its quality is retained, managers might fall into the trap of thinking it can last forever.

Decline

The potential problems to watch for, any of which can result in slow or rapid decline, include the following:

The audience has gradually shifted toward lower spenders, undesirables who cause problems, or those with no particular interest in the theme or specialties.

The product has changed for reasons other than to improve quality and marketability.

The product has not changed at all, even though competition has increased and visitors have expressed dissatisfaction or changing preferences.

Maintenance and replacement costs are escalating, while revenue is leveling or falling off.

Crowding suggests that the site or facility capacity has been reached.

Community support wanes, owing to negative social or environmental impact, bad public relations, or boredom and apathy.

Promotions fail to attract new audiences and the proportion of repeat visitors rises—or the opposite!

There is no established rule of thumb for the ideal ratio of repeat to first-time visitors, but it is clear that a healthy attraction has to maintain enough appeal to bring people back—in other words, develop brand loyalty—and enough novelty to lure new customers. In tourism, new customers are vital because they should include many tour groups and passersby who have traveled a long distance and cannot be considered as potential repeat visitors. A significant proportion of repeat visitors should be long-distance tourists, as this group maximizes tourism benefits.

Marketing Strategies for Adapting the Event

Research has yet to prove that decline is inevitable, for either a destination area or a specific attraction. More research will be needed to demonstrate any hard rules of product evolution in this sector. Some preliminary research by Getz and Frisby (1988) has discovered that many community-run festivals experience repeated cycles of growth and decline, attributable mostly to volunteer burnout and lack of resources for adequate production or promotions. Howell (1987) has found that local festivals seem to stagnate within five or six years of initiation, and that stagnation or decline is more likely in areas with declining population or income. He advised that events in such circumstances must either increase promotions or change the product.

Sound management and marketing can ensure that the event adapts and either grows in keeping with expanded capacity and attractions or stabilizes for an optimal supply-demand balance. Several marketing strategies are available for extending the life cycle of the event, and these provide important options to be integrated in the strategic marketing plan.

Market Penetration

This strategy is one of attracting more users to the same event, without necessarily changing the types of users or the market area. Managers of static attractions and resorts can use special events to get patrons to return more frequently, but the challenge for annual events is quite different. It can be accomplished through more successful promotions, price discounting, improved sales to special-interest groups, or delivery of better value for the customers' money. Aggressive marketers might take aim at luring customers from the nearby competition, through direct comparison and boasting of advantages. This has obvious limited possibilities for onetime events or community festivals that lack obvious competition. Indeed, the uniqueness of events should be a fact, not a promotional fantasy, so there should really be little direct competition. Another technique is to use visitor and market surveys to identify nonusers within established market segments—organizers should have already identified customer needs and desired benefits—and promote to them more aggressively, such as through direct person-to-person sales.

Product Reformulation

If established audiences are losing interest, modifying the program or other fundamental elements of the product, such as the setting, can stimulate repeat visits. Just as theme parks regularly add new rides or special events, annual festivals can adopt a long-range plan to keep adding new and appealing features. Arts festivals do this when they upgrade the quality of performances or attract big-name headliners. If the product improvements are consistent in theme, the same market segments can be lured back. Care must be taken not to drastically alter the event program to the point where returning customers are not just surprised but disappointed with the changes.

Market Development

This strategy seeks out new target markets, often in geographic terms or by benefit-defined segments. For annual events, it means tapping the day-tripping market and then going after tours and independent travelers from farther afield than established market areas. Cooperative efforts with tourist organizations and regional or national promotional bodies are necessary. Most special events find that direct marketing to bus tours is an excellent way to break into new tourist markets.

Product Development

An alternative is to modify the event so as to broaden its appeal, or offer variations of the event aimed at somewhat different interests. For example, an arts festival can easily modify its program to add different types of performance, and can schedule each type to avoid conflicts among different types of audience. Some events have winter and summer versions, catering to different tourist markets, while others use multiple sites.

Diversification

This is the most radical marketing strategy, and it is seldom used for festivals or special events. There are examples, however, of festivals going on the road, so to speak, in effect becoming touring theatrical companies. Others have directly or indirectly spawned other events, such as so-called fringe festivals or events with completely different themes. The result is new products for new markets. Although it is a marketing strategy, it also requires planned organizational change.

Choices when Festivals and Events Go Bad

Occasionally the media focus on events that have clearly gone bad, presenting the organizers with serious problems. Examples are annual events at which drinking, drug use, rowdy behavior, and even rioting have become almost institutionalized. Others have experienced very bad publicity from accidents or injuries, overcrowding, political protests, boycotts, terrorism, blatant rip-offs, or organizational failure resulting in substandard services and a very poor visitor experience. Once the media have the troubled event in their sights, a cautious approach to adaptation and improvement must be abandoned. *Demarketing,* which is a planned shift in target markets or demand reduction, often requires more time than is available, and ordinary approaches to market development or product innovation will not work in a crisis situation.

Several choices are available, but none of them is easy to swallow. Termination of the event is the most radical solution but probably the only choice in desperate situations. The risk is that the crowds looking for the usual outlet for their bad behavior will simply go elsewhere—or will continue to show up at the same location. This phenomenon appears to be associated with particular holidays or other significant dates, and at resorts popular with youth.

A change in name or theme, with the attempt to convey the message that a completely new event has been developed, might work. If it replaces a terminated event, several years of absence might be required to discourage the unwanted types and to remove the negative image associated with the failed event.

A change in name, theme, and venue has greater promise. It appears that the setting is part of many event problems, and that a new location with different physical features will discourage some groups and attract others. For example, street or park festivals always have to face the problem of crowd control. Illicit behavior is hard to detect and even harder to control. But an indoor setting, or an outdoor environment with gates and tickets, can solve the problem. Resorts with an image that attracts action-seekers will likely have a more difficult job of security than will sedate, rural villages.

With the increasing linkage of events and corporate sponsors, the possibility exists for problems linked to the sponsor's image. Where alcohol is formally identified with the event, a strong image of partying and boozing might be created. Sponsors do not want problems, so the interests of organizers and sponsors alike require that advertising and image-making work toward a different atmosphere. Changing the sponsor, however, remains an option when dealing with a crisis.

Changing themselves might not occur to event managers or organizers, but they must ask themselves if they are part of the problem. Naturally this will not do much good if the new management fails to take new action. Open, democratically elected organizations have a built-in mechanism for removing management, but many structures do not. Political pressure or public embarrassment might be required to get rid of unwanted and unresponsive organizers.

Other Types of Change

Some changes are permanent, as in the case of an annual theater festival that builds its own facility, expands the program, and becomes a fixed cultural attraction. Although the name *festival* might be retained, the product is quite different, and its management and marketing must be adapted.

Goal displacement is the term given to a shift in purpose or goals over time. A real risk is that organizers begin to think their status and privileges are more important than the event, or professional staff alter the goals to reflect their needs for security and advancement. In open organizations there is also the possibility that power groups will form, with the purpose of changing the event for any number of artistic, economic, or political reasons. The only good defense against unwanted shifts in goals is to establish firm statements of the purpose and goals and how they relate to all aspects of the organization and production, as well as firm policies on how they can be changed. Stakeholders must be partners to such changes, so developing strong networks ensures greater stability. Managers must not stifle planned change, however, because evaluation and adaptation are essential.

Growth and decline are common, particularly in public festivals (Getz and Frisby 1988). Occasional lapses in an annual production can also be found, with some years being missed due to poor weather, lack of money, volunteer burnout, or other reasons beyond the organizers' control. Such peaks and troughs can be anticipated, particularly in the early years of development. They do not necessarily follow the nice curve of the product life cycle model, so that model should not be taken as absolute truth.

EVALUATION: ARE WE SUCCESSFUL?

Defining success is not necessarily a simple task, nor is measuring it. Because there are different perspectives on events, conflicts of interpretation or priorities tend to arise, as in the case where event organizers stress their event's success in stimulating local interest in the arts, but the city council believes it was a failure in attracting tourists. In addition, goals and priorities often change over time. The first-time event might be considered successful if it manages to survive for a second year. After a while, goals will be refined and new ones added. Often tourism does not or realistically cannot become an important consideration until basic funding and operational problems are resolved.

When evaluating event tourism policies and programs, the tourist organization has a broader challenge. The success of each event is obviously important, leading to the need to assist some organizers in conducting reliable evaluations. But there is the additional need to assess the overall contribution of events to destination development, as well as to evaluate the effectiveness and efficiency of assistance, marketing, and promotions.

Goal Attainment

The logic of evaluating goal attainment requires that the evaluator prove that the desired impact, or output, was created by the event or program. In practice, however, proof is difficult to determine with total validity. Rather, it is common to develop indicators of success, each of which stems from one or more of the event or program goals. For example, if there is a stated goal to attract foreign tourists, then related success indicators could be the number or proportion of foreign tourists observed in attendance, or perhaps the increase in foreign arrivals to an area over a given period of time. These indicators are called performance objectives, or criteria, when they are stated quantitatively—for example, to attract 10 percent more foreign tourists in the next calendar year. But general indicators are also often useful, particularly where precision of measurement would be difficult; for example, the goal "to foster community-based tourism development" could be measured through qualitative or quantitative evaluation of the number and types of organizations engaged in tourism-related activities.

One of the limitations of goal attainment evaluation is that analysis is determined by the range and nature of stated goals, which means that certain types of impact might be ignored. If tourism goals are not adopted by an event organization, then visitor surveys might not bother to note the home addresses or overall spending patterns of tourists. If the tourist agency has no goals on community development or environmental protection, then methods for detecting social and ecological changes probably will not be developed. It is also a question of resources, because evaluation costs money. Consultants are often required to conduct reliable surveys and analysis, but it is possible for event organizers to do their own evaluation with limited costs. Every goal should be evaluated, but judgment will be needed to determine the best frequency and depth of research. Informal evaluations, sometimes involving nothing more than postevent meetings or annual goal-setting sessions, are also important.

Evaluation Steps

Tables 5-1 and 5-2 described sample goals for event tourism, and Table 7-2 detailed sample goals and indicators of success for individual festivals and special events.

These examples are the starting point in evaluation. Each goal must be written unambiguously. Then a series of success indicators is listed. Note that each has to show how the goal is to be met by stating performance indicators, such as by specifying that attendance is to be increased by a certain amount or percentage. Time criteria can be added, as in specifying an increase of 25 percent within one year.

The evaluator next has to decide which data types and measures are both needed and obtainable; these will vary with the type of event and the resources available. To illustrate, consider a goal calling for increased attendance at an event. This requires a reliable measure or estimation of total attendance and a comparison over time. The measurement of attendance might be easy, consisting of ticket sales. More difficult would be the need to take a sampling of crowds at several venues over the duration of the event. Turnover rates and multiple visits might have to be calculated to get a good estimate (see Chapter 10). Measurement can be complicated, and skilled researchers and analysts might have to be employed.

Appropriate and practical sources of data must then be determined. An attendance count and visitor survey are basic methods, but there are choices in how to conduct them, and how often.

Finally, the evaluator faces the task of pulling together all the evidence and making good use of it. Concluding Chapter 10 is a discussion of how to make the best use of evaluation results, with a focus on marketing and tourism promotion.

A PRACTICAL SEGMENTATION AND MARKETING STRATEGY

Segmentation and marketing can be carried to illogical extremes, producing more confusion than anything. It can also be a complex and expensive process, requiring extensive market research and analytic expertise. Few events have this capability, and most will not benefit from exploratory segmentation studies. Consequently, a more practical approach to segmentation is needed. This is provided in Table 8-1. It is based on the findings of available event research and all the previous related discussions.

The Local Market Area

The basic premise of the strategy is that most events depend on local and day-tripping regional markets. Even the largest of world's fairs and the Olympics have adhered to this pattern, although mega-events draw a higher number and proportion of overnight tourists than do small events. So for all events, partic-

Table 8-1. A Practical Marketing and Segmentation Strategy for Festivals and Special Events

Local Market	Regional Market	Long-Distance Market
Residents of host community	Mostly day-trippers	True tourists

Key Target Segments

Local Market	Regional Market	Long-Distance Market
Participants	Up to 100 miles	Those staying in area
Interest groups	Bus tour groups	Passers-through
Known or repeat users	Special-interest groups	Second-home or seasonal residents
Immediate neighbors	Repeat visitors	Special-interest groups
Families and general audiences	Participants	Participants

Marketing Needs

Local Market	Regional Market	Long-Distance Market
Free publicity	Cultivated tour organizers: packages	Cooperative promotions
Public relations	Targeted ads, all media	Media attention
Community ownership	Predictable date	Destination promotions
Local sponsors	Linkage to other events or attractions	Enlisted residents, to bring visiting friends or relatives
Ease of access	Cooperative promotion	Developed hallmark image for the event
Free events or price discounts	Compatibility with destination theme	Pricing to encourage long stays
Newspaper and radio advertising	Visitor information	
	Competitive pricing	

ularly new and struggling ones, the local and regional markets have to be cultivated.

Key target segments in the local market include the obvious, such as participants, competitors, special-interest groups related to the event theme, known users of related events or attractions, and repeat visitors to the event in question, along with the segments known to frequent festivals and special events, such as families and seniors for festivals, young males for sports, and educated females for arts. Residents in the most immediate neighborhood of a festival or family-oriented event constitute the primary segment. It does not take much research to identify these basic target segments, nor will it require unusual effort to reach them.

The key marketing needs for these local target groups are shown in the table. Because the community should be interested in all local events, it is possible and also highly desirable to keep the population aware of the event year-round, relying most on free publicity and word-of-mouth contacts. A sense of community involvement and ownership can pay better dividends than advertising. This can be accomplished through a theme meaningful to the residents, taking the planning and the event itself into the community, a good volunteer recruitment and reward system, open management, and wide, interorganizational networking. Local sponsors can provide most of the necessary advertising, with emphasis on last-minute reminders—residents can and will engage in impulse eventgoing. Ensuring that the event program and directions to get there are readily available, for example in the local newspaper the day before the event, will facilitate impulse attendance. Because residents will also know all about traffic and parking problems, they might fear extra congestion near events, so organizers must overcome this barrier through well-publicized tranportation and parking solutions. Finally, ensuring high visibility for the event, such as parades, Main Street locations, banners, and posters, can be a lure for impulse attendance.

The Regional Market

The regional market might best be considered only when the local potential has been developed, unless the event has a tourism mandate or is in a small community without a sufficient local population base to support the event. An event's main regional market, geographically, is within an easy day-trip. Nearby cities, particularly those with quick road access, are the prime targets. Surveys have found that a 50- to 100-mile radius is about the maximum market area for most small to medium-sized events, but a visitor survey or even casual conversations with visitors can define the main market area.

Segments in this day-trip zone will be similar to the local target groups, but with an emphasis on repeat visitors—get a list of addresses!—and bus tours. Seniors' clubs are frequent day-trippers by bus, and many special-interest groups can be encouraged to hire a bus or use special shuttle transport. They can be reached through community-group directories, parks and recreation departments, and other readily available public sources. Organizers should not forget that participants, such as in sports tournaments, also constitute target markets.

Charter companies and tour wholesalers should be approached to organize tours, and these groups should be afforded special reception and services. A shuttle service that is cheap and reliable can be important.

Marketing to these regional segments should emphasize year-round cultivation of tour companies and special-interest groups, with seasonal awareness and reinforcement messages in paid advertising. There is probably little value to most events in trying to maintain year-round visibility throughout a regional market. Many events put on a publicity drive, gaining momentum in the months and days before the event. Publicity stunts and numerous press releases are also used to attract media attention.

Predictability is important to the regional market, especially in encouraging repeat visits and where organizers rely on word-of-mouth promotions. Holding the event on the same date, such as the first weekend in April, and at the same place will eventually pay off in developing local and regional markets. It is not so important in other tourist markets, where last-minute trip decisions are less likely. Brand-name loyalty can be developed, again through predictability, but also through reliability. If consumers know that an annual event, or various events put on by certain organizers, is always of high quality, repeat visits from a distance are likelier. As more and more events develop, competition for regional markets can only increase, and these factors become crucial.

The regional market requires special communications channels and information sources. Develop linkages with other attractions and events to maximize impact. Cooperative promotions can go a lot further than the promotion of a single event, especially if a coherent destination theme can be developed that features events. Ensure that the information available to out-of-town visitors is adequate to their special needs.

People traveling a distance might also be willing to pay an admission price, but not if it is out of line with similar events and attractions; so the price must be competitive. Special-interest target markets, such as people interested in certain types of music, or in antiques, might prefer paying an admission to events, or specific elements of an event, if higher quality or exclusiveness is thereby ensured.

Long-Distance Tourist Markets

A component of the regional market will be a prime tourist market, as these visitors can be lured to stay overnight or longer in the host community. In addition to long-distance travelers who can be attracted to the event, true tourists will include people already staying in the area, such as those visiting friends and relatives or staying at second homes. Enlist residents to bring friends and relatives, or at least to send them information.

The likeliest target for long-distance travel to an event as the main purpose of a trip is composed of participants, especially in sports, and people with a known special interest in the event theme or program, such as arts or music club members. Membership lists of clubs and associations can be a powerful marketing tool, and local clubs and associations can be used to promote the event to their wider memberships.

Higher-level cooperative promotions, linking events to regional and national campaigns, are needed to reach the long-distance tourist. More than likely, the general-purpose tourist, such as those on a touring trip or package, will be lured to a small event only if it is included in a preplanned itinerary, brought to the visitor's attention early in the trip to a new destination area, or held in a place convenient to the tourist. Promotion of the destination itself is essential, and event organizers should take the lead in ensuring that events are promoted at the same level as other attractions and services.

Mega-events rely on a must-see image linked to their uniqueness, but lesser events can stress unique features as well, thereby catching the eye of casual tourists. If there are several events in a touring area, the tourist might be lured by the self-proclaimed biggest, best, or only one of its kind. But organizers have to weigh the potential advantages of exaggeration and gimmicky image-making against the need to inspire residents' confidence in the event and the thoughtful tourist's desire to experience authentic cultural festivities.

Developing a hallmark image has a potentially similar effect, but only if the event and the host community are inseparably linked together. This strategy has to inspire an instant association between the community and the event, as in the New Orleans Mardi Gras or Stratford's Shakespearean Festival.

Finally, pricing for tourists has to include package deals and other incentives, such as long-stay discounts, to encourage at least overnight visits. Wholesalers might have to be offered special prices linked to the volume of tourists they bring to the event. The economic benefits will be magnified greatly as the number of overnight tourists increases.

SUMMARY

Chapter 8 concluded the discussion of the traditional marketing mix and added consideration of interactive and internal marketing. Promotions were covered first, with emphasis on the fact that promotions really means the communications mix. Practical advice was given on advertising, personal selling, sales promotion, publicity, and public relations.

Special attention was required for the subject of sponsorship. Drawing on available literature and limited research, some conclusions were stated on what is required to attract corporate sponsors and how they might affect the organization.

The first dimension of place, applicable to events, is the setting. With reference to the model of the event product from the visitor's perspective (Fig. 7-2), generic characteristics of festival settings were scrutinized. Basically, the setting must facilitate a public celebration, and it was noted that festivals take place in specially marked areas that are removed temporarily from normal functions— a process called valorization. The setting must also accommodate and promote games, ritual, and the feeling of belonging and sharing. Some basic design criteria were then specified, relating specifically to the needs of tourists.

The second aspect of place is that of distribution. As applicable to events, this requires consideration of communications, direct contacts with customers, and the use of intermediaries for packaging and tours. Owing to the importance of tour groups for most events, the discussion focused on ways to attract and host them. It was stressed that tourists must be made to feel like honored guests, and tour groups and the wholesalers should receive special treatment.

Interactive marketing was delimited by reference to several relationships that have particular significance to festivals and special events: visitors interacting with the host population, which usually includes staff and volunteers; visitors and the setting; customers with other customers. Much of the event experience is shaped by these interactions, the synthesis of which can be called ambience, or atmosphere. Organizers and event producers should therefore seek to manage the interactions to increase event attractiveness.

Internal marketing is focused on staff and volunteer training. The primary consideration is developing a customer-oriented philosophy so that tourists and residents are all treated as honored guests.

Managing change was handled by first reintroducing the concept of product life cycle and highlighting its application to event marketing planning. For each stage in the theoretical life cycle—introduction, growth, maturity, and decline—there are appropriate marketing and planning implications. Much of the discussion dealt with ways to assess and prevent decline through several marketing strategies: market penetration, product reformulation, market development, product development, and diversification. An additional consideration is how to cope with an event that goes bad. A number of possible emergency actions were assessed, such as changing the names, the settings, or the management.

Evaluation is the process that ensures the event will adapt to changes in the environment, including shifts in the market. Some practical advice was given on conducting evaluations and making the process a permanent part of marketing planning.

Finally, Chapter 8 offered a simplified, practical approach to segmentation and marketing (Table 8-1). The key local, regional, and tourist market segments were identified and advice given on how to cultivate them.

CHAPTER NINE

Case Studies

A select group of case studies cannot possibly do justice to the full range of festival and event types, settings, and issues, yet it is the best way to illustrate key points made throughout this book. The major criterion used in picking these particular events was the availability of good, recent information. An attempt was also made to provide some degree of international coverage of different types of events.

The first case is that of the America's Cup defense, a special sporting event and onetime opportunity for Western Australia to develop the infrastructure and image for a major surge in tourism. In some ways it is comparable to other mega-events such as the Olympics or a world's fair. Particular emphasis is placed on the planning and marketing process and the multiplicity of impacts.

A community festival, Dickens on the Strand in Galveston, Texas, illustrates how events, tourism, heritage conservation, and economic development are mutually reinforcing. It is also an excellent example of a high-quality, totally themed festival. Data on its customers, effectiveness, and economic impact are presented, based on research commissioned by the organizers.

The third case actually involves multiple festivals and events in Canada's National Capital Region. Many cities have sought to develop an attractive tourist image, as well as to develop their cultural life through festivals and events, and this is particularly important in a national capital. Eight festivals were studied in 1988 for a consortium of public agencies, and data are presented on their marketing effectiveness and economic effects. Two large festivals, Winterlude and Festival of Spring, are profiled in greater detail.

Completing this chapter are profiles of two events held annually in New Zealand. Speight's Coast to Coast triathlon illustrates the roles of corporate sponsorship in developing a sporting event, and it also illustrates how an event's theme can reinforce the country's image. The Otago Goldfields Heritage Celebration is a new festival involving a number of communities. It was organized to promote tourism in a remote destination region with a strong heritage theme.

What is different in this set of case studies, compared to our earlier discussion on destination event tourism development, is the emphasis on how individual events can develop and market themselves as tourist attractions, as well as on their specific effects. To date, not very many such cases have been documented comprehensively, and more research along these lines will help develop some general concepts and conclusions.

THE 1987 AMERICA'S CUP DEFENSE, PERTH/FREMANTLE, WESTERN AUSTRALIA

Perhaps no sporting event has brought greater interest in Australia than this 1987 world-class yachting event, held in Fremantle and Perth, Western Australia. It also attracted great public debate about tourism and events, generating for the first time a substantial body of event-related research. As a case study, this event epitomizes many of the costs and benefits associated with the mega-event, and sports events in particular.

What made this set of yacht races remarkable was that the America's Cup had never previously been won by non-Americans, so this was the first foreign-venue challenge. To the non-yachting observer, it is clear that the excitement and touristic appeal of the event was definitely not that of watching the races— which were mostly inaccessible to those without air support or boats of their own. Rather, the races became a global media event, attracting the top American news anchors, TV documentary crews, and all the commercial hoopla normally associated with carnivals and political conventions. In a way, the races were like a mini-Olympics, involving not only the best that technology and money could create, but also pitting nation against nation in reasonably friendly rivalry— unlike the subsequent New Zealand challenge, which degenerated into technological farce and much negative legal tacking.

For the host state and cities, the challenge was the opportunity of a tourism planner's lifetime to get onto the world tourism map, develop infrastructure, renew declining urban areas, celebrate relatively newfound wealth and maturity—and to make a profit. It was also a lesson in politics, public participation and protest, urban renewal dynamics, free-enterprise economics, and marketing management. Much has already been written on this event and its aftermath,

1987 America's Cup defense, Perth and Fremantle, Western Australia: Visitor spending and new money from competitors, sponsors, grant-givers, and investors generate income for the host community (Western Australian Tourism Commission).

1987 America's Cup defense, Perth and Fremantle, Western Australia: The event was a catalyst for new recreational and tourism infrastructure (Western Australian Tourism Commission).

so this chapter documents only selected highlights pertaining to destination planning, marketing, image-making, and event impact.

Planning and Marketing the America's Cup

Western Australia and the host cities of Perth and Fremantle were in large part forced partners in the ambitions of business tycoon Alan Bond, whose motives for entering the America's Cup were said to include the promotion of a major resort development near Perth. But with success in the United States, and the necessity of a defense in Australia, the potential benefits were clear. The research manager of the Western Australian Tourist Commission observed (E. Smith 1986, 77):

The Government—Commonwealth, State and Local—appreciated early in 1984 that this event was undoubtedly to be not only a major sporting exercise but also an unprecedented opportunity to expose Australia to the world as a modern, technologically advanced, industrial nation with natural and man-made features abounding to attract the most world-weary tourist.

Planning for the cup defense posed unique challenges. It had to be a loose partnership among all levels of government, the private syndicates racing the yachts, the sponsoring yacht club, and commercial participants in the travel and hospitality sectors. In addition, the venue—Fremantle is a separate local authority that provides the harbor for metropolitan Perth—is isolated from other cities and had no previous experience with mega-events. To cope, the state established an America's Cup unit within the Western Australian Tourism Commission, complete with its own seconded staff and operations room.

The cup unit saw as its overall goal the "responsibility to spread the tourism-related effect of this catalytic event" (E. Smith 1986, 80). To maximize its impact required some imagination and enormous planning and coordination efforts. The year prior to the defense was itself important, including hosting of the curtain raiser, the twelve-meter yachting championships that attracted most of the America's Cup syndicates. Then 1987 was designated Year of the Visitor in Western Australia. The defense itself was a five-month series of qualifying races, allowing great scope—and perhaps creating the necessity—for complementary events. These included an international finance symposium, called PACRIM; the Perth America's Cup International Exposition; and highlighting of the annual Festival of Perth, a major arts event already well established in the city.

The cup unit's specific tasks involved coordination of all the participating bodies, promotions, media relations, information dissemination (such as a calendar of events and accommodation register), fund-raising through sponsorships, and work in association with the tourist industry.

The official record of the state's involvement (Government of Western Australia n.d.) noted other planning initiatives. Two new legislative acts were required to deal with the novel problems of yachting, and other acts involving, for example, health and liquor regulations had to be amended. A total of $66 million (Australian) was spent by the Commonwealth and state governments on the event and related projects, plus an additional $7.8 million by local authorities. Among the major projects covered by this spending binge were the following:

- Harbor improvements and a new marina
- Community services and facilities, such as transport, public housing, and infrastructure
- Restorations of historic sites
- Shoreline protection
- Maritime safety and policing
- Communications, including a state-of-the-art media center and an information center
- Arts development

The state government both desired and supported aggressive marketing. Packages were developed for the international market and made available as early as 1985. The yachting fraternity was targeted for promotion, but general exposure was achieved through the device of inviting numerous journalists and travel writers to Perth/Fremantle prior to the events, thereby seeding free articles and news coverage. In the end, almost 3,000 members of the media from thirty-five countries were accredited at the site.

Several critical variables pertaining to the marketing of the cup defense or other mega-events were noted (E. Smith 1986). Smith said it is important to understand the event, its history, and the needs of all participants thoroughly. Considerable public relations skills are required to deal with the various groups and keep them all satisfied and working effectively. Participants such as airlines and the racing syndicates, for example, did considerable promotion of their own; others, such as the arts festivals, did not make good use of the potential for joint marketing. Most important is the issue of image building. The marketing efforts had to achieve a balance between too much hype and too little. Too much could result in the so-called Los Angeles Olympics Syndrome, with people staying away out of fear of high prices, crowds, and lack of accommodation; too little could result in failure.

Also on the subject of image building for the event, Smith (1986, 89) noted, "It is the media backed up by word-of-mouth which generates and controls the hype." While travel writers can reach target audiences, in this case the yachting crowd, news reporters reach the widest audience and thereby influence general perceptions of the event. The cup defense did in fact experience distorted, misinformed, and biased local and interstate media coverage, necessitating continual public relations efforts for damage control. Contingency plans also had to be in place to cope with the unpredictable outcomes of the qualifying races. As countries dropped out, the target markets changed. One last piece of advice from Smith is pertinent here. Securing good media coverage during the event is also important, both to generate last-minute visits, especially as finalists are determined, and to stimulate postevent tourism. The halo effect of mega-events is well known, as tourists are often influenced to visit the host city and actual sites of past mega-events that had received high media exposure.

Visitor Forecasts

Demand forecasting and impact evaluation were contracted by the state government to the Centre for Applied and Business Research at the University of Western Australia, Perth. Its researchers felt that accurate predictions of visitor numbers could not be based on the experience of previous hallmark or sporting mega-events, given the unique venue. Consequently, the center undertook within Australia two surveys of intentions, in which respondents were asked by telephone to state the likelihood of their visiting Perth/Fremantle and the races in particular. Probability factors ranging from .15 (possibly) to 1.0 (certain) were assigned, and a formula devised to estimate volumes. Local residents in the Perth region were also surveyed to determine the scale of expected visitation from friends and relatives. Past tourist trends for the state were analyzed to arrive at an estimate of incremental volumes attributable to the event. But it was unknown whether the event would actually keep away visitors who would have come to the area in the absence of the event. It was also unknown whether cup visitors would spend more or less than the usual tourist. International travel forecasts were very difficult to make. The researchers observed that other mega-events seemed to attract approximately 10 percent of total visits from abroad, so this proportion was used (Centre for Applied and Business Research 1987).

Controversy erupted over the visitor forecasts, and estimates were revised upward at least once. The tourist industry, and others with vested interests, naturally wanted to see large crowds; their own investments required them! Some journalists and community groups, however, were afraid of crowds and all the perceived negative impact. The researchers were not likely to please anyone in these circumstances.

The official postevent estimates indicate that large numbers of tourists were attracted—about 930,000—but approximately 22 percent fewer visitors came to Western Australia for the five-month period than had been forecast. Foreign visitation had been forecast at 146,000, with the postevent estimate set at 134,900. The foreign market accounted for 14.5 percent of all visitors. Interstate visitors were calculated to be approximately 43 percent less than the forecast. Even the postevent figures could contain significant errors, however, especially in the difficult-to-measure domestic categories. Economic impact assessment based on the estimates must therefore be interpreted with some caution.

Impact

The official summary of the impact of the America's Cup defense (Government of Western Australia n.d.) listed key conclusions of the visitor surveys, longitudinal household surveys in Fremantle, and economic impact assessment. It was estimated that visitors spent $95 million in the state, resulting in a total effect—after applying appropriate multipliers—of $454 million; this spending generated the equivalent of 9,500 full-time jobs.

Fremantle residents were found to be largely supportive of the event and the idea of future mega-events. Major negative effects were judged by the citizens to be higher prices and congestion. The benefits were thought to include more to do, the general carnival atmosphere, and improved business opportunities.

Comparing responses before and after the event was revealing. The researchers from the Centre for Applied and Business Research (1987) found that neither the level of economic activity nor the amount of physical problems that were created were perceived to be as high following the events as they were prior to the defense.

Independent researchers also examined the America's Cup, and their observations add to the official conclusions about impact. Hall (1988) noted that there had been no true cost-benefit evaluation of the event, only an estimation of economic gains. He argued that opportunity costs should have been examined (for example, what else could have been done with the money invested and what opportunities were forgone to hold the event), that leakage from the state economy due to external investments had not been calculated, and that administrative and social costs were not fully explored.

One additional point emerges from the America's Cup experience. Hall and Selwood (1987) documented the public debate and protests associated with the event, including direct opposition to developments and aboriginal protests regarding land claims. This is an almost inevitable side effect of attracting attention, and event organizers and tourism agencies must be prepared to cope with it; the cynic would call it damage control. But any public event will generate open discussion, and protests of various kinds should be expected. The wise event and tourism planner will anticipate and constructively accommodate the inevitable.

Long-Term Effects

Hall and Selwood (1987) examined the potential consequences of the event on the image and long-term touristic attractiveness of the Perth region. They believed that a great deal of media and promotional noise faces the tourism marketer, and establishing a clear, competitive image for the destination is therefore difficult. The hallmark event, "with its high intensity coverage and its concentrated time exposure, can achieve the objective" (Hall and Selwood 1987, 6). They hypothesized that the full range of events and promotions associated with the cup defense, as produced by the tourism agencies, could "very rapidly boost the area through the development stage" of Butler's model of the destination area cycle of evolution (see Chapter 6).

This accelerated tourism growth is not without potentially adverse effects, however. Hall and Selwood (1987, 7) cautioned that "redevelopment of facilities disrupts pre-existing patterns of activity and lifestyle. The hallmark event thus represents a quantum jump in the amounts of change and the rates of change." It is also quite possible that the successful event could have such a profound impact on the host community that the consequences for tourism might be unpredictable.

The official government evaluation of the defense concluded that intangible benefits were realized for the state's industry and business, owing to heightened international awareness, new business contacts, and the demonstration of Australian technology. Boat-building and marine technology in particular gained.

Update: An Interview with Mark Sparrow

Two years after the event, in 1989, the Western Australian Tourism Commission was giving advice to New Zealand and others regarding their experience with the America's Cup. No doubt one of the first things an event planner should do is talk to those who have had firsthand experience, because one cannot get all the necessary knowledge from a textbook. So let's do the same.

Mark Sparrow, director of research and planning for the Western Australian Tourism Commission, was asked to comment for this book on the long-term impact of the America's Cup defense, and how the commission's planning and marketing had been influenced by their valuable experience.

Q: "What has happened in the two years following the defense?"

A: "In general, the America's Cup took a long time to leave Perth/Fremantle. As this was a major hallmark event for us, and one that received unprecedented publicity, both nationally and internationally, it was able to generate a halo effect. Tourism did not decline in a short space of time, as some negativists gibed. Tourists who either did not or could not visit Perth when the America's Cup was on came afterward. Our data show that despite a 12 percent increase in rooms available, occupancies took some time to decline to average levels. In short, one can conclude that our image was positively projected for these halo visits that followed the actual defense series."

Q: "You said that available rooms had increased 12 percent?"

A: "Yes, there were five hotels completed in Perth just before the defense. The event caused a peak in occupancy, but the subsequent drop-off was not great, even with expanded capacity. Our data also showed that the number of international air arrivals have continued to grow, while domestic air arrivals peaked in 1987."

Q: "What other long-term impacts are noticeable?"

A: "The area certainly acquired international credibility for hosting events, particularly in sailing. We have attracted the Whitbread Round the World event, and the Australia Cup Match Racing Series at Fremantle. The World Bridge Federation Championships are here in 1989, and the World Shotgun Championships in 1990. Also, quite a few convention bids have been successful, both national and international in origins. Twelve significant conventions are lined up for 1989 and 1990. Increased tourism infrastructure and exposure are making these possible."

Q: "On balance, was it good or bad?"

A: "Despite pre-event negative comments on the social and economic impacts, and alarmists on visitor forecasts, the America's Cup was a positive force for change. Business gained overall, with many new contacts and increased retail trade. The community gained, with more associated infrastructure, increased employment, preserved and refurbished heritage, new thinking, increased shopping and licensing hours, and pride. The Western Australian economy gained over $454 million over the defense period."

Q: "Have you any lessons on mega-event planning to pass on?"

A: "Perth and Fremantle, all levels of government, and the private sector all learned valuable lessons for the planning of future hallmark events of various scales. On reflection, when presented with the necessity to do something similar again, I am sure we are now better positioned to respond quicker, adapt better, and in all plan more effectively. There is no right or wrong way to handle the planning of a mega-event of this caliber, but the following are basics: Start planning as early as possible. Undertake proper research rather than rely on speculators. Establish a private/public coordination group to look at the big picture and take action; it has to be linked to power and financial resources. Call in experts as needed, but don't establish too many subsidiary specialized task groups who will tend to duplicate or frustrate each other's efforts. Above all, know that you will not do things exactly according to the master plan, so learn from the experience."

DICKENS ON THE STRAND, GALVESTON, TEXAS

This is an excellent example of a festival created for a specific purpose, in this case to draw attention to and help preserve Galveston's historic waterfront commercial district. The idea was conceived by the Galveston Historical Foundation, and the Dickens theme was a logical extension of the district's nineteenth-century cotton-trading connections with England and heritage of Victorian architecture. The Strand is a famous street in London, and also the name of the main thoroughfare in Galveston's historic district.

When the event was first held in 1974, the run-down historic district on Galveston Island was in need of money for restoration, and that required greater public awareness and support. The historical foundation had established a revolving fund to assist in restoration work, and the notion of a special event to attract publicity and tourists was a natural extension of its work. The first Dickens on the Strand was really a block party, but it has evolved into a major annual community festival and tourist attraction.

Not only is the historic district a beneficiary of the festival, but sixty nonprofit community groups participate and raise money for their own purposes. About 6,000 volunteers make it all possible, and over 100,000 visitors attend annually.

Many sponsorships are important to an event of this size and quality. For example, in 1989 Eastman Kodak was sponsor of the handbell concerts, and the University of Texas Medical Branch sponsored the beach race. American Airlines provided a round trip for two to London, which is won by a draw. Whataburger sponsored the costume contest, and local Galveston and even Houston businesses are involved in a number of promotional activities.

The Setting and Festival Atmosphere

The festival takes place every December, during the first weekend of the month, in a seventeen-block section of the Strand National Historic Landmark District. By 1987 some $60 million had been invested in renovations of most of the fifty designated historic structures, which now contain numerous restaurants, night-spots, and shops (Meyer 1987). Work on the remaining buildings continues as money is raised. The island has other attractions as well, including an arts center, historic residences open for touring, and two ships docked there permanently, the tall ship *Elissa* (circa 1877) and the replica paddlewheeler *The Colonel*.

During the two days of the festival, eleven gates are erected along side streets and on the Strand, to control activities and permit the charging of admission. This is somewhat unusual for street festivals, and elsewhere it could be managed only in similar settings where vehicular traffic flow is not essential and local businesses not adversely affected. The daily admission price in 1989 was set at six dollars for adults, three dollars for senior citizens and children six or older, and free for younger children. Advance orders receive discounts, and people arriving in suitable Victorian costume are admitted free—a benefit to regular local customers. Theatrical performances at Galveston performing arts organizations have an admission charge, and merchandising is another source of revenue.

The physical layout of the area permits the separation of activities, the holding of parades, and the creation of themed areas such as Covent Garden and the Dickens Posting Station. A number of information booths are erected at key points. Parking has been a problem in the past, leading to introduction of trolley service from outlying parking areas and a shuttle bus service from Houston.

The architectural character of the Strand resembles Victorian London, and the event organizers have carried this flavor into all other elements under their control, including authentic Victorian costumes, entertainment, food, beverages, games, rides, and music. Besides any Galveston residents who wish free admission and eligibility for prizes, all participating volunteers are also costumed appropriately. Dickens's characters are an integral part of the attraction; visitors can chat with Scrooge or Tiny Tim. Christmas shopping is a highlight of the festival, and strolling carolers set the mood. A parade is held each day, featuring Queen Victoria and Dickens's characters.

Other activities at Dickens on the Strand add to the authentic Victorian atmosphere. The Dickens Handbell Festival brings bell ringers from across Texas to participate in "the world's largest outdoor handbell concert" (Meyer 1987, 8). Four concerts, with over 340 ringers each, take place in a corner plaza highlighted by a huge Tannenbaum, or Christmas tree. Each year theatrical performances are held, featuring Dickens's *A Christmas Carol* in the restored Opera House. In 1988 the Strand Street Theater presented the musical *Oliver!*, followed in 1989 by *The Mystery of Edwin Drood*. Children are treated to special fun and entertainment in the Railroad Museum. The 1988 program also included a morning tea with Cedric Dickens, grandson of the famous author; a Victorian Organ Extravaganza in the 140-year-old Episcopal Church; and a five-kilometer Victorian Beach Race—in costume!

From the Dickens on the Strand brochure for 1989, the following quotations summarize the mood and attractiveness the organizers try to create:

Celebrate the Season! For just one weekend each December, you can step back in time, back to the days of horse-drawn carriages and hot wassail, to the land of Charles Dickens.

Games to play, jugglers to watch, contests, dancers, costumed characters—even a dancing bear are the fun of Dickens.

Enjoy food for every palate, from tea-time treats with Daughters of the British Empire to the full-course feasts of British fare.

Costumed Victorian vendors line the streets to offer gifts, decorations, clothing and artwork reminiscent of 19th century England. Craftsmen demonstrate their trade, and treasures fill the festive shops and carts.

Planning and Marketing

The Galveston Historical Foundation maintains a permanent staff of four with responsibility for special events, including Dickens on the Strand, augmented by marketing, accounting, and other administrative staff. Ann Anderson, in 1989 the events director, relies on volunteers and over thirty community organizations to do much of the preparation and on-site production of the Dickens festival.

Year-round effort is required, consisting of postevent evaluation, promotion and publicity, marketing studies, and production planning. Improving transportation and on-site services demands considerable attention. Sponsors must be recruited and their needs satisfied.

Direct promotions include news releases, an annual poster, and attractive color brochures, at a cost of around $8,000 annually. The Discover Historic Galveston Island color brochure also features Dickens on the Strand. More important, perhaps, is the value of free publicity. After the 1988 festival, Ann Anderson said, "We've received some wonderful coverage, both in Texas and across the country." The Cable News Network featured the event, and it was covered in a *USA Weekend* insert in 307 newspapers across the United States. *Texas Highways* magazine ran an eight-page lead story on the festival. In all, 50 magazine articles and over 550 newspaper articles publicized the event. Total advertising value of free coverage was estimated to be in the area of $1,700,000!

Market Research

In 1987 the foundation commissioned a major market-research effort, with surveys conducted by a team from the Department of Recreation and Parks at Texas A&M University. Both on-site interviews and longer mail-back question-naires were used to develop profiles of visitors and measure their motivations, reactions, and spending patterns.

A random sampling of visitors was obtained at the entrance gates by over fifty costumed volunteers from the foundation and the university. The surveys went to every one hundredth adult visitor on the Saturday of the event and every fiftieth on the Sunday, although the flow of visitors at particular gates neces-sitated some adjustments. A total of 630 short questionnaires were completed, with a refusal rate of less than 10 percent of those asked. In the mail-back survey, a total of 562 of 735 were returned, for a response rate of 76 percent.

Table 9-1 (from Ralston and Crompton 1988b) displays some of the main findings from both surveys and enables a direct comparison of the results. On most points, the two survey methods yielded quite similar results, as would be expected given the random sampling technique. But a mail-back questionnaire has the advantage of permitting the respondents to answer questions about their entire trip after it has been completed, which produces different results on some questions. Total spending, length of stay, and activities undertaken at the event should be more reliable when obtained by postevent survey compared to on-site, or intercept, surveys, although the accuracy of recalled information will likely diminish over time. The two surveys also resulted in differences in the gender and age of respondents, which can be attributed to the nonresponse bias and to the likelihood that different persons completed the mail-back form than had been given it.

It can be seen that Dickens on the Strand attracted a very high proportion of repeat visitors to Galveston: half of all visitors had been to the event previously. Over one-quarter said they had visited the event at least five times, and another 25 percent had been there on three or four previous occasions, which constitutes a loyal tourist audience. The vast majority of tourists came to the city specifically for the event (28 percent came from beyond the Galveston/Houston area), which demonstrates its high drawing power in an otherwise slow tourism month. Approximately one-quarter of the visitors were found to have stayed overnight, which has obvious advantages for local commercial accommodation, catering, and entertainment establishments. Groups without children were predominant among those staying overnight.

The audience was upmarket in terms of incomes and ages. There was a good variety of party types, with many families, and 6 or 7 percent came as part of a tour group. Hardly anyone attended alone (1 percent and 4 percent in the two surveys), which shows the importance of festivals as a social leisure outlet.

Data were also obtained on information sources used by respondents, which

Table 9-1. Dickens on the Strand: Comparison of Findings From On-Site and Mail-Back Visitor Surveys (by percentage)

Question	On-site	Mail-back
Two or more prior visits to Galveston	69	71
Prior visit to Dickens on the Strand	50	50
Festival was main reason for trip	75	80
Information sources:		
Television news	42	44
Radio	24	24
Newspapers	41	47
Magazines	8	6
Poster display	11	17
Brochures	10	17
Friends	40	43
Other	17	16
Staying overnight	28	23
Income:		
Less than $19,999	13	9
$20,000–$39,999	29	28
$40,000–$59,999	29	31
over $60,000	30	32
Knew that festival was sponsored by the Galveston Historical Foundation	72	71
Gender:		
Male	47	38
Female	53	62
Age:		
34 and under	45	35
35 to 44	30	32
45 and over	25	33
Type of visitor group:		
Family with children	21	20
Adults without children	36	35
Family, friends, and relatives	17	23
One person alone	4	1
Group of friends	19	17
Other	3	4
Origin:		
Galveston	15	12.5
Houston	67	59.5
Other	18	28

Source: Ralston, L., and J. Crompton. 1988. *Profile of visitors to the 1987 Dickens on the Strand emerging from an on-site survey (and mail-back survey).* Report to the Galveston Historical Foundation.

indicated that television, newspapers, and friends were the most useful. Organizers learned exactly which newspapers and TV and radio stations were good sources; this can be valuable in target advertising.

Turning to motivations, a very interesting set of questions included in the mail-back questionnaire were used to probe the reasons for attendance at Dickens on the Strand. Based on the literature concerning leisure motivations, the researchers developed a set of forty-eight statements that covered the domains of stimulus seeking, family togetherness, social contact, meeting or observing new people, learning and discovery, escape from personal and social pressures, and nostalgia. Respondents were asked to indicate the degree of importance of each statement in leading to their decision to attend, assigning a score from 1 for not important to 5 for very important.

The full list of the motivation statements is shown in Table 9-2, revealing a blend of very general statements, such as "Because it is stimulating and exciting"; some pertaining to the specific attributes and elements of Dickens on the Strand, such as "To experience the Victorian period"; and two pertaining to temperature and the beach, which were deleted from the final analysis. Also eliminated, after testing for their relationship to the leisure motivation domains, were a number of weak statements. Table 9-2 includes the mean, or average, score and lists the statements in order of rank, from highest to lowest averages.

It should be noted that an alternative approach could have been based on common travel motivations, such as the two statements on specific area attractions (climate and the beach), and others related to prestige, family connections, health, freedom, fantasy, challenge, exploration, or even business. This might result in a somewhat broader understanding of reasons for visits, especially among those who had traveled a long distance to the event.

Using cluster analysis, an attempt was made to identify market segments, defined by origins, age, income, and family group type, that shared similar motivations. But it was found that discrete segments did not exist, leading to the conclusion that "the motivations dimensions were generic across all groups" (Ralston and Crompton 1988, 3). This conclusion might say something about festivals in general, confirming our three-level model that describes generic benefits common to public festivals and special events.

Ranked in descending order, the most important motivational groups were family togetherness (mean: 3.19); meeting or observing new people (2.81); nostalgia (2.76); learning and discovery (2.68); social contact (2.64); stimulus seeking (2.51); and escape from personal and social pressures (2.38). None of these averages, which are composites of the responses to all forty-eight statements, was particularly high, as means of between 4 and 5 could have been obtained. Perhaps this is a product of the scale itself, or it could suggest the absence of single, strong attractions as opposed to a group of generic benefits.

These findings are not a real surprise, as other festival visitor surveys have found family and social benefits to be the most important. Knowing this, organizers can shape the production to facilitate family togetherness and other

Table 9-2. Dickens on the Strand: Motivation Statements and Mean (Average) Scores

Statements	Mean (5 highest)	Rank
Because I like the variety of things to see and do	3.62	1
Because the Dickens festival is unique	3.57	2
Because the atmosphere of Dickens is special	3.54	3
To see the entertainment	3.52	4
To experience new and different things	3.50	5
Because I had heard about the festival and it sounded like fun	3.49	6
Because I enjoy special events	3.48	7
To see the costumes	3.45	8
Because it is stimulating and exciting	3.38	9
Because I thought the entire family would like it	3.36	10
So the family could do something together	3.35	11
So I could do things with my companions	3.32	12
For a change of pace from everyday life	3.27	13
To get away from the usual demands of life	3.26	14
To have a change from my daily routine	3.16	15
To be with people who enjoy the same things I do	3.05	16
For a chance to be with people who are enjoying themselves	2.96	17
Because I like history and am interested in historical things	2.95	18
To experience the Victorian period	2.94	19
Because I like to "eat, drink, and be merry"	2.91	20
So I could be with my friends	2.90	21
To celebrate Christmas	2.89	22
Because I have been here before and had a good time	2.85	23
Because I was curious	2.85	24
To help bring the family together more	2.84	25
To observe the other people attending Dickens	2.84	26
To see the characters from the Dickens books	2.83	27
Because I enjoy history	2.79	28
Because of the sense of discovery involved	2.77	29
To kick off the Christmas season	2.76	30
Because I enjoy a festival crowd	2.68	31
Because Dickens on the Strand is a tradition	2.66	32
To be with people of similar interests	2.57	33
To be "where the action is" in Galveston	2.37	34
To learn more about historic Galveston	2.32	35
Because it is educational for the children	2.31	36
To contribute my time to a community event	2.18	37
Because I make weekend trips to special events often	2.13	38
To go Christmas shopping	1.96	39
To eat British food	1.84	40
Because I like to party	1.82	41
To be near the beach and the Gulf of Mexico	1.75	42
Because I saw it on television	1.67	43
Because I like to wear costumes	1.63	44

(Continued)

Table 9-2. (*Continued*)

Statements	Mean (5 highest)	Rank
To have an opportunity to dress up in costume	1.59	45
Because I like to drink alcohol	1.36	46
To meet members of the opposite sex	1.26	47
Because the weather is warmer here than where I live	1.16	48

Source: Ralston, L., and J. Crompton. 1988. *Motivations, service quality, and economic impact of visitors to the 1987 Dickens on the Strand emerging from a mail-back survey.* Report to the Galveston Historical Foundation.

social opportunities. Had the cluster analysis revealed differences among important segments of the market, or if the organizers wish to attract distinct segments, such as tourists interested in theater, or local teenagers, then a different strategy might be in order.

Looking at individual statements, these were the five most important: "Because I like the variety of things to see and do" (mean: 3.62); "Because the Dickens festival is unique" (3.57); "Because the atmosphere of Dickens is special" (3.54); "To see the entertainment" (3.52); and "To experience new and different things" (3.5).

Another insight into the attractiveness of the event comes from the listing of mean scores on the relative importance of five features of the festival. Respondents were asked to assign 100 points among these items (with average results indicated in parentheses): (1) people in costume (25.7); (2) entertainment (23.7); (3) the historical setting (22.2); (4) the special foods and beverages (17.4); and (5) holiday shopping (12.6).

Ralston and Crompton (1988) noted that the motivation scales mostly pertain to so-called push factors, which make people want to travel or attend an event, whereas the five specific features listed above are pull factors, drawing people to the Dickens festival. They also found that the general attractiveness of Galveston was part of the draw for visitors, and this fact could show a potential for cross-selling the other attractions and the festival.

Service quality was tested by asking respondents to score thirty-one items on a five-point scale. The statements were based on previous research, which determined that important components of service in the leisure industry were reliability, or the ability to perform the promised service dependably and accurately; tangibility, or the appearance of the physical site and staff; responsiveness, or willingness and ability to provide prompt service; assurance, or employee knowledge, courtesy, and ability to inspire trust and confidence; and empathy, or caring and individualized attention. It might well be asked if these measures are totally applicable to a community festival as opposed to a commercial tourism or leisure business, but they are a good starting point. More research will be required to determine whether festivalgoers have different expectations because of the nature of the event, its sponsors, or its goals.

Results showed that the audience was very impressed with entertainers' friendliness and costumes, the ease of finding the site, safety, vendors, and visual amenity. Mid-level service ratings were given for not enough places for sitting or parking, dirty and insufficient numbers of portable rest rooms, and parking costs that were too high. No item scored really low, showing a generally high level of satisfaction.

Open-ended questions were also provided. It was found that 86 percent of respondents indicated a desire to return to Galveston because of the festival, which suggests that Dickens on the Strand builds a positive image for the city as a destination (Ralston and Crompton 1988c, 10). The most often mentioned positive aspects of the event were found to be costumes, food and drinks, atmosphere, the variety of entertainment, and shopping and stores. Most disliked were crowding, the amount and price of parking, dirty and few toilets, lack of variety and high prices of food, and rain. These reinforce data collected in the other parts of the surveys. Suggestions were also obtained, many of which were creative additions to the existing theme and range of activities, rather than clear alternatives.

Economic Impact

Visitor expenditure data were collected in the mail-back survey, covering food and beverages, admission fees, nightclubs, lounges and bars, retail shopping, accommodations, automobiles, commercial transportation, and an "other" category. Dollar amounts were also broken down by location: the festival site, the remainder of Galveston Island, and elsewhere.

For each of the six visitor group or party types, an average expenditure was estimated. This requires knowledge of the average number of members in each type of group, or making an assumption on its average size, because the survey collected information on an individual's total trip expenditures. Next, the average spending for each group type was weighted to reflect its proportion of the total attendance. Also, because almost 9 percent of the sample visited during both days, the calculations had to be converted to reflect the total number of visitors, 100,329, rather than the total number of visits, 110,000. See Chapter 10 for additional discussion of this visitor and visitation problem.

Table 9-3 shows the main findings of this analysis. The total amount of visitor expenditure was estimated to be approximately $7.5 million, of which 54 percent was spent at the festival site and an additional 28 percent was spent on Galveston Island. The researchers noted that the average per capita spending of $40.55 at the festival site is high compared to that at a theme park, which might expect $25 per person per day (Ralston and Crompton 1988c, 21). This reflects both the affluence of visitors to Dickens on the Strand and the fact that theme parks

Table 9-3. Dickens on the Strand: Summary of Total Visitor-Incurred Expenditures, by Geographic Area and Category

Expenditure Category	At the Festival	Galveston Island	Elsewhere	Total Amount	% of Total
Food and Beverages	$1,148,691	932,749	288,299	2,369,939	32
Admission fees	563,606	62,857	30,410	656,873	9
Nightclubs, etc.	173,691	59,124	18,340	251,155	3
Retail purchases	1,391,266	238,885	243,241	1,873,352	25
Lodging	368,512	576,708	46,954	992,174	13
Private auto	251,768	160,237	249,361	661,366	9
Commercial transport	88,772	39,811	357,035	485,618	6
Other	82,591	42,979	67,171	192,747	3
Total	4,068,857	2,113,350	1,301,011	7,483,218	100
% of total	54	28	18	100	
Per capita spent	$40.55	$21.06	$12.97	$74.58	

Source: Ralston, L., and J. Crompton. 1988. *Motivations, service quality and economic impact of visitors to the 1987 Dickens on the Strand emerging from a mail-back survey.* Report to the Galveston Historical Foundation.

usually attract a younger audience. A very interesting observation was that families with children resulted in only 10 percent of spending but constituted 22 percent of all groups. Adults without children were the highest spenders, partly because a higher proportion of them stayed overnight.

The Galveston Historical Foundation realizes a large revenue of close to $500,000, mostly on ticket sales, compared to approximately $140,000 in direct costs. Revenue is used to support a multitude of historical foundation projects and programs. The research did not include either an estimation of the total economic impact of the festival on the city or a cost-benefit analysis.

Local news reports indicate that substantial benefits accrue to the tourism industry, with the *Galveston Daily News* (1987) reporting that hoteliers were able to sell rooms easily and at premium rates during the festival weekend. Store owners and restaurateurs also experienced abnormally large sales. The business community in the Strand area has to compete with the beach area of Galveston Island; the Dickens festival, along with February's Mardi Gras and the November Jazz Festival, were being looked on as an excellent way to offset the normal wintertime slump in business.

Use of Marketing Research

Dickens on the Strand organizers have used the survey analysis to help improve the product and its promotion. The event area has been expanded and new performance areas added, new rest room facilities were created, and the park-and-ride shuttle service and new trolley line were introduced to ease congestion. Programming caters to the key target market: older adults with higher-than-average incomes.

Potential sponsors are recruited with this information; in addition, grant-giving foundations want to know exactly who attends. For example, one major corporation was very interested in the fact that 9 percent of spending was on automobiles. To satisfy another major sponsor, children's programs were being expanded.

Perceived crowding and parking problems required the greatest attention. Not only was it necessary to introduce the shuttles and a new trolley system to the site, but potential customers had to be convinced in advance that the experience of getting to the event would not be a hassle.

CANADA'S NATIONAL CAPITAL REGION

The National Capital Region of Canada—metropolitan Ottawa and Hull—is a unique festival and event setting. As the country's capital it is a natural tourist destination, and the National Capital Commission exists to ensure that the region's image and status are national in character. Population of the capital region is approximately 600,000, with the City of Ottawa accounting for 300,000. Two provinces are involved—Ontario and Quebec—along with regional and local governments.

Festivals and events have been prominent elements in the area's attractiveness to tourists, and this case study enables us to examine their collective role in destination image-making and development, as well as the development, marketing, and impact of individual events. Several studies have been undertaken on the region's events, and this author has obtained supplemental information from interviews and other sources.

A major impact and marketing assessment of eight festivals and events in the region was undertaken in 1988 (Coopers and Lybrand 1989) for the Ottawa-Carleton Board of Trade, Province of Ontario, City of Ottawa, and National Capital Commission. Its purpose was to establish a data base for event planning and management, thereby assisting the events in fund-raising, evaluation of product quality, and potential improvements. In addition, the study was to enable public and private sector funding bodies to make decisions concerning assistance to the events, and to help organizers and funding bodies develop a strategy for revenue generation and funding. These multiple objectives make the study unique in its breadth and applications. Other sources of information include previous studies of the two largest festivals, Winterlude in 1985 (Ekos Research Associates 1985) and the 1986 Festival of Spring (DCH Consultants Inc. 1986), and an unpublished case study of the Festival of Spring by this author.

Winterlude, Canada's National Capital Region: A unique festival in a unique setting brings tourists in the off-season and bolsters the capital's image as a people place (National Capital Commission).

Winterlude, Canada's National Capital Region: specialist activities on the ice (National Capital Commission).

Profiles of Eight Festivals

Eight festivals were included in the major 1988 research; a brief profile of each one follows.

Winterlude

Winterlude, also called Bal de Neige, is the region's most successful tourist event attraction, partly because of the major funding provided by the National Capital Commission. Started in 1979 as a winter carnival or festival and held annually over ten days each February since, it makes heavy use of the NCC-operated Rideau Canal, which for many years had been a popular ice-skating venue. Formal objectives of Winterlude reflect the commission's mandate: to enhance the capital as a showplace for all Canadians and improve its quality of life; to stimulate the local economy; to strengthen the image of the commission; and to promote winter recreational activities.

In recent years the commission has attempted to make its event more of a community festival; to do this it established the Winterlude Festival Association

Inc. in 1986. It is a nonprofit body with a large board of governors involving all the local municipalities and members from separate public- and private-sector advisory boards. It has full-time staff, including a general manager and positions for programming, fund-raising, and marketing. An eleven-person executive committee and the general manager are the key organizers. The National Capital Commission continues to be the main supporter of Winterlude, with provincial grants assisting. Some of the participating municipalities take financial responsibility for their own Winterlude events. In addition, at least 500 volunteers, both individuals and groups, support Winterlude every year.

Events and activities in Winterlude are carefully controlled to ensure they meet strict criteria: they must celebrate winter, be nonpartisan—important in a national capital!—and be complementary to the whole program. All activities must also be open to the public and efforts made to ensure accessibility for populations with special needs. Some events have an admission fee, while others are free. Bilingualism—French and English—is encouraged, and all materials and promotions are in both official languages of Canada. All sponsorships must be approved by the Winterlude Festival Association, and are carefully screened to ensure compatibility with the Winterlude objectives and image.

The 1989 Winterlude program boasted over 200 "lively activities and amusements for the whole family!" Some of the major events were public skating, shows, and horse racing on the frozen canal; a snow village and ice sculptures; opening-night fireworks, music, and celebrations; and competitions in iceboating, speed skating, barrel-jumping, and much more. Clowns, performers, and the Winterlude mascots, the Ice Hog Family, are regular features. A winter playground is set up for children, and there are sleigh rides to enjoy. Although the main festival sites are along the NCC-controlled canal in Ottawa, the participating municipalities also host activities.

Promotion of Winterlude stresses the image of a family-oriented winter celebration in the National Capital Region. Through attendance at many other festivals and parades, the Ice Hog Family mascots have become well known.

Winterlude is the most successful of the region's events in attracting tourists. The Coopers and Lybrand (1989) study of eight events concluded that in 1988 Winterlude attracted 605,000 participants (who made over 1 million visits), of whom 170,000, or 28 percent, were from at least fifty miles outside the region. Most important, fully 82 percent of nonlocal visitors reported that Winterlude was a major factor in their decision to visit the region, which greatly influenced the economic impact calculations.

The earlier study of Winterlude (Ekos Research Associates Inc. 1985) determined that the 1985 production of the festival attracted 185,000 such nonlocals out of a total of 576,000 participants. The study also noted significant growth, with an increase of 185,000 participants since the 1982 event, and 80 percent of this due to nonlocal visitation. The consultants concluded that effective marketing and high levels of visitor satisfaction had accounted for the substantial gains.

The Festival of Spring

The Festival of Spring began in 1953 as a tulip festival celebrating the wartime presence of the Dutch royal family in Ottawa. Over the years the annual event grew in attendance but was plagued by underfinancing. Volunteers from the business community and tourist industry in Ottawa, who operated the Tulip Festival since its inception, also felt that there was a lack of community support for it and that it did not have enough festival-like attractions to encourage staying tourists. Other perennial problems were the weather and the unpredictability of the main attraction—tulips!

In 1975 a reorganization occurred and the event became the Festival of Spring, with a mandate to expand its attractiveness to tourists and become a community-based festival for the whole capital region. A unique series of free events, combined with promotion of the large tulip displays, was the program concept. Initially a number of municipalities in both Ontario and Quebec participated, but several of them withdrew, leaving the City of Ottawa as the main financial backer. The National Capital Commission has also been involved, mainly through the use of its land, equipment, and staff for festival venues. Occasional grants from the Province of Ontario and corporate sponsorships have also been important sources of funding.

From 1974 through 1986, professional management was obtained under contract, after which the first full-time staff members were hired. This change was attributable in large part to continued financial losses and the insistence of the City of Ottawa that changes be made in management and the program. A city-sponsored study (DCH Consultants Inc. 1986) made recommendations on programming, staffing, financing, and organizing the festival, including some reminiscent of the Winterlude transformation: to obtain better community support and promote the event more as a tourist attraction. That study also evaluated the festival theme and concluded that the image and program should return to the original springtime flower celebration. The 1986 festival, for example, had been themed around *The Wizard of Oz*, and some visitors criticized this as being childish, irrelevant, or poorly developed. After the major reorganization in 1986, festival staff more aggressively pursued innovative programming and sponsorships. One idea was to have corporate sponsors create large floral displays as a form of advertising.

Two major anchors for the festival are a popular Flotilla—a boat parade on the canal—and the National Capital Marathon. A craft fair is held each year, along with a number of parties and concerts. The Festival of Spring primarily uses National Capital Commission parkland near the Parliament Buildings and along the Rideau Canal, but since 1987 there has been increasing use of indoor facilities and outlying sites, to make the event more community-oriented and to protect against bad weather. A related objective has been to bring the festival atmosphere to Ottawa's downtown through cooperation with merchants.

Advertising for the festival is done through newspapers, posters, brochures, and radio; TV commercials were planned for 1987. Coach tours are important, so staff members cover travel marketplaces. Members of the festival board are expected to promote the event through direct contacts and media interviews. Media kits are prepared annually, and press releases made. A kickoff party and media conference have also been used to generate publicity.

In 1988 the Festival of Spring was estimated to have attracted almost 350,000 visitors (generating 684,000 visits), of which about 73,500, or 21 percent, were nonlocals; 66 percent of the sampled nonlocal visitors indicated the festival was a major factor in their decision to visit Ottawa (Coopers and Lybrand 1989).

Other Festivals and Special Events

The other festivals covered in the study are all arts and cultural events in theme. Homelands is an annual multicultural festival held in June. Its attractions include arts, food, and entertainment representing some twenty-five nationalities and featuring wedding traditions. Italian Week is an annual ethnic festival held in June in a specific Ottawa neighborhood. Concerts, sports, open-air street activities, and of course food and wine are popular attractions.

Festival Franco-Ontarien celebrates French-Canadian culture and traditions during a week in June. In 1988 over 400 artists and 150 performances were presented, together with children's activities and art shows. The Canada Dance Festival runs over the end of June and into July. It began in 1987 as a national celebration of modern and traditional dance, with performances at the National Arts Centre and a number of outdoor sites.

The Ottawa International Jazz Festival, held in July, presents hundreds of entertainers on stages throughout the region. The Festival of Arts runs for seventeen days in September and October and highlights the cultural uniqueness of the capital and region.

Other special events held annually in the National Capital Region include the Children's Festival in June; Oh Canada Days on the national holiday weekend, around July 1; National Capital Airshow in July; Central Canada Exhibition in August; International Cycling Festival in August; Hot Air Balloon Festival in September; Fall Rhapsody, a celebration of autumn foliage through special tours; Ottawa Winter Fair in October; Festival of Christmas Lights in December; and the New Year's Eve party on Parliament Hill.

Without doubt this is an impressive collection of special events and festivals, truly worthy of a national capital. Most are concentrated during the traditional tourist season, however, from late spring through early autumn. This provides a lot of potential activity for summer tourists, with Winterlude and the Festival of Lights intended to provide off-season attractions.

Economic Impact

Research in the Coopers and Lybrand (1989) study included on-site surveys of participants at each of eight festivals, plus telephone surveys of the regional population to help estimate total attendance and obtain some marketing data. The on-site interview samples ranged from 1,107 at Winterlude to 305 at Home-lands, while telephone surveys in the region totaled 1,952. A telephone survey was also conducted in the cities of Toronto and Montreal to determine the level of awareness about the capital region's event attractions. Additional data came from a survey of the local tourist and hospitality industry and organizational and marketing reviews of the festivals themselves.

Some visitor data for Winterlude and the Festival of Spring were presented earlier; Table 9-4 allows a comparison of all eight festivals covered by the Coopers and Lybrand study. The top two rows show the estimated total number of participants—not visitation or total attendance—and estimated percentage who were nonlocal, visiting from more than fifty miles beyond the region.

The third and fourth rows show the percentages and the expenditure amounts used in estimating total economic impact. *Incremental* means the amounts can be attributed to the festivals, so it can be called new money (i.e., comparable to an export). Obviously, nonlocal expenditures are the most important, and of that only the proportion that can be reasonably attributed to the event itself. Based on information provided by survey respondents—namely, what percent of their trip was motivated by the festival—the consultants worked out a percentage of all expenditures that could be deemed incremental.

A small proportion of the spending of regional residents was also deemed to be incremental. Respondents at the festivals were asked if their spending during the festivals was higher or lower than it would have been ordinarily; for all but two of the events, the respondents indicated it was somewhat higher. For the Festival of Arts the negative incremental spending by locals, combined with very small incremental spending from nonlocals, actually yielded a negative total incremental expenditure and resulted in no macroeconomic benefit at all.

The final line shows an estimation of total macroeconomic benefits accruing to the capital region because of the events. Rather than employ a simple income multiplier, the consultants based their estimates on a five-year econometric simulation, which enabled them to take into account the actual strength of the economy during the time of the events and subsequently. This technique generated a conservative estimate of a $61 million (Canadian) contribution to the region's gross domestic product.

In addition, the festivals generated 1,881 person-years of employment, including 20 full-time employees of the festivals, and substantial tax revenues. Corporate income tax was not covered, but it was estimated that the festivals generated $8.8 million in federal and provincial income and sales tax revenues. This can be compared to the eight festivals' combined total budget of $5.8 million.

Table 9-4. Economic Impact of Eight Festivals in Canada's National Capital Region

	Festivals*							
	Winter	Spring	Home	Italian	Franco	Dance	Jazz	Arts
Attendance (in thousands)	605	350	17	47	234	27	129	58
Nonlocal attendance (%)	28	21	9	5	15	25	19	13
Incremental spending (%)	75	58	19	49	25	51	11	8
Incremental spending**	$35.3m	$14.4m	.048m	$.26m	$1.6m	$1.8m	$1.3m	−$.16m
Macro impact	$40.6m	$14.4m	$.048m	$.26m	$1.9m	$2.2m	$1.6m	nil
Total macroeconomic impact = $61,041,000								

* See text for full names of the festivals.
** Dollar amounts expressed in millions.
Source: Coopers and Lybrand Consulting Group 1989. *NCR 1988 festivals study final report.* Report to the Ottawa-Carleton Board of Trade.

The Attribution Problem

One aspect of this economic impact assessment that requires comment is the attribution problem, specifically the inclusion of incremental spending by residents based solely on their impressions of whether or not they tend to spend more on festivals than on ordinary days. This accounted for only a minor amount of the actual incremental expenditures used in the calculation of macroeconomic benefits, but it is a questionable inclusion. Respondents can hardly be expected to have accurate knowledge of their average daily expenditures and how they are affected by festivals and special events. Moreover, any additional spending might otherwise have been spent at any other attraction in the region, making it an internal transfer, not new money. There are too many unknowns in this type of calculation, and it might be prudent to exclude spending by locals.

The calculation of incremental expenditures by nonlocals is also subject to debate. In this study the total spending of tourists at the events was discounted to reflect the fact that many said they did not come to the region primarily because of the events. Nevertheless, they did come as tourists and they did spend money that is considered new. In fact, they might not have spent anything in the region if there had been no events for them to attend, or they might have spent more than other tourists who came when there were no events on. There is also the problem of truly knowing festivals' image-enhancing role in attracting people to the capital. Therefore, to eliminate that spending completely from the calculation of macro or total economic benefits has the effect of arbitrarily and unjustifiably reducing the impact of event tourism. A better approach would be to estimate total tourist spending and its economic benefits, including an estimate of the amounts that can be directly attributable to event-motivated tourists and the amounts attributable to spending at events.

Willingness to Pay and Social Worth

At five of the eight festivals, respondents were asked about their willingness to pay for the free events. At two events that have entry fees (Franco-Ontarien and Dance), respondents were asked if the price was too high, low, or just right. This information was used to estimate what the study called a "social worth" of the events.

Total social worth was calculated for each of the five free events by assuming that it equaled the average amount people said they would be willing to pay, multiplied by total visitation. The average amounts were substantially affected by the fact that 20 percent of the respondents at all free festivals would not pay any price at all. The consultants attributed this to a "contingency valuation" problem and assumed that respondents feared the introduction of user fees. Of course, it could also be that many respondents would not think of paying for a public festival even though it has a high social worth to them, simply because they equate a public festival or celebration with an open, free atmosphere. Paid events would be equated with entertainment, like going to a theater.

The calculations revealed an "average willingness to pay" ranging from $4.51 for the Festival of Arts to a low of $2.58 for the Homelands Festival. This range can be assumed to reflect, at least in part, the perceived benefits to be obtained from each event. When adjusted to reflect total visitation, the social worth of each festival ranged from a low of $64,000 for Homelands to a high of $4,670,000 for Winterlude. The total of all five free events was estimated to be $9.3 million, which would be in addition to the macroeconomic benefits discussed above.

It might be asked, however, if this hypothetical social worth should be discounted to reflect the actual amounts visitors spent at, or in getting to, the events. The consumer might very well be willing to pay a given sum for an event experience, which has to be allocated to travel, accommodations, entry fees, food, souvenirs, and so on. If one element in the total package is free, that permits higher spending elsewhere. On the other hand, for those events found to have low economic impact otherwise, it might be useful to stress their so-called social worth.

Certainly there is a value to free events, but assigning a dollar amount to it is a dubious exercise. In Chapter 10 this issue comes up again, in reference to the so-called psychic benefits calculated for the Grand Prix of Australia.

Organizational and Marketing Audit

Coopers and Lybrand (1989) reviewed each festival's organization, planning, financing, and marketing. The marketing audit, of particular interest here, was aided by data from the visitor surveys. Because of the range of scale in the eight events, there were wide variations in staffing and marketing efforts. Winterlude is the largest, with six full-time staff and a budget of about $3.5 million. By contrast, Homelands and Italian Week had small annual budgets of $43,000 and no full-time staff. Festival Franco-Ontarien was unique in its use of two private firms to handle sponsorship recruitment, marketing, and promotions, while the dance festival was unique in having a private firm produce the entire event. Volunteers are important to all the events, with Winterlude annually relying on approximately 3,000.

Grants or sponsorships or both were important to all the festivals, but several depend greatly on other sources of revenue. Table 9-5 shows the funding picture for the eight festivals; it can be seen that total estimated revenues for 1988 varied from large to tiny. Government grants accounted for half or more of the revenue of four festivals, but less than one-third for two of them. Sponsorships generated very small revenues overall, but they did figure prominently in Winterlude and the Festival of the Arts. Other sources, including ticket, advertising, and food and beverage sales, were highest (78 percent) for Italian Week, which had the smallest revenues and budget.

The balance between these revenue elements will reflect management priorities and the style of the event, but sponsorships must figure prominently for larger festivals and special events. The Festival of Spring sought to overcome its chronic financial problems by increasing its sponsorship component, but achieved only a low 3 percent in 1988 and in 1989 found itself in a difficult deficit position. Coopers and Lybrand (1989, 43) noted that a "cluttered and competitive market for sponsorship funds" had developed and that cooperation among the festivals might improve overall success in raising funds.

Consultants found the marketing plans of most of the eight festivals to be weak or nonexistent, which conforms to findings of the Getz and Frisby (1988) research concerning community-run festivals in Ontario. The main problem was in translating goals and objectives into concrete action plans. An exception was the jazz festival, which had developed a marketing plan with goals and objectives, a communications strategy, market research plan, sponsorship data, budgets, and scheduling. Advertising media options were linked to target markets, and information requirements were identified for obtaining funding.

Awareness of the festivals among the capital region's residents was found to be high, especially for the two largest: Winterlude (97 percent awareness) and the Festival of Spring (87 percent). Others ranged from 51 to 76 percent, but Homelands, the smallest, was known by only 14 percent of the telephone survey sample. In the surveys conducted in Toronto and Montreal, much lower levels of awareness were discovered, with Winterlude having the highest (46 percent in Montreal and 38 percent in Toronto). The consultants suggested that low levels of awareness in these two cities argued in favor of using ads in well-targeted media to get at key segments, rather than the broad-scale advertising that had been employed.

Table 9-5. Revenues and Sources of Funding for Festivals in Canada's National Capital Region

Festival	1988 Revenue (estimated)	Revenue from Government Grants (%)	Sponsorship (%)	Other (%)
Winterlude	$3,500,000	42	27	31
Franco	879,800	47	14	39
Dance	563,225	67	7	27
Spring	305,495	50	3	47
Jazz	284,900	32	13	55
Arts	223,300	62	22	16
Italian	38,715	13	9	78
Homelands	42,600	57	*	43

*Goods and service only; no dollar estimate made.
Source: Coopers and Lybrand Consulting Group 1989. *NCR 1988 festivals survey final report.* Report to the Ottawa-Carleton Board of Trade.

Visitor surveys found that newspaper coverage was the most frequently mentioned source of information about the events, followed by word of mouth, radio, and promotional brochures. Word of mouth was very important to nonlocals—as high as 58 percent, for Italian Week—and this could be exploited through direct marketing, asking residents to send material to friends and relatives.

Profiles obtained of customers at the eight festivals revealed a great similarity among the festivals and between locals and tourists. The exception was language—French or English—which varied with the location and type of events. Festivalgoers in Canada's National Capital Region tended to be more from higher-income families with higher levels of education. They were also younger than the population norm for the region.

Levels of satisfaction also were elicited from visitors concerning the services and facilities at each festival, with respondents asked to state their level of agreement with a number of statements on quality, benefits, adequacy of information, and problems. Overall levels of satisfaction were high, but some rated better than others.

Relations with the Local Tourist and Hospitality Industry

Another interesting aspect of this comprehensive study was its attention to relationships between the festivals and the local tourist and hospitality industry. From a survey of 206 hotels, restaurants, and nightclubs, it was found that their awareness of the festivals was quite high—up to 100 percent, for Winterlude.

Only Homelands (33 percent) and the dance festival (53 percent) scored below 78 percent.

The opinions of the business community regarding the festivals were largely favorable. They believed the festivals were significant tourist attractions and added to the quality of life. But while these businesspeople thought government support for the events was reasonable, they were divided on whether or not local hotels and restaurants should be more actively involved as festival sponsors. A small proportion also thought the festivals had a negative impact on their businesses, and the consultants did acknowledge that some of the events had the potential to redirect business from one area to another during the events.

Hotels and restaurants were involved in special promotions or advertising for some of the events, particularly Winterlude, but hardly at all for the smaller ones. This fact, combined with the mixed attitudes of the industry concerning sponsorships, suggested to the consultants that more could be done to link the festivals and the business community, and that the festivals had to do a better job in making the businesspeople aware of the significance of the events—something that the study itself would facilitate.

Image Enhancement

Visitors at the three ethnic festivals—Homelands, Italian, Franco-Ontarien—were asked to indicate their level of agreement with this statement: "Events like the festival make one proud of the nation's capital." Between 86 and 88 percent of respondents agreed, showing a very positive image-enhancing role for the festivals.

The earlier study of Winterlude (Ekos Research Associates Inc. 1985) similarly measured the festival's role in creating a favorable image of the capital. That research found that 75 percent of tourists agreed that their image of the National Capital Region had improved. Over 90 percent of locals and nonlocals alike agreed with the statement that events such as Winterlude make them proud of the nation's capital. Consultants on that project concluded that Winterlude itself reflected well on the region, and also that it attracts people to the area who are subsequently impressed. This combination was thought to increase tourism potential.

TWO NEW ZEALAND EVENTS

Two short case studies from New Zealand deserve mention; one is a multicommunity festival linked to the development of a regional touring route, the second a special event that demonstrates the importance of sponsorship. Both have received financial support from the event tourism unit of the New Zealand Tourist and Publicity Department (NZTP) as part of a national strategy to foster special events capable of enhancing the country's image, attracting tourists, and spreading tourism benefits geographically and seasonally.

The Otago Goldfields Heritage Trail and Goldfields Celebrations

The Otago region of New Zealand's South Island experienced a gold rush in the 1800s, and there remains a legacy of historic sites and communities, which are being promoted as a themed tourist region. In 1987, the 125th anniversary of the discovery of gold, the first Goldfields Heritage Celebrations were held. The initiative came from individuals in the region and featured visits by a replica stagecoach to the area's historic sites and goldfield towns, with each community holding special commemorative reenactments. The twenty separate sites of the existing Otago Goldfields Park, managed by the Department of Lands and Survey, were highlighted, and the ceremonies served to inaugurate the region's Heritage Trail.

In 1988 the participating communities of Otago formed a legal trust and assumed responsibility for the celebrations, but it was later opened to all interested businesses and individuals. These initiatives were assisted by an event tourism grant from NZTP—the first regional and cultural event to receive money under the new program. A sum of $10,000 was granted as seed money, to be used for developing the festival and attracting international interest and a profile for its future. Additional grants were secured from the 1990 Commission, set up for the country's 150th anniversary in 1990, and the Lottery Board Heritage Fund. Sponsorships were also being sought.

The Otago Goldfields Heritage Trust has the goal of developing and promoting the historic sites, trails, and events of the region, both to preserve the heritage and to expand tourism. It is hoped that the trail will become a year-round tourist attraction, and the trust planned to construct appropriate roadside signposts, interpretive plaques, and town trails, as well as to develop brochures and guides. Within a year, the organizers reported increased tourism to the smaller towns on the trail, which are off the main highways.

An evaluation of the 1988 festival was undertaken to satisfy NZTP grant conditions. The trust reported that twelve communities had participated during a ten-day celebration. In five communities a committee had formed, but others relied on individual organizers and more unstructured community involvement. The community of Arrowtown, which already had a high profile owing to its historic character and proximity to the international resort of Queenstown, made its event run at a profit. Proceeds go back into community facilities, promotions, and other events.

Promotions were undertaken by the trust, including posters, giveaway maps, regional newspaper ads or supplements, and a news media kit. Individual communities obtained additional paid—or free—local advertising, in both print and radio media. The November timing of the event, during New Zealand's spring, does not guarantee a captive tourist market in the region.

As a festival, the Otago Goldfields Heritage Celebrations is unique in its multicommunity structure. The theme, however, is a natural one to link the towns and historic sites, just as the stagecoach reenactment physically links the venues and makes the theme tangible. Period costumes, gold panning, cancan dancing, old-time circuses, staged robberies, vintage rallies, barn dances, demonstrations of old crafts and skills, and street parades provide the activities and atmosphere. Each day in each community is bound to be different.

It is also unique in its linkage to the development of a regional, themed touring route. Most of the sites and towns on the route are not resorts, and some are quite out of the way, so the promotion of a common theme and circuit is bound to help disperse tourism more widely. The festival provides a highly promotable, tangible image for the region and the Heritage Trail. Its timing also serves to attract tourists in a shoulder season, with potential economic benefits for many businesses.

Speight's Coast to Coast

Some would say that only New Zealanders could invent an endurance sporting event like the Speight's Coast to Coast! It boasts of being the toughest multidisciplinary event in the country, combining a mountain run, canoeing, and cycling, from one side of South Island to the other. It began in 1983, organized then—and now—by a private entrepreneur, and grew quickly in terms of the number of participants and sponsorships.

The endurance character of the competition, similar to triathlons and the iron man types of contests that have become internationally popular in recent years, suits New Zealand's image of an outdoor paradise. This flavor also attracted sponsors and helped elevate the special event into an annual attraction and image maker. NZTP awarded an event tourism grant of $8,500 (NZ) to the Coast to Coast in 1988 to help the organizer generate international interest and publicity. With the plan to create parallel events in other countries and hold an annual world championship in New Zealand, there is considerable potential to develop a world-class sporting attraction.

An assessment of this competition (Harland 1989) revealed an interesting relationship between corporate sponsorship, evolution of the event, and its growing tourism value. Harland documented the role of the major sponsor, New Zealand Breweries, in giving the event a high profile by associating it with three different brands of beer, in sequence, and ultimately naming it after the Speight's brand. The brewery also sought out a limited number of major and associate sponsorships in 1988 to attract greater financial support, thereby elevating the event's publicity and permitting higher prizes in order to attract more or better competitors.

The switch from one brand of beer to a lesser-known brand (from Steinlager to Speight's) was at first looked upon as a loss of prestige, but the change actually resulted in more money being pumped into the event's promotion. The brewery used the Coast to Coast to promote Speight's into new markets. Publicity was also achieved through TV documentaries about the event and stories in international magazines. The sponsors established a comprehensive marketing program to obtain even wider coverage.

Referring to the product life cycle, Harland contended that a new special event can benefit from a high-profile sponsor to create awareness, and this in turn will increase its tourism potential. It is also ideal if the event and the sponsor's product or image match, and this was clearly the case in the association of beer with the rugged, outdoors image of the Coast to Coast.

SUMMARY

The selected cases in Chapter 9 illustrated many of the points made previously in the book about product development, marketing, and event impact.

An example of a mega-event was presented first. The America's Cup defense, held in 1987 in Perth and Fremantle, Western Australia, had a tremendous impact on that destination by launching it to the forefront of attention in the sporting world. The planning and marketing process was reviewed, benefiting from personal insights provided by key players in the process. A discussion of the event's impact revealed some controversy about the balance between costs and benefits, but the general conclusion appeared to be highly favorable for the region, even in the opinion of residents affected by developments. The Australian experience generated useful lessons about mega-event planning, not the least of which is the need for long-term, flexible planning involving all levels of government, industry, residents, and the sporting interests.

Dickens on the Strand, held annually in Galveston, Texas, was shown to be an excellent example of a community festival created to foster heritage conservation. It is comprehensively themed and attracts loyal resident and tourist markets. Visitor surveys were conducted to identify marketing needs and estimate economic impact. Results were used to influence sponsors and develop the product and customer services, such as through the improvement of access and addition of new events. A unique part of the research was the examination of visitor motivations and benefits.

Canada's National Capital Region hosts numerous festivals and special events, placing it in league with many other cities striving to become known as festival communities. The active involvement of the government's National Capital Commission also ensures that a truly national flavor is provided, and the commission consciously seeks to strengthen the region's image. Research concerning eight of the region's main festivals was conducted in 1988, yielding valuable data on economic impact, marketing, and organization. In our case study we illustrated some of the findings, pointing out conceptual and methodological issues involved in impact assessment. Evidence was also presented to prove that the festivals were enhancing the National Capital Region as a tourist destination.

Two examples from New Zealand completed the case studies. The Otago Goldfields Heritage Trail and Goldfields Celebrations was created as a unique blending of a multicommunity festival and the promotion of a regional touring route. With assistance from the event tourism unit of the New Zealand Tourist and Publicity Department, small communities were striving to develop a destination theme, attract off-season tourists, and spread tourism demand to out-of-the-way places.

The second New Zealand case was Speight's Coast to Coast, a rugged triathlon sporting event that complements the outdoors image of the South Island. Particular attention was given to the influence of corporate sponsorship on development and promotion of the event.

CHAPTER TEN

Methods for Evaluation and Impact Assessment

Evaluation steers the entire planning and marketing process. It is the way to constantly learn more about the organization's environment, an event's or destination area's potential market, the intended and unintended outcomes of events, and ways in which to improve the event. Very practical reasons for evaluation can be simply stated:

- Identify and solve problems
- Find ways to improve management
- Measure success or failure
- Identify costs and benefits
- Identify and measure impacts
- Satisfy sponsors and authorities (accountability)
- Gain acceptance, credibility, and support

In the context of event tourism, the desired outcome of events is the focus of evaluation: their touristic attractiveness, success in drawing target markets, tourist expenditure and other economic impact, image enhancement for the destination, and stimulation of other development. Organizers and sponsors of events typically have other priorities, particularly meeting attendance and financial targets. They also need to measure consumer motivations and satisfaction, along with the extent of repeat visitation; so marketing considerations figure prominently.

In this chapter we focus on the achievement of tourism-related goals, although the wise event tourism planner and event manager will take into account all the perspectives on festivals and events that have been discussed. Community, social, and cultural impact should be assessed and environmental effects evaluated.

In preceding chapters we delimited specific evaluation needs for destination tourism planning and for developing the tourism potential of festivals and special events. This chapter covers the key methods used in event evaluation and impact assessment, and gives advice on how to analyze and effectively utilize the data. Advice on how to conduct successful research and analysis within small or unsophisticated organizations is included, as only the largest and most prosperous will be able to devote major resources to surveys, analysis, and complex evaluation processes. Others can rely on simple checklists, key indicators of performance and impact, and an open management style that maximizes input and feedback from all the stakeholders.

BASIC DATA NEEDS AND METHODS

Table 10-1 lists the major types of data needed to evaluate the tourism-related impact and effectiveness of festivals and special events, together with an indication of the methods generally required to obtain the data. The main categories of data pertain to the event visitor, the trip, motives and marketing, activities and spending, and the various kinds of impact. Within each of these categories are listed the important types of data, specific measures, and methods of obtaining the data. For example, the most basic piece of information needed about visitors is the attendance at events—both total attendance and attendance at individual subevents. This can be measured by total number of customers, number of visitations, turnover rate, and peak attendance. Methods used to obtain these measures include ticket sales, turnstile counts, vehicle counts, crowd estimates, and random market area surveys.

Destination Perspective

There are differences between evaluation from the perspective of tourist destination organizations and that undertaken by event organizers. Destination evaluators want to know the same things as event organizers, but for all events in the destination area. They also want to know about broader patterns of tourism, particularly the relationships between different events and between events and other attractions. Usually a destination exit survey, involving interviews with tourists as they leave the region, is the best way to obtain this information. We

Table 10-1. Basic Data Needs and Methods

Data Types	Specific Measures	Methods
Attendance		
Total festival or event attendance	Total number of customers	Ticket sales
Attendance at subevents	Number of visitations	Turnstile counts
	Turnover rate	Vehicle counts
	Peak attendance	Crowd estimates
		Market area surveys
Visitor Profiles		
Profile of each visitor	Age in years	Visitor survey
	Male or female	Market area survey
	Employment status	Direct observation
	Educational level	
	Income level	
Type of party	Family only	
	Family and friends	
	Friends only	
	Alone	
	Tour group	
	Tour group plus family or friends	
Size of party	Number of visitors traveling together	
Market Area and Trip Type		
Home address	Country, state, city, or town	Visitor survey
Origin of trip	Origin on day of survey	
	Stops on the trip	
	Accommodation used	
Type of trip	Number of nights	
	Packages used	
Mode	Type of vehicle	Observation
Marketing, Motivations		
Information sources	Media consulted	Visitor survey
	Importance of word of mouth	
Reasons for trip	To the area	
	To the event	
	Importance of event in motivating trip	
	First time or repeat visit	
Benefits sought	Desired experiences, activities, goods and services	
Satisfaction	Things that pleased	Suggestion box
	Things that displeased	
	Suggestions	
	Intent to return	

(Continued)

Table 10-1. (*Continued*)

Data Types	Specific Measures	Methods
Activities and Spending		
Activities at the event Activities outside the event	Attendance at event attractions and sites Activities in the host community; on the trip	Visitor survey Turnstile counts Ticket sales Observation Business survey Financial record
Expenditures	At the event and on the trip: Accommodation Food and beverages Entertainment Souvenirs Other shopping Travel related	
Economic Impact		
Total incremental visitor expenditure at event; in community	Total attentance × average expenditure at event and outside	Visitor survey Attendance count Accommodation occupancy survey
Macroeconomic impact	Total incremental income plus secondary and induced effects	Income multiplier
Profit or surplus revenue Employment created	Revenues minus costs Full- and part-time Direct and indirect Total person-years	Financial record Employment multiplier
Other Impacts		
Ecological	Conservation Pollution Habitat loss	Observation Environmental research
Social and cultural	Resident attitudes Heritage loss Traditions altered or preserved Amenity loss or gain Public behavior Change in aesthetics	Resident survey Public meeting Police records Fire records
Cost-Benefit Evaluation		
Tangible costs Tangible benefits Intangibles	Ratio of tangible costs to benefits Qualitative evaluation of net value	

do not cover that type of survey here specifically, but Table 10-1 and subsequent discussion of methods do indicate how the destination perspective can be accommodated. Usually it is a matter of getting the same basic information plus a few additional points.

Table 10-1 shows that several vital methods are necessary for event tourism evaluation: attendance counts and estimates, visitor surveys, and economic impact assessment methods. Most of this chapter is devoted to these methods and ways to analyze the data. Cost-benefit evaluation is covered as a method by which the net worth of one or more events can be determined, taking into account intangibles as well as economic costs and benefits. Direct observation can also have value, particularly for quick and simple evaluation, so we will discuss some appropriate techniques.

ATTENDANCE COUNTS AND ESTIMATES

Mega-events are commonly launched or promoted with considerable fanfare and inflated attendance forecasts. Why some do not reach their targets, and why some such as Vancouver's Expo '86 and Brisbane's Expo '88 exceed them, is not the point here. Small events also have trouble forecasting attendance, but more serious is the difficulty in accurately measuring or estimating attendance. Without reliable numbers, organizers cannot estimate total spending, nor can tourism planners calculate the impact; the proportion of repeat visitors cannot be determined, nor can market segments be estimated; trends cannot be established, and forecasting is hindered.

Visitors versus Visitation

As a general rule, organizers of events with gates and ticketed admissions have little trouble calculating total paid attendance, which can also be called the gate or total visitation. But they might have more difficulty knowing how many individuals attended, because visitors are likely to attend more than one activity, at multisite events, or on more than one day, in events lasting longer. If only total visitation is known, organizers will be unable to estimate total tourist spending, which can be calculated only by multiplying the average spending of all visitors by the total number of visitors.

To illustrate this problem, consider a two-day event with a total attendance of 10,000 each day, as measured by paid admissions. A random visitor survey on the second day found that 50 percent of the sample had actually attended on both days, so 5,000 of the second-day crowd were repeaters, and therefore the total number of individual visitors was not 10,000 but only 7,500—5,000 the first day plus 2,500 new visitors on the second. If average visitor spending of the sample was $10, covering both days, then the total visitor spending was

$10 × 7,500, *not* $10 × 10,000. Of course, this problem could be avoided by taking separate random surveys each day and calculating separate estimates of average visitor spending per day.

With an event at multiple sites or over more than one day, the estimation of average and total visitor spending can get quite complicated. Not only will a complex sampling frame be required, but a statistician will be needed.

Benchmarks and Indicators

A benchmark is the initial or occasional count—or estimate—of attendance against which future counts or estimates are compared, in order to establish trends. Other indicators, or surrogate measures, of attendance can be linked to this onetime attendance figure, and the indicators can be monitored to make future estimates. One common indicator is that of total sales, based on the assumption that if x number of visitors generated y amount of sales, then in the future $y + 1$ sales indicates that attendance has increased proportionately.

The best indicators are those thought to be directly dependent on the size of the crowd, such as total receipts, number of items consumed, and attendance at one easily measured activity or site. Over time it is probable that the linkages between total attendance and these indicators will change, so if they are used it must be with caution and with monitoring of the factors that might cause divergence. For example, total sales or receipts will certainly vary with gross attendance, but might also rise or fall with promotion, accessibility to the outlets, competition from new items in other events, or even the weather.

Parade Counts

The simplest approach is to determine the depth of the crowd at a point (e.g., five deep) and apply this figure to the parade length. Big errors are likely, however, if any of the following occur: people bunch together in clusters; attendance peaks just as the parade passes; viewers move along with the parade; or some points on the route are highly favored, while others are avoided or viewing is impossible.

To overcome these common complications, a more systematic but complex technique is needed, as described in the following steps:

1. Measure the length of the parade viewing route; omit portions where viewing is impossible.
2. Divide the viewing length into equal segments within which accurate counts can be made.
3. Isolate those segments known or judged likely to attract significantly fewer or greater numbers of viewers; they require separate counts.

4. Randomly select (draw numbers from a hat) at least thirty segments for the whole parade, excluding the separate sections for significantly larger or smaller anticipated crowds.

5. Make a 100 percent count of the sample segments and all the atypical, separate segments; make counts at the time the parade passes; exclude from the count all people moving along with the parade into the segment.

6. Calculate the average crowds for all the sample segments and multiply the average by the total number of segments along the parade route, except the ones counted separately; now add the estimate to the full counts obtained from the separate segments.

Static Crowds

Where a crowd occupies a space and there is no significant coming and going, a simple grid sampling can be used to make a reliable estimate of attendance. Divide the space into equal cells by fixing reference points along the perimeters. It does not matter much that the site is irregular, so long as there are cells covering all places where visitors will stand or sit. Again, sample at least thirty segments. If the cells are small, there is no need to worry about clustering, since the differences in cell occupancy will be small. If clustering is a problem, it will be necessary to separately count the cells where bunching occurs or where occupancy is abnormally low. The estimate is then derived the same way as for parades, by multiplying the average cell occupancy by the total number of cells, then adding the counts from separated cells.

If an aerial photo of the site can be taken, a complete count might be possible, or the grid lines for sampling can be drawn onto the photo. This technique is less reliable for parades because attendance peaks as the parade approaches— unless it is a very short parade.

Where movement is unrestricted, as in Main Street events, the grid sampling technique can be used to estimate the peak attendance, or several counts can be taken to determine general trends. But for most open events this will be impractical, owing to site arrangements. Besides, an estimate of total attendance is desired. The main problem is turnover—the fact that the people in the crowd are constantly changing as some arrive and others leave. Three techniques can be used in these situations: vehicle counts, pedestrian counts, and market area surveys.

Vehicle Counts

In some cases it might be possible to count all vehicles arriving at the event site or multiple sites. Buses, boats, trains, or planes would be counted separately, so that total arrivals by these modes are known. For autos, an average number of passengers must be estimated by counting how many are in, say, every twentieth car. The average is then multiplied by the total number of cars. To make this work will require one or more observers to count all arrivals; all entrances must be covered. Automatic vehicle counters can be used so that observers have to worry only about occupants.

But some vehicles might make multiple visits. The only way to take this into account is to mark all arrivals somehow, as with window or bumper stickers, or to give first-time arrivals a parking ticket to show upon return. But returning vehicles might bring back different people! The only way to find out is to ask. Also requiring consideration are pedestrians and bicyclists. They must be counted separately, but this will be impractical unless all entrances can be observed.

A third complication, particularly acute for Main Street festivals, is local traffic unrelated to the event. One way to separate visitors from locals or normal business travel is to stop all arrivals at road entrances and issue visitor stickers, or perhaps channel visitors to designated parking lots. General traffic surveys can also be used to estimate normal local volume, which can be subtracted from total counts on the day of the event, but there will be errors attributable to normal fluctuations in local traffic.

Counts of Moving Pedestrians

Like vehicles, pedestrians can be counted as they enter or leave the event area, even if there are no gates. In this system observers must cover all entrances and either count all arrivals and departures or take sample counts regularly. For example, over an 8-hour event, a 1-minute sample every 15 minutes would yield 32 separate counts. Much like the parade segments and crowd cell counts, the average count for the 32 sample minutes is multiplied by the total number of minutes in 8 hours—480—to obtain an estimate of arrivals. As with the other methods, blocks of time known to have very high or very low arrivals should be isolated and counted separately.

A similar system called the police method (Indiana Department of Commerce and Indiana State Festival Association 1988) is to count people in a defined area (e.g., ten square yards) three times over the event's duration. This should be done in the peak flow area, not at entrances. The totals of the three counts are added up, then divided by three to yield the average count. This average is multiplied by the total number of cells in the entire event area through which people are moving, and finally this figure is multiplied by the number of hours of pedestrian flow.

Both techniques yield very rough estimates, and neither one copes with the problem of some people being counted more than once. They are actually measures of total flow, rather than total attendance, and can be heavily influenced by site design.

Market Area Surveys

If the primary market area is known, from visitor surveys, then a postevent random household survey, most easily undertaken by telephone, can be used to estimate total attendance. Selected respondents must be asked who in the household attended what events, when, and how many times. The problems are twofold: long-distance tourists will have to be ignored, or estimated by some other means; and telephone-based sample frames contain errors because of unlisted numbers and households that have no phones.

It should be clear by now that estimating attendance at open events is difficult. No 100 percent reliable count is possible unless there is complete control of entrances and exits, and statistically reliable estimates are possible only for static crowds where a random sample can be taken. For most open events, only a rough estimate can be obtained, and even then the evaluations must take into account the problems of multiple entrances, turnover, and counting procedures.

VISITOR SURVEYS

Whether by self-completed questionnaire or direct interview, on-site or off-site visitor surveys provide the most useful information for evaluation of events and event tourism. They are relatively easy and inexpensive to undertake and analyze, at least at a basic level; but they do present challenges of design, sampling, and interpretation. There are some essential requirements for visitor surveys, and if they cannot be met it is better not to attempt one.

It is now quite easy to get access to event surveys and professionals capable of advising organizers or tourism officials on how to implement them. But experience in conducting and reviewing numerous surveys has convinced this author that it is a mistake to use somebody else's questionnaire, or to fit bits and pieces from surveys together and call it your own. Instead, it is essential that each visitor survey be formulated for specific purposes, and in such a way that the evaluators or planners get exactly the information they need. The following steps provide a simple guide to this process of custom-designing the survey.

General Purposes of the Survey

Different purposes require different methods and measures. It is efficient to accommodate multiple purposes, but only with the resources to do it properly. Joint ventures among event organizers, tourist agencies, and other stakeholders should be pursued for these reasons. A visitor survey can help with all three basic types of planning and marketing evaluations: formative, process, and summative.

In formative evaluations, the visitor survey is intended to help formulate and evaluate options for event development. These types stress marketing issues, such as identification of benefits desired by target segments, and suggestions for improvements or new events.

Process evaluations focus on the actual operations, including staffing, infrastructure, services, and visitor-related problems. For short-duration events, visitor surveys aimed at identifying and correcting problems might be impracticable, and direct observations will have to suffice. For longer-duration events, it is a good idea to sample visitors over the duration of the event to monitor satisfaction and facilitate correction of any problems.

Summative, or outcome, evaluations identify, measure, and determine the significance and implications of event impacts. Both intended and unintended effects must be included. For specific events, the emphasis in the visitor survey will be on determining the effectiveness and efficiency of promotions, satisfaction with event attributes and the setting, spending, and likes, dislikes, and suggestions.

Destination planners will also benefit from event evaluations, although this will probably take the form of summarizing visitor surveys from various events. If these are not being done, the destination planners must work with event organizers to secure them. Standardization of measures will help the destination planner's analysis. Destination planning benefits from evaluation of specific events by revealing potential markets, assessing impact, and coming up with ideas for new events. The destination planner will want all the summative evaluation from existing events, as well as an appraisal of event organizations and potential community support for events.

Data from many surveys can also be used to evaluate the areas's image, the effectiveness of events in promoting and channeling tourism, and the success of efforts to develop better event organizations. Questions on overall travel motivations and patterns, on general spending, and on impressions of the region or nation must be added to those concerning the specific event. Tourism planners will use the data in conjunction with exit or approach surveys and general market research.

Most common are the onetime event visitor surveys, which have to satisfy as many evaluation purposes as possible. It therefore becomes necessary to set priorities for all the options.

Determination of the Specific, Ultimate Uses of Data

The worst mistake is to try to do too much, and that unfortunate outcome often occurs when a committee designs a survey. If a committee is in charge of evaluation, a smaller subcommittee should be established to work out the options and design and test the survey. Include at least one experienced survey methodologist, and try to get representation from the tourism industry.

To avoid becoming overambitious, the evaluators must carefully specify exactly who wants the data, and in what ways it will be used. The interests of tourism and the arts community will coincide in some areas, but conflicting needs are likely. So the group must arrange the possibilities in an order of priority; a good way to do that is to ask each stakeholder to rank his or her key objectives or questions. If too many questions remain after accommodating all the top priorities, it may be necessary to launch more than one survey. A master survey can be formulated with inserts of questions, to meet different needs, randomly mixed in; or a short on-site survey can be augmented by a longer take-home form.

Key Data Requirements, Measures, and Other Collection Methods

Any goal or question can be converted into specific data requirements. For example, to evaluate the effectiveness of promotions it will be desirable to ask visitors how they heard about the event, or what information sources they consulted. The objective of determining economic impact requires data on visitor spending. The measures must be developed next. Visitor spending can be measured in a number of ways: for example, on- or off-site, by place, by type of expenditure, or by time of day or day of week. The unit of measurement is normally monetary in nature, and it can be aggregated by party or kept at the individual level (see Table 10-1).

To collect each type of data might require different methods, and the visitor survey might not be best for all of them. Logbooks have been used to measure tourist spending, but they would require very special expertise to attempt at a special event, because visitors might stay only a short time and may be difficult to contact in advance. Direct interviews on the site or at exit points will work, as will self-completed questionnaires. An interesting alternative is the conducting of a postevent, random telephone survey in the market area. Each method has both merit and limitations, but the intent at this stage is to screen all the options and determine the list of measures to be covered in the visitor survey.

Methods and Feasibility

Which method will be most cost-effective in obtaining the data needed? Can the organization provide the human resources, funds, and technical expertise necessary to do the job right? It might be a matter of cost or convenience that determines the choice of survey methods. And the comfort and convenience of visitors must not be forgotten. There is no point in giving them self-completion questionnaires but not pencils, or forms that are hard to write on or take an hour to read and complete. Are there convenient places to sit and write, or in which to be interviewed? Will questionnaires be picked up, or are there places at exits for drop-offs?

Selecting the sampling method is a crucial decision, and it will be an important factor in determining feasibility. Options are presented later; each has implications for cost, timing, personnel, and ultimate use of the collected data. So-called quick-and-dirty surveys, without random sampling, do yield useful insights for minimal cost, but they cannot be used to measure impact or convince sponsors of success.

Another factor to weigh is the need for support data. A random survey of visitors is meaningless without accurate attendance counts or estimates. Logbooks cannot be used for reliable estimates unless the participants are known to represent all eventgoers proportionately.

Survey Design

Those in charge of survey design, having followed these steps so far, will now have arrived at some decision about survey content and format, and how it will be implemented. This will be a far different survey from one derived by asking a committee for suggestions or by borrowing a few questions from another event.

Some art is involved in formulating the questions and formatting the survey, but whatever its form it should be given a pilot test. The best tests are at events, but for many organizers that is impossible. Instead, a sample of ordinary people, the organization committee, and some experts could all be asked for feedback. Revisions will likely be in order, and if they are major ones another test should be attempted. Finally, arrangements for production, personnel, and equipment can be made. Evaluators also must not forget to evaluate their own efforts, particularly the survey itself.

Is there a model visitor survey that events can use? It is too dangerous to provide a standard questionnaire, as some reader might ignore the previous steps and simply borrow the author's form. Rather, a list of basic and optional questions is provided at the end of this chapter. These can form the basis of a customized survey for the user's specific needs.

The Sampling Method

Choosing the sample frame is a crucial decision, and once it is determined the survey staff must faithfully adhere to it. Volunteers must be trained, and all participants in the visitor survey must have the right attitude if bias is to be avoided. The most common on-site sampling frames for events are described below.

Turnstile Intercept Sampling

In the turnstile sample, every, say, tenth or one hundredth person passing through the gate can be given a questionnaire or interviewed. This guarantees absolute randomness, although care must be taken to avoid coverage of the same person twice if people are allowed to leave and return. It must also be decided if only adults are to be covered, and if one member of each family or party is to be covered.

As a rule of thumb, at least 200 completions should be sought for even the smallest of events. It is possible to estimate statistical levels of confidence for the sample only if it is known what proportion of the total attendance was sampled, and then only if there was no response bias, such as only certain types of people completing the forms. Because of the nonresponse problem, interviews are often preferred. The interviewer can determine what types of people refused to participate, and can generally get a higher response rate than from impersonal questionnaires. However, interviews are restricted by the number of available interviewers, and at peak times the turnstile interview sample might break down due to the sheer volume of arrivals.

On-Site Intercept Sampling

An alternative to the turnstile method is to intercept visitors as they move about an open site, or where they congregate on the site. Wherever people line up, surveyors have a good chance to systematically select every nth person. It is important to avoid arbitrary selection of respondents, or a selection bias can occur—for example, there might be a natural tendency to approach people of a certain type. Lines are particularly good because the people are waiting anyway and might not mind filling out a form. The alternative is to select every nth person past a given point, such as the entrance to a building or area.

Personal questions present a problem, however, so verbal interviews should be concerned only with general matters, unless privacy can be assured. A combination of interview and self-completed questionnaire is a possible solution, with personal matters relegated to the latter.

The big problem is to ensure that the whole site and all activities are covered, over the duration of the entire event. Keep in mind that the composition of the crowd will vary over time and around the site, depending on the attraction, services, and accessibility. To overcome this problem requires time sampling, in which interviewers conduct the survey during specified times throughout the event; and spatial sampling, in which they are assigned specific sectors covering the whole site.

Because these on-site intercept methods do not ensure a truly random sample, but do apply strict selection criteria, they are called systematic. In terms of reliability they are not as good as random samples, but potentially they can be better than quota samples.

Quota Sampling

Given the daunting problems of obtaining a random or systematic sample, some evaluators might choose a quota sample instead. If 200 respondents are desired, interviewers can be told to collect 10 or 20 each, subject to getting a balance between the genders, along with an age spread. Other characteristics such as race or ethnicity might be important to specific events and can be incorporated in the quotas.

While this is a simple and useful approach, there is no basis for estimating the characteristics of the whole crowd from a quota sample. Of course, none of the nonrandom methods can be used for estimating the characteristics of the whole crowd, at least according to strict statistical practices. The evaluator must try to get the most representative sample possible, then qualify the final estimates by noting the limitations of the sample and resulting response bias.

Other Survey Problems

A special problem in tourism surveys is that of selection bias attributable to a visitor's length of stay in the area or at the event. Those who are in the area or on the grounds longest will have the greatest chance of being intercepted for questioning. Turnstile sampling avoids this problem, assuming that repeat visitors are not covered more than once. Approaching visitors as they leave the site or area also overcomes this problem, assuming a random or systematic sampling frame. If an on-site quota sample is used, the length-of-stay bias cannot easily be avoided.

If self-completion questionnaires are used, the respondents must be provided with suitable places and the means to complete the forms and get them back to the evaluators. Some events invite respondents to visit a central place, and provide a reward for those who comply. Others provide drop-off points at exits— but don't use receptacles that look like waste bins! If possible, ask for the address of everyone given a form, then write to those who don't return it in time. This might be viewed as a breach of confidentiality, however. The best approach might be to use a short interview or questionnaire that can be completed in the presence of the interviewer.

The possibility of selection and interview bias has already been mentioned. Once a sampling frame has been selected, the interviewers, or those selecting questionnaire recipients, must follow the system. If a quota sample is used, there is a lot of room for selection bias, even though the quota might stipulate an even number of males and females and age groups. What about race or party type? To be effective, the quota cannot leave room for a bias to creep in, yet it is extremely difficult to construct and adhere to a very detailed quota sampling frame.

Self-completed questionnaires can fail if their design or format suffers from any of the following:

- Print too small for some recipients to read
- Language or words that some visitors do not understand
- Too much detail or a format that appears too complicated
- Questions that are too personal
- Failure to provide pencil or pen
- Flimsy paper that is hard to write on

Design is in part a matter of necessity, determined by the purpose, number of questions, and intended recipients. In part it is an art, helped by trial and error and examination of other surveys. As a general rule, the shorter and simpler the questionnaire, the better and more accurate the responses will be. If an incentive can be offered to complete and return the questionnaire, that is desirable. Another good rule of thumb is to commence with easy, descriptive questions and leave personal ones to the end. Restrict open-ended write-in questions to a minimum; otherwise the forms can get messy and coding will be complicated. People in a hurry often ignore write-in questions.

Personal interviews can eliminate or reduce some of the problems associated with self-completion questionnaires. Skilled interviewers can shift the order of questions, probe where necessary, and double-check key points. Unless the interview is done in private, however, personal questions should be limited to self-completion forms. The survey form must therefore be well organized and easy for both interviewer and respondent to use.

OBSERVATION TECHNIQUES AND APPLICATIONS

Using standard checklists, event staff and volunteers can gain a great deal of quantitative information as well as an enhanced subjective evaluation of the event. For some organizers, observational research might be a necessary substitute for visitor and market surveys. At any rate, it should be a formal part of all evaluation strategies. Observations have several advantages over surveys:

All staff and volunteers can participate, each contributing a unique perspective on the event, the customers, and the impact.

Customer behavior is sometimes a better indicator of problems, preferences, and attitudes than are formal responses to surveys.

Key elements of the event product can be evaluated only by means of direct observation: how people behave under different circumstances; how transport and movement controls actually work; the quality of the experience actually delivered, including food and entertainment; the quality of service delivered by staff and volunteers as measured against management criteria; the use of information or directional material and signs; the effectiveness of waste, litter, and pollution controls.

The atmosphere or ambience of the event, which is a vital but intangible element of the product, can be evaluated best by a combination of direct observation and visitor comments; everyone associated with the event is likely to have a valuable opinion on the overall effectiveness of the atmosphere, or at least on specific factors that create atmosphere, and sometimes talking about these things and their synergistic effect is the only way to decide if the atmosphere can be improved.

It is a mistake, however, to rely too heavily on casual comments and unsubstantiated observations. At a minimum, each employee and volunteer participant in the event should be provided with an evaluation checklist covering those items for which evaluation is expected, probably in conjunction with a listing of operational tasks required by each participant. The checklist can include several types of measurement:

Items that are present or absent, adequate or inadequate, as determined by performance criteria, not subjective opinion; for example, are there sufficient litter bins, and are they emptied frequently enough to avoid spillage?

Items judged to be good or bad, such as the quality of food

Items requiring lengthy observation and analysis, such as the behavior of visitors under specific circumstances; for example, what was the effect of signposting on pedestrian flow?

Items requiring a summary conclusion, such as the overall quality and visitor satisfaction with entertainment, as determined by observation of visitor reactions and comments

Some checklists can be completed during the event, though not by all workers; every volunteer and staff member should complete a form after the event. An alternative, or additional step, is to have so-called cruisers or shoppers on staff for the sole purpose of making observations. Fast-food chains use shoppers to secretly evaluate food, service, and facility quality, and wise event managers can do the same. These people ideally should be trained observers; there are advantages and disadvantages in using known observers as opposed to those who will be strangers to other staff and volunteers.

A major consideration is ethics. Some forms of secret observation can be violations of human privacy or dignity, so observers should be told the limits of their assignments. On the other hand, casual and unobtrusive observers can fit into the crowd without any influence whatsoever. And if staff evaluations are included, there is merit in making them open and obvious so that staff members know they are being observed. Everyone subject to evaluation should, of course, have advance knowledge of the criteria being used, and should not be expected to perform duties they are not trained and qualified to handle. With volunteers this is often not possible, so informal, postevent evaluation is a reasonable option.

PUBLIC FORUMS AND STAKEHOLDER SURVEYS

In keeping with the principle of community-based tourism planning, and for good public relations as well, event evaluators should include all stakeholders in the process. This covers the public, participating groups, organizations providing grants, sponsors, performers, and business and tourism associations. A survey of each participating group would reveal useful information from a variety of perspectives, while a public forum gives everyone the opportunity to discuss issues and generate ideas. Event organizations that become closed and unresponsive will probably lose public support.

Impact assessment must involve some kind of public survey or forum to reveal any hidden and unexpected outcome such as property damage, social disturbances, incidence of crime, or accidents. This can be combined with marketing research, including measurement of local attendance and attitudes. Specific types of impact will require quantitative input from sources as diverse as the police, health and security agencies, and transportation services. Police data on accidents and crime are also important.

In addition, organizers of every event should maintain a clippings file to record the media publicity, analysis, and commentary given the event and its impact. From a tourism point of view, coverage in national and international magazines, in newspapers outside the host community, and in widely circulated promotional materials are important. Many event managers make estimates of the monetary value of free publicity.

Household surveys, by telephone or mail, can also be used for a number of purposes: to estimate attendance at events, collect information on event impact, measure awareness of and attitudes toward events, assess the competition, and even test new product ideas. Market surveys logically will be confined to the known principal market areas or aimed at potential and developing market areas. Target markets having specialized interests, rather than a geographic base, must be reached through specific membership lists.

ECONOMIC IMPACT ASSESSMENT

This is a special type of evaluation that focuses on the economic costs and benefits generated by the event or by event tourism. All too often it is the only type of evaluation undertaken, leaving social, cultural, and environmental effects undocumented.

Much of the data for economic impact assessment must come from reliable visitor surveys, including the following:

- Total spending on the trip by tourists
- Total spending at the event by all visitors
- Spending per day, per visit, or per night
- Party size, to determine spending per visitor or party
- Length of stay by visitors to the area, and accommodations used
- Where money was spent at the event
- Where money was spent on the trip—accommodations, transportation, meals, shopping, entertainment

Other useful information on economic impact can be collected from: gate receipts; the revenue, profits, and expenditures of vendors and performers at the event; employee pay records; and financial statements of participating groups and sponsors.

Visitor Expenditures

A mistake that event organizers sometimes make is to boast of the total amount of expenditure by all event attendees, as if this was a measure of the economic value to the community or destination area. Given that much of the total was derived from residents of the area, it is a very misleading figure and has little value in the tourism field. The real economic benefits of events are from visitors who come to the area primarily because of the event or who stay longer and spend more because of it.

When attendance is known, the results of regional or national tourist expenditure surveys can be used to estimate the amount of money brought into the area. This is an easy shortcut, but it has a major limitation in that average expenditures for tourists might not apply to eventgoers in general or visitors to any particular event. That is why visitor surveys are required; even if they do not include spending data, they can still be used to check if eventgoers are similar in important characteristics to the average tourist. As discussed in earlier chapters, however, it has been found that event tourists are often different and tend to spend more.

Multipliers

Economic impact assessments often include a multiplier calculation to demonstrate that incremental tourist expenditure has what are called direct, indirect, and induced benefits for the local economy. The idea is that new money ripples through the economy, changing hands many times, thereby having a cumulative impact greater than the initial amount of tourist expenditure. Unfortunately, it is not that simple.

The direct income for an area is the amount of tourist expenditure that remains locally after taxes, profits, and wages are paid outside the area and after imports are purchased; these subtracted amounts are called leakages. The remaining money is income to the area, which immediately starts to circulate, thus creating indirect income. Again, much leakage from the area occurs, so this round of spending creates much less income. The overall effect on the economy beyond these first two rounds of monetary flow is called the induced income, related mostly to consumer spending. Indirect and induced income is often lumped together and called secondary local area income.

Types of Multipliers

A source of much confusion is the use of different types of multipliers and different ways of expressing them. It also appears that some tourism and event boosters use multipliers incorrectly, to exaggerate the benefits. Archer (1982) examined the misuse of multipliers, and his article is essential reading for those who want to use the technique in impact assessment.

The type usually used in tourism impact studies is the income multiplier; it "is basically a coefficient which expresses the amount of income generated in an area by an additional unit of tourist spending" (Archer 1982, 236). For example, if tourists attracted to an area by a festival spend $100,000, which is considered to be new or incremental income for the area, and if this spending is found to generate $50,000 of income for the area, after subtracting leakages, then the income multiplier is 0.5.

Archer (1982) cited a number of income multipliers from various studies: for small island countries, they ranged from 0.58 to 1.30; for counties and American states, they were 0.88 to 1.30. In Great Britain, small-town, county, and regional tourism income multipliers ranged from 0.18 to 0.47. These examples show clearly that the size of the area is an important factor in shaping the multiplier. The same applies for underdeveloped economies; a great deal of leakage occurs owing to imports and other types of outbound monetary flow.

Some economists prefer the value-added multiplier, which is similar to the income multiplier. It represents the wages, profits, and salaries of all the producers in the chain of production begun by incremental tourist expenditure. It cannot exceed a value of 1.0 unless induced consumption is included; then it can have a value up to 1.5 (Burns, Hatch, and Mules 1986, 14).

Other types of multipliers are based on the effects of incremental tourist spending on economic activity—sales, transactions, output, gross domestic product—rather than income to residents. These can have high values, which can be misused to exaggerate the true value of tourism to a local area. Archer (1982, 239) gives the example of a small town that was calculated to have a sales multiplier of 1.46 and an income multiplier of 0.36 in its hotel sector. This meant that an incremental tourist expenditure of $100 in a hotel would generate $146 of sales activity in the area, but only $36 of local income! Another important point from this example is that sectors of the economy have different multipliers. They also vary with other factors, as illustrated in subsequent examples.

Employment multipliers are also commonly cited in tourism studies; these can be expressed as the number of jobs created per unit of tourist expenditure, such as one job created for every $100,000, or as the ratio of jobs created indirectly by tourist spending to jobs created directly in the tourism sector. All multipliers are linked, because they all measure the effects of incremental tourist expenditure. And income is what creates jobs, although how many jobs depends on other factors besides the total amount of tourist spending. Tourist expenditure in commercial accommodations creates many service-sector jobs, but tourists staying with friends and relatives, and day-trippers, have a much lesser impact.

A Model of the Income Multiplier and Events

Figure 10-1 illustrates the process of money exchanges, or flows of incremental income, that generate wealth for a local area. The money spent by tourists at the event, and elsewhere in the local area, is respent possibly many times and ultimately contributes to general economic growth. Also beneficial to the local economy is revenue obtained from external funding sources such as sponsors and government grants, unless that money would have come to the area anyway, in which case some other opportunity has been forgone.

Tourist expenditure and other external revenue are easy to measure, but to calculate income for the area requires detailed knowledge of what happens to the tourist expenditure and revenue as it ripples through the local economy. The double lines in the diagram represent the flows of particular interest in creating local income, starting with new or incremental revenues and tourist expenditures, which go to the event and other sectors of the tourist industry. The direct income created by this revenue is the money available to local residents after taxes, imports, and profits leak out of the area from the direct recipients of the revenue and tourist spending. The event and other tourism-related businesses then spend money on necessary goods, services, and wages, which also results in leakages from the area. The money left over for local income after the spending among the various interbusiness linkages is called the indirect income. Beyond this, it is difficult to trace exact flows, but it is known that the ripple effect continues, albeit with greatly diminished impact, creating induced local income as part of general economic growth. Investments made from event profits are part of this economic growth process.

As with all multipliers, the focus is on money brought into the area by tourists,

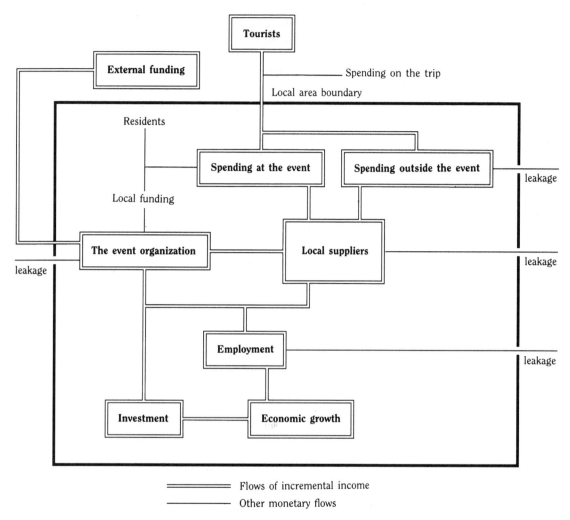

Figure 10-1. The income multiplier and events: flows of incremental income.

plus other external revenue. This is a crucial point, as money spent by residents is not necessarily contributing to economic growth; their money might have been spent elsewhere in the area if not for the event. There is some evidence, though, to suggest that major events do keep some residents at home who otherwise would leave the area for a trip. And it is also probable that a community with attractive events encourages more local spending for entertainment and merchandise. This is why some economic impact assessments include a portion of resident spending in the multiplier calculations.

Generally, small areas and small economies have high amounts of leakage, so their multipliers are small. An event in a major city usually will have a greater effect on the local economy, because more of the tourist expenditure will stay in the city owing to linkages between various sectors of the economy and to more wages and profits staying locally.

This diagram can be a powerful planning tool, as it highlights the ways in which tourism and event organizers can seek to maximize the value of the event to the area. Evaluators can then devise measures to monitor the process and determine elements for improvements.

Enhancing the Local-Income Multiplier Effect

A coordinated event tourism strategy, which seeks to maximize local economic benefits, should strive to meet the following objectives:

Make the event long enough and attractive enough to encourage overnight stays in the host community or destination area.

Ensure sufficient accessibility and accommodations so that both tours and individual travelers are able to make convenient overnight stopovers specifically for the event.

Encourage residents to invite guests to stay with them during the event and to take guests to the event.

Provide sufficient merchandising to attract visitor spending at the event.

Coordinate events and other attractions to build a "critical mass" sufficient to attract and hold visitors in the area.

Conduct research to identify and measure the linkages and leakages, and exactly where gains can be realized.

Employ mostly local people for staff and performers.

Require the licensing of merchants, vendors, and exhibitors so that locals can be given priority, or at least so that a share of profits can be kept locally.

Make purchases from local suppliers.

Put profits back into community projects.

Make sure all visitor needs—food, entertainment, souvenirs, accommodations, gasoline—are provided for at the event or locally.

A few guidelines on types of visitors can also be stated. For creation of local income, the ideal event visitor stays at least one night in the area, preferably at serviced commercial accommodations; comes in a group, all members of which spend money; consumes merchandise, food, and beverages at the event and in the community; prefers local produce, arts, crafts, and so forth over imported foods; and spends a substantial portion of all travel costs—gasoline, bus fares, and the like—locally.

Shortcut Method

A shortcut method to determining the net economic benefit of an event, or tourism in a community, was developed by Howell (1987) at Clemson University. The formula is

$$(x - y) \times z = \text{net benefit}$$

where x is the number of dollars spent per capita multiplied by total attendance; y is the amount of leakage, in dollars; and z is a multiplier.

Event organizers must determine average visitor spending and total attendance, then make a list of the amounts considered to be leakage. The total amount of money spent outside the community or taken away by performers and merchants is probably going to be easy to determine, but not leakages attributable to imported goods and services used in the event production, such as the amount of leakage attributable to food or beer bought at local stores. More difficult is knowing what multiplier to use.

Many researchers borrow multipliers derived from some other area or event and apply them to their own, with little thought given to the problems and assumptions this entails. Nevertheless, using a multiplier derived from general studies of a regional economy might be the only way organizers of an event can calculate the total economic effects.

Examples of Multipliers Used for Events

A few examples can be cited to demonstrate the different approaches, types, and sizes of multipliers used for events; nevertheless, this can all be confusing to those unfamiliar with the field. Event organizers would be wise not to undertake this type of analysis without expert economic advice.

Vaughan (1979) studied the Edinburgh Festival in Scotland and worked out income multipliers for different types of visitors. He calculated that each pound sterling of tourist spending yielded 29 pence (hundredths of a pound) of local income. In other words, the aggregate multiplier was 0.29. But spending by Scottish visitors resulted in a higher multiplier (0.32), owing to different spending patterns. Overseas tourists generated more expenditure per day, even though the resultant multiplier was slightly less.

Hatten (1987) applied a value-added multiplier of 1.215 for off-site spending and one of 0.882 for on-site spending at Vancouver's Expo '86. It was assumed that 10 percent of the spending by Vancouver residents and 50 percent of the spending by other residents of British Columbia was incremental to the provincial economy, compared to 100 percent of the spending of visitors from outside the province. These multipliers were derived from an input-output model for the provincial economy that measures all the linkages and leakages that relate to each sector of the economy. Why should the multiplier be higher for off-site tourist spending? It depends a lot on the event, and at Expo '86 the on-site consumption of souvenirs, food, and other services resulted in a lot of leakage to U.S. companies.

A major examination of the Calgary Exhibition and Stampede (DPA Group Inc. 1988) included a multiplier analysis that distinguished between effects on the City of Calgary and on the Province of Alberta. A 1985 visitor survey had found that 72 percent of non-Calgary residents of Alberta and 47 percent of non-Alberta residents gave the stampede as the main reason for their visit, so their spending on the trip and at the event could be considered incremental. In addition, the consultants assumed that 10 percent of the spending of Calgary residents at the event was incremental because the event kept money in the city that would have been lost through travel. But the incremental effect was lower at the provincial level, because in the absence of the stampede some tourist spending at the event would have been diverted elsewhere in the province. Consequently, in calculating the provincial multiplier, only 10 percent of the spending of Calgary residents at the event, 10 percent of the spending of other Alberta residents at the event, and 38 percent of the spending of non-Albertans at the event was considered to be incremental.

Based on the estimation of incremental expenditure, three types of multipliers were used to estimate the total economic impact of the exhibition and stampede events for Calgary and Alberta. To be even more precise, multipliers were applied to on-site and off-site purchases, to staff wages respent in the city, and to other expenditures. Table 10-2 shows the results. The GDP, or gross domestic product multiplier, is really a value-added multiplier. The household income multiplier is of particular interest, as it demonstrates the creation of wealth for Calgary and Alberta residents, mostly in the form of wages and salaries. For example, an estimated $.559 in local household income was created by each dollar of on-site incremental expenditure.

The employment multiplier shows the person-years of employment generated per $100,000 of incremental expenditure. Employment is measured in person-years because so many event and tourism jobs are seasonal and/or part-time. It was calculated that 3.45 person-years of employment were generated for every $100,000 of off-site incremental visitor spending.

This type of study is complex, and not without problems. Multipliers for cities are usually not available and have to be estimated. Multipliers for regions and countries can be applied to local areas only by making assumptions of validity. Refinements are desirable to take into account the differences between types of tourist, types of goods, and services consumed, as well as between local and

Table 10-2. Calgary Exhibition and Stampede: Multipliers

To be applied to	Alberta Multipliers		
	GDP[a]	Household Income[b]	Employment[c]
On-site purchases[d]	.925	.559	2.53
On-site wages respent[e]	.555	.296	1.10
Off-site expenditures[f]	1.051	.692	3.45
Other expenditures[g]	.925	.559	2.53
	Calgary Multipliers[h]		
On-site purchases[d]	.79	.48	2.1
On-site wages respent[e]	.47	.25	0.9
Off-site expenditures[f]	.89	.59	2.9
Other expenditures[g]	.79	.48	2.1

[a] Gross domestic product per $ expenditure.
[b] Household income per $ expenditure.
[c] Person-years employment per $100,000 expenditure.
[d] Weighted average of component multipliers, with weights determined by sourcing pattern of on-site expenditure.
[e] Applied to the assumed 70 percent of direct wages respent; the rest goes to taxes, savings, and out-of-province expenditures.
[f] Weighted average of component multipliers, with weights determined by pattern of visitors' expenditures.
[g] Assumed equal to multipliers for on-site purchases.
[h] Calgary multipliers estimated to be .85 times Alberta multipliers.
Source: DPA Group Inc. 1988. *Economic impact of the Calgary Exhibition and Stampede.* Report to the Calgary Exhibition and Stampede.

regional or national impact. At best, the use of such multipliers yields a rough estimate, although economists can usually determine if it is a conservative or generous estimate.

COST-BENEFIT ANALYSIS

The multiplier concept has value primarily in revealing structural weaknesses in the economic unit under study, and as a planning and evaluation tool to help make the event more beneficial to the local economy, in terms of both income and employment. It is usually used, however, for political reasons: to demonstrate the significance of tourism, an event or other tourist attraction, in contributing to economic development. Unfortunately, the effects are sometimes exaggerated and all kinds of assumptions and problems can complicate the exercise.

There is also a tendency to use the multiplier to demonstrate only macroeconomic benefits, without consideration of economic costs or evaluation of intangibles and noneconomic items. That makes the multiplier a tool for generating misleading conclusions.

Cost-benefit analysis has the advantage of being able to draw conclusions about the net benefit of the event after costs have been subtracted, and of incorporating intangibles and noneconomic measures. It can be used in postevent evaluations or in feasibility studies conducted to help determine the overall worthiness of a proposal.

The method is not without difficulties. Several general problems always arise, including how to measure or compare tangibles, such as revenue, with intangibles such as psychological benefits; how to subtract intangible costs from tangible benefits; and how to determine the parameters of the calculations, such as what area to cover, what time period, and whether benefits and costs should be measured for the whole community or just the public sector.

In addition, events give rise to special problems. A major study of the Adelaide (Australia) Grand Prix by the Centre for South Australian Economic Studies (Burns, Hatch, and Mules 1986) highlighted these issues:

Demand is primarily for related services, not the event itself; therefore, data acquisition must be broad.

A peaking of demand is typical of short-term and occasional events; impact might therefore be difficult to isolate from general trends.

Peaking also affects the level and distribution of benefits.

Special attention must be given to the reallocation, or switching, of funds locally, which is not a real benefit.

The benefits of events might occur over a long time period—for example, as a heightened tourism image leads to increased travel—but investments will often be short-term; therefore, the discounted present value of benefits must be compared with costs.

Justification of costs for event infrastructure might have to be made by considering future use, such as the legacy of an event facility.

Major beneficiaries of events are both the customers and, potentially, the entire host community; therefore, external factors are of major interest.

A cost-benefit analysis should be undertaken for all events, but very sophisticated analyses will be possible only for major events. Some guidelines for simple cost-benefit analyses are given later in this section. It is also important to note that the analysis of costs and benefits will be quite different if it is assumed that the aim is the creation of tourism revenue, or other external revenue, as opposed to events unconcerned with tourism. Where tourists are not at all involved, what is mostly being considered is the reallocation of resources within the study area, rather than the creation of new wealth.

The methods used from the Australian Grand Prix cost-benefit analysis provide a good model, although circumstances and resources will be important factors in shaping methods for different events. One final product of the analysis was a chart (see Table 10-3) showing an upper and lower estimate of the benefit-cost ratio, from the State of South Australia's perspective.

Two ratios for tangible economic benefits and costs are shown: an upper estimate of 3.8:1 and the so-called lower bound, 3.1:1. These ratios can be interpreted as follows: for every dollar of cost, or investment in the event, between 3.1 and 3.8 dollars of benefit to the State of South Australia were realized. Intangibles were treated separately, and perhaps controversially, so we will discuss them later in this chapter. A more detailed examination of the tangible costs and benefits is required here.

Tangible Costs

The Grand Prix researchers (Burns, Hatch, and Mules 1986) had to wrestle with the very definition of costs, as applicable to an event like the Grand Prix. Typical of many mega-events, different levels of government were involved. Grants from the Commonwealth of Australia were counted as benefits, as they constituted new revenue made available only because of the event. But grants by the state to the event were counted as costs, because that money could have been used for other state purposes; it had a so-called opportunity cost, stemming from the opportunities forgone in order to assist the event. If the City of Adelaide had been the area for which the cost-benefit evaluation was undertaken, then state grants might have been considered benefits—if they were not simply diverted from some other payments to the city.

The Grand Prix costs were of the following types:

Grants from within the state that could have been used for other purposes

Construction and demolition expenditure, minus applicable grants

Amounts written off as depreciation

Planning, marketing, and operating costs, minus applicable grants

Cost of borrowing: interest payments

External factors, including costs to other government agencies—police, fire, health, transport, waste disposal, and so on—that can be attributed to the event as being above and beyond the norm; costs of damage to private property caused by the event; and economic losses to businesses adversely affected by the event

Table 10-3. Benefit-Cost Ratio: 1985 Grand Prix in Adelaide (tangible economic benefits and costs only, in millions of dollars)

	Upper Bound	Lower Bound
Benefits		
Visitor expenditures (including multiplier effects)	$ 9.865	$ 9.865
Event and construction costs (funded from outside the State and including multiplier effects)	$14.941	$13.765
Total	$24.806	$23.630
Costs		
Event and capital costs funded from state sources	$ 6.571	$ 7.520
Benefit-cost ratio	3.8:1	3.1:1

Source: Burns, J., J. Hatch, and T. Mules. 1986. *The Adelaide Grand Prix: The impact of a special event.* Adelaide: The Centre for South Australian Economic Studies.

One could also include the costs resulting from crime associated with an event and inflationary effects on housing, property, food, and so forth, if caused by the event and related development.

Tangible Benefits

Care is required when defining and measuring benefits. External grants are benefits to the region only if they constitute new, not diverted, sources of funds. Spending by residents is mostly a redistribution of local wealth rather than a benefit, although we have already seen that a portion of their spending might be considered incremental revenue. Some researchers have found that major events do keep people at home rather than traveling on vacation, and others have suggested that resident spending increases because of events, so to that extent the spending by residents is beneficial. The Australian Grand Prix researchers (Van der Lee and Williams 1986, 46) concluded: "The 'once in a lifetime' character of the first Grand Prix and the relatively limited time to change consumption and savings habits leads to the suggestion that it was likely that some increased expenditure was financed from existing savings, thereby providing some additional economic stimulus in the short term." But they did not include any resident spending in their calculations of tangible benefits, yielding conservative estimates.

Benefits of the Grand Prix attributed to the State of South Australia included grants received from outside the area to construction or event operations; tourist expenditures attributable to the event, using the value-added multiplier to estimate total impact on the state; and private investment attracted by the event. Most events by themselves lack the ability to attract new hotels or other private investment, but they might have the effect of accelerating development; any development boom, however, might also result in a subsequent glut, with weaker businesses experiencing actual losses.

Another problem with attribution of benefits involves time switching. Events can motivate people to visit an area earlier or later than a planned visit. Should the resultant spending be included in the multiplier or in cost-benefit calculations? Visitors should be asked if they would have come to the area during the year, but at a different time; those replying yes can legitimately be eliminated from the event impact calculations. But some visitors might not know for certain if the event influenced the timing of a visit, so a bias could be introduced. In theory it is correct to eliminate the expenditures of time switchers, but in practice it is difficult to assess.

A useful and relatively easy measure of the incremental impact of an event is the difference between normal visitor numbers to the area, or occupancy rates, and numbers during the event. Assuming this type of data is available, and assuming that established trends would have continued, then the expenditures of the *increased* number of tourists would be included in the event impact analysis. Even this has a problem, however, because eventgoers often spend more than regular tourists. Some adjustment would have to be made to account for the average difference.

Multipliers derived from state input-output tables for various industry sectors were used. These ranged from 1.109 for expenditures in the food sector to 1.212 for transportation, with a weighted average for all sectors of 1.192. This approach is more accurate than using a gross regional or national multiplier.

Intangible Costs and Benefits

Intangibles—things not measurable in dollars or other comparable units—can be dealt with in either of two ways: analyze them subjectively, and separately from the items measured in dollars, or attempt to give them a surrogate monetary value. Some items might actually contain elements that can be treated quantitatively or subjectively. For example, events can have an impact on local housing. The inflation of rents or property values can be measured in dollars, which makes it a tangible cost. But human costs associated with eviction, reduced choice, homelessness, or despair require either a surrogate measure, such as trying to give a dollar value to time spent homeless, or treatment in a purely qualitative way.

Several intangible costs were dealt with in the Australian Grand Prix research. Traffic congestion and parking problems experienced by the general population were at times serious. A household survey of residents attempted to measure time lost by residents, and a monetary value was given to this time. Noise disturbances from the races were actually measured, in decibels, and the household surveys determined the degree of public inconvenience caused by noise in several zones around the racecourse. The public was also asked to measure the level of inconvenience arising from crowding.

The most interesting intangible cost of the races was that of motor accidents. The researchers analyzed trends in road accidents in the Adelaide area and determined that the Grand Prix did have a psychological impact that led to an increase in accidents and injuries, over and above what could be attributed to increases in traffic volume alone. Dollar values were assigned to deaths and injuries; but this measurement will be offensive to some and meaningless to others.

Giving surrogate monetary value to the intangible costs is useful but fraught with problems. It is also hard to argue that intangible costs are sufficient to neutralize the economic benefits. This line of cost-benefit assessment can be done only in a political forum where values are explicitly stated and weighted. For example, can a motor race be justified if it leads to riots, crimes, accidents, or deaths?

A major intangible benefit was also considered in the case of the Australian Grand Prix. Surveys revealed a very high level of support for the event, stemming from the excitement, entertainment value, and pride that the races generated for Adelaide residents. The researchers called this a psychic benefit and tried to measure its value in monetary terms. The calculations were based on the fact that even those people who complained of noise or traffic delays were strongly in favor of the Grand Prix—as much as the population as a whole. From this fact, a daring hypothesis was formulated: that the monetary value of the psychic benefit was at least equal to the estimated monetary costs of noise and traffic congestion. The actual estimates made in the study are not important here, but it is an example of what can be done, creatively, to make cost-benefit analysis more comprehensive and quantitative. It can be challenged, certainly, on the basis that psychic benefits can never have monetary value, as they lie in the realm of unmeasurable and fleeting emotions. It can also be suggested that a better way to measure psychic benefits would be to ask people how much they would be willing to pay for an experience. (See the case study of festivals in Canada's National Capital Region, in Chapter 9.)

Another related issue is that of long-term attitudinal changes. General tourism research has found that in many circumstances, residents become more concerned with the costs, and more antagonistic to tourism and development, over time. Doxey (1975) developed an "Irridex," or irritation index, to describe this process, and several researchers have found evidence to support the hypothesis. It is possible that Adelaide residents will eventually come to view the Grand Prix as more of a nuisance than an exciting novelty. Onetime events, such as the Olympics, do not face this problem, but all periodic events must. Organizers must address this potential for waning public support.

Some potential long-term benefits associated with events are very difficult to measure. In the Adelaide case, researchers looked at possible advantages accruing to the region and concluded that the races might have increased local entrepreneurial activity and interest in investment, as well as an improved attitude of residents toward local products. The analysts concluded: "Perhaps the major long term benefit would be an attitude change on the part of local businessmen and workers, the development of confidence and pride in one's ability." (Burns, Hatch, and Mules 1986, 28). In this way events can be an enabling mechanism for broader and more ambitious changes. Other mega-events have been seen in this light, and even small community festivals could achieve similar improvements in attitude, resulting in real gains for the viability of the economic and social community. Such gains are not easily quantifiable.

Other intangible costs and benefits have been cited in the tourism and event literature, and any of these could be important under certain circumstances. Costs might include an increase in crime and prostitution, which are almost always associated with large crowds. The so-called demonstration effect might also come into play, as residents of the host community adopt the values or consumer habits of richer tourists. Or actual hostility for tourists might arise if residents feel they are being exploited.

The Distribution of Costs and Benefits

The question of who benefits and who pays the costs is often more important than determining and measuring the actual costs and benefits. It is partially an issue of scale, as tourism is often promoted by senior levels of government and by the industry, with local governments and communities picking up many of the costs. And it is an issue of values, as in the case where the severity of some costs is seen to outweigh anticipated benefits. Unfortunately, these distributional questions are often not asked in impact assessments or in feasibility studies that forecast the costs and benefits of a proposal.

Regarding festivals and events, we have already listed some of the key distributional issues in the earlier discussion of the multiplier concept. There it was argued that the multiplier is a planning tool, to be used to help maximize benefits to the host community. By tracing the linkages and leakages that determine the multiplier, the evaluator can learn where the costs and benefits lie, then take measures to correct problems or realize opportunities. The goal should be to modify the event or its organization to achieve widespread benefits for the community and to minimize costs and disruptions.

Externalities are the most difficult problem. Is it justifiable for event organizers to attain their goals or profits at the expense of property damage, noise, traffic congestion, or other disruptions to uninvolved residents? Can ecological damage or pollution be accepted? What about changes in the social fabric of a community, as a result of annual exposure to a large influx of tourists? The tourism industry gains, but the community is forced or encouraged to change. These are not easy issues to resolve, but they should be considered and debated.

A Simplified Cost-Benefit Evaluation Process

As will be clear by now, detailed and reliable economic impact assessment and cost-benefit evaluation require considerable expertise and a sophisticated research program. For organizations unable to undertake such an effort, a simplified process of cost-benefit evaluation is desirable.

First, accurately calculate capital and operating costs, including debt charges. Capital costs and debt charges can be prorated to yield an annual event cost.

Next, assess external costs. Who is paying for police, fire, and emergency services? Is there any property damage, loss of amenity, or crime that is attributable to the event? These costs are normally excluded from the event's cost-benefit calculation, but they must be considered for an evaluation of the costs and benefits to the area.

Third, determine visitor expenditures. Estimate how much of this is attributable to the event, as that amount is incremental or new money to the area. Add external revenues from grants and sponsors, unless that money would have come to the area anyway.

For a very basic cost-benefit evaluation, compare the estimate of annual incremental revenues to the annual event cost. Subtract any external costs that can be quantified. Calculate the ratio of benefits to costs. Separately consider the intangible costs and benefits, and the issue of who gains and loses. Keeping these separate will greatly simplify the analysis, but it also introduces the necessity for political input.

For a more thorough evaluation, use one or more multipliers to estimate the total or macroeconomic benefits of incremental revenues; a properly formulated multiplier builds in the normal leakage from the area being considered. Since these benefits are areawide, they must be balanced with quantifiable estimates of all costs to the area. Surrogate values can be assigned to some of the intangibles, but others will remain for a final subjective evaluation.

Finally, consider potential long-term benefits and costs. Keep in mind that the multiplier does not estimate long-term benefits and is useful only where the economy has extra production capacity to translate new spending into income.

USE OF EVALUATION RESULTS

Evaluation results often get filed and forgotten—especially if they are negative. But nobody learns and nothing progresses without open and honest evaluation, so the evaluator must try to maximize the usefulness of research and analysis in both practical and political ways. This concluding section will concentrate on how to get the most out of an evaluation for marketing events as tourist attractions, although we start with principles that have wider applications.

General Principles

To maximize the effectiveness of all evaluations, the entire process must be firmly institutionalized. In other words, evaluation must not be viewed as an occasional job for solving problems or generating new ideas. It must be a permanent and important responsibility of senior managers. It goes hand in hand with planning, goal setting, and budgeting. Marketing takes its lead from evaluation, and so does production of the event. To get to this level of management sophistication, several key principles should be followed:

Set up an evaluation committee, or assign the specific responsibility for evaluation to the main planning committee.

All committees must have an evaluation task, with input to the main evaluation committee.

Establish clear goals and objectives, with measurable performance standards or criteria each year.

Start the planning of each event through evaluation of the previous one.

Train all volunteers in observation and evaluation techniques; every volunteer and staff member has an evaluation role to play.

Evaluate with all stakeholders in the event, including the public at large.

Never cover up problems or minimize costs; it always comes back as a problem or scandal! Gain credibility and support by meeting problems head-on.

Start out with modest evaluation exercises and work slowly toward more complicated research and evaluation; consult research experts and get advice from event associations.

At a minimum, get a onetime grant or sponsorship to conduct a benchmark visitor survey and impact assessment; it can be updated periodically.

SWOT Analysis to Help Improve Touristic Attractiveness

SWOT, which stands for strengths, weaknesses, opportunities, and threats, is an evaluation tool often used in strategic planning at the stage of environmental scanning or situational analysis (see Chapter 7). We discuss it here to demonstrate the usefulness of evaluation in helping to improve the attractiveness of events and destinations to tourists.

An evaluation of the product can be oriented to reveal strengths, weaknesses, opportunities, and threats. This can be done with either a simple checklist or a detailed survey of every aspect of the organization and production.

Strengths

Tourism strengths are likely to consist of any or all of the following:

- Unique theme or setting
- Large and diverse program or activities
- Existing large audiences, many of whom are regulars
- A good reputation outside the community or destination area
- Specialized appeal
- High-quality performances or activities
- A captive tourism audience, at resorts, convention centers, with friends or relatives, at cottages or second homes
- A range of complementary attractions and services in the area
- Widespread promotion through media coverage
- Sponsors with national or international interests
- Existing packages and services for tour groups
- Solid support from the community, including volunteers and political support
- Organizational and management capability to expand, improve, and innovate
- A high ratio of benefits to costs

Weaknesses

Tourism weaknesses, naturally, are the absence of the abovementioned strengths. It cannot be assumed, however, that the absence of direct criticism in visitor surveys is an indication that there are no weaknesses. Potential trouble spots should be singled out for direct questioning, and observational techniques should also be used to reveal problems.

Weaknesses will also show up in impact assessment, especially where it is revealed that incremental revenues are low and leakages are high. Remember that the multiplier concept is most useful in demonstrating how such weaknesses can be overcome, and strengths capitalized upon, to create more local area income and economic development.

Political weaknesses must also be identified. They can arise from inadequate public relations and networking; from negative, externalized impact; and from failure to demonstrate the economic or other significance of events.

Opportunities

Tourism opportunities are anything that can be taken advantage of to enhance tourist attractiveness, such as new or developing tourist attractions in the area, which can be either a new lure or a competitive threat; newly emerging target markets; opportunities for joint promotions and packages; and the potential addition or improvement of new event activities or attractions.

Evaluation tends to reveal opportunities, just as it highlights strengths and weaknesses. To be positive, list each identifiable strength and weakness and then suggest ways to eliminate or lessen each weakness and to build upon each strength. Other opportunities will be suggested if the evaluation process is open to all stakeholders, especially to the tourist industry and the general public.

Threats

Tourism threats are emerging or potential obstacles to achieving goals, including the following examples:

- Competition
- Market changes toward other types of event or attraction
- Declining quality due to age, neglect, or poor management
- Inability of event management or volunteers to adapt and innovate
- Loss of community and volunteer support if benefits are not obvious, or if costs or problems grow
- Lack of support and promotion from tourist organizations

Market Evaluation

To augment SWOT, analysis of visitor surveys can be used to help evaluate existing markets and reveal implications for marketing planning.

Why do people come to the event now? Explore the customers' interests, activities, and preferences and develop a picture of the generic benefits customers obtain from the event experience. Think of the event as a leisure experience having a value in time and money to clients. Are they getting their money's worth? Then examine the existing and potential targeted benefits that the product provides and how these specialized interests can be used to attract tourists. Several forms of analysis are helpful.

Quantify the market in terms of the percentage of local residents, day-trippers, and overnight tourists attracted to the event, as well as other tourists. How many group tours are attracted? Where do most repeat visitors come from? Is each of these markets different in socioeconomic or spending characteristics?

Map the market area of the event. What distance from the site encompasses 50 percent of the audience? What about 75 percent? Are there any obvious gaps, such as nearby cities from which few visitors attend? Why do some areas generate more visitors than others? Is it due to promotion and advertising or to socio-economic patterns?

Is the event catering to a narrow audience of teenagers or young males, or does it have very wide appeal? Develop profiles of the main types of individuals and visitor parties, using demographic data such as age, gender, marital status, and family composition, socioeconomic data such as income, occupation, and education, trip characteristics, and activity and spending patterns.

Develop profiles of motivations and preferences for each major market group. What are they looking for, and have they obtained those benefits? What did they like or dislike? What new products would please them?

SAMPLE QUESTIONS FOR VISITOR SURVEYS

It would not be useful to provide a model visitor survey, as no single instrument could satisfy all the possible information requirements of researchers and evaluators. The steps suggested earlier should be followed to develop a survey that will answer the main questions of the organizers or tourist organization. Academic researchers, consultants, or government officials should also be approached for advice, particularly to ensure that reliable methods of data collection and analysis are followed and to test the validity of the questions, so that they will help evaluators get the information needed.

The following list of sample questions is organized under major headings reflecting the primary uses of the data. Some questions would have to be modified depending on whether the survey was to be completed by event visitors or through interviews. In general, interviewers can probe beyond the questions to elicit desired information, although this risks the introduction of interviewer bias. A different instrument—the survey form—is also required for interviews, as it will contain instructions for interviewers rather than respondents. A great deal of skill and art is involved in questionnaire design, and experienced researchers have accumulated tricks and rules of thumb that novices can easily miss.

The order of questions can be important. Personal questions, such as age, gender, and income, are usually left until the end. In some cases there is no point in collecting personal data at all, especially if direct observation of event-goers is possible; interviewers can also note the gender and approximate age of respondents without asking. Key questions should be placed early in the survey, although a few easy warm-up questions might be useful at the very beginning.

The number of questions that can be asked will be governed by the nature of the event, the way respondents are approached, the conditions under which the interview or surveying takes place, and consideration of the respondents' receptiveness. People waiting in long lines might appreciate the diversion of a questionnaire, and it is an excellent circumstance for interviews. But a survey will be inconvenient to people involved in an activity or hurrying to enter or leave a site. For these reasons, some researchers have used both a short on-site questionnaire and a long take-home questionnaire, given either to the same people or to different random samples. Take-home surveys can be longer and ask for more detailed information about the entire trip, but they will also probably get lower response rates.

Ideally, the visitor survey consists of a random sample of individual adults or youths old enough to understand all the questions, rather than groups or parties. If the sample frame is systematic, such as every tenth visitor, this will ensure a representative picture of all the types of groups present. Some information about both the individual and the group can be obtained, but spending in particular is best handled at the individual level.

Visit and Trip Characteristics

These initial questions distinguish the true tourist from the local and give useful information on party and trip characteristics that can be cross-tabulated with other information. Attendance estimates require knowledge of the average number of days each visitor showed up at events lasting more than one day. How many times the average person entered the event area is also important. Following are some key questions:

Is this the first year you have attended this event?

How many years have you been here previously?

Is this the first day of this event you have attended?

How many days have you been to the event?

Is this your only trip to the event today? How many trips to the event have you made today?

Where is your permanent home?

Where did you travel from today to get to the event? How far away is that?

How did you travel to the event?

Are you staying in this area (or city) overnight? For how many nights?

How many nights in total are you away from home during this trip?

Where are you staying? (Specify type of commercial accommodation versus staying with friends or relatives.)

Did you come to this event alone, or with a group? What kind of group—family? Friends? Tour group? How many adults are in your group? How many children?

How long have you been here so far? How much longer are you planning to stay? (Option for take-home questionnaires: How many hours or minutes were you at the event in total?) (For longer events: How many days did you come to the event?)

Motivations and Information Sources

This is an important group of questions for marketing and impact assessment.

Are you in this area (or city) mainly to attend this event, or is there some other reason? (Option: Please indicate how important this event was in your decision to travel to this area (or city): not at all; somewhat important; very important; the only reason.)

Why did you come to this event? (Leave open-ended or provide possible reasons, such as for the music; the food; a family outing.) (Option: Which of these things attracted you to this event? List the main features.)

How did you find out about this event? (Leave open-ended or provide a list of sources, including friends or family and "don't remember.") (Option: Do you remember hearing about this event from the following sources? List advertising and promotional sources.)

Have you been to a similar event recently? Which ones?

Economic Impact

More accurate and complete information on expenditures can be obtained from postevent surveys. If it is an on-site survey, all that can be requested is an estimate of what the respondent is likely to spend. The intention is to calculate average visitor spending at the event, in the area, and on the trip. Tourist expenditures must be separated from those of residents. The amount spent by those who came to the area for reasons other than the event should be eliminated or discounted from multiplier and tourism cost-benefit calculations. Expenditures by tourists who would have come to the area at some other time in the year (time switchers) can be eliminated from tourism multiplier and cost-benefit calculations.

Please record all the expenditures you have made at this event. (List all possible categories.)

What did you spend while in this area (or city) during this trip? (Include accommodations, transportation, dining, shopping, other attractions and entertainment.)

What else did you spend on this trip? (Options: You can ask for total party spending, but then divide by party size to determine average per-visitor spending.) A logbook supplied to a small sample of visitors prior to the event is likely to obtain more accurate information, and interviews with prompting will also be better.

Activity Patterns

It is very useful to know what visitors actually see, do, and spend money on while attending the event. Relying on memory will produce errors, so it is best to provide a list (if space and time permit) of all the possible activities, then let the respondent check off those completed or attended, and possibly those that are planned. For multisite or multiperformance events, it is very important to know how many visitors responded to each opportunity, just as it is important to know how many days each person attended; otherwise, accurate attendance and spending estimates are impossible.

What have you done or visited at the event? Please check off all those things listed below. Anything else? What else do you plan to do before you leave?

What else have you done or visited in this area?

Consumers' Evaluation

Evaluators can have a lot of fun playing with various measures of customer satisfaction, preference, and problems experienced. These questions must be adapted to the particular needs of each event, and should reflect current marketing, production, and management goals. At the simplest level are open-ended questions asking visitors to state likes, dislikes, problems, and suggestions. Wise evaluators will confirm the answers by means of direct observation and staff evaluations. More elaborate scales can also be used, as in our case study of Dickens on the Strand (Chapter 9). If desired, the evaluation can apply to the whole destination area.

Please tell us about any problems you have experienced at the event.

What did you particularly like about the event?

What did you particularly dislike?

Do you have any suggestions for improving the event?

What else would you like the event to offer in the future?

Was the event exactly what you expected? What was different?

Do you plan to return in the future?

Would you recommend the event to someone else?

Please indicate how satisfied you were with all the following activities, events, or attractions. (Respondents can be asked to rank them in order of satisfaction, or to indicate from 1 to 5 their degree of satisfaction with each.)

Personal Data

If the sample is of individuals there is less need to add questions about the whole visiting party, but it does add useful profiles for marketing purposes. Each question can be modified to obtain data on the whole group.

Please tell us (or write in) your age, in years. (Categories can be used.)

Are you male or female?

Are you married? Do you have children?

What is your occupation or type of employment (including student, home-maker, retired, unemployed)?

What is your highest level of completed education? (Show categories.)

What is your annual income? (It is probably best to use broad categories.)

Please describe the group you came with today (number, age, gender, relationship).

Be sure to thank, and if possible reward, all respondents. Remember that a survey can be a public relations tool, as well as an evaluation device.

SUMMARY

Basic data needs and methods were covered first (Table 10-1), illustrating the importance of multiple methods and the interdependence of attendance counts, visitor surveys, and on-site evaluation by managers and staff. The perspective of destination planners was not ignored. Their interests are similar to those of event managers, but in addition they cover broader market research, exit surveys, and trend monitoring to assess the overall importance of events to the tourist industry and economic development. It was strongly emphasized that all perspectives on festivals and events must be included, with specific methods developed to evaluate social, cultural, and environmental effects.

Techniques for estimating attendance were compared, taking note of the difficulty in obtaining reliable estimates in the absence of ticket sales or controlled gates. Nevertheless, reasonable estimates can be made through various sampling procedures. Without trustworthy attendance numbers, impact assessment and market evaluation become guesswork.

Considerable attention was paid to visitor surveys—how to prepare and conduct them, and their analysis. All festivals and events should conduct regular, though not necessarily annual, visitor surveys. Choices of sampling methods were discussed, entailing a comparison of the advantages of on-site and off-site surveys, quota versus random and systematic sampling frames, interviews versus self-completion questionnaires, and the role of general household surveys in the market area. Although organizers were strongly advised to follow the provided steps in developing their own survey questions, a final section in Chapter 10 listed sample questions that can be adapted to many situations.

To complement visitor surveys, observational techniques and staff or volunteer checklists are desirable. Basic guidelines were given on these points, followed by a recommendation to include public, stakeholder evaluation forums and media scans.

Economic impact assessment is a subcategory of evaluation focusing on costs and benefits in monetary terms. The complications of determining incremental revenue, or new money to the area under study, were examined. In particular, there is room for judgment in attributing portions of visitor and resident expenditures based on the perceived importance of the event in stimulating the spending.

Uses and abuses of various multipliers, used to estimate macroeconomic effects, were also scrutinized. Of greatest interest are income or value-added multipliers, which show the total, cumulative effect of incremental revenue in creating personal or household incomes for area residents. Organizers were cautioned to employ expert advice when assessing economic impact and especially when applying multipliers, as many pitfalls can occur. Too often estimates of total or macroeconomic impact are greatly exaggerated or based on faulty assumptions. Examples of multipliers applied to events were provided to demonstrate valid approaches.

More important than the actual formulas and calculation of multipliers is an understanding of how incremental revenue generates wealth for the host area. Figure 10-1 illustrated the process, clearly demonstrating the important monetary flows. Elaborating upon the model, we developed criteria for events to use in attempting to maximize the creation of local area income, such as by relying on local goods and services, keeping wages and profits in the area, and attracting external grants and sponsorships. In addition, what is considered the ideal eventgoer, from the perspective of enhancing local economic benefits, was profiled.

Cost-benefit analysis is necessary to account for intangibles, particularly the social, cultural, and environmental effects of events. Using the example of a cost-benefit analysis of the first Australian Grand Prix at Adelaide, conclusions were drawn as to the types of costs and benefits that must be considered, how intangibles should be treated, and the important issue of determining exactly who gains or loses. A simplified cost-benefit evaluation process was outlined, for organizers unable to conduct the elaborate research and sophisticated analysis.

In conclusion, Chapter 10 provided advice on using evaluation to enhance the event. This included an outline of a SWOT analysis to assess strengths, weaknesses, opportunities, and threats, and a discussion of how to use it to maximize the attractiveness of events to tourists.

CHAPTER ELEVEN

Conclusions and Future Perspectives

This final chapter looks ahead to possible future developments in this exciting field of festivals, special events, and tourism. It includes interviews with several professionals in the field. We begin with a synthesis of conclusions on the "specialness" of some events.

QUALITIES THAT MAKE SOME FESTIVALS AND EVENTS SPECIAL

A special event can be defined contextually, from the perspectives of the organization and the visitor. But what makes some events more special than others? Is there a set of attributes, or planning and marketing criteria, that can be used to create or increase specialness from the visitor's perspective?

In one sense, all festivals are by definition special, as they are infrequent and outside normal work and life experiences. But all special events are not festivals, because festivals require a focus of celebration, theming, and public involvement. More and more events are adding festive qualities to expand their appeal, however, so the distinction is blurring somewhat.

A final synthesis of all the pertinent points made throughout the text is now possible, and this is really the only way to come to grips with the specialness issue. There is no simple, concise way to define specialness, except with the contextual approach we used as a working definition. What follows, therefore, is a description of all the attributes or characteristics of festivals and events that can elevate them above the commonplace and make them unique leisure and cultural experiences, powerful travel motivators, and facilitators of community pride and development.

A multiplicity of roles: Events have the potential to foster tourism, conservation, heritage, arts, leisure, community development, and other social or cultural goals; events can be catalysts for economic and infrastructure development, and they can support urban renewal efforts. To the resident market, therefore, specialness is related to the diversity of goals that festivals and events successfully pursue.

Festive spirit: Specialness increases with the ability of events to create a true festive spirit, the qualities of which include the celebration of shared values, ritual, games, spectacle, and a feeling of belonging and sharing. The ambience must encourage joyfulness—even revelry—along with freedom from routine constraints and an inversion of normal roles and function. An important aspect of the festive spirit is the role of interactions: customers with staff and volunteers; customers with other customers; customers with the setting. These interactions can be managed, to a degree, but also generate an unpredictable and potentially special atmosphere.

Satisfying basic needs: All the basic human needs and related leisure and travel motivations can be satisfied in part through festivals and events. This is related to the festive spirit, but it also encompasses the full range of physical, interpersonal or social, and personal or psychological needs. Attention to needs and motives can make events more special.

Uniqueness: Mega-events rely on a must-see, once-in-a-lifetime sense of uniqueness to attract visitors; all festivals and events, to some degree, can manage their product and promotions or image-making to create the specialness associated with a unique happening. Special events must be perceived to be outside normal experience and above the commonplace. Events are inherently different from static attractions, and the differences must be enhanced. Adding specialties to the product—whether merchandise, food and beverages, activities, or entertainment—increases the sense of uniqueness and thus the competitive advantage.

Authenticity: This is related to uniqueness, in that events based on indigenous cultural values and attributes will be inherently unique. To the tourist, specialness will be heightened by a feeling of participation in an authentic community celebration. The participation of the community as organizers, staff, and performers enhances authenticity.

Tradition: Many events have become traditions, rooted in the community, and attractive to visitors because of the mystique associated with traditions. To a degree, the mystique can be fabricated, but unless the event is special to the host community it will not become a tradition with special appeal to tourists. Hallmark events, which are closely associated with the host community so that event and destination images are mutually reinforcing, are traditional by nature.

Flexibility: Events can be developed with minimal infrastructure, moved in space and time, and adapted to changing markets and organizational needs. This special character of events makes them particularly well suited to provide high-quality experiences to visitors and residents in many circumstances. An abundance of events in a destination contributes to the feeling that it has a special quality of attractiveness.

Hospitality: Flexibility and the involvement of the host community enable events to maximize customer orientation and make each attendee feel like an honored guest. In other words, the tourist is provided with community hospitality and the resident customer is made to feel part of the hospitality.

Tangibility: From the perspective of tourism destination themes and images, festivals and events have a unique ability to provide a tangible manifestation of ambient resources, especially culture and hospitality. The tourist can experience the specialness of a destination through its events.

Theming: All elements of the event production or performance can be themed to maximize festive spirit, authenticity, tradition, interactions, and customer service. The theming of static attractions almost certainly leads to the addition of special events. Theming makes festivals and events special in a very tangible way.

Symbolism: Elements of the production, or the event itself, can provide symbolism related to cultural values or to political and economic objects. This relates to tradition and authenticity, but symbolism can also be manipulated for self-serving reasons. The use of rituals and symbols together adds to the festive atmosphere, but it can also give an event special significance above and beyond its immediate purpose and theme.

Affordability: Although high-cost, high-quality events will have tourist and resident appeal, events providing affordable leisure and social or cultural experiences will become increasingly special to large segments of the population who lack the means to pay for alternatives.

Convenience: Events are special opportunities for spontaneous, unplanned leisure and social opportunities. This is of increasing importance in a hectic, work-oriented world, especially in urban environments. Flexibility is a related quality.

With these attributes or qualities of specialness in mind, the event organizer and manager can seek to create a more appealing and satisfying event, for both residents and tourists. For the most part, specialness means similar things for tourists and residents, although, as shown in this book, a customer orientation requires somewhat different treatment for visitors to the host community.

The other dimension of specialness should not be forgotten: festivals and events have special roles to play in tourism development, as was repeatedly stressed throughout the book.

RESEARCH NEEDS

Research and data on festivals and events and related marketing factors have not kept up with the explosion in the number and significance of events. Governments and the industry will have to tackle this problem in the 1990s if event tourism is to reach its potential and if event organizers are to meet their multiple goals. The principal research needs are summarized below.

Basic statistics: Governments and event associations must combine efforts to conduct complete inventories and classifications of festivals and events, measure demand for them, reliably estimate attendance, and monitor trends in numbers, types, and impacts of events. Included in the category of basic statistics should be a segmentation of the markets to reveal eventgoers' characteristics and the value of events in satisfying different tourist needs. Destination planners must also learn more about the growth and evolution of event tourism products—events and related packages or tours.

Needs and motives: This book speculated on how events can potentially satisfy all the basic human needs and related leisure and travel motives, but more focused research is required to corroborate the hypothesis. This problem is at the heart of specialness and is vital to understanding the appeal of events. Attitude and motivation (or psychographic) research has been conducted, but without sufficient attention to the event sector.

The event experience: We explored a model of the event product from the visitor's perspective, but can it be substantiated or improved through research? The nature of the experience as shaped by the setting, program, and interactions must be subjected to research. Possible lines of inquiry include visitor interviews, direct observations of customer behavior, and controlled manipulation of event components—in other words, field experiments. The disciplines of sociology and environmental psychology, as well as the design professions, can contribute valuable insights.

Marketing effectiveness: Related to the need for research on needs and motives is that of evaluating the effectiveness of event marketing and promotions, particularly image-making. What messages and images work best for destinations and individual events? Again, this book suggested appropriate strategies, but without the benefit of background research.

Case studies: Although the results of case studies do not have generalized application, they are vital in providing background data, stimulating ideas, and allowing comparisons in support of hypotheses. All the roles of events require examination, in various settings and for different types of festivals and events. In particular, there is a need for case studies that comprehensively document event history, organization, production, and impact. Do certain types of events create more benefits for the host community? Not enough is known to answer this question.

Visitor surveys: These are essential research tools, and their validity and reliability must be constantly improved. Case studies have to be documented and evaluated, and various methods must be tested in a variety of event settings. Results of high-quality visitor surveys should be published. Considerable room for improvement exists in the areas of attendance counts, on which reliable analysis of impact and markets depends, and on-site sampling methods for surveys.

Economic impact assessment: A number of good studies have been reviewed in this book, but the state of the art is weak. An overemphasis on multipliers and inappropriate use of them have given rise to exaggerated and unreliable claims of macro event impacts. The allocation problem must be addressed, especially with regard to determining the appropriateness of including a portion of resident spending as incremental revenue. In addition, the practice of discounting visitor spending, to reflect the visitor's attribution of the importance of an event in drawing him or her to an area, requires further examination. It must be asked if self-attribution by visitors is valid and reliable, and if event-related spending by tourists who have not been motivated by an event should nevertheless be included in impact assessment.

Cost-benefit evaluation: Given the weaknesses of typical economic impact assessment, refinement of cost-benefit evaluation techniques is required. Research on the assigning of surrogate monetary values to intangible effects is warranted. Is it valid to include any indirect impact on social phenomena, such as accidents and crime? More attention to the distribution of costs and benefits of events is definitely required, particularly to external factors in the context of long-term effects. There has been too much unsubstantiated imputation of long-term benefits to host communities, especially with regard to so-called legacies. Social and cultural effects have not been well researched. How frequent are the examples of commercialized events, events that have failed, or events that have caused social problems?

Policy and planning evaluation: As event tourism policies and planning become more common, and perhaps more sophisticated, they must be subjected to open monitoring and evaluation. Destination planners, for example, have to establish a system for monitoring individual events, the development of tours and packages, and general impact. Experiments in community-based tourism planning through the medium of festivals and special events should be undertaken. The roles of various levels of government have to be examined.

Management effectiveness: Although beyond the scope of this book, it is apparent that more research is needed on the practical organization and management of events and how their effectiveness can be increased to meet various goals, including those pertaining to tourism. The role of grants and sponsorships must be assessed, as well as the use and training of volunteers. How well events adapt to change is another area deserving attention. Event associations have a responsibility to base their information-sharing and professional training on systematic evaluation of common practices.

FUTURE PERSPECTIVES

Forecasts pertaining to events and event tourism have already been summarized at the end of Chapter 3. To obtain a broader perspective on trends and likely developments in the 1990s, several experts from the festivals and events field were asked to share their insights.

Interview with Don Lunday, executive director of the International Festivals Association

Q: "Looking to the future, where is IFA headed?"

A: "The hope is to see IFA become truly international. We already have a strong American and Canadian component, and at our recent conference in Palm Springs we had attendance from Great Britain, Australia, New Zealand, and the Netherlands. Recently IFA exchanged membership with the Foundation of European Carnival Cities, and we are developing links between our members. In fact, in 1992 our conference will be in Rotterdam. We are also moving closer to related associations such as the Children's Festivals group that is very active in North America."

Q: "And what about festivals in general—what are the trends for the 1990s?"

A: "The festival world is becoming a more integral part of the free world, linked to more leisure time and discretionary income. This is certainly true in North America, and appears to be emerging in Western Europe. For example, they are very active in the Netherlands in taking a tourism-based interest in festivals. In Japan, where the government has recently been encouraging people to take more leisure time and holidays, there will be a symposium in 1990 on leisure-time festivals. And generally, cities are creating festivals as a component of leisure and community development policy."

Q: "Is it just a big-city phenomenon?"

A: "Absolutely not. North American society is highly mobile, and its cities lack the traditions that European cities have, so festivals are an important way to get people involved and help develop roots in the community. But small towns are also big on festivals and events, because they do not want the people and the leisure money to leave them for other opportunities. Also, senior governments are in the business of developing national-level events."

Q: "Sponsorship is increasing as a factor in shaping festivals and special events. Is this a good trend?"

A: "I think so. It tends to give the festival more freedom to develop its own goals and programs. Local sponsors are best for many events, but large sponsorships can help make the festival national or international in scope. More will be tourist-oriented."

Q: "Speaking of tourism, what is the key to a festival becoming a tourist attraction?"

A: "Well, I think the key is to set a clearly defined goal—to be local or national or even international in scope. For example, the Pasadena Tournament of Roses, for which I have worked many years as a volunteer, has changed its mission as it gained first national and then international stature. It is now broadcast live to between four hundred and five hundred million people in ninety countries, and it has attracted major sponsors as it grew. And there is the small Monrovia, California, Armed Forces Day Parade near here, which is televised but has the goal of not trying to compete with the big events. Instead, they aim to get ten thousand kids on the streets each year to see the parade and have a good time as a sign of community pride and involvement."

Interview with Doug Little, president of Festivals Ontario and chairman of the Leacock Heritage Festival (Orillia, Canada)

Q: "What do you think is in the future for festivals?"

A: "They have tremendous potential, both as a medium of culture and community arts and for their tourism potential. The problem is getting recognition of their importance. Governments have not been providing the funding or assistance we need. It seems that cultural agencies are only interested in performing arts, and not community festivals, while some tourism organizations see festivals as being purely cultural in nature! There isn't agreement on how to approach festivals, especially community festivals, and that is hindering their development. On the other hand, more and more municipalities are getting active in developing and helping community events, and that might cause the other governments to take more notice."

Q: "What are Festivals Ontario and the Canadian Association of Festivals and Events doing about this problem?"

A: "We are trying to convince the provincial and federal governments that community-based festivals have as much potential as other events. They are the fastest growing type of festival, are not expensive, have broad appeal, and help keep people traveling in Canada."

Q: "Your new festival in Orillia, the Leacock Heritage Festival—how do you market it?"

A: "Our idea with the Leacock festival, which emphasizes Orillia's connection with the famous Canadian humorist, was to add a strong attraction to our summer tourist season, to get people to stay in this town and shop here. We are working with our tourist associations to maximize regional promotions, and with the local media to get their support as sponsors. All-year public relations are important, and so are gimmicks to get coverage. Our marketing committee has this job. But like most community events we do not have the budget for major advertising. Involving the local community is the key to successful marketing and a successful festival."

Q: "What can festivals and events do to increase their tourist attractiveness?"

A: "The cost of effective tourist marketing is the main limitation. It's fairly easy to reach the local and regional audience, but support is needed from tourist organizations and government to help fund wider promotions. Also, better promotions are required. Simple calendars of events don't sell the ambience, the sizzle, of events. Special festival and event publications are far better for communicating what each event really has to offer."

Interview with Lesa Ukman, executive editor of the Chicago-based *Special Events Report*

Q: "What types of festivals and special events are likely to gain from increasing corporate sponsorship?"

A: "There will always be certain types of events that are trendy for a few years, but what is important is that in a broad sense, any events with authenticity will continue to see increases in corporate support. The idea behind event sponsorship is for companies to associate themselves with something that has meaning to consumers. As product differences become less and less distinct, consumers are basing purchasing decisions on the company behind the product and their perceptions of the company's image. Given that atmosphere in the marketing climate, legitimate events that have meaning to consumers apart from their sponsors will continue to thrive."

Q: "How will this affect their marketing and their attractiveness to tourists?"

A: "The effect that increasing sponsorship will have on event marketing abilities is really up to the organizers. They must put the money to good use. Overall, increased revenue should be beneficial to their marketing efforts, allowing them to provide better programming, improve collateral materials, hire professionals to help their sales efforts, etc. Also, since it is in the sponsor's best interest to have a successful, well-attended event, a corporation will often lend its expertise to the event personnel."

Q: "Do you feel that corporate sponsorship changes the nature of some festivals and special events?"

A: "No, it does not. As a general rule, there is no danger to festivals in these alliances. The reason is that sponsors are now sophisticated enough to understand that changing the nature of what they sponsor will diminish its inherent value, i.e., the affinity the event has with its audience. The entire notion of sponsorship is to align with arts, sports, or causes that appeal to a target market. To offend this audience by meddling with programming would only generate ill will toward the sponsor, and so it is utterly self-defeating."

The three interviews express a common faith in the positive future of festivals and special events. They also demonstrate the need for improved support from governments, and the value of sponsorships, in elevating community festivals— both for social and cultural reasons and as tourist attractions.

Final Remarks

Festivals and special events have tremendous potential as tourist attractions, development catalysts, image makers, animators of attractions, and facilitators of community-based tourism planning. The links to tourism and economic development should not, however, overshadow their roles in fostering community development, the arts, leisure, health, and improved understanding among cultures. Partnerships among all these interests are growing and should be cultivated by all the related interest groups. Tourism will benefit to the extent that all the other perspectives on festivals and events grow and flourish.

The prospects are exciting. In festivals and special events there is the opportunity to use tourism as a force for sustainable development and cultural growth. Through tourism, festivals and events have the potential to generate revenue, attract attention to causes, and develop their product to everyone's advantage.

With so much potential for positive outcomes, the tourism-event partnership must become more prominent and receive more attention from governments.

Considerable effort is required, in research, funding, advice, and support. Attention to potential costs and negative impact must also be an integral part of event tourism planning and marketing.

In the decade of the 1990s, great expectations can be realized in the special blend of tourism, festivals, and events.

Glossary

Activity outlet: An event, facility, or service that provides an opportunity for tourists in the area to engage in desired activities—and therefore spend money.

Alternative tourism: Forms of tourism that are more socially, culturally, and environmentally developmental, and less destructive, than contemporary mass tourism. Related terms: *community-based; organic; soft tourism; sustainable development.*

Ambience: Qualities of the environment, setting, or event that make it special or attractive; the intangible atmosphere of the place or event, including emotional responses of the participants and visitors that foster a festive or celebratory mood.

Ambient attractions: Qualities of the general destination environment, including scenery, culture, climate, wildlife, and hospitality, that have appeal to tourists. Festivals and special events can be tangible expressions of culture and hospitality.

Animation: Bringing a static attraction or facility to life through interpretation, events, and activities.

Attendance: The total number of customers or visitors, or the size of the crowd. This amount should be distinguished from the total number of visitations, which is a measure of person-visits; for example, one person attending an event three separate times equals three person-visits.

Attraction: A site, facility, or event with attributes capable of drawing tourists and satisfying their expectations. Regarding events, a hierarchy of mega-event, regional attraction, and local attraction can be identified. Touring attractions can be at any level, as can programs of events at permanent attractions.

Attractiveness: A measure of the relative strength of attractions in terms of the number of people drawn, the geographic spread of the market area, or appeal relative to that of the competition.

Attribution: Determining the proportion of eventgoers' expenditures that can be considered new or incremental revenue to the area, for purposes of calculating economic impact. Tourists attracted to an area totally or primarily by an event generate the greatest benefit. Discounts can be made for those with multiple motives.

Authenticity: The property of being a genuine cultural event, artifact, or landscape; uncommercialized; not a tourist trap; reflecting the host community's way of life and self-image.

Benefits: The experiences or personal rewards of travel, or of a visit to an event, that are sought by customers and tourists; the economic or other effects of tourism or events that are considered to be positive outcomes when conducting cost-benefit evaluations, and are expressed in monetary terms, or intangibles. Generic benefits of festivals and events include sharing and belonging, spectacle, games, ritual, and authenticity. Targeted benefits are specialties that make the event unique and give it competitive advantage.

Capacity: For a site or facility, the absolute or legal maximum attendance; more generally, capacity to absorb tourism refers to the issue of how much, what kinds, and what pace of tourism development an area can or wants to tolerate.

Carnival: Originally a religious feast or festival and associated revelry celebrating a farewell to the flesh just before Lent, as typified by Mardi Gras; a traveling midway or show, with rides and amusements.

Catalyst: An event or policy that serves to induce or bring together the elements conducive to other forms of development or change.

Cavalcade: A procession, as on horseback; often used to describe a sequence of events, as in a cavalcade of sports. Related terms: *flotilla; parade.*

Celebration: Solemn rites to mark or make famous an observance; joyfulness and a mood of excitement in commemoration of an important cultural event or shared cultural attribute. Celebration is generic to all festivals.

Ceremony: A sacred rite, formal observance, formality, or public or private function. Most events include elements of formal ceremony, religious, metaphysical, or secular in nature.

Circus: A traveling entertainment show, usually with clowns, trained and wild animals, and acrobatic performers; a place in which entertainment occurs.

Commemoration: A remembrance; celebration of someone or an event by way of solemn acts of devotion. Commemorations, as in remembrances of war dead, generally do not include elements of festivity, but might be associated with a festival. Anniversaries, centennials, memorials, remembrances, and holidays are all popular forms of commemoration.

Community-based festivals: Events controlled by the host community, usually through volunteer and nonprofit organizations.

Community-based tourism: Tourism planning based on the goals of the host community or destination, including identification of the tourism product most suitable to the area.

Community development: The process of fostering local democracy, economic and administrative self-sufficiency, leadership, organizational and interorganizational development, and social harmony.

Conference; congress; convention; meeting: Business-related events attracting people to a particular destination for the specific purpose of doing business, exchanging views, obtaining information, or conducting association affairs.

Contest; competition: An event in which prizes are awarded or recognition given for specific accomplishments, such as reaching a level of performance, or for victory over competitors. Many special events include contests in forms such as beauty pageants, bake-offs, trials, awards, examinations, tournaments, playoffs, Olympics, classics, marathons, races, field days, rallies, championships, grand prix, and meets. Some contests are scheduled, as in league play, while others are special events. Some sporting contests have taken on festive qualities or have festivals built around them.

Cost-benefit evaluation: Analysis that compares all costs—capital, operating, opportunity, and external—with all benefits to determine a ratio of one to the other; requires expression of all costs and benefits in monetary terms and/or a subjective evaluation of intangibles.

Cultural performance: Any public display, such as parades, festivals, and other special events, that expresses shared cultural values.

Cultural tourism: Tourism motivated by cultural, as opposed to natural resource, attractions.

Customer: Someone who has paid an admission price or is making a purchase; a guest at a public festival or event. A customer orientation is vital to event marketing.

Day-tripper: Excursionist; one who leaves home for an activity and returns the same day. This often constitutes the most important market for events.

Demonstration effect: The influence tourists have on the attitudes and cultural characteristics of host populations. Most authors have viewed it as a negative process, leading to acculturation, increased import propensity due to emulation of tourists' consumptive life-style, and eventually hostility toward tourists and tourism development.

Destination planning: The planning of all facets of tourism and its impact in a resort, region, or nation for purposes of creating attractions and infrastructure to make it a popular tourist destination.

Distribution: Using intermediaries and tour packages to facilitate travel to events and destinations.

Diversification: A marketing strategy in which new products are developed or added to appeal to new markets.

Essential services: Necessities for all events and attractions, the absence or poor quality of which can disappoint and discourage customers; examples include safety, health, comfort, access, information, communications, food, and beverages.

Evaluation: The analytic and judgmental process of determining the worth or success of an event by comparing outcomes with goals (i.e., goal attainment), or by comprehensive cost-benefit analysis (i.e., systematic); evaluation includes impact assessment.

Event: Affair; effect; happening; notable occurrence. Events are clearly different from permanent attractions in several respects: they have a fixed, usually short duration; they are usually public or at least subject to media coverage; they are often independent from built facilities.

Event tourism: The systematic planning, development, and marketing of festivals and special events as tourist attractions, development catalysts, and image builders for attractions and destination areas.

Exhibition: A public show or display. Traditional fairs and exhibitions are closely related in origin, form, and settings.

Exposition: Display; exhibit; act of expounding or explaining; a fair; a world's fair is commonly called an exposition, or Expo.

Externalities: The costs or problems not normally encompassed by event or tourist organizations, but directly and indirectly created by the event or event tourism; examples include pollution, crime, loss of community amenity, and costs for other levels of government.

Facilitation: The use of special events to help achieve other goals, such as fostering the arts or sports or contributing to urban renewal or conservation; similar to *catalyst*.

Fair: Periodic exhibitions or expositions, often competitive in nature, of produce or manufactured goods; sale of articles. World's fairs are a special class of exposition in which nations participate. Trade fairs are designed to bring manufacturers and suppliers in contact with potential purchasers or consumers. Agricultural fairs, fall fairs, and county fairs combine rural traditions with entertainment and contests. Related terms: *bazaar; flea market; market; mart; sale; show.*

Feasibility study: Analysis of the practicality, suitability, and desirability of attracting or creating an event. It usually includes a cost-benefit evaluation.

Feast: Rich and elaborate meal. Related terms: *barbecue; feed; party; picnic; roast.* The original meaning of a feast is that of a religious festival, but it is now seldom used in that sense.

Festival: A public, themed celebration. Falassi (1987) has summarized the various popular meanings of this word as "(a) a sacred or profane time of celebration, marked by special observances; (b) the annual celebration of a notable person or event, or the harvest of an important product; (c) a cultural event consisting of a series of performances of works in the fine arts, often devoted to a single artist or genre; (d) a fair; (e) generic gaiety, conviviality, cheerfulness. Related terms: *feast; fest; festivities; fete; fiesta*. Common types or themes of festival: arts (visual and performing), children's, education, ethnic, folk, food, harvest, heritage, multicultural, music, recreational, seasonal, sporting, street, and technology.

Gala: A show or festivity; often used as an adjective, rather superfluously, as in a gala event.

Games: Sports; athletic competitions or meets; a generic term to describe a wide range of activities pursued for fun; humorous activities or situations. Some games have become institutionalized with organizing bodies and detailed regulations, as in the Olympics or Pan-Am Games.

Hallmark event: An event that gives a destination a high profile or provides the tourism theme for the destination; the event and its host community possess mutually reinforcing attractiveness.

Image-making; image enhancement: Using festivals and events to create positive or favorable expectations about the destination and related tourist experiences; marketing efforts intended to correct or improve the image of an event.

Impact assessment: The process of identifying, measuring, and evaluating the significance of both the intended and unintended outcomes or effects of events and event tourism. It should be directed at assessment of organizational effectiveness and effects on the environment, economy, and society.

Incremental income: The expenditures of visitors, or other revenue, that is new revenue for the destination or host community, and therefore equivalent to export earnings. Money that would have been invested, spent, or given to the destination regardless of an event cannot be considered as a benefit of the event. All the expenditures of visitors who came to a community because of an event, and who would not have traveled otherwise, can be considered to be incremental. See also *Attribution* and *Multiplier*.

Intangibles: Costs or benefits that must be evaluated qualitatively, or for which surrogate monetary values must be assigned, to conduct a cost-benefit assessment; examples include social disruption and prestige.

Interactive marketing: A process aimed at improving the interactions between hosts and guests, employees and customers, tourists and other tourists, and tourists with the environment, as factors shaping the travel experience and customer satisfaction.

Internal marketing: Marketing that focuses on the role of employees and volunteers in creating satisfying customer experiences.

Jamboree: A noisy revel; a large assembly.
Jubilee: An anniversary (twenty-fifth or fiftieth); a celebration.

Legacy: The physical, financial, psychological, or social benefits that are permanently bestowed on a community or destination region by virtue of hosting an event. The term can also be used to describe negative impact, such as debt, displacement of people, pollution, and so on.
Leisure: Free or discretionary time; a state of mind marked by a feeling of freedom from obligation; the property of a personally satisfying experience undertaken for its intrinsic value.

Market area: The geographical area from which the bulk of demand is generated.
Market development: Seeking new target markets or an expanded market area.
Market penetration: A marketing strategy aimed at attracting more users to the same product or gaining increased market share through maximizing competitive advantages; the proportion of the population attending an event.
Market positioning: Based on product-market matching and segmentation, the product is positioned for maximum competitive advantage. This might involve modifications to any element in the marketing mix to differentiate the event or event tourism products from the competition.
Market potential: The size of the market for events; potential demand. It can be measured by reference to expected attendance, sales, or a proportion of the population likely to attend—which can be termed *market penetration*.
Marketing mix: The traditional marketing mix consists of product, price, place, and promotion; a broader interpretation includes *interactive* and *internal marketing*.
Marketing planning: The process of orienting the organization to identification and meeting of the needs—desired benefits—of target markets. The process, or the strategic marketing plan, should include situational and environmental analysis; purpose and goals; specific objectives and criteria for evaluating performance; marketing strategies, or ways to meet goals and objectives; an action plan; financial implications and budget; evaluation, feedback, and revision mechanisms.
Mega-event: A popular expression describing the largest and most visible of events, such as world's fairs and the Olympics. In the context of event tourism, they are events that attract the largest number of tourists or a proportion of tourists substantially higher than other events, or have a major impact on the image of the destination.
Multiplier: Of particular interest to event impact assessment is the income or value-added multiplier, which measures the cumulative impact of incremental tourist spending as it ripples through the destination economy—the direct,

indirect, and induced effects—creating income for area residents. Linkages between local producers and services increase the effects, and leakages through imports and through profits or wages removed from the area weaken the effect. Other multipliers include measurement of the effects of tourism on employment, sales, output, imports, or government revenue.

Olympics: A special class of athletic competition for national teams only, divided into Summer and Winter Games, and regulated by the International Olympic Committee. The term also has been used to describe other events that represent the summit of competition in a particular field.

Packaging: Combining elements of the event or tourist experience to improve customer convenience, or to influence travel or use patterns. A packaged tour is most applicable to events.

Pageant: A show of people in costume, taking part in processions or dramatic scenes; a spectacle; a brilliant display; pomp.

Parade: Public procession; to make a display or spectacle of something or someone. Parades are integral parts of many festivals, and may be special events in their own right.

Party: A private or public time of merrymaking. Related terms: *affair; ball; bash; capers; fete; fling; follies; frolic; fun day; gala; happening; hootenanny; occasion; revel; spree; strut; wingding.*

Performance: A single artistic act or show; often part of a performance series or season. Related terms: *concert; extravaganza; hootenanny; pageant; production; spectacular; tattoo; theater festival.*

Pilgrimage: Journey to a holy place; travel for a sacred purpose.

Place (setting): The event site; locations of events in a destination area; environmental factors, both tangible and intangible, that shape the event experience and help create its ambience.

Pricing: Determining the role of price in the marketing mix. Price can be used to influence overall demand, and as a communication tool for target segments. Pricing might have to change to reflect stages in the product life cycle.

Procession: Any moving display of people, animals, or objects; a parade. Related terms: *cavalcade; cruise; flotilla (on water); invasion; pilgrimage; tour; trek.*

Product: A good, service, or package of goods and services offered to potential tourists; the benefits realized by visitors to events; the consequences of special events for tourism, community development, and organizational development.

Product life cycle: Stages of introduction, growth, maturity, and decline in the evolution of an event or tourist product.

Product-market matching: A process by which the choice of viable and suitable products is matched against viable target markets to generate priorities for development or promotions.

Product reformulation: Modifying the product or elements of the program to sustain appeal to the same target markets.

Promotion mix (or communications mix): The choices in methods of communicating with potential customers, including paid advertising, public relations, publicity (often free), personal selling, and sales promotions.

Reenactment: Performing an historical event, such as a battle, as entertainment or as an interpretive tool.

Ritual: Solemn rites; ceremonies with a set form.

Rodeo: Public exhibition of cowboy skills and associated contests and entertainment. Related terms: *roundup; shoot-out; stampede.*

Seasonality: The annual flow of travel, caused by institutional factors, fad, or climate, often resulting in peak, shoulder, and off-peak seasons; the dominance of one or more seasons for holding events.

Segmentation: Analysis of potential markets to identify relatively homogeneous groups as target markets. Common segmentation criteria include geographic (market areas); demographic (age, gender, marital status, race, life cycle); socioeconomic (education, income, social class, occupation); psychographic (personality, attitudes, travel philosophies, life-style); benefits sought (preferred products and experiences); consumer behavior (preferred ways of buying, travel mode, frequency of travel, season of travel).

Show: Any display or exhibit; performance; demonstration; entertainment act.

Socials: Assemblies for primarily social reasons. Related terms: *bee; congregation; gathering; get-together; homecoming; jamboree; powwow; reunion; revival.*

Special event: A onetime or infrequently occurring event outside the normal program or activities of the organizers; for consumers, a leisure, social, or cultural opportunity outside the normal range of choice or beyond everyday experience.

Specialness: Qualities that make some festivals and events more attractive than others (see Chapter 11 for a full discussion).

Spectacle: An event or show emphasizing visual display; larger-than-life events.

Sponsorship: The payment of fees, in-kind payments, or other forms of investment in an event, usually by profit-seeking companies, as part of an advertising, sales, or public relations strategy.

SWOT analysis: Evaluation of the strengths and weaknesses of the product or organization and the opportunities and threats likely to influence it. SWOT is an evaluation device and can be used as part of strategic marketing planning.

Tangible product: The event theme, program, activities, merchandise, and experiences, or event tours and packages, available for customers' consumption.

Target marketing: Selecting the market segments to which the event and its promotion will be directed. Segmentation is used to identify relatively homogeneous groups.

Theme: The object or meaning of a celebration; the unifying philosophy or concept that blends the name, program, promotions, symbols, and event experiences into a coherent package; a name or concept for a destination area that is intended to convey an attractive image and differentiate it from that of the competition.

Tourist: A visitor to the host community or destination area; someone traveling for pleasure. Some governments use criteria of a minimum distance traveled and minimum number of nights away from home in the definition of a tourist. Generally, only pleasure travel is considered, and this criterion can be used to distinguish visitors from tourists.

Travel motives: Factors that cause people to seek travel, generally in pursuit of a desired experience while at the same time escaping undesirable circumstances—so-called push and pull factors. Basic human needs—physical, social, and psychological—are motivators, as are attractions such as special events and festivals.

Visitation: See *Attendance*.

Visitor: Anyone attending an event; people from outside the host community or destination area.

World's fair: A special class of fair, often called an exposition or expo, regulated by the International Bureau of Exhibitions under international agreements.

References

Abrahams, R. 1987. An American vocabulary of celebrations. In *Time out of time: Essays on the festival,* ed. A. Falassi, 173–83. Albuquerque: University of New Mexico Press.

Adams, R. 1986. *A book of British music festivals.* London: Robert Royce.

Anderson, R., and E. Wachtel, 1986. *The expo story.* Madeira Park: Harbour Publishing.

Archer, B. 1982. The value of multipliers and their policy implications. *Tourism Management* 3 (4): 236–41.

———. 1989. Trends in international tourism. In *Tourism marketing and management handbook,* eds. S. Witt and L. Moutinho, 593–97. Englewood Cliffs, N.J.: Prentice-Hall.

Arkansas Department of Parks & Tourism. N.d. *Building a festival.* Little Rock.

Armstrong, J. 1985. International events and popular myths. In *International Events: the real tourism impact.* Proceedings of the 1985 Travel and Tourism Association (Canada Chapter) annual conference, Edmonton, 9–37.

Arthur, M.-A. 1989. Personal communications with the author.

Arts Council for Oklahoma City. 1987. *Annual report.*

Ashworth, G., and B. Goodall. 1988. Tourist images: Marketing considerations. In *Marketing in the tourism industry: The promotion of destination regions,* eds. B. Goodall and G. Ashworth, 213–38. London: Croom Helm.

Australian Bicentennial Authority. N.d. *Australian bicentennial calendar notes.*

Australian Bureau of Tourism Research. 1988a. *Australian tourism forecasts, international visitor arrivals.* Canberra.

———. 1988b. Frontiers in Australian tourism. Papers from a conference held in Canberra.

———. 1988c. *Tourism and the economy.* Canberra.

————. *BTR Tourism Update,* various issues. Canberra.

Australian Department of the Arts, Sport, the Environment, Tourism and Territories. 1988. Directions for tourism—a discussion paper. Canberra.

Australian Department of Sport, Recreation and Tourism. 1985. Economic impact of the World Cup of Athletics, held in Canberra in October, 1985. A discussion paper. Canberra.

Australian Standing Committee on Tourism. 1986. The impact and marketing of special events. Papers of the Australian Travel Research Workshop at Mount Buffalo Chalet.

Australian Tourism Research Committee. 1987. Strategic planning for tourism, an Australian travel research workshop. Papers and workshop notes.

Australian Tourist Commission. N.d. *The Australian Bicentenary 1788–1988, Come along for the party.* Brochure.

Australian Travel Research Workshop. 1986. The impact and marketing of special events. Proceedings.

Badders, H. 1984. *South Carolina—a festive state. A survey of festivals in 1984.* South Carolina Festival Association.

Baltimore Area Convention and Visitors Association and the Baltimore Office of Promotion. 1989. *Baltimore Clipper,* summer/fall. Newsletter.

Baud-Bovey, M. 1982. New concepts in planning for tourism and recreation. *Tourism Management* 3 (4): 308–13.

Baud-Bovey, M., and F. Lawson. 1976. *Tourism master plan.* Toronto: Ryerson Polytechnical Institute.

Beioley, S. 1981. *Tourism and urban regeneration: Some lessons from American cities.* London: English Tourist Board.

Bellerose, P., and J. Pelletier. 1988. Tourism and multiculturalism: Impact of ethnocultural attractions and events. Paper presented at the National Conference on Tourism, Culture and Multiculturalism, Montreal.

Benedict, B. 1983. *The anthropology of world's fairs.* Berkeley: Scolar Press.

Benson, J. 1985. Mall marketing. In *Banking on leisure transcripts,* ed. L. Ukman, 45–49. Chicago: International Events Group.

Blackorby, C., R. Ricard, and M. Slade. 1986. The macroeconomic consequences of Expo '86. In *The Expo Story,* eds. R. Anderson and E. Wachtel. Madeira Park: Harbour Publishing.

Blank, U. 1989. *The community tourism industry imperative.* State College of Pennsylvania: Venture.

Blum, E. 1989a. Research shows a strong link between tourism and the arts. *Travel Weekly,* May 29.

————. 1989b. Tourism officials cite growing appeal of culture-related travel. *Travel Weekly,* May 18.

Boissevan, J. 1979. Impact of tourism on a dependent island: Gozo, Malta. *Annals of Tourism Research* 6:76–90.

Boorstin, D. 1961. *The image: A guide to pseudo-events in America.* New York: Harper and Row.

Bos, H., C. van der Kamp, and A. Zom. 1987. Events in Holland. *Revue de Tourisme* 4:16–19.

Brissenden, C. 1987. Expo '86 . . . scenario for success. *Tourism Management* 8 (1): 49–53.

Britten, S., and W. Clarke, eds. 1987. *Ambiguous alternatives: Tourism in small developing countries.* Suva, Fiji: University of the South Pacific.

Buck, R. 1977. Making good business better: A second look at staged tourist attractions. *Journal of Travel Research* 15 (3): 30–31.

Burak Jacobson. 1986. *Canadian tourism attitude and motivation study.* Ottawa: Tourism Canada.

Burns, J., J. Hatch, and T. Mules, eds. 1986. *The Adelaide Grand Prix: The impact of a special event.* Adelaide: The Centre for South Australian Economic Studies.

Butler, R. 1980. The concept of a tourist area cycle of evolution: Implications for management of resources. *Canadian Geographer* 24 (1): 5–12.

Butler, R., and J. Grigg. 1987. The hallmark event that got away: The case of the 1991 Pan American Games in London, Ontario. In *Paper '87, Conference on People and Physical Environment Research.* Centre for Urban Research, University of Western Australia, Perth.

Camacho, J. 1979. *Festivals, commemorations and anniversaries. A study and report.* London: British Tourist Authority.

Cameron, C. 1989. Cultural tourism and urban revitalization. *Tourism Recreation Research* 14 (1): 23–32.

Canada Council. 1980. *The impact of culture on tourism in Canada: A review of travel and festival surveys.* Ottawa.

Canada, Minister of State, Tourism. 1985. *Tourism tomorrow.* Ottawa.

Canada's capital, celebrating the seasons in Ottawa-Hull. N.d. Brochure.

Canada's Wonderland. 1989. Guidebook to Canada's premier theme park.

Canadian Government Office of Tourism. 1982. *Planning festivals and events.* Ottawa.

Canadian Olympic Association. 1989. *Toronto's proposal to host the 1996 Olympic Games.* Toronto.

Canadian Press. 1989. Alberta natives want to cash in on area's tourism. *Kitchener Waterloo Record,* June 25.

Cann, J. 1986. The Wellesley Apple Butter and Cheese Festival: A study of organizational development and socio-cultural impacts. Bachelor's thesis, Department of Recreation and Leisure Studies, University of Waterloo.

Carpenter, G., and C. Howe. 1985. *Programming experiences: A cyclical approach.* Englewood Cliffs, N.J.: Prentice-Hall.

Centre for Applied and Business Research, University of Western Australia. 1987. *America's Cup defence series, 1986/87, impact on the community.* Perth.

Centre for Urban Research, University of Western Australia. 1987. Paper '87, conference on people and physical environment research. Perth.

Charlottetown Department of Tourism and Parks. 1988. *Prince Edward Island 1988 visitors guide.* Charlottetown.

Cheska, A. 1981. Antigonish Highland Games: An ethnic case study. Paper presented at the North American Society of Sport History, ninth annual convention, Hamilton.

Chick, C. 1983. Tourism Canada. *Recreation Canada* 41 (5): 24–25.

Cohen, E. 1972. Towards a sociology of international tourism. *Social Research* 39 (1): 164–82.

———. 1979. Rethinking the sociology of tourism. *Annals of Tourism Research* 6 (1): 18–35.

———. 1989. "Primitive and remote," hill tribe trekking in Thailand. *Annals of Tourism Research* 16 (1): 30–61.

Colbert, F. 1988. The economic impact of festivals and major events: Who benefits? Paper presented at the National Conference on Tourism, Culture and Multiculturalism, Montreal.

Conserve Neighborhoods. 1980. Community events and how to organize them. Newsletter of the National Trust for Historic Preservation, no. 13. Washington, D.C.

Cooke, K. 1982. Guidelines for socially appropriate tourism development in British Columbia. *Journal of Travel Research* (Summer): 22–28.

Coopers and Lybrand Consulting Group. 1989. *NCR 1988 festivals study final report.* Report for the Ottawa-Carleton Board of Trade. Ottawa.

Corcoran, T. 1988. Advantages and considerations in staging a major sporting event: World cup skiing competitions at Waterville Valley, New Hampshire. In *Tourism research: Expanding boundaries,* 101–2. Travel and Tourism Research Association Nineteenth Annual Conference, Montreal. Salt Lake City: University of Utah.

Cowell, D. 1984. *The marketing of services.* London: Heinemann.

Crompton, J. 1979. An assessment of the image of Mexico as a vacation destination and the influence of geographical location upon that image. *Journal of Travel Research* 17 (4): 18–23.

Crompton, J., and C. Lamb. 1986. *Marketing government and social services.* New York: John Wiley and Sons.

Cunneen, C., and R. Lynch. 1988. The social meanings of conflict in riots at the Australian Grand Prix Motorcycle Races. *Leisure Studies* 7 (1): 1–19.

D'Amore, L. 1983. Guidelines to planning in harmony with the host community. In *Tourism in Canada: Selected issues and options,* ed. P. Murphy, 135–59. Western Geographic Series. University of Victoria.

Dann, G. 1971. Tourist motivation: An appraisal. *Annals of Tourism Research* 8 (2): 187–219.

Davidson, L., and W. Schaffer. 1980. A discussion of methods employed in analyzing the impact of short-term entertainment events. *Journal of Travel Research* 18 (3): 12–16.

DCH Consultants Inc. 1986. *Study of the 1986 Festival of Spring.* Report for City of Ottawa Recreation Branch.

DeKadt, E., ed. 1979. *Tourism: Passport to development?* Oxford: Oxford University Press.

Derek Murray Consulting Associates Ltd. 1985. *A study to determine the impact of events on local economies.* Report for Saskatchewan Tourism and Small Business. Regina.

Dewar, K. 1989. Interpretation as attraction. *Recreation Research Review* 14 (4): 45–49.

Dexter, K. 1978. *Bazaars, fairs, and festivals, a how-to book.* Wilton, Conn.: Morehouse-Barlow Co.

Dickens on the Strand. N.d. Brochure of the Galveston Historical Foundation.

Doxey, G. 1975. A causation theory of visitor-resident irritants, methodology and research influences. In *The impact of tourism,* 195–98. Sixth Annual Conference Proceedings of the Travel Research Association.

DPA Group Inc. 1988. *Economic impact of the Calgary Exhibition and Stampede.* Report for the Calgary Exhibition and Stampede.

Duffield, B., and J. Long. 1981. The development of a schema for identifying the nature of tourism impact. *Etudes et Memoires* (September): 81–100.

Dunbar, P. 1989. Major special events planning: Collingwood's World Youth Wrestling Championships. *Recreation Canada* 47 (4): 9–15.

Dungan, T. 1984. How cities plan special events. *The Cornell H.R.A. Quarterly* (May): 83–89.

Economic Planning Group of Canada. N.d. *Tourism is your business: Market management.* Toronto: Canadian Hotel and Restaurant, Maclean Hunter.

Economist Intelligence Unit. 1989. *International tourism reports,* no. 2.

Economist Intelligence Unit. 1986. *International tourism reports, New Zealand.*

Editorial Services Co. 1989. *Kentucky travel guide.*

Ekos Research Associates Inc. 1985. *Ekos report on Winterlude: Executive summary.* Report for the National Capital Commission. Ottawa.

Elrod, T. 1988. Marketing the magic kingdom. In *The complete travel marketing handbook,* ed. A. Vladimir. Lincolnwood, Ill.: NTC Business Books.

Encyclopedia Britannica. 1988. Vol. 26. See Feasts and festivals; Rites and ceremonies.

Encyclopedia of Associations: International Organizations. 1989. 23rd ed.

Epperson, A. F., ed. 1986. *Private and commercial recreation.* State College of Pennsylvania: Venture.

Falassi, A., ed. 1987. *Time out of time: Essays on the festival.* Albuquerque: University of New Mexico Press.

Fanshawe, S. 1989. A tale of two towns: Festivals. *The Weekend Guardian,* June 3.

Farber, C. 1983. High, healthy and happy: Ontario mythology on parade. In *The celebration of society: Perspectives on contemporary cultural performance,* ed. F. Manning, 33–50. Bowling Green, Ky.: Bowling Green Popular Press.

Faulkner, B. 1988. An overview of tourism research in Australia. In *Frontiers of Australian tourism,* eds. B. Faulkner and M. Fogenie. Canberra: Bureau of Tourism Research.

Fennell, D., and P. Eagles. 1989. Ecotourism in Costa Rica: A conceptual framework. *Journal of Parks and Recreation Administration* (December).

Florida Department of Commerce, Division of Tourism. 1989. *Florida festivals and events media guide, 1989.* Tallahassee.

Folklorama. N.d. *Book your world tour.* Brochure.

Foster, D. 1985. *Travel and tourism management.* London: Macmillan.

Frechtling, D. 1987. Assessing the impacts of travel and tourism: measuring economic costs; measuring economic benefits. In *Travel, tourism and hospitality research,* eds. J. Ritchie and C. Goeldner, 333–61. New York: John Wiley and Sons.

Frisby, W., and D. Getz. 1989. Festival management: A case study perspective. *Journal of Travel Research* 28 (1): 7–11.

Gale Research Co. 1984. *Festivals sourcebook,* 2nd ed. Detroit.

Galveston Daily News. 1987. Various issues.

Gartner, W., and D. Holecek. 1983. Economic impact of an annual tourism industry exposition. *Annals of Tourism Research* 10:199–212.

Gauthier, M. 1987. Festivals: A new clientele. Paper presented at the annual conference of the Travel and Tourism Research Association, Canada Chapter.

Geffen, A., and C. Berglie. 1986. *Food festival: The ultimate guidebook to America's best regional food celebrations.* New York: Pantheon Books.

Georgia Department of Industry and Trade. N.d. *Georgia on my mind: The official travel guide for the state of Georgia.*

Getz, D. 1983. Capacity to absorb tourism: Concepts and implications for strategic planning. *Annals of Tourism Research* 10:239–63.

————. 1984. Tourism, community organization and the social multiplier. In *Leisure, tourism and social change.* Edinburgh: Centre for Leisure Research, Dunfermline College.

————. 1986a. *Manual on measurement and visitor surveys for festivals.* Ottawa: National Task Force on Tourism Data.

————. 1986b. Models in tourism planning: Towards integration of theory and practice. *Tourism Management* (March): 21–32.

————. 1987. Tourism planning and research: Traditions, models and futures. In *Strategic Planning for Tourism.* Papers of the Australian Travel Research Workshop, Bunbury, Australia.

————. 1989a. Special events: Defining the product. *Tourism Management* 10 (2): 125–37.

————. 1989b. Festival and special event sponsorship: A systems approach. Paper presented at the annual conference of the Travel and Tourism Research Association, Honolulu.

Getz, D., and W. Frisby. 1988. Evaluating management effectiveness in community-run festivals. *Journal of Travel Research* 27 (1): 22–27.

Gillespie, A. 1987. Folk festival and festival folk in twentieth century America. In *Time out of time: Essays on the festival,* ed. A. Falassi, 153–61. Albuquerque: University of New Mexico Press.

Goeldner, C. 1987. Travel and tourism information sources. In *Travel, tourism and hospitality research,* eds. J. Ritchie and C. Goeldner. New York: John Wiley and Sons.

Goeldner, C., and P. Long. 1987. The role and impact of mega-events and attractions on tourism development in North America. In *The role and impact of mega-events and attractions on regional and national tourism development,* 119–31. Editions AIEST, vol. 28. St. Gallen, Switzerland.

Goodall, B., 1988. How tourists choose their holidays: An analytic framework. In *Marketing in the tourism industry: The promotion of destination regions,* 1–17. London: Croom Helm.

Goodall, B., and G. Ashworth, eds. 1988. *Marketing in the tourism industry: The promotion of destination regions.* London: Croom Helm.

Government of Western Australia. N.d. *Master record of the government's role in Australia's defence of the America's Cup—1987.* Perth.

Gray, C. 1987. *The economic impact of arts and crafts festivals in selected northeast Minnesota communities.* St. Paul: College of St. Thomas.

Great Britain Year Book 1989. 1988. London: HMSO.

Greater Montreal Convention & Tourism Bureau and Quebec Ministry of Tourism. N.d. *Montreal tourist guide.*

Greenwood, D. 1972. Tourism as an agent of change: A Spanish Basque case study. *Ethnology* 11:80–91.

Grimes, A. 1987. *The economic impact of the arts on Oklahoma City, 1987 update.* Report for the Arts Council of Oklahoma City.

Gunn, C. 1982. Destination zone fallacies and half-truths. *Tourism Management* 3 (4): 263–69.

————. 1988. *Tourism Planning,* 2nd ed. New York: Taylor and Francis.

Gutowski, J. 1978. The protofestival: Local guide to American folk behaviour. *Journal of Folklore Institute* 15:113–31.

Hall, M. 1988. The politics of hallmark events: A review. Paper presented at APSA, at the University of New England, Armidale.

————. 1990. The definition and analysis of hallmark tourist events. *Geojournal.* Forthcoming.

Hall, M., and H. Selwood. 1987. America's cup lost, paradise retained? The dynamics of a hallmark tourist event. In Paper '87, Conference on People and Physical Environment Research, Centre for Urban Research, University of Western Australia, Perth.

Hanna, M. 1981. The performing arts and tourism in Britain. In *The arts and tourism, a profitable partnership,* 57–61. New York: American Council for the Arts.

Harland, J. 1989. Festival and special event sponsorship: Case studies from New Zealand. Paper presented at the annual conference of the Travel and Tourism Research Association, Honolulu.

Hatten, A. 1987. *The economic impact of Expo 86.* Victoria: British Columbia Tourism and Provincial Secretary.

Haywood, M. 1986. Can the tourist-area life cycle be made operational? *Tourism Management* 7 (3): 154–67.

Heenan, D. 1978. Tourism and the community: A drama in three acts. *Journal of Travel Research* 16 (4): 30–32.

Helber, L. 1985. Marketing development strategies for tourist resort development. In *Tourist resort development: Markets, plans and impacts,* ed. K. Hollinshead, 27–32. Proceedings of Conference, the Centre for Leisure and Tourism Studies, Kuring-gai College of Advanced Education, Sydney.

Henry, M., and G. McMullen. 1987. Some economic impacts of equine activities in Aiken County. In *Hospitality and tourism invitational proceedings,* ed. R. Howell. Department of Parks, Recreation and Tourism Management, Clemson University.

Heritage Inns Australia. 1988. Prospectus.

HIDB (Highlands and Islands Development Board). 1989. *Joint events and festivals scheme guidelines, 1 April 1989 to 31 March 1990: Tourism marketing.* Inverness.

Hiller, H. 1987. The urban impact of the 1988 Winter Olympics: Calgary, Canada. In Paper '87, Conference on People and Physical Environment Research, Centre for Urban Research, University of Western Australia, Perth.

Hillman, S. 1986. Special events as a tool for tourism development. *Special Events Report* 5 (16): 4–5.

Hipkins, M. 1987. How Fremantle coped with the challenge. In Paper '87, Conference on People and Physical Environment Research, Centre for Urban Research, University of Western Australia, Perth.

Holgerson, R. 1988. The economic impact of festivals and special events in Canadian communities. Paper presented at the annual conference of the Canadian Parks/Recreation Association, Vancouver.

Howell, R. N.d. *Small town tourism development.* Department of Parks, Recreation and Tourism Management, Clemson University.

Howell, R., and T. Bemisderfer. 1982. *South Carolina tourism development handbook: A primer for local communities.* Department of Recreation and Park Administration, Clemson University.

Hughes, H. 1987. Culture as a tourist resource—a theoretical consideration. *Tourism Management* (September): 205–16.

Hunt, J. 1975. Image as a factor in tourism development. *Journal of Travel Research* 13 (3): 1–7.

Indiana Department of Commerce and Indiana State Festival Association. 1988. *Indiana's how to of festivals and events.* Indianapolis.

Indiana Department of Commerce Tourism Development Division. N.d. *Indiana, the wander book.* Indianapolis.

International Amateur Athletic Federation. *Handbook 1988–1989.* London.

International Bureau of Exhibitions. 1989. *The IBE and regulations respecting international exhibitions.* Paris.

International Events Group. 1984. *The official 1984–1985 directory of special events and festivals,* 1st ed. Chicago.

———. 1985. *Banking on leisure transcripts.* Chicago.

———. 1990. *The official directory of festivals, sports and special events,* 3d ed. Chicago.

International Federation of Festival Organizations. N.d. Brochure.

International Festivals Association. N.d. *Festival! Ideas for community festival organizers.*

International Olympic Committee. *Olympic Charter '87.*

Irwin, D. 1985. Expo '86: the research. In *International events: The real tourism impact.* Proceedings of the Canada Chapter of the Travel and Tourism Research Association annual conference, Edmonton.

Iso-Ahola, S. 1980. *The social psychology of leisure and recreation.* Dubuque: Brown.

———. 1983. Towards a social psychology of recreational travel. *Leisure Studies* 2 (1): 45–57.

Jafari, J. 1983. Tourism today. *Leisure Today* (April): 25–54.

———. 1988. Retrospective and prospective views on tourism as a field of study. Paper presented at the meeting of the Academy of Leisure Sciences, Indianapolis.

James, E. 1961. *Seasonal feasts and festivals.* London: Thames and Hudson.

Janiskee, B. 1979. Harvest and food festivals in South Carolina: Rural delights for day-tripping urbanites. Paper presented at the annual meeting of the Association of American Geographers, Philadelphia.

———. 1980. South Carolina's harvest festivals: Rural delights for day tripping urbanites. *Journal of Geography* (October): 96–104.

———. 1985. Community-sponsored rural festivals in South Carolina: A decade of growth and change. Paper presented to the Association of American Geographers, Detroit.

Jeanne V. Beekhuis and Co. 1988. *Expenditures and characteristics of visitors to the inner harbor and related downtown sites Baltimore, Maryland* Summer 1988. Report for City of Baltimore Office of Promotion and Tourism.

Jefferson, A., and L. Lickorish. 1988. *Marketing tourism, a practical guide.* Harlow, England: Longman.

Jewell, B. 1976. *Fairs and revels.* Tunbridge Wells, England: Midas Books.

Johnson, W. 1986. The effects of festivals on the host community: A case study of the Bala cranberry festival. Bachelor's thesis, Department of Recreation and Leisure Studies, University of Waterloo.

Jordan, J. 1980. The summer people and the natives: Some effects of tourism in a Vermont vacation village. *Annals of Tourism Research* 7 (1): 34–55.

Junker, J. 1989. Fiesta bowl. Paper presented at the annual conference of the Travel and Tourism Research Association, Honolulu.

Kamloops Travel Information Centre. 1988. *Take time in Kamloops, tournament capital of British Columbia.*

Kelly, J. 1985. *Recreation business.* New York: Macmillan.

———. 1987. *Recreation trends.* Champaign-Urbana, Illinois: Management Learning Laboratories.

Kentucky Department of Travel Development. 1987. *Market and economic analysis of the 1987 bluegrass music festival.* Tourism Research Series, no. 39. Frankfort.

Kerslake, B. 1987. Garden festivals: Good for tourism? In *The Tourism Industry 1987/88,* 66.

Korza, P., and D. Magie. 1989. *The arts festival work kit.* University of Massachusetts Arts Extension Service. Amherst.

Kosters, M. 1987. Big international events of tall ships and their coastal sisters. In *The role and impact of mega-events and attractions on regional and national tourism development,* 189–98. Editions AIEST, vol. 28. St. Gallen, Switzerland.

Kreag, G. 1988. Festival, fair and event marketing. Paper presented at Festivals and Events Seminar, University of Minnesota.

Krippendorf, J. 1982. Towards new tourism policies. *Tourism Management* 3 (3): 135–48.

——. 1987. *The holiday makers.* London: Heinemann.

Kujat, D. 1989. Kamloops: Tournament capital of B.C. *Recreation Canada* 47 (4): 6–8.

Kurtzman, J., and J. Zauhar. 1987. New vistas in marketing mega events. *Revue de Tourisme* 4:22–24.

Lambert, B. 1988. An evaluation of the special events program. Unpublished draft report for the Yukon Territory Department of Tourism. Whitehorse.

Lariviere, M., and H. Vachon. 1989. Festivals and events: A position paper (and annexes to the position paper). Ottawa: Tourism Canada.

Law, C., and J. Tuppen. 1986. *Tourism and greater Manchester: The final report of the urban tourism research project.* Department of Geography, University of Salford.

Leathers, C., and W. Misilek. 1986. Cost-benefit analysis in planning for tourism development: The special problem of socio-cultural costs. *Tourism Recreation Research* 11 (2): 85–90.

Lee, J. 1987. The impact of Expo '86 on British Columbia markets. In *Tourism: Where is the client?* eds. P. Williams, J. Hall, and M. Hunter. Conference papers of the Travel and Tourism Research Association, Canada Chapter.

Levin, J. 1989. How cities play off their main events. *Meetings and Conventions* (February): 70–91.

Lewis, R., and T. Beggs. 1988. Selling Bermuda in the off season. In *The complete travel marketing handbook,* ed. A. Vladimir. Lincolnwood, Ill.: NTC Business Books.

Ley, D., and K. Olds. 1988. Landscape as spectacle: World's fairs and the culture of heroic consumption. *Environment and planning D: Society and space.*

Little, D. 1989. Personal communication with the author.

Livability Digest 1 (1). 1981.

Lorentzen, S. 1981. *Building a cultural tourist industry in America: The launching of a Wagner festival.* Washington State Department of Commerce and Development.

Louviere, J., and D. Hensher. 1983. Using discrete choice models with experimental data to forecast consumer demand for a unique event. *Journal of Consumer Research* 10 (3): 348–61.

Ludwig, J. 1976. *The great American spectaculars.* Garden City, N.Y.: Doubleday & Co.

Lunday, D. 1989. Personal communication with the author.

MacAloon, J. 1984. Olympic Games and the theory of spectacle in modern societies. In *Rite, drama, festival, spectacle: Rehearsals towards a theory of cultural performance,* ed. J. MacAloon, 241–80. Philadelphia: Institute for the Study of Human Issues.

MacCannell, D. 1976. *The tourist: A new theory of the leisure class.* New York: Schocken Books.

MacIntosh, R., and C. Goeldner. 1986. *Tourism, principles, practices, philosophies,* 5th ed. New York: John Wiley and Sons.

Macleans. 1986. Sending in the clowns. (May): 54.

Macnaught, T. 1982. Mass tourism and the dilemmas of modernization in Pacific island communities. *Annals of Tourism Research* 9:359–81.

Mahoney, E. N.d. (a). Designing a promotion strategy. Mimeograph. Michigan State University.

———. N.d. (b). Marketing parks and recreation: The need for a new approach. Mimeograph. Michigan State University.

Mahoney, E., D. Spotts, and D. Holecek. 1987. *Economic impact of Christmas at Crossroads Village 1986.* Report for the Genesee County Parks and Recreation Commission. East Lansing: Michigan State University, Travel, Tourism and Recreation Resource Center.

Mannell, R., and S. Iso-Ahola. 1987. Psychological nature of leisure and tourist experiences. *Annals of Tourism Research* 14:314–31.

Manning, F., ed. 1983. *The celebration of society: Perspectives on contemporary cultural performance.* Bowling Green, Ky.: Bowling Green Popular Press.

Marris, T. 1987. The role and impact of mega-events and attractions on regional and national tourism development: Resolutions of the 37th Congress of the AIEST, Calgary. *Revue de Tourisme* (4):3–12.

Marsh, J. N.d. The economic impact of a small city annual sporting event: An initial case study of the Peterborough church league atom hockey tournament. Trent University.

Martin, B., and S. Mason. 1988. Current trends in leisure. *Leisure Studies* 7 (1): 75–80.

Maryland Department of Economic and Employment Development, Office of Tourism Development. N.d. *Maryland event resource guide.* Baltimore.

Maslow, A. 1954. *Motivation and personality.* New York: Harper and Row.

Mathieson, A., and G. Wall. 1982. *Tourism: Economic, physical and social impacts.* New York: Longman.

Mayo, E., and L. Jarvis. 1981. *The psychology of leisure travel.* Boston: CBI.

McLaren, J. 1989. The buskers are coming! *Recreation Canada* 47 (4): 20–23.

McLeod, P., and J. Syme. 1986. Forecasting the economic impact of the America's Cup. In *The impact and marketing of special events, papers of the Australian Travel Research Workshop,* 45–74. Australian Standing Committee on Tourism.

McConkey, R. 1986. Attracting tours to special events. Paper presented to the annual conference of the Canadian Association of Festivals and Events, Hamilton.

McDermott Associates. 1985. *The economic determinants of tourist arrivals in New Zealand and Australia.* Report for the Tourist Industry Federation.

McDermott Miller Group Ltd. 1988. *The implications of tourism growth in New Zealand.* Report for the New Zealand Tourist and Publicity Department. Wellington.

McIntosh, L. 1987. An analysis of the economic impacts of the 1986 Wellesley Apple Butter and Cheese Festival. Bachelor's thesis, Department of Recreation and Leisure Studies, University of Waterloo.

McNulty, R., ed. 1986. *The return of the livable city: Learning from America's best.* Washington, D.C.: Acropolis Books and Partners for Livable Places.

McWilliams, E., and A. Mills. 1985. *Evaluation of festivals, special events and visitor attractions.* Recreation and Parks Department, Texas A&M University.

Mendell, R., J. MacBeth, and A. Solomon. 1983. The 1982 world's fair—a synopsis. *Leisure Today, Journal of Physical Education, Recreation and Dance* (April): 48–49.

Meyer, O. 1987. Dickens on the Strand. *Heritage,* a publication of the Texas Historical Foundation (Autumn): 6–11.

Meyer, R. 1970. *Festivals: USA and Canada.* New York: Ives Washburn.

Michigan Travel Bureau. N.d. *Michigan Travel Bureau cooperative advertising program guidelines and application form.* East Lansing.

Middleton, V. 1988. *Marketing in travel and tourism.* Oxford: Heinemann.

Mill, R., and A. Morrison. 1985. *The tourism system, an introductory text.* Englewood Cliffs, N.J.: Prentice-Hall.

Minnesota Office of Tourism. 1988, 1989. *Minnesota Explorer.* Various issues. St. Paul.

Minnikin, R. 1987. World Expo 88—an economic impact study. In Paper '87, Conference on People and Physical Environment Research, Centre for Urban Research, University of Western Australia, Perth.

Mirloup, J. 1983. The fete and its decline in France: A geographical study based on a regional example. In *Leisure, Tourism and Social Change,* vol. 1, Congress proceedings. Edinburgh: Tourism and Recreation Research Unit.

Mitchell, C., and G. Wall. 1985. *The impact of the Three Centuries Festival.* Department of Geography, University of Waterloo. Report for the Ontario Ministry of Culture and Communications.

———. 1986. Impacts of cultural festivals on Ontario communities. *Recreation Research Review* 13 (1): 28–37.

Moscardo, G., and P. Pearce. 1986. Historic theme parks, an Australian experience in authenticity. *Annals of Tourism Research* 13 (3): 467–79.

Munich Tourist Office. N.d. *Incentives travel manual, 1988/89.*

Murphy, P. 1985. *Tourism, a community approach.* New York: Methuen.

National Trust for Historic Preservation. 1980. *Conserve Neighborhoods:* Community events and how to organize them. Newsletter, no. 13, Washington, D.C.

Nevada Magazine. 1989. Nevada events, a guide for travelers (January/February).

New Brunswick Department of Tourism. 1976. *Economic impact study of Loyalist Days, 1975.* Saint John.

———. 1987. *Canadian Midget Softball Championships, Nelson-Miramichi.* St. John.

New South Wales. 1986. *Tourism Development Strategy.* Sydney.

New South Wales Bicentennial Council. *Bicentennial Bulletin.* Various issues 1987–1988.

New South Wales Government Bicentennial Secretariat. 1987. *Bicentennial celebrations New South Wales government programme.* Sydney.

New York State Office of Parks and Recreation. 1981. *New York urban cultural park system, summary plan.* Albany.

New York State Department of Economic Development. 1988. *Tourism master plan, 1988 evaluation and review, and 1989 annual strategy.* Albany.

———. N.d. *Application for festival designation.* Albany.

New Zealand Tourism Council. 1986. *Growing pains: Current issues facing New Zealand tourism.* Wellington.

New Zealand Tourist and Publicity Department. 1987. *New Zealand Tourism Report* no. 38 (November).

———. *Tourism Research Newsletter.* Various issues 1987–1989. Wellington.

———. N.d. *What's on in 1990.* Wellington.

———. N.d. *The New Zealand Book 1989/90.* Wellington.

———. N.d. *1989/90 strategic plan.* Wellington.

———. N.d. *Making you New Zealand's star attraction.* Wellington.

New Zealand Tourist and Publicity Department and New Zealand Tourism Council. 1984. *New Zealand tourism: Issues and policies.*

Noronha, R. 1979. Paradise reviewed: Tourism in Bali. In *Tourism: Passport to development?* ed. E. de Kadt, 177–204. Oxford: Oxford University Press.

North Carolina Department of Commerce, Division of Travel and Tourism. 1989. *North Carolina calendar of events,* vol. 1. Raleigh.

Nova Scotia Department of Tourism. 1987. *1986/87 Highland heart evaluation: Antigonish Highland Games.* Halifax.

Ontario, Ministry of Citizenship and Culture. N.d. *Let's put on an arts festival.* Toronto.

———. 1985. *How to draw the tourist.* Toronto.

Opportunity West Development. 1985a. *Festival du Voyageur tourism development plan.* Winnipeg.

———. 1985b. *Folklorama development project.* Winnipeg.

O'Reilly, A. 1987. The impact of cultural hallmark/mega-events on national tourism development in selected West Indian countries. *Revue de Tourisme* 4:26–29.

Otsego County Tourism Bureau. *Travel guide: 1989 I love New York summer festival.* Brochure.

Palmer, P. 1989. Attracting major tournaments, the Saint John experience. *Recreation Canada* 47 (4): 44–46.

Papson, S. 1981. Spuriousness and tourism: Politics of two Canadian provincial governments. *Annals of Tourism Research* 8 (2): 220–35.

Patton, G. 1986. A marketing policy for New Zealand tourism. In *Tourism: Prospects and challenges for local government,* ed. J. Taylor, 132–40. Proceedings from a course at Lincoln College.

Pearce, D. 1987. *Tourism today: A geographical analysis.* Harlow, England: Longman.

———. 1989. *Tourist development,* 2nd ed. Harlow, England: Longman.

Pearce, P. 1982. *The social psychology of tourist behaviour.* Oxford: Pergamon Press.

Pearce, P., and G. Moscardo. 1986. The concept of authenticity in tourist experiences. *Australia/New Zealand Journal of Sociology* 22 (1): 121–32.

Pieper, J. 1973. *In tune with the world: A theory of festivity.* Chicago: Franciscan Herald Press (Translated by R. and C. Wilson, from the 1963 German original).

Plant, B. 1984. Elmira Maple Syrup Festival, profile of a success story. Department of Recreation and Leisure Studies, University of Waterloo.

———. 1985. Visitor profile analysis 1985 Elmira Maple Syrup Festival. Bachelor's thesis, Department of Recreation and Leisure Studies, University of Waterloo.

Plog, S. 1972. Why destination areas rise and fall in popularity. Paper presented to the Southern California Chapter of the Travel Research Association, San Diego.

———. 1987. Understanding psychographics in tourism research. In *Travel, tourism and hospitality research,* eds. J. Ritchie and C. Goeldner, 204–13. New York: John Wiley and Sons.

Price Waterhouse. 1986. *A report for the Canberra Festival Committee on the benefits of staging the Canberra Festival.* December 1986, final report.

Prince Edward Island Department of Tourism and Parks. N.d. (a). *Prince Edward Island 1988* (and 1989) *visitor's guide.* Charlottetown.

———. N.d. (b). *Touch nature 1988.* Charlottetown.

Quebec Ministry of Tourism. 1988. *Quebec vacation guide.* Quebec City.

Queenan, L. 1989. Ohioana. *Ohio* (August): 13–15.

Ralston, L., and J. Crompton. 1988a. *Profile of visitors to the 1987 Dickens on the Strand emerging from an on-site survey.* Report to the Galveston Historical Foundation.

———. 1988b. *Profile of visitors to the 1987 Dickens on the Strand emerging from a mail-back survey.* Report no. 2 for the Galveston Historical Foundation.

———. 1988c. *Motivations, service quality and economic impact of visitors to the 1987 Dickens on the Strand emerging from a mail-back survey.* Report no. 3 for the Galveston Historical Foundation.

Redfoot, D. 1984. Touristic authenticity, touristic angst, and modern reality. *Qualitative Sociology* 7 (4): 291–309.

Reed, T. 1980. *Indy—Race and ritual.* San Rafael, Calif.: Presidio Press.

Rey, P. 1986. Economic impact of special events. In *The impact and marketing of special events,* papers of the Australian Research Workshop, 36–45. Australian Standing Committee on Tourism.

Reynolds, P. 1987. Arts festivals for a new world. *Connections Quarterly* 6:29–34.

Ritchie, J. 1984. Assessing the impact of hallmark events: Conceptual and research issues. *Journal of Travel Research* 23 (1): 2–11.

Ritchie, J., and C. Aitken. 1984. Assessing the impacts of the 1988 Olympic Winter Games: The research program and initial results. *Journal of Travel Research* 22 (3): 17–25.

Ritchie, J., and D. Beliveau. 1974. Hallmark events: An evaluation of a strategic response to seasonality in the travel market. *Journal of Travel Research* 13 (2): 14–20.

Ritchie, J., and M. Lyons. 1987. Olympulse iii/Olympulse iv: A mid-term report on resident attitudes concerning the XV Olympic Winter Games. *Journal of Travel Research* 26 (1): 18–26.

Ritchie, J., and J. Yangzhou. 1987. The role and impact of mega-events and attractions on national and regional tourism: A conceptual and methodological overview. In *The role and impact of mega-events and attractions on regional and national tourism development,* 17–57. Editions AIEST, vol. 28. St. Gallen, Switzerland.

Ritchie, J., and M. Zins. 1978. Culture as a determinant of the attractiveness of a tourist region. *Annals of Tourism Research* 5 (2): 252–67.

Roberts, J. 1989. Green mantle. *The Weekend Guardian,* June 17–18.

Ronkainen, I., and J. Farano. 1987. United States' travel and tourism policy. *Journal of Travel Research* 25 (4): 2–8.

Rooney, J. F. 1988. Mega-sports events as tourist attractions: A geographical analysis. In *Tourism research: Expanding boundaries,* 93–99. The Travel and Tourism Research Association Nineteenth Annual Conference, Montreal.

Rosenow, J., and G. Pulsipher. 1979. *Tourism: The good, the bad, and the ugly.* Lincoln, Neb.: Century Three Press.

Rusk, M. 1989. *Market product match: Determining the international market for Canada's annual festivals and events.* Ottawa: Tourism Canada.

Sallee, B. 1985. The basics of festivals and events management. Paper presented at the Festivals and Events Seminar 1985, Texas A&M University.

Saskatchewan Department of Economic Development and Tourism. N.d. *The great Saskatchewan vacation book.* Regina.

Saskatchewan, Ministry of Tourism and Small Business. N.d. *Planning, organizing and evaluating an event in Saskatchewan.* Regina.

Savannah Leisure Services Bureau. 1987. *Economic impact study 22nd Air National Guard Softball Tournament 1987.* Savannah, Georgia.

Schwaninger, M. 1989. Trends in leisure and tourism for 2000–2010: Scenario with consequence for planners. In *Tourism marketing and management handbook,* eds. S. Witt and L. Moutinho, 599–605. Englewood Cliffs, N.J.: Prentice-Hall.

Scottish Tourist Board. 1989. *Survey of visitors to the Glasgow garden festival tourist information centre.* Edinburgh.

Shaw, G., J. Greenwood, and A. Williams. 1988. The United Kingdom: Market responses and public policy. In *Tourism and economic development, Western European experiences,* eds. A. Williams and G. Shaw, 162–79. London: Pinter.

Shemanski, F. 1984. *A guide to fairs and festivals in the United States.* Westport: Greenwood Press.

———. 1985. *A guide to world fairs and festivals.* Westport: Greenwood Press.

Shepard, D. 1982. Community organizations and hallmark events, a case study of the Wellesley Apple Butter and Cheese Festival. Bachelor's thesis, Department of Recreation and Leisure Studies, University of Waterloo.

Simmons, D. 1988. Destination area residents' participation in tourism planning: An unachievable ideal? Department of Geography, University of Waterloo.

Simmons, D., and P. Devlin. 1986. *The socio-cultural impacts of tourism.* Department of Parks and Recreation, Lincoln College, Christchurch. Report for the New Zealand Tourist and Publicity Department.

Smith, E. 1986. Marketing techniques for hallmark events (the first defence of the America's Cup). In *The impact and marketing of special events, papers of the Australian Travel Research Workshop,* 76–96. Australian Standing Committee on Tourism.

Smith, S. 1988. The festival visitor: It may not be who you think it is. *Feedback, the Official Publication of the Waterloo (Ontario) Chamber of Commerce* (November): 1.

———. 1989. *Tourism analysis: A handbook.* Harlow, England: Longman.

Smith, V., ed. 1977. *Hosts and guests: The anthropology of tourism.* Philadelphia: University of Pennsylvania Press.

Snow Country. June 1989.

Socher, K., and P. Tschurtschenthaler. 1987. The role and impact of mega-events: Economic perspectives—the case of the Winter Olympic Games 1964 and 1967 at Innsbruck. In *The role and impact of mega-events and attractions on regional and national tourism development,* 103–10. Editions AIEST, vol. 28. St. Gallen, Switzerland.

Soutar, G., and P. McLeod. 1987. Fremantle residents' perception of the impact of the America's cup on their city. In Paper '87, Conference on People and Physical Environment Research, Centre for Urban Research, University of Western Australia, Perth.

South Carolina Department of Parks, Recreation and Tourism and the South Carolina Festivals Association. 1982. *Festival planning handbook,* 2nd edition.

South Dakota Department of Tourism. N.d. *South Dakota vacation guide, official centennial edition.*

Sparrow, M. 1987. A planning model for hallmark events. Workshop paper for Paper '87, Conference on People and Physical Environment Research, Centre for Urban Research, University of Western Australia, Perth.

———. 1989. Personal communications with the author.

Special Events Report. May 9, 1983. Festival survey.

———. December 6, 1982. Telluride, Colorado . . . How one town has profited from festivals.

Spicer, D. 1958. *Festivals of Western Europe.* New York: Wilson.

Spivak, C., and R. Weinstock. 1986. *Gourmet food and wine festivals of North America.* Ventura, Calif.: Printwheel Press.

Stabler, M. 1988. The image of destination regions: Theoretical and empirical aspects. In *Marketing in the tourism industry: The promotion of destination regions,* eds. B. Goodall and G. Ashworth, 133–61. London: Croom Helm.

Statistics Canada. 1989. *National task force on tourism data: Final report.* Ottawa.

Stanton, M. 1989. The Polynesian Cultural Center: a multiethnic model of seven Pacific cultures. In: V. Smith, ed., *Hosts and Guests: The Anthropology of Tourism,* 2nd ed. Philadelphia: University of Pennsylvania Press, 247–62.

Stevens, T. 1989. Battlefield interpretation: War & peace, tourism's dilemma. *Leisure Management* 9 (1): 60–64.

Stewart, B. 1983. Canadian Association of Festivals and Events (CAFE). *Recreation Canada* 41 (5): 20–21.

Stoll, D. 1963. *Music festivals of the world.* Oxford: Pergamon Press.

Taylor, J., ed. 1986. *Tourism: Prospects and challenges for local government.* Proceedings from a course at Lincoln College, Christchurch, New Zealand.

Taylor, P., and C. Gratton. 1988. The Olympic Games: An economic analysis. *Leisure Management* 8 (3): 32–34.

Texas Department of Commerce. N.d. *The Texas visitor industry and the State Tourism Division programs and services.*

———. N.d. *Texas: It's a whole other country.*

Teye, V. 1987. Developing Africa's tourism potential, prospects and issues. *Tourism Recreation Research* 12 (1): 9–14.

Thorburn, A. 1986. Marketing cultural heritage. *Travel & Tourism Analyst* (December): 39–48.

Tomlinson, G. 1986. The staging of rural food festivals: Some problematics with the concept of liminoid performances. Paper presented to the Qualitative Research Conference on Ethnographic Research, University of Waterloo.

Toronto Ontario Olympic Council. 1989. *Toronto '96: Toronto's proposal to host the 1996 Olympic Games.* Toronto.

Tourism Canada. 1986. *The U.S. pleasure travel market study, Canadian potential highlights report.* Ottawa.

———. 1987. *Pleasure travel markets to North America: Japan, United Kingdom, West Germany, France, highlights report.* Ottawa.

———. 1989. *Discussion paper on a national tourism strategy.* Ottawa.

Travel and Tourism Research Association (Canada Chapter). 1986. *International events: The real tourism impact.* Proceedings of the 1985 conference.

TravelArctic, Government of the Northwest Territories. N.d. *Canada's Northwest Territories explorer's guide.* Yellowknife.

Travis, A. 1989. Tourism destination area development (from theory into practice). In *Tourism marketing and management handbook,* eds. S. Witt and L. Moutinho, 487–98. Englewood Cliffs, N.J.: Prentice-Hall.

Tuppen, J. 1985. *Urban tourism in France—a preliminary assessment.* Urban tourism project, working paper no. 3, Department of Geography, University of Salford.

Turner, V., ed. 1982. *Celebration: Studies in festivity and ritual.* Washington, D.C.: Smithsonian Institution Press.

Ueberroth, P. 1985. *Made in America: His own story.* New York: William Morrow.

Ukman, L. 1985. Opening remarks. In *Banking on leisure transcripts.* Chicago: International Events Group.

———. 1989. Personal written communications with the author.

UNESCO. 1977. The effects of tourism on socio-economic values. *Annals of Tourism Research* 4:74–105.

University of Illinois at Urbana-Champaign. N.d. *Planning community-wide special events.* Cooperative Extension Service, College of Agriculture, Circular no. 1123.

University of Minnesota Extension Service Tourism Center. 1989. *Festivals and events, information and resource book.* St. Paul.

University of Missouri, Department of Recreation and Park Administration. 1986. *Tourism USA: Guidelines for tourism development.* Washington, D.C.: U.S. Department of Commerce, USTTA, Economic Development Administration.

U.S. Department of Housing and Urban Development. 1981. *The urban fair: How cities celebrate themselves.* Washington, D.C.

U.S. Travel Data Center. 1989a. *Discover America 2000.* Travel Industry Association of America. Washington, D.C.

———. 1989b. *The 1988–89 economic review of travel in America.* Washington, D.C.

Uzzell, D. 1984. An alternative structuralist approach to the psychology of tourism marketing. *Annals of Tourism Research* 11:79–99.

Vallee, P. 1987. Authenticity as a factor in segmenting the Canadian travel market. Master's thesis, Department of Recreation and Leisure Studies, University of Waterloo.

Van der Lee, P., and J. Williams. 1986. The grand prix and tourism. In *The Adelaide Grand Prix: The impact of a special event,* eds. J. Burns, J. Hatch, and T. Mules, 39–57. Adelaide: Centre for South Australian Economic Studies.

Van Esterik, P. 1982. Celebrating ethnicity: Ethnic flavor in an urban festival. In *Ethnic Groups* 4:207–27.

Vanhove, D., and S. Witt. 1987. Report of the English-speaking group on the conference theme. *Revue de Tourisme* 4:10–12.

Vaughan, R. 1979. *Does a festival pay? A case study of the Edinburgh Festival in 1976.* Tourism Recreation Research Unit, working paper no. 5, University of Edinburgh.

Vermont Statehood Bicentennial Commission. 1989. *Vermont Bicentennial,* vol. 2, no. 1.

Victorian Tourism Commission. 1986. *Goldfields development program.* Melbourne.

———. 1987. *Wine and high mountain country tourism development program.* Melbourne.

Victorian Tourism Strategy. 1984. Statement by the minister responsible for tourism. Melbourne.

Wall, G., and C. Knapper. 1981. *Tutankhamen in Toronto.* Department of Geography Publication Series no. 17, University of Waterloo.

Wallis-Smith, M. 1987. Major international sporting events, characteristics and criteria for selection: A South Australian viewpoint. In Paper '87, Conference on People and Physical Environment Research, Centre for Urban Research, University of Western Australia, Perth.

Wang, P., and R. Gitelson. 1988. Economic limitations of festivals & other hallmark events. *Leisure Industry Report* (August): 4–5.

Wasserman, P., E. Herman, and E. Root, eds. 1977. *Festivals sourcebook.* Detroit: Gale Research Co.

———, 1984. *Festivals sourcebook,* 2nd edition. Detroit: Gale Research Co.

Waters, S. 1988. *Travel industry world yearbook, the big picture—1988.* New York: Child and Waters.

Watt, C., and R. McCarville. 1985. *1985 survey of Texas festivals.* Texas A&M University.

Watt, C., and B. Wicks. 1983. *Texas county fairs: A report of survey results.* Texas A&M University.

Western Australian Tourism Commission. 1985. *Tourism development plan Midlands region.* Perth.

Wicks, B., and C. Watt. N.d. *Texas festivals and events: A report of survey results.* Department of Recreation and Parks, Texas A&M University.

Wilkinson, D. 1988. *The event marketing process.* Willowdale, Ontario: Event Management and Marketing Institute.

Wilson, J., and L. Udall. 1982. *Folk festivals: A handbook for organization and management.* Knoxville: University of Tennessee Press.

Witt, S., and L. Moutinho, eds. 1989. *Tourism marketing and management handbook.* Englewood Cliffs, N.J.: Prentice-Hall.

World Expo '88. N.d. *World Expo '88 report.* Brisbane.

York Tourist Bureau. N.d. *York, yesterday in a day.*

Yukon Territory. N.d. *Yukon tourism special events program, 1988/89 program guidelines.* Whitehorse.

Credits

The author gratefully acknowledges permission from the following to reproduce material:

Journal of Travel Research, published by the Travel and Tourism Research Association and the Business Research Division, University of Colorado: for reproduction of tables and text from D. Getz and W. Frisby. 1988. "Evaluating Management Effectiveness in Community-run Festivals." 27 (1): 22–27; and for the definition of hallmark events from J. Ritchie. 1984. "Assessing the Impact of Hallmark Events: Conceptual and Research Issues." 23 (1): 2–11.

Don Lunday, Executive Director of the International Festivals Association; Doug Little, President of Festivals Ontario; Lesa Ukman, International Events Group; and Mark Sparrow, Director of Research and Planning for the Western Australian Tourism Commission, for permission to quote at length from personal interviews.

The Ottawa-Carleton Board of Trade: National Capital Region Festival Study, for permission to reproduce tables and text from Coopers and Lybrand Consulting Group. 1989. *NCR 1988 festivals study final report.*

The Calgary Exhibition and Stampede for permission to reproduce tables and text from DPA Group Inc. 1988. *Economic Impact of the Calgary Exhibition and Stampede.*

The Galveston Historical Foundation for permission to reproduce photographs of Dickens on the Strand, and tables and text from three reports by L. Ralston and J. Crompton. 1988.

The University of New Mexico Press, Albuquerque, for permission to quote from A. Falassi, ed. 1987. *Time Out of Time: Essays on the Festival.*

Butterworth Scientific Limited for permission to reproduce text and illustrations from D. Getz. 1989a. Special events: Defining the product. *Tourism Management* 10 (2): 125–37.

Tourism Canada, for permission to reproduce tables and data from *The U.S. Pleasure Travel Market Study, Canadian Potential Highlights Report;* from *Pleasure Travel Markets to North America: Japan, United Kingdom, West Germany, France Highlights Report;* from M. Lariviere and H. Vachon. 1989. *Festivals and Events: A Position Paper,* and annexes to the position paper; from M. Rusk. 1989. *Market Product Match: Determining the International Market for Canada's Annual Festivals and Events.*

National Capital Commission, Ottawa, for permission to reproduce photographs of Winterlude.

New Zealand Tourist and Publicity Department for permission to reproduce photographs of the Otago Goldfields Celebration and the Speight's Coast to Coast.

The US Travel Data Center, for permission to reproduce selected data and the table "Seven Generational Groups" from *Discover America 2000.*

The Baltimore Area Convention and Visitors Association for permission to reproduce photographs.

The Western Australian Tourism Commission for permission to reproduce photographs of the America's Cup defense facilities.

Index